OPERATION BAGRATION

OPERATION BAGRATION

AN INCOMPLETE TRUTH

B.V. SOKOLOV

Translated and Edited by RICHARD W. HARRISON

Pen & Sword
MILITARY
AN IMPRINT OF PEN & SWORD BOOKS LTD.
YORKSHIRE · PHILADELPHIA

First published in Great Britain in 2024 by
PEN AND SWORD MILITARY
An imprint of
Pen & Sword Books Limited
Yorkshire – Philadelphia

Copyright © B.V. Sokolov, 2024

ISBN 978 1 39905 092 0

The right of B.V. Sokolov to be identified as Author of this work has been asserted by him in accordance with the Copyright, Designs and Patents Act 1988.

A CIP catalogue record for this book is available from the British Library.

All rights reserved. No part of this book may be reproduced or transmitted in any form or by any means, electronic or mechanical including photocopying, recording or by any information storage and retrieval system, without permission from the Publisher in writing.

Typeset in Times New Roman 9.5/11.5 by
SJmagic DESIGN SERVICES, India.
Printed and bound in the UK by CPI Group (UK) Ltd.

Pen & Sword Books Limited incorporates the imprints of Atlas, Archaeology, Aviation, Discovery, Family History, Fiction, History, Maritime, Military, Military Classics, Politics, Select, Transport, True Crime, Air World, Frontline Publishing, Leo Cooper, Remember When, Seaforth Publishing, The Praetorian Press, Wharncliffe Local History, Wharncliffe Transport, Wharncliffe True Crime and White Owl.

For a complete list of Pen & Sword titles please contact
PEN & SWORD BOOKS LIMITED
George House, Units 12 & 13, Beevor Street, Off Pontefract Road,
Barnsley, South Yorkshire, S71 1HN, England
E-mail: enquiries@pen-and-sword.co.uk
Website: www.pen-and-sword.co.uk

or
PEN AND SWORD BOOKS
1950 Lawrence Rd, Havertown, PA 19083, USA
E-mail: uspen-and-sword@casematepublishers.com
Website: www.penandswordbooks.com

Contents

Foreword vi

Chapter 1　Why Was the Western Front Command Removed
　　　　　　in April 1944? 1
Chapter 2　The *Poles'ye* Tragedy 41
Chapter 3　The Belorussian Partisan Movement through the Eyes
　　　　　　of a Cadre *Chekist* 46
Chapter 4　The Prelude to 'Bagration' 49
Chapter 5　The Rout 88
Chapter 6　The Voyage of the *'Wiking'* 163
Chapter 7　The Voyage of the 'Pseudo *Wiking*' 191
Chapter 8　The Salvation of Army Group Centre 203
Chapter 9　The Sides' Losses 241

Notes 263
Index 277

Foreword

Operation 'Bagration', during the course of which the Red Army routed the main forces of the Germans' Army Group Centre (actually, three of its four armies were destroyed) during the summer of 1944 and liberated the greater part of Belorussia, almost all of Lithuania, part of Latvia and the eastern regions of Poland, and reached the East Prussian border, is rightly considered one of the most successful Soviet operations of the Great Patriotic War. During 'Bagration' a group of forces was routed which, by the way, exceeded in strength that which had been destroyed at Stalingrad, and in a significantly shorter period of time. 'Bagration', according to its degree of success in 1944, can only be compared to the second Iasi–Kishinev operation in August, during which Army Group South Ukraine was routed and Romania joined the anti-Hitler coalition. In 1945 the Vistula–Oder operation of January–February, when Army Group Vistula was routed and Soviet forces seized bridgeheads over the Oder River 60–70km from Berlin, can be compared to 'Bagration'.

By the summer of 1944 the higher Soviet headquarters had learned to adequately coordinate troop operations. Four Fronts, 26 armies, two cavalry-mechanized groups, 168 divisions, 12 corps, 20 independent brigades and seven fortified areas took part in Operation 'Bagration'. During the course of the operation two-pronged enveloping attacks were launched, as a result of which three major enemy groups of forces – Vitebsk, Mogilev–Minsk and Bobruisk – were surrounded and basically destroyed. Since the attacks were launched almost simultaneously, the Germans were deprived of the opportunity to manoeuvre their very scanty reserves. Moreover, the Soviet command managed to achieve strategic surprise, insofar as almost to the very start of 'Bagration' the German command assumed that the main attack would be launched not along the entire perimeter of the 'Belorussian balcony', but in the Kovel' area.

The main factor in the success of Operation 'Bagration' was the overwhelming Soviet superiority in men and materiel. And this superiority, in turn, became possible thanks to the fact that 16 days before the start of Operation 'Bagration' Anglo-American forces began Operation 'Overlord' – the landing in Normandy, an amphibious invasion of the continent of Europe unprecedented in its scale. The Germans were forced to shift the main forces of their panzer divisions and Luftwaffe to repel the landing, which could not but have a most negative effect on the stability of the German Eastern Front. Under the Soviet regime it was not acceptable to speak about the influence of 'Overlord' on 'Bagration'. Nor is this subject now a central one in the works of Russian historians. By the way, were it not for 'Overlord', then Operation 'Bagration' might not have taken place at all, particularly if the Germans had employed on the 'Bagration' front all of the forces they were forced to throw in to repelling 'Overlord'.

FOREWORD

In this book I will attempt to answer the following questions. Did the Germans have a chance, given another method of operations, if not to repel the Soviet offensive within the confines of Operation 'Bagration', then at least to minimize the damage from it? What did the Germans know of Soviet plans before the start of 'Bagration'? Was the choice of the axes of the Soviet forces' attacks during Operation 'Bagration' an optimal one? Could more favourable results have been achieved given a different method of operations? What was the influence of Operation 'Overlord' on Operation 'Bagration' and, on the other hand, how did 'Bagration' in its turn influence 'Overlord'? Why during the second phase of 'Bagration', following the arrival of elite German panzer divisions, did the Soviet forces' successes become much more modest? What were the actual losses of both sides during Operation 'Bagration'?

Chapter 1

Why Was the Western Front Command Removed in April 1944?

Operation 'Bagration' was preceded by the unsuccessful attempts by the Soviet Western Front, with the support of the Kalinin Front, which lasted for half a year, from the autumn of 1943 to the spring of 1944, to slice off the 'Belorussian balcony', which covered the route to Berlin. In the same fashion an entire series of unsuccessful counterblows from August to October preceded the large Soviet offensive around Stalingrad (Operation 'Uranus'), which began on 19 November 1942. At that time these failures brought the *Stavka* of the Supreme High Command to the conclusion as to the necessity of repeating the offensive with even greater forces simultaneously along a greater number of axes. In a similar fashion, the failures along the Belorussian direction brought Stalin and his marshals in the spring of 1944 to a conclusion as to the necessity of organizing a general offensive with the maximum amount of men and materiel and the launching of simultaneous attacks along different axes. This was preceded by quite threatening organizational measures.

In April 1944, following a series of unsuccessful offensives against the important rail junctions of Vitebsk and Orsha, the commander of the Western Front, General V.D. Sokolovskii, was removed from command, along with a number of other generals.

The Western Front's chief of staff, Colonel General A.P. Pokrovskii, recalled:

> When the train carrying the commission arrived, the members of the commission – these included Malenkov as head of the commission, as well as Fedor Fedotovich Kuznetsov, at that time chief of the intelligence directorate, as well as several others – at first spoke with the military council, and then they summoned us, including myself in my capacity as Front chief of staff.
>
> I remember how Malenkov calmly asked Sokolovskii: 'How did all these failures come about. Here they are saying that there were insufficient forces, that there was insufficient materiel and that these operations should not have been carried out with these men and materiel. What can you say about that? This was clear to you. Why did you not once during all this time pick up the telephone and call comrade Stalin and state your opinion as to why these operations should not have been conducted, why there were insufficient forces and why the assigned tasks could not be carried out?'

OPERATION BAGRATION: AN INCOMPLETE TRUTH

There was a long pause. Sokolovskii failed to reply. I was thunderstruck. But facts are facts. He did not utter a single word. And he really did not call . . .

Sokolovskii did not utter a single word in reply to the question. I don't know how to explain that. Either he could not bring himself to call Stalin, or he believed that he would be able to carry out the tasks assigned to the Front with the insufficient amount of men and materiel that he possessed. And we were short of everything during that final operation, after which he was removed. There were few tanks. There were not enough shells. There were not enough men. There was nothing with which to carry out the assignment.

Perhaps the fact that he believed Gordov, and that he would carry out the task assigned to the 33rd Army, played a role in this. Perhaps he (Gordov) promised him, and he (Sokolovskii) believed him. It's hard to say.[1]

The commission's members included State Defence Committee member G.M. Malenkov (chairman), Colonel General Shcherbakov (chief of the Red Army's political administration), Colonel General S.M. Shtemenko (chief of the General Staff's operational directorate), Lieutenant General F.F. Kuznetsov (chief of the General Staff's intelligence directorate), and Lieutenant General A.I. Shimonaev (chief of the General Staff's operational rear directorate).

One of the reasons for the purge of the Western Front command was the letter from Lieutenant General L.Z. Mekhlis, a member of the Western Front's military council, to Stalin, which remains unpublished. Stalin particularly trusted Mekhlis as his former assistant. However, aside from Mekhlis, other generals and officers had written to Stalin about the shortcomings in the Western Front's conduct of offensive operations. For example, at the end of March 1944, the deputy chief of the 33rd Army staff's operational section, Colonel I.A. Tolkonyuk, wrote to Stalin:

> . . . some of our leading generals with the Western Front and 33rd Army, upon whom literally everything regarding the preparation and conduct of an operation depends, are unable or either do not want to understand that one cannot count on the success of an unprepared operation, and that one must approach the conduct of an operation extremely seriously, and that here one needs to rationally calculate the required men and materiel that may be expended without any kind of benefit and which cannot be reconstituted except over an extended period, and that a lost engagement or battle reduces an army's strength greatly and for a long time, and that one cannot win simply by the wish to defeat the German enemy. They are unable to understand that we have not become so rich as to expend our men and material on petty matters without thinking beforehand about the possible dire consequences. Finally, some of our ranking comrades are unable to understand that the training of troops, that is, of the actual executors of the engagement, is one of the chief and basic prerequisites for success and that the ability to train subordinate forces for the forthcoming fighting is one of the most important qualities of a commander . . .

WHY WAS THE WESTERN FRONT COMMAND REMOVED

In the second half of 1943 and the beginning of 1944 (from September 1943 through March 1944) the 33rd Army, in conjunction with the Western Front's other armies, carried out five major offensive operations (and many lesser operations) with the objective of breaking through the enemy's defence and capturing first Orsha (operating east of Orsha) and then the city of Vitebsk (operating south-east of Vitebsk). The overwhelming majority of the army's generals and officers undertook this mission with great zeal and desire, but did not achieve the desired results after suffering colossal losses. During this period the 33rd Army alone lost 20,975 men killed, and overall lost 103,011 men killed, wounded and missing, including three division commanders killed and one wounded, eight deputy division commanders and chiefs of staff killed and wounded, 38 regimental commanders and their deputies, and 174 battalion commanders, while during the same period it lost 419 tanks and 60 self-propelled guns burned and destroyed by enemy artillery and air directly on the battlefield; the 2nd Guards Tatsinskaya Tank Corps suffered heavy losses and has been rendered ineffective due to its unsuccessful commitment into the fighting to develop the success.

Five to ten days were allotted to the preparation of each of these operations, with the operations lasting from 5 to 22 days. The enemy's defence was to be broken along a front from 4.8 to 9km, with each first-echelon division accorded a zone of 1–2km along the front. The artillery density in each of the operations conducted ranged from 126 to 206 guns per kilometre of front (not counting 45mm guns, regimental artillery and 82mm mortars). A total of 1,801,600 shells and mortar rounds was expended. As a result of the heavy and extended fighting, which was accompanied by heavy losses, the army advanced 2 to 13km into the depth of the enemy's defence, while in some operations it did not advance at all. During all of this time the army occupied 148km^2 of territory and liberated 82 inhabited locales. Taking into account the large amount of men and materiel expended and the extremely insignificant success achieved, many of us are weighed down by failures, some rush around, 'pulling out their hair', getting nervous and upset and, finding no satisfaction in fighting, and with regret and disappointment curse the existing situation on our sector of the front, while often employing the fateful word 'unlucky'.

What are the chief reasons for these failures, which have resulted in the breakdown of not badly planned operations and heavy losses in men and materiel and desired results?

1) The first and main reason was the fact that men and materiel were expended on petty things, and instead of a serious and shattering attack on the enemy, 'pinpricks' were launched, from which he very rapidly recovered, while materiel was also expended on petty matters and in packets, and were thus unable to deliver a serious result. If you strike a man with a log he will undoubtedly be killed, but if you break up this log into splinters and beat this man at different times with

these splinters, then he will easily withstand these blows and will in no way lose his viability. Figuratively speaking, this is how one may describe the attacks against the enemy by our 33rd Army.
2) Shortcomings in planning, preparing for and conducting the operations. In planning the forthcoming operations, the Front would indicate to the army the makeup of the forces being employed and the breakthrough sector. The breakthrough area was determined simply on the basis of the configuration of the front, without taking into account terrain conditions. The army sector and the breakthrough sector were determined by the Front commander and were so narrow that they excluded any kind of choice for a favourable breakthrough location by the army commander. Moreover, the narrow breakthrough front (4–6km) put our attacking units that had penetrated into his defence under crossfire and flanking aimed fire from all types of enemy weapons. This is one of the important reasons for our lack of success and heavy losses. The divisions launching the main attack were given attack sectors of 1–2km in width, while a division's combat formation was, as a rule, deeply echeloned and the divisions almost always initially attacked with two battalions and then the remaining elements were consecutively committed into the fighting; that is, the divisions were committed into the fighting by battalion. Under these conditions, neither a division's firepower nor its shock force were employed simultaneously, but were expended in detail. In the majority of cases, only the forward battalions actually took part in the fighting, while the division's remaining units, echeloned in depth, were scattered by the enemy's artillery fire before they reached the forward edge of the defence and, suffering heavy losses, they completely lost their combat effectiveness.

Your Order No. 306 on new combat formations in the army was not carried out and the army commander either did not understand its importance and the benefit of the new combat formations, or did not recognize them (we are speaking here of the former army commander, Colonel General Gordov). Operations, as a rule, were prepared in haste and there was never enough time to reconnoitre the enemy defence (aerial photographs were often received 1–2 days before the beginning of the operation and often on the day of the operation's start).

The troops were committed into the fighting with unassimilated and untrained reinforcements, which constituted the main mass of the combat elements. The officers assumed command of these elements on the go and went into battle with them, without knowing their subordinates, who also did not know their officers.

Divisions went into battle half-armed: there were few automatic weapons, while each division had from 16 to 30 heavy machine guns, with one magazine for each automatic rifle and light machine gun. If one takes into account the fact that the majority of the troops were armed with rifles, which they handled poorly, as was the case with the already small number of automatic rifles, then it becomes clear that a division's firepower was extremely low. These circumstances and the foolish combat employment of the artillery, as we will show later, created conditions in which the cooperation of the combat arms on the battlefield was completely absent. The artillery fired and the infantry did not move, then the infantry would rise to attack and the artillery would cease firing and remain silent. The untrained subunits and officers did not undertake any kind of manoeuvre and would lie down under enemy fire and allow themselves to be destroyed, thus encouraging the enemy, who got satisfaction by shooting up with impunity our immobile infantry which, aside from everything else, did not even have shovels for entrenching. The division would lose nearly all of its infantry in one or two days of fighting, without achieving any results. Between ten and fifteen infantrymen would remain in each regiment, while the higher commanders would always demand an attack and awaited the results with impatience. Personnel losses were mainly due to the enemy's artillery and mortar fire. This is confirmed by the fact that fragmentation wounds accounted for from 70–90 per cent of the entire number of wounded.

In our combat employment of artillery there exists a harmful and illiterate tendency – to count the density of artillery pieces according to the number of guns (barrels) per kilometre of front, and not according to the amount of ammunition designated for use. For the sake of this, a large number of artillery units and formations would be brought up to the front and the breakthrough front and the division attack sectors would be narrowed in the extreme. Shells were allotted for the beginning period of the operation to the tune of one to 1.5 units of fire, which could be effectively fired by four to five times less the number of artillery pieces. A reduction in the amount of artillery units and strength for supporting the division and their complex control equipment by increasing the expenditure of munitions for each gun would have greatly simplified the organization of cooperation and troop control during the heat of the fighting and would have increased the effectiveness of fire. The length and order of the artillery preparation were determined not by some kind of well-founded calculation based on the character of the enemy's defence, the number of artillery pieces and the quota of the allotted munitions, but haphazardly, according to a shopworn routine that has been learned by the enemy. (The start of the artillery preparation, as a rule, was signalled by a salvo from 'rocket artillery', and then the so-called 'destruction' period was conducted, lasting several tens of minutes to about a half-hour, although none of the artillerymen actually knew what he was supposed to destroy, or if there was anything to destroy. Then a 10–20 minute fire onslaught against the forward edge of the enemy defence would be conducted, and then, as a rule, the artillery would cease firing and the infantry would begin its attack.)

The work of the artillery was arranged so that our artillery along our sector of the front was never able to suppress the enemy's artillery, while the latter, upon choosing a favourable moment, would come

OPERATION BAGRATION: AN INCOMPLETE TRUTH

down on our infantry along previously registered lines and would almost completely wipe it out. During the most important times on the battlefield the enemy's (the defender's) fire dominated, and not ours (the attacker's). Our army's artillery proved to be nearly powerless to take on the enemy's tanks and self-propelled guns. Attempts were made with the attacking companies to bring up by hand guns for firing over open sights, but they always fell behind, were often put out of action by enemy fire, and had no effect. Practical preparation for the forthcoming operations was carried out in an extremely unskilled manner, in view of the enemy: the troops designated for the breakthrough were moved up to the forward edge (along the breakthrough sector) a few days before the start of the operation, while over the course of several days materiel supplies would be accumulated. We should have done this the other way around: first, accumulate materiel, reconnoitre the enemy's defence, move the artillery into position and prepare it, while the troops should be moved into their assembly positions no earlier than a day before the start of the attack. This is one of the important guarantees of surprise.

The opinion exists among some of the ranking officers of our army that, given the overall strategic situation, we did not have the time and opportunity for serious preparation and sufficient materiel support for the operations and that we fully achieved the goal assigned to us, by tying down the enemy along our front and preventing him from transferring his forces to the south, where large-scale operations are underway. Such an opinion strikes me as incorrect and I disagree with it. A simple calculation shows that one could conduct one or two serious and well-prepared operations with the men and material expended by the Western Front during the time described, to break through the enemy defence along at least a 20–30km front, to develop the success and not only tie down the enemy, but to liberate a large amount of territory, or to draw in a significant portion of the enemy's forces from other directions, or, as the result of great major defeats, force him to undertake an operational withdrawal. The failures of the operations conducted may be explained by their extremely unskilled and primitive planning, preparation and practical conduct. Neither the scale of the operations, nor the means of their preparation and conduct corresponded to the goals assigned.

For the purpose of supporting future operational success, Tolkonyuk immediately made ten proposals:

1) Prohibit attempts to break through the enemy's defence along a front less than 12km; that is, along a front which enables us to keep the enemy under fire with flanking and oblique fire throughout the entire breakthrough zone.
2) Divisions which have been reduced to 4,500 men or less should be pulled out of the fighting, as combat ineffective, for replenishment.

WHY WAS THE WESTERN FRONT COMMAND REMOVED

3) Allow no less than 30 days to train and knock together divisions that have received more than 50 per cent of their elements' strength in reinforcements.
4) In order to economize on our infantry, engagements which cannot be supported by a sufficient amount of munitions for suppressing the enemy's artillery and mortars should not be conducted during daytime.
5) The planned operation should be planned in detail at a level no less than the Front staff, which will offer a greater opportunity for choosing favourable terrain, a breakthrough sector and the concentration of that equipment necessary (it's often impossible to do this at the army level).
6) The infantry's combat formations during the breakthrough of the enemy's field defence should be organized in strict accordance with your Order No. 306 on new combat formations. To forbid (most of all, army and corps commanders, who are the main violators of the order in question and who cover up their violations of Order No. 306 and the infantry combat manual with the term 'deep combat formations'), by echeloning the divisions' combat formations in depth and expending these divisions in detail, without employing their entire shock strength.
7) In planning and carrying out artillery support for the operation, to first of all take into account the possibility of complete suppression for the necessary time and the partial destruction of the enemy's artillery and mortar batteries as the main killers of our infantry. An attack by infantry and tanks should be forbidden under conditions of the enemy's artillery and infantry superiority on the battlefield.
8) In order to combat the enemy's self-propelled guns and tanks, which remain the main 'bugaboo' of our infantry in the depth of the enemy's defence, it is necessary to create special units, armed with self-propelled guns and tanks, which would accompany the attacking infantry, with the task of destroying the enemy's tanks and self-propelled guns operating in small groups against our infantry. The rifle divisions' anti-tank artillery should be moved by light tanks or special armoured personnel carriers, in order to support the movement of anti-tank weapons in the infantry's combat formations.
9) The employment of tank formations in wooded and swampy terrain (the Belorussian forests and swamps) is to be prohibited.
10) To demand a special written account by the army commander for each operation conducted, with a conclusion by non-interested (neutral) parties. This will increase responsibility and broaden the operational-tactical view of the higher command element and will help to unearth in time deficiencies and mistakes, as well as to take them into account in future combat operations.[2]

How much were I.A. Tolkonyuk's proposals adopted and employed in Operation 'Bagration'? Let's examine them in reverse order. The idea of finding some kind of neutral observer capable of evaluating an account by an army commander was utopian and inapplicable in practice. Such a neutral but sufficiently authoritative general simply did not exist in nature. In reality, the Front commanders and also *Stavka* representatives, such as Marshals Zhukov and Vasilevskii during Operation 'Bagration', evaluated the army commanders' accounts.

Of course, the employment of tanks in wooded and swampy terrain is not desirable, but actually during 'Bagration' they were employed in precisely such terrain simply because there was no other type of terrain in Belorussia. The employment of armoured equipment was made easier by the fact that the offensive took place at the height of summer, which in 1944 in Belorussia was exceptionally hot. The supremacy of Soviet aviation also made the employment of Soviet armoured equipment easier. Soviet tanks, forced to concentrate along the roads, were only rarely subjected to attacks by the Luftwaffe. The idea of transporting anti-tank guns directly in the infantry's combat formations with the aid of armoured personnel carriers and light tanks, while in and of itself a good idea, was difficult to realize in the actual conditions of 1944. Due to the small number of armoured personnel carriers in the Red Army, they were used only in rare instances for transporting anti-tank guns. Light tanks were part of tank and motorized units, so in order to drag the rifle units' anti-tank guns around with their assistance required coordination at the level of the commanders of tank and rifle units, which by no means was always achieved in practice. There actually existed units designed for fighting the enemy's armoured equipment. These were self-propelled artillery regiments and self-propelled artillery brigades. The first such brigade was created as early as August 1943. By the beginning of 1944 there were two such brigades, and by the start of Operation 'Bagration' there were six, of which only two were employed in Belorussia as part of the First Belorussian Front. This is explained by the fact that there was less armoured equipment in Army Group Centre than in Army Groups North Ukraine and South Ukraine, which in the opinion of the *Stavka* did not require the special concentration of anti-tank equipment along the 'Bagration' front. With the appearance of new German panzer divisions, including elite ones, along Army Group Centre's front the Soviets' shortage of mobile anti-tank formations played a negative role. They were actually able to achieve the suppression of the enemy's artillery and mortar fire at the start of Operation 'Bagration', but this was a consequence of the Soviet side's overwhelming superiority not only in artillery, but in tanks and infantry. During the first days of the Soviet offensive the German artillery was forced to fire on too many targets simultaneously and rapidly shot off its unit of fire. After this they either had to abandon their guns or to pull them back to new positions, calculating that they would be able to bring up munitions there. However, the delivery of shells was made more difficult by Soviet air superiority, which heavily bombed the supply columns, which were almost entirely without anti-aircraft equipment.

Stalin's Order No. 306, 'On the Improvement of the Tactics of the Offensive Engagement and on the Combat Formations of Small Units, Units and Formations', issued as people's commissar for defence on 8 October 1942, demanded:

> Prohibit the echeloned organization of the combat formation in the platoon, company, battalion, regiment, and division in the offensive engagement. The demand for the maximum and simultaneous participation of infantry and its firepower in the engagement, from the

beginning to the end of the engagement, must be the cornerstone of the organization of the infantry's combat formations.

The section and platoon are to be deployed as skirmishers for the engagement. The distance between soldiers on the move should be 6–8 paces.

With the start of the offensive all of the platoons in the rifle company should be placed in a single echelon. Depending on the situation, the rifle platoons may be deployed either in one line (all of the platoons side by side), or in echelon formation; for example, one platoon forward and two echeloned behind its flanks, but not directly behind the lead one; two platoons forward and one behind in the space between them.

Heavy machine guns and mortars, both organic and attached, and anti-tank rifles, if available, are to be employed to fire from the flanks and in the spaces between the platoons.

The rifle companies in the battalion are also to be deployed in a single echelon and, depending on the situation, guide them: either all of the companies in a line (company next to company), or at an angle behind (two companies in a single line, with one company behind with a space between the lead companies), or echeloned to the right (two companies side by side in a line and one echeloned behind the right flank), or echeloned to the left (two companies side by side in a line and one echeloned behind the left flank).

Rifle battalions in the regiment's (brigade's) combat formation are to be deployed as follows: either all three battalions in a line or at an angle forward or an angle backward, or either echeloned to the right or left.

Rifle regiments in the division's combat formation are also to be placed in a single echelon (all the regiments in the combat line, next to each other, at the start of the engagement) . . .

In order to avoid excessive crowding of the combat formations, and from this heavy losses, during an offensive a standard-sized division (7–8,000 men), as part of an army's shock group, is to be assigned a zone of about 4km and under no circumstances less than 3km along the front.

Aside from the single fire and firing in bursts from rifles, as called for in our manuals, restore the practice of volley fire for the rifle section, platoon and, in certain cases, for the company as well.

Volley fire is to be employed against tight concentrations and combat formations of the enemy's personnel in all varieties of the engagement and on the march – for beating off surprise cavalry attacks and the enemy's columns, against low-flying enemy aircraft, and sometimes as a means of discipline, which helps the commander at the necessary moment in the engagement to rapidly take his section in hand.[3]

In practice, those complex combat organizations, including those that called for delivering machine-gun fire and fire from anti-tank weapons through the infantry's combat formations, were not for the Red Army's soldiers, whose level of training, as well as the level of training for NCOs and for platoon and company commanders, was too low. Thus, as opposed to Order No. 306, the troops continued into 1944 as well to attack in dense combat formations, because they were not sufficiently trained for the more complex, thin combat formations. As regards the idea of conducting volley fire, this was a purely office organization, relying on the experience of the Civil War but having no relation to the realities of 1944. There was no need for repulsing cavalry attacks due to the absence of cavalry among the Germans. Moreover, the allied Romanian and Hungarian cavalry divisions had long been fighting dismounted. While attacking fortified positions, even if they are no more than fully-outfitted trenches, the enemy is always under cover and volley fire has no effect.

In Operation 'Bagration' 172 Soviet rifle divisions (including four Polish divisions) attacked along an approximately 1,100km front. If we assume that two-thirds of their strength would be in the first echelon, that is, about 115 divisions, then each division had on average a 9.6km front. Naturally, the offensive was not to be conducted along the entire front, but only along previously-selected breakthrough sectors, where the troop density, of course, was different. In reality all of the rifle divisions were often thrown into the offensive, without creating a second echelon. Here, for example, the former artillery commander for the First Baltic Front, Colonel General N.M. Khlebnikov, recalls:

> According to General Bagramyan's plan, the offensive was built on an extremely high density of men and materiel along the breakthrough sector. By sharply weakening the remaining sectors of the front, 75 per cent of the formations and units and 87 per cent of the artillery and all of the tanks were concentrated here. The breakthrough sector accounted for only 15 per cent of the front line. At the same time, for the men and materiel which we disposed of, the breakthrough sector itself was very broad – about 25km (18km for the 6th Guards Army and 7km for the 43rd Army). Thus the Front's forces had to attack in single-echelon formation.[4]

I.Kh. Bagramyan himself states that 'four rifle corps from the 6th Guards Army and two from the 43rd Army were brought in, as well as the 3rd Air Army, and all the reserves and a tank corps. Insofar as the 43rd Army had twice as few forces for breaking through the defence as did the 6th Guards Army, only a 7km breakthrough sector was set aside for it, while the remaining 18km were reserved for the 6th Guards Army.'[5]

Moreover, the 43rd Army's offensive sector was 5km less than I.A. Tolkonyuk's recommended width of attack front of 12km and enabled the Germans to enfilade the entire breakthrough zone with flanking and oblique fire. As of 1 July 1944 the 43rd Army had eight rifle divisions in three corps, and the 6th Guards Army nine rifle divisions in three corps. But the latter still had attached to it the Front-subordinated 22nd Guards Rifle Corps, consisting of three divisions.[6] Thus one may draw the conclusion that along the 43rd Army's offensive sector there were six rifle divisions (1.17km per division) along the 7km breakthrough zone, and along the 6th Guards Army's offensive sector there were 12 divisions along 18km (1.5km per division). In both cases these indices were very far from those recommended by Order No. 306 of 'no less than 3km along the front'. Here it's worth noting that of the 6th Guards Army's 12 divisions, six were Guards units. In 1944 the authorized strength of a Guards rifle division (10,670 men) was greater than the authorized strength of an average rifle division (9,435 men) by 1.13 times.[7] By taking into account this difference, a single average rifle division in the 43rd Army had an attack zone of 1.4km. If one accepts that spaces were left between the divisions of at least 100m, in order to avoid getting tangled up in the neighbouring divisions' combat formations, then actually there was 1.08km per division in the 43rd Army and 1.25km in the 6th Guards Army. One should not doubt that an analogous situation existed in the other Fronts. Although Order No. 306 was not too bad in a number of places, from the point of view of military theory, it did have one major shortcoming – it was practically never put into practice. Thus heavy personnel losses during the conduct of 'Bagration' were inevitable. However, not one of the Front commanders suffered for this, or for violating Order No. 306 during the course of 'Bagration'. Of the army commanders, the unlucky ones were the commander of the 5th Guards Tank Army, P.A. Rotmistrov, and the commander of the 33rd Army, V.D. Kryuchyonkin. Rotmistrov was blamed for his heavy losses, not in personnel, but in tanks. Besides this, his conflict with the commander of the Third Belorussian Front I.D. Chernyakhovskii also played a role. Kryuchyonkin, who was formally relieved of his position due to illness, had a reputation among the higher commanders of being a poor commander. For example, the former chief of staff of the Third Belorussian Front, Colonel General A.P. Pokrovskii, in a conversation with the writer Konstantin Simonov, characterized Vasilii Dmitrievich as follows: 'Kryuchyonkin was a poor commander. He . . . was a man of a different scale and not an army commander. He was a typical cavalryman, but did not evolve. He was a cavalry corps commander at the beginning of the war. This was the height of his capabilities. He was a poor commander.'[8]

Nor did the idea of prohibiting infantry and tank attacks in the face of the enemy's battlefield superiority in artillery and mortar fire catch on. Attacks against the enemy's unsuppressed artillery and mortar fire system continued right up to the end of the war and here 'Bagration' was no exception. On the other hand, beginning with 'Bagration' the incidences in which they were unable to suppress the German artillery fire system became much fewer.

Tolkonyuk's idea that an army operation should be planned together with the Front headquarters received support. It was during Operation 'Bagration' that joint planning was carried out.

No one was prepared to adopt Tokonyuk's proposal not to undertake attacks during daylight, if there was a shortage of munitions for suppressing the enemy's artillery. The same went for the idea to allow a division which had received more than 50 per cent of reinforcements for its combat elements no less than 30 days for training and knocking the units together. They actually did try to pull divisions whose strength had fallen to 4,500 men out of the front line, but they were not always able to do this. Before the beginning of the 12 October 1943 offensive on Orsha, the Western Front command allotted the armies very narrow attack sectors not exceeding 5km in width. The armies attacked in 2–3 echelons consisting of rifle divisions. There was even another success-development echelon made up of mobile formations. Similarly, the divisions and regiments organized their combat formations in 2–3 echelons. This was supposed to help in augmenting the strength of the attack while breaking through the German defence. But the main reason for the extremely narrow offensive sectors and the deep echeloning of forces was that the arriving reinforcements had not been trained in either defensive or offensive fighting. Thus the Western Front command sought to get the rank and file to attack 'in dense masses, while directly feeling one's neighbour to the left and right', insofar as 'a poorly trained and untested soldier would immediately hit the dirt and not move upon hearing the first explosions of shells and mortar rounds. The presence of second and third echelons advancing behind the first supported a non-stop forward advance.'[9] However, such an offensive method inevitably led to extremely heavy losses among the attackers, whose dense combat formations served as excellent targets for the German artillery and attack aviation. On 13 October the Polish Tadeusz Kosciuszko 1st Infantry Division, which was part of the 33rd Army, suffered heavy losses from air attacks. During 12–13 October the division lost more than 500 killed, more than 1,680 wounded and 661 missing in the Lenino area.[10] According to the Polish historian Robert Wroblewski, during 11–12 October, according to Soviet reports, the Polish 1st Division lost 2,009 men, the 33rd Army's 42nd Rifle Division lost 379 men and the 290th Rifle Division lost 423 men. According to Wroblewski's calculations, during 11–12 October the German 337th Infantry Division lost about 500 men. On 12 October this division lost 124 men killed and died from wounds. Of this number, 85 were killed in the Lenino–Trigubovo–Polzukhi–Punishche area, while nine men died of their wounds at the Yurkovo–Kurtasy main medical station.

In the fighting on 12–13 October the Polish infantry division suffered losses amounting to 23.7 per cent of its initial strength, or 3,054 men, of which 510 were killed or died from their wounds, including 51 officers, while 1,776 were wounded, including 100 officers, and 652 men were missing, including 13 officers, and 116 men were captured.

On 13 October the 337th Infantry Division reported destroying 36 Soviet tanks (26 T-34s, five KVs, one T-70, one General Lee, two T-60s, and three self-propelled guns), of which eight were knocked out in close-quarters fighting. The division took 39 prisoners from the 153rd Rifle Division's (21st Army) 556th Rifle Regiment (to the north of Azarovo), the 150th Punishment Company (to the south of Polzukhi), the Polish 1st Tank Regiment (around Trigubovo), the Polish 2nd and 3rd Infantry Regiments (around Polzukhi and Trigubovo), and the Soviet 20th Fighter Regiment. Also, 13 deserters from the Polish 2nd Infantry Regiment turned themselves over to the division's elements. Besides this, documents (two Red Army booklets) were found on dead soldiers from the 42nd Rifle Division to the south-east of Polzukhi. On 13 October the 337th Infantry Division lost 70 men killed and died of wounds, of which 33 died in the Lenino–Trigubovo–Polzukhi–Punishche area, and 14 died from their wounds at the Yurkovo–Kurtasy main medical station.

During the night of 13/14 October the Polish 1st Infantry Division was relieved by the Soviet 164th Rifle Division. On 14–15 October the Soviet 21st Army undertook an unsuccessful attempt to break through along the sector Height 217.6–Azarovo with the forces of the 62nd and 157th Rifle Divisions and the 33rd Army in the Lenino–Polzukhi area on 14–16 October. At 1600 on 14 October the Germans recaptured the eastern part of the village of Polzukhi, which had been seized earlier by the Polish 2nd Infantry Regiment.

The German 337th Infantry Division (8,761 men on 9 October, including 2,953 in combat units) was attacked on 12 October by five Soviet divisions from the 21st and 33rd Armies. The Soviet forces suffered heavy losses in killed and wounded and the 337th Infantry Division captured 441 prisoners and deserters from the Polish 1st Infantry Division's 1st and 2nd Regiments, as well as from the 290th Rifle Division's 882nd and 885th Rifle Regiments, one pilot from the 49th Fighter Regiment and

WHY WAS THE WESTERN FRONT COMMAND REMOVED

one pilot from the 321st Assault Air Regiment. The division also destroyed 26 tanks (16 T-34s, four KVs, one BT-7, and five other unidentified tanks), of which five were destroyed in close-quarters fighting by elements of the 313th Grenadier Regiment.

During 12–18 October the Western Front's losses, according to highly understated data from the Front headquarters, amounted to 5,800 men killed and 17,500 wounded. It's not clear whether this includes the losses of the Polish 1st Infantry Division, or whether they were counted separately. The second variant is more likely, because the Poles suffered heavy losses in missing in action, while missing in action are not listed at all in the Western Front's report on losses.[11] During 11–20 October 1943 the German Fourth Army, which faced the Western Front along the Orsha axis, lost 786 men killed, 3,478 wounded and 308 missing in action.[12]

In the Western Front's combat journal the reasons for the unsuccessful offensive are described as follows:

> The offensive organized on 12 October along the Orsha axis was not developed successfully for the following reasons: The enemy found out through a deserter about the breakthrough preparations and took countermeasures (prepared a large aviation group, reinforced the axis with tanks and self-propelled guns, and during our artillery and air preparation he hid his personnel and weapons in shelters). And he put up all of this during our forces' attack . . .
>
> The Front continued to experience great difficulties in bringing up auto fuel, ammunition, food, and air aviation fuel to the troops. The railway as far as Smolensk was still working poorly and yielded 6–7 trains per day. Dirt supply roads were very long and required a lot of time and fuel for a round trip.
>
> The artillery, mortars and infantry conducted the battle, while there were few tanks for operating with the infantry, and they were quickly put out of action. Having failed to achieve the necessary success in this operation, the troops . . . were forced to halt offensive activities . . .[13]

So, what caused all the commotion in the *Stavka*, General Staff and SMERSH? Why was it necessary to immediately replace the leadership of the Western Front? In the Malenkov commission's report the specific failures of Sokolovskii's forces during the operation against Orsha and Vitebsk were analysed in detail. There, it was noted in particular that:

> Beginning on 12 October 1943 and continuing through 1 April 1944, the Western Front, under the command of General Sokolovskii, conducted 11 operations along the Orsha and Vitebsk axes, namely: the Orsha operation of 12–18 October 1943; the Orsha operation of 21–26 October 1943; the Orsha operation of 14–19 November 1943; the Orsha operation of 30 November–2 December 1943; the Vitebsk operation of 23 December 1943–6 January 1944; the Bogushevsk operation of 8–24 January 1944 [Bogushevsk is a town in the Vitebsk Oblast', halfway between Vitebsk and Orsha, B.S.]; the Vitebsk operation of 3–16 February 1944; a local operation along the Orsha axis during

OPERATION BAGRATION: AN INCOMPLETE TRUTH

22–25 February 1944; the Vitebsk operation of 29 February–5 March 1944; the Orsha operation of 5–9 March 1944; and the Bogushevsk operation of 21–29 March 1944.

All of these operations ended unsuccessfully and the Front did not carry out the tasks set by the *Stavka*. Nor was the enemy defence broken through in a single one of the enumerated operations and, at best, the operations would conclude with an insignificant penetration into the enemy's defence in the tactical depth, which cost our forces heavy losses.

Then the results of the operations were listed, along with the losses suffered:

The offensive along the Orsha axis during 12–18 October concluded with a penetration of 1–1.5km. Our losses: 5,858 men killed and 17,478 wounded, for a total of 23,336 men.

The offensive along the Orsha axis during 21–26 October, with an advance of 4–6km. Our losses: 4,787 men killed and 14,315 wounded, for a total of 19,102 men.

The offensive along the Orsha axis during 14–19 November, with an advance of 1–4km. Our losses: 9,167 killed and 29,589 wounded, for a total of 38,756 men.

The offensive along the Orsha axis during 30 November–2 December, with a penetration of 1–2km. Our losses: 5,611 killed and 17,259 wounded, for a total of 22,870 men.

The offensive along the Vitebsk axis during 23 December–6 January, with an advance of 8–12km. The enemy fell back to previously-prepared lines. Our losses: 6,692 killed and 28,904 wounded, for a total of 35,596 men.

The offensive along the Bogushevsk axis during 8–24 January, with a penetration of 2–4km. Our losses: 9,651 killed and 32,844 wounded, for a total of 42,495 men.

The local operation along the Orsha axis during 22–25 February yielded no result. During this operation the units of the 52nd Fortified Area themselves got into an encirclement and the initial situation was reestablished with heavy losses. Our losses: 1,288 killed and 4,479 wounded, for a total of 5,767 men.

The offensive along the Vitebsk axis during 29 February–5 March, with an advance of 2–6km. Our losses: 2,650 killed and 9,205 wounded, for a total of 11,855 men.

The offensive along the Orsha axis during 5–9 March was unsuccessful. Our losses: 1,898 killed and 5,639 wounded, for a total of 7,537 men.

The offensive along the Bogushevsk axis during 21–29 March, with a penetration of 1–3.5km. Our losses: 9,207 killed and 30,828 wounded, for a total of 40,035 men.

During these unsuccessful operations from 12 October 1943 through 1 April 1944 the Front lost along the active sectors alone 62,326 men killed and 219,419 wounded, for a total of 281,745 men. If one adds to this the losses along the passive sectors of the front, then the Western Front's losses during the period from October 1943 to April 1944 were 330,587 men. Aside from this, 53,283 sick entered the Western Front's hospitals during this time.

I want to direct the reader's attention to the fact that there is no mention in the report about the Western Front's missing in action. And they must have been considerable, if only in the local operation along the Orsha axis during 22–25 February, when our forces themselves fell into an encirclement.

Such disappointing results were achieved in spite of an overwhelming superiority in men and materiel. The Malenkov commission's report particularly emphasized the inordinate expenditure of a large amount of munitions:

> In the operations listed above, from October 1943 through March 1944, the Front expended a very large amount of munitions, namely 7,261 train cars. During the year from March 1943 through March 1944 the Front expended 16,661 train cars of ammunition. During this time, that is during a year, the Belorussian Front expended 12,335 train cars, the First Ukrainian Front 10,945 train cars, and the Fourth Ukrainian Front 8,463 train cars, while each of the remaining Fronts expended less ammunition than the above-named Fronts. Thus the Western Front expended more ammunition than any other front [one should note that it was the absence of success – the breakthrough of the enemy front, which led to the increased expenditure of ammunition; the enemy facing the other Fronts was forced to fall back significant distances and during the pursuit the expenditure of ammunition was significantly less than during the storming of fortified positions, B.S.].
>
> The Western Front's unsuccessful actions during the preceding half-year, the heavy losses and the great expenditure of ammunition can be explained not by the presence of a powerful enemy and an unassailable defence facing the Front, but exclusively by the unsatisfactory leadership on the part of the Front command. The Western Front, while conducting all the operations, always enjoyed a significant superiority in men and materiel over the enemy, which undoubtedly enabled it to count on success.

Further on, the members of the commission presented concrete data about the sides' correlation of forces in the various operations.

> The Orsha operation of 12–18 October 1943 – 19 rifle divisions, a tank corps, a cavalry corps, 12 artillery brigades, 20 artillery regiments from the high command reserve, three tank brigades, and six tank and self-propelled artillery regiments. In all, there were 134 tanks. The artillery density was 150–200 tubes per kilometre of front. The enemy had two infantry divisions, 3–5 artillery regiments and about 30 tanks. A single infantry division, two panzergrenadier divisions and 3–4 artillery regiments were later brought up.

OPERATION BAGRATION: AN INCOMPLETE TRUTH

The Orsha operation of 21–26 October 1943 – 11 rifle divisions, a tank corps, 13 artillery brigades, 19 artillery regiments from the high command reserve, two tank brigades, and three tank and self-propelled artillery regiments. In all, there were 172 tanks and there was a density of 115–260 tubes per kilometre of front. The enemy had four infantry divisions, an SS brigade, 6–7 artillery regiments, and up to 60 tanks.

The Orsha operation of 14–19 November 1943 – 32 rifle divisions, a tank corps, 16 artillery brigades, 32 artillery regiments from the high command reserve, four tank brigades, and seven tank and self-propelled artillery regiments. In all, there were 410 tanks and a density of 120–260 tubes per kilometre of front. The enemy had four infantry divisions, two panzer divisions, an SS brigade, and up to 12 artillery regiments. In all, he had about 70 tanks.

The Orsha operation of 30 November–2 December 1943 – 34 rifle divisions, 13 artillery brigades, 24 artillery regiments from the high command reserve, four tank brigades, and ten tank and self-propelled artillery regiments. In all, there were 284 tanks and a density of 120–170 tubes per kilometre of front. The enemy had four infantry divisions, two panzer divisions and up to ten artillery regiments. In all, he had about 200 tanks.

The Vitebsk operation of 23 December–6 January 1944 – 11 rifle divisions, a tank corps, ten artillery brigades, four artillery regiments from the high command reserve, four tank brigades, and five self-propelled artillery regiments. In all, there were 147 tanks and a density of 110 tubes per kilometre of front. The enemy had two infantry divisions, up to five artillery regiments and about 60 tanks. Another three infantry divisions had been thrown in by the close of the operation.

The Bogushevsk operation of 8–24 January 1944 – 16 rifle divisions, one rifle brigade, a tank corps, 12 artillery brigades, six artillery regiments from the high command reserve, six tank brigades, and eight self-propelled artillery regiments, for 295 tanks. The enemy's forces were four infantry divisions, parts of two panzergrenadier divisions, up to nine artillery regiments, and up to 130 tanks.

The Vitebsk operation of 3–16 February 1944 – 16 rifle divisions, a tank corps, 12 artillery brigades, nine artillery regiments from the high command reserve, two tank brigades, and two self-propelled artillery regiments, for a total of 129 tanks and 115–140 tubes per kilometre of front. The enemy had five infantry divisions, up to nine artillery regiments and about 140 tanks. About two infantry regiments were later thrown into the fighting.

The Vitebsk operation of 29 February–5 March 1944 – 15 rifle divisions and one rifle brigade, seven artillery brigades, ten artillery regiments from the high command reserve, and six tank brigades, for a total of 87 tanks. The enemy had five infantry divisions, ten artillery regiments and about 90 tanks.

The Orsha operation of 5–9 March 1944 – eight rifle divisions, three artillery brigades, six artillery regiments from the high command

WHY WAS THE WESTERN FRONT COMMAND REMOVED

reserve, one tank brigade, and two tank regiments, for 80 tanks and a density of 100 tubes per kilometre of front. The enemy had one infantry division, three artillery regiments and up to 35 tanks.

The Bogushevsk operation of 21–29 March 1944 – nine rifle divisions, ten artillery brigades, six artillery regiments from the high command reserve, five tank brigades, and four self-propelled artillery regiments, for 73 tanks and a density of 100–150 tubes per kilometre of front. The enemy had two infantry divisions, up to five artillery regiments and up to 40 tanks.

Insofar as there were no panzer subunits in the German infantry divisions, in the majority of cases the report calls self-propelled guns tanks, which were actually attached to infantry formations as battalions.

And just what were the losses suffered by the Germans from October 1943 to April 1944? We have data only for the number of killed for all of the German ground forces which were involved in combat during this time, not only on the Eastern Front, but in Italy and also in the Balkans against Josip Broz Tito's partisans. From 1 October 1943 through 1 April 1944 Germany's ground forces lost in killed, including those who died from wounds, disease and other causes, but without counting those missing in action, 252,793 men, four times less than the Western Front lost during the course of the unsuccessful offensive operations. Taking into account the losses along the passive sectors of 48,842 men, the overall number of killed on the Western Front during the period in question was approximately 72,000 men, which was 3.5 times less than the losses suffered by the German ground forces along all the fronts. But can one determine the losses suffered by precisely those German divisions which opposed the Western Front? Let's try. As is clear from the report by the Malenkov commission, during all of the unsuccessful operations by Sokolovskii's armies they were opposed by approximately two panzer divisions, two panzergrenadier divisions and about 11 infantry divisions, as well as one SS brigade. Here double counting is possible, insofar as the Germans could have moved divisions from the Orsha area to Viteþsk or Bogushevsk, or vice versa. Besides this, Western Front intelligence had the habit of significantly exaggerating the enemy's forces. To be sure, the commission sought to cleanse the intelligence information of fanciful divisions, but where's the guarantee that they did it for all of them? Nonetheless, we will take as the maximum strength of the German group of forces facing Sokolovskii's armies along the active sectors of the front as 15.5 estimated divisions. In this case I counted the infantry divisions' combat groups as full-strength divisions, while taking into account that for a large part of the period from October 1943 to April 1944 they operated as more or less full-strength formations. Moreover, during the period from November 1943 to April 1944 another 22 divisions were disbanded on the Eastern Front due to heavy losses, so that the overall number of divisions operating against the Red Army (excluding the formations in Norway and Finland) amounted to about 174.5 during this period.

It is still necessary to determine what kind of losses German forces suffered in Italy. From July 1943 to the beginning of December 1944 they lost in killed and died of wounds 47,873 men. Taking into account the intensity of the fighting during the period from October 1943 to April 1944, one may place the losses at about 20,000 dead. Then the losses on the Eastern Front for these months may be calculated at 232,000 men.

OPERATION BAGRATION: AN INCOMPLETE TRUTH

Fifteen and one-half divisions out of 174.5 amount to about 8.9 per cent. Accordingly, their losses can be defined at most as 21,000 killed and died from wounds. But this is only in the case that one accepts that the average losses of a single division in Army Group Centre during this period were not lower than the average losses in the other Army Groups on the Eastern Front. By the way, the Germans were suffering their heaviest losses then in Ukraine, and not in Belorussia. For example, of the 22 divisions disbanded during this period, only four of them came from Army Group Centre. The same number of divisions was disbanded in Army Group North, while the remaining 14 were from Army Groups A, South, South Ukraine and North Ukraine. At the same time, in May Army Group Centre numbered 41.5 divisions, with 37 divisions in Army Group North, and 74 divisions in Army Groups South Ukraine and North Ukraine. Thus Army Group Centre contained 27.2 per cent of all the divisions on the Eastern Front, but only 18.2 per cent of the overall number of disbanded divisions. Thus one must note that by no means were those disbanded divisions in Army Group Centre those that faced the Western Front. One can assume that the divisions fighting against this Front lost in killed and died from wounds, at a minimum, one and a half times less than the average for all German forces on the Eastern Front. Then the losses for the 15.5 divisions fighting along the active sectors of the front may be defined as 14,000 killed and died from wounds. No less than 15 per cent of this number is those who died from their wounds, so that the number of those killed may be calculated as approximately 13,000 men.

This is approximately five times less than the losses suffered by the forces of the Western Front attacking Vitebsk, Orsha and Bogushevsk – 62,000 killed. Taking into account the significant undercounting of Soviet irreparable losses, the actual correlation was more than likely even more unfavourable for Sokolovskii's forces.

It was emphasized in the report by Malenkov's commission that the illiterate, in the tactical and operational sense, actions of the headquarters and troops of the Western Front led to the failures:

> As opposed to the established experience of the war, the Western Front command in certain operations organized the breakthrough along very narrow sectors: along a 6km front in the Vitebsk operation of 23 December and along a 5km front in the Orsha operation of 5 March. This enabled the enemy to concentrate a destructive flanking fire and, in conjunction with counter-attacks by small reserves, to exclude the possibility of our infantry's advancing and inflicting heavy losses.
>
> The Front headquarters was removed from planning the operations and was fixed only upon the course of events developing according to the army plans. The Front headquarters does not have any kind of operational planning documents for conducting the operation. All the operations conducted were planned only in the armies and were orally confirmed by the Front commander. As a result, the Front headquarters did not make any proposals to the command for planning and conducting the operations and did not carry out the required control for fulfilling the command's decisions. As concerns operational preparation, here there were very major shortcomings which negatively influenced the outcome of the operation. The regrouping of forces and preparation for the operations were carried out without the necessary secrecy and

disinformation of the enemy, as a result of which the element of surprise was lost in almost all the operations and the operations unfolded in conditions of the enemy's readiness to meet our offensive, although no documents of any kind were formally issued and everything was supposedly held in absolute secret.

In some operations the rifle divisions and the reinforcements were committed into the fighting from the march. In the 5th Army's operation during 22–25 February, the 184th Rifle Division, on the night of 20/21 February, turned over its defensive sector to the 158th Rifle Division and by the morning of 22 February had reached the assembly point for the offensive and at 0800 on the same day and, following a ten-minute artillery assault, went over to the offensive and, of course, was unsuccessful. In the 33rd Army's operation of 3–16 February the 222nd, 164th, 144th and 215th Rifle Divisions were each reinforced with 1,500 men on the eve of the offensive and committed into the fighting on the following morning. The officer element that arrived with the reinforcements took command of its subunits in the jumping-off area and led them into the attack within a few hours.

The higher headquarters allocate to themselves and their work a large part of the time allotted for the preparation, so that almost no time remains for the conduct of reconnaissance and drawing up the tasks for the lower levels on site and the organization of cooperation . . .

In the majority of operations conducted by the Front the armies, especially the 33rd Army, attacked while deeply echeloning their combat formations and created an excessive density of personnel, thus violating Order No. 306. Such an organization of combat formations led to a situation in which 2–3 battalions in a division attacked, while the remaining battalions remained behind. In these conditions, the shock divisions were not employed simultaneously, but were expended in detail, and their firepower remained idle. All of this led to heavy losses before the troops even entered the fighting and upon suffering such losses and being under constant fire, the units lost their combat effectiveness even before the start of the fighting.

I should note that heavy losses among the troops, even before they are in a condition to come to grips with the enemy, is a long-standing Russian tradition. Let's recall Andrei Bolkonskii's regiment in *War and Peace*, during the Battle of Borodino, which lost more than a third of its rank and file from French artillery even before entering the fighting.

The special commission, headed by Malenkov, having studied the activity of the Western Front's headquarters, concluded:

> As a result of the positional situation on the Western Front and the advance by neighbouring Fronts, a configuration of the front line along the Smolensk–Minsk direction was created which is extremely unfavourable for us. The enemy along this direction has a salient in our direction of up to 150km in depth. Such a situation exerts an

unfavourable influence on the neighbouring Fronts and enables the enemy to keep its aviation in the Lepel' – Mogilev–Minsk triangle and operate with it along the shortest routes against the rear of the Baltic and Belorussian Fronts. As regards the Western Front, the enemy is closest of all to Moscow.

It was from this then, in April 1944, that there arose the idea of Operation 'Bagration' – the launching of the main attack in Belorussia simultaneously with the forces of several Fronts. The Germans, as we will see later, immediately learned of this plan, but were unable to undertake any kind of effective countermeasures. The Malenkov commission also noted the completely unsatisfactory condition of the intelligence organs:

> Reconnaissance in the Western Front is conducted quite unsatisfactorily. The data which it produces is often unreliable. The intelligence section of the Front's headquarters does not control the activities of the armies', corps' and divisions' intelligence organs and has ruined agent intelligence. Colonel Il'nitskii, the chief of the intelligence section, put out doubtful and exaggerated information as reliable. Troop intelligence is not organized and is conducted without a plan. Intelligence operations are prepared and conducted poorly, with heavy personnel losses of an average of up to five men for a single prisoner captured, while troop intelligence does not gather information necessary for the command.
>
> Reconnaissance in force is carried out in a non-purposeful fashion and is conducted without careful preparation and organization and is often not backed up by fire support, as a result of which a large portion of the Front's intelligence activities finish unsuccessfully and with heavy losses. There are major shortcomings in the preparation and conduct of intelligence search operations, particularly in the enemy rear. The main task of a search is to capture a prisoner for confirmation purposes, but this is not carried out in many cases. For example, in December [1943, B.S.] the 192nd Rifle Division carried out 23 intelligence operations in order to capture a 'tongue'. Not a single prisoner was taken as the result of these operations and losses among our intelligence group were 26 men killed and wounded. From 1 January through 15 February [1944, B.S.] the 192nd, 247th and 174th Rifle Divisions carried out hundreds of intelligence search operations and not a single prisoner was taken. In the 331st and 251st Rifle Divisions our scouts often blew themselves up in our minefields, because their location was not pointed out to them.
>
> The observation service among the Front's forces is organized formally. Nobody is in charge of this type of intelligence and observation is carried out by untrained people and often turns into the pointless viewing of the terrain, while actual observation of the enemy is absent.
>
> The *Stavka*'s instructions prohibiting the employment of intelligence elements in battle as common infantry are systematically violated at the front. For example, in January 1944 all of the 33rd Army's intelligence subunits of units and formations took part in the offensive as line subunits and were almost completely destroyed.

There are particularly great shortcomings in agent intelligence. Agent intelligence in the Western Front has become polluted by doubtful people and is conducted in a primitive manner and by rote. The information collected by this kind of intelligence is often not confirmed and is often the source of disinformation.

The recruitment of agents is conducted without sufficient checking and is not individualized. Agents are often recruited by groups of people who have not been vetted and who do not have life experience. Among the agents there are often found people who are politically doubtful, unreliable and who are counter-recruited by the Germans immediately after their insertion.

The training of agents is conducted in an unorganized manner and hurriedly, without sufficient training. Many agents, lacking sufficient preparation, are quickly uncovered. The elementary rules of conspiracy are violated. Large groups of agents socialized among themselves and knew each other well. For example, the intelligence groups of Khristoforov, Yurchenko, Kalnibolotskii and Sitnikov, which were destined for work in the enemy rear in various areas and numbering overall 28 men, were housed together in a single dwelling throughout their entire training. The equipping of agents sent into the enemy rear was often standardized and enabled the Germans to easily spot our agents. Agents were dispatched in 1942 and 1943 to territory occupied by the Germans in 1941 and were dressed in clothes labelled that they had been produced by the Moscow Sewing Factory in 1942 and 1943. The standardized nature of their clothes, in the event of the unmasking of one agent, enabled the enemy to easily unmask our other agents.

The Front's intelligence section did not seek to insinuate agents into the enemy's headquarters and military establishments. The agents' work was carried out along the lines of least resistance and was limited to simple observation and the gathering of rumours amongst the local population. The intelligence section's communications with its agents working in the rear is in very poor condition. Many agents have ceased sending reports entirely because there is no power for their radio sets. The intelligence section, while having every opportunity for the uninterrupted supply of power for the radio sets, treats this important matter carelessly and irresponsibly.

Although aerial reconnaissance is carried out formally, the data received from aviation is not analysed in a timely manner and is not checked against other sources and is often not communicated to the troops. Aerial photos and aerial maps get stuck in the higher headquarters and are not sent to the troops in a timely manner.

Radio intelligence, despite the large amount of radio equipment, works poorly and often yields absolutely incorrect data and leads our headquarters into making mistakes.

The intelligence section of the Western Front's headquarters is not coping with the tasks assigned to it. Overestimating the enemy's forces, the lack of planning in intelligence work, lack of contact with the troops, the inability to acquire the necessary information in a timely manner, and to distinguish what is false from what is true – these are typical features in the work of the intelligence section of the Western Front's headquarters. The chief of the Front headquarters' intelligence section, Colonel Il'nitskii, systematically exaggerates the strength of the enemy facing the Western Front. This was expressed in the increase of the number of divisions and the numerical strength of the enemy's divisions facing the Western Front.

Nor did anything remain of the reputation of the Western Front's chief of staff, General Pokrovskii:

> The Western Front's headquarters is not carrying out its role. The staff lacks a leader, is cut off from the Front command and from the important tasks being decided by the troops and essentially functions as some kind of statistical bureau, only gathering data according to the situation and in a tardy manner. Questions of planning operations, the organization of the battle and controlling the achievement of decisions made by the command have actually been removed from the staff's competence. During the course of four months the chief of staff and the entire staff have been located about 100km from the location of the Front command and during this time the commander and the chief of staff met no more than 3–4 times. There is one colonel from the staff with the commander at his VPU [temporary command post, B.S.] (although in this case the name does not fit), who essentially carries out the duties of an adjutant. The Front commander, comrade Sokolovskii, considers such an unheard of practice quite normal.
>
> Not only the Front commander has bought the headquarters to such a state, but the chief of staff, Lieutenant General Pokrovskii, who is afraid of responsibility and is unable to make independent decisions on even small matters, is also guilty. Pokrovskii does not undertake any kind of measures to fix the abnormal situation with the staff and works in a formalistic and bureaucratic manner. The chief of the operational section, Major General Chirkov, lacks initiative and is no good as the leader of the Front's operational section.

The Western Front command as a whole came in for criticism from the Malenkov commission:

> The chief reason for the operational failures on the Western Front is the unsatisfactory troop control on the part of the Front command. The Western Front command, instead of learning from its shortcomings and eliminating them, has manifested self-satisfaction and conceit and has failed to uncover these shortcomings, has not taken mistakes into account, has not trained people and has not raised commanders in the spirit of truthfulness. The most glaring shortcomings and mistakes were repeated in all the operations. The examination of the operations and the

WHY WAS THE WESTERN FRONT COMMAND REMOVED

issuing of summation orders on the shortcomings and results of combat operations on the Western Front were not practised.

Despite the fact that one of the major shortcomings in conducting operations was the artillery's poor work, this shortcoming was not overcome and continued to repeat itself. In all of the operations conducted by the Front the artillery did not suppress the enemy's fire system and, it followed from this, did not support the infantry's advance. The Front command knew of the heavy losses in personnel as the result of the artillery's poor work, of the enormous expenditure of ammunition, but, however, did not take measures to correct the artillery's work.

The Front command is intolerant of criticism and attempts to criticize shortcomings are met with hostility. Typical of this are the comments by General Sokolovskii on the report by a General Staff officer, in which the shortcomings in preparing and controlling the operation, which was conducted by the 31st Army on 29 October 1943, were highlighted. The comments are as follows: 'The value of this document is quite insignificant, even on a good market day'. 'Colonel Nekrasov evidently did not think about what he was writing'. 'This man has evidently gotten used to babbling'. 'Lies!' 'Stupid lies'. 'Lies'. 'The writer completely misunderstands the battle to break through the defence'. 'Words, and nothing more!' Such an atmosphere has arisen at the front and people are trained in such a way that they are afraid to put forward to the Front command questions concerning shortcomings. There were timid attempts on the part of individual combat arms commanders to point out the shortcomings in the troops' activities and to examine them in an order, but the Front commander rejected such attempts.

The command's instructions for eliminating the shortcomings took the form of oral and informal admonitions which never obliged anyone to do anything. For example, the situation in Gordov's army did not change up until his removal by the *Stavka* from the position of commander of the 33rd Army, although comrade Sokolovskii assures us that he issued oral instructions to Gordov to eliminate the outrages prevalent in the army. The Front command did not present a report to the *Stavka* on the shortcomings and reasons for the failure of the operations and in such a manner failed to truthfully uncover for both itself and the *Stavka* the reasons for the failure to carry out the tasks set by the *Stavka*. The hushing up of the true reasons for the failure of these operations was, in this case, nothing more than a form of deceiving the *Stavka*.

The Front command poorly understood people and uncritically related to their shortcomings. This is explained by the fact that Colonel General Gordov was completely and without foundation considered the best army commander and Colonel General of Artillery Kamera is considered a good artillery officer, despite the fact that the artillery did not carry out its tasks, and that Colonel Il'nitskii is considered a good intelligence officer, while the work of the Front's intelligence section is actually in a decrepit condition.

OPERATION BAGRATION: AN INCOMPLETE TRUTH

Front commander comrade Sokolovskii is removed from his closest assistants – the commanders of the combat arms and service chiefs – for days at a time and does not receive them and does not resolve their questions. Some of the commander's deputies did not know of their troops' tasks in connection with ongoing operations, not to mention that they were not brought in to draw up the operations. For example, the commander of the armoured and mechanized forces, Lieutenant General of Tank Forces Rodin, declared: 'Not once did they ask me how to best employ tanks. I'm only a dispatcher and send tanks to this or that army. I learned of the tank troops' tasks in the armies or from subordinate tank troops.' The Front command does not react in a timely manner to the troops' needs. As a result, for example, in certain of the attacking divisions, particularly in the 33rd Army, there was only a single disk for the light machine guns and a single belt for the heavy machine guns. This led to a situation in which at the height of the fighting the machine guns were unable to support the infantry and spent a good deal of time loading disks and belts. In a number of operations the artillery fell behind the infantry as a result the lack of transport for the guns. At the same time, the Front has a sufficient quantity of transport in order to completely cover the attacking troops' artillery. The Front command only had to react to the army's needs and to manoeuvre the equipment to the front in a timely manner. There was a shortage of radios in the lower artillery and infantry echelons, as a result of which cooperation between the infantry and artillery was disrupted. At the same time, there was a sufficient amount of radios in the front and armies' rear and headquarters to support the attacking forces. It is the fault of the Front commander that in November–December 1943; that is, at the height of the operations, there were serious breakdowns in food supply in many divisions. Taking into account the existing supply of products in the divisions, armies and the front, there was no more than a 5–7 day supply of food, according to a number of basic products (meat, fish, bread, and groats).

There then followed the overall and depressing conclusion:

Since October 1943 to April 1944 the Western Front, despite a superiority in forces over the enemy and the great expenditure of ammunition, did not move forward. All of the operations conducted during the half-year failed, due to the Front command. The Western Front failed to carry out the tasks set by the *Stavka* of the Supreme High Command and has been weakened as the result of the heavy losses in men and materiel, which are the result of the unskilled leadership of the Front command. At present time the Western Front is in need of reinforcements and assistance.

Such a situation in the Western Front is the result of the unsatisfactory leadership of the Front command on the part of the commander, General Sokolovskii, the former member of the Western Front's military council, Lieutenant General Bulganin, and the current member of the military council, Lieutenant General Mekhlis.

WHY WAS THE WESTERN FRONT COMMAND REMOVED

The Western Front command has become conceited and does not approach its mistakes in a critical manner. Despite the failure of eleven major and minor operations during the course of a half year, the Front command did not draw lessons from this and did not truthfully report to the *Stavka* on the situation at the front.

General Sokolovskii proved himself to be not up to the task as a Front commander. Comrades Sokolovskii and Bulganin bear, first of all, responsibility for the fact that in the Western Front there was lacking the necessary training of command cadres in the spirit of truthfulness and antipathy toward shortcomings [actually, this training was lacking throughout the entire Red Army, B.S.].

The mistake of the current member of the Western Front's military council, Lieutenant General Mekhlis, is that he did not report to the *Stavka* on the true nature of the situation at the front.

There are particularly major shortcomings in the artillery's activities. The artillery troops in the Western Front do not uncover their mistakes or correct them, while at the same time the poor work of the artillery was the main reason for the failures of the offensive operations. In this regard, besides the Front command, the Front artillery commander, Colonel General of Artillery Kamera, is to blame most of all. The mistake by Chief Artillery Marshal Voronov is that he, while at the Western Front, did not uncover major shortcomings in the artillery and failed to report to the *Stavka* on the poor work of the Western Front's artillery.

The Western Front headquarters is faceless and is removed from the command and the troops and demands strengthening. The current chief of staff, Lieutenant General Pokrovskii, cannot cope with his duties.

The situation in the intelligence section of the Front's headquarters is completely unfavourable. Colonel Il'nitskii, the chief of the intelligence section, is in need of special verification and he should be replaced.

In the interests of the cause, it is necessary to: a) remove General Sokolovskii from the post of Western Front commander, as he has failed to cope with a Front command and to reduce him in rank to Colonel General. A new commander should be appointed to the Western Front, capable of correcting the situation at the Western Front; b) the Central Committee of the All-Union Communist Party (Bolsheviks) should issue a reprimand to comrade Bulganin because for a lengthy period of time as a member of the Western Front's military council, he did not report to the *Stavka* on the presence of major shortcomings at the front; c) strengthen the Western Front's headquarters and, most of all, remove the front chief of staff, Lieutenant General Pokrovskii, from his position, and the chief of the operational section, Major General Chirkov, and to place in these positions people who are capable of organizing the work of the Front's headquarters and to increase its role; d) remove from his post the commander of the Front's artillery, Colonel General of Artillery Kamera, and to reduce him in rank to Lieutenant General of Artillery. To appoint to the Western Front a new artillery commander capable of eliminating the shortcomings in the artillery's work. To oblige Chief Artillery Marshal Voronov to immediately take on the matter of eliminating major shortcomings in the Western Front's artillery; e) remove Colonel Il'nitskii from the post of chief of the Western Front's intelligence section and to appoint in his stead an experienced and tested commander. To oblige the chief of the General Staff's intelligence directorate, Lieutenant General Kuznetsov, to take all necessary measures to correct the state of affairs in the Western Front's intelligence section; f) taking into account Colonel General Gordov's major errors in the command of the 33rd Army, as well as a number of his incorrect actions, decide the matter of his transfer to a lesser position and to reduce him in rank to Lieutenant General.

Of the Western Front's various combat arms, the artillery came in for the greatest criticism in the report:

> Our artillery in the operations conducted, despite its concentration in large numbers and its superiority over the enemy's artillery, both during the artillery preparation and during the fighting, was unable to suppress the enemy's fire system. The artillery often fired on empty spaces, without carrying out the infantry's requests, lost connection with it, and sometimes even fired on its own infantry. The infantry would go into the attack against the enemy's unsuppressed fire system, suffered enormous losses and failed to advance. Our artillery's fire activity, particularly counter-battery fire, was inferior during all phases of the fighting and did not meet the demands placed upon it. There were repeated cases in the 33rd, 31st and 5th Armies, when the artillery carried out area fire (by quadrants) based on data issued by army artillery headquarters, while there were actually no targets in these quadrants and the army fired on empty spaces and our infantry was fired upon by the enemy's firing positions from other areas. In the 33rd Army's operation of 23 December 1943 there were no officers at some of the artillery regiments' observation posts, but only enlisted men. Nor were there observers everywhere in the infantry's first echelon. As a result of this, the 194th Rifle Division was bombarded by its own artillery. In this army things came to such a pass the guns firing over open sights fired on their own infantry . . .
>
> The Western Front commander, General comrade Sokolovskii, the former member of the Front's military council, Lieutenant General comrade Bulganin, and the chief of the Front's artillery, Colonel General comrade Kamera, are guilty of failing to uncover major shortcomings and mistakes in the artillery's work. Self-satisfaction, arrogance and conceit reign among the artillerymen. The artillerymen do not uncover their mistakes, do not study them and attempt to paint over them. The Front and armies have not issued orders regarding shortcomings in the artillery's actions and have not indicated measures for eliminating them. As a result of such an incorrect attitude by the Front command towards the matter of commanding artillery, the same crude mistakes and shortcomings in the artillery's actions were repeated in each operation.

WHY WAS THE WESTERN FRONT COMMAND REMOVED

> While preparing the operation, the artillerymen at all levels carry out reconnaissance of their targets in a very bad way and fail to discover the enemy's fire system. As a result of this lack of knowledge of its targets, the artillery is unable to carry out aimed fire against specific targets and, as a rule, wages ineffective area fire. During this period the artillerymen slowly employ the intelligence organs, carry out reconnaissance by means of passive observation and rarely employ mobile observation posts and those moved up to the forward edge of the enemy's defence.

Nor was there any order amongst the Western Front's tank troops:

> As is known, the experience of the war has shown that major tank formations must be employed for developing the success following the breakthrough of the enemy's major defensive belts. As opposed to the experience of the war and instructions from the *Stavka* on the matter of employing tank formations, the Western Front command threw its 2nd Guards Tatsinskaya Tank Corps against the enemy's undisrupted defence, as a result of which the tank corps could not advance and suffered heavy losses.
>
> In the operation along the Orsha axis during 14–19 November, the tank corps was committed into the fighting when the infantry along a 3km front had penetrated to a depth of 2–3km into the defence. In the 33rd Army's operation along the Vitebsk axis on 23 December, it was planned to commit the tank corps into the fighting after the infantry reached the Luchesa River (18km in the defensive depth). For this reason, the tank corps was not committed into the fighting during the first three days of the infantry's advance to a depth of 8–10km, and when the infantry was halted by the enemy's organized fire from previously-prepared positions and the Luchesa River still remained ahead, the tank corps was thrown into the fighting and, following the loss of 60 tanks and not having achieved success, was pulled back behind the infantry's combat formations. In the operation along the Bogushevsk axis of 8 January, a tank corps was committed into the fighting when the infantry had essentially failed to achieve any successes. Upon suffering up to 70 per cent losses, the tank corps advanced 2–4km along with the infantry and after this was removed from the fighting.
>
> Thus the constant striving by the Front command to achieve the breakthrough of the enemy defence by means of the premature commitment of a tank corps into the fighting has not yielded results and has led to a situation in which the tank corps currently has two tanks left.
>
> Very heavy losses are observed in all the battles among the tank brigades operating directly with the infantry. The chief cause of these losses is that the enemy's anti-tank weapons are not suppressed by our artillery fire and coordination between the tanks, supporting artillery and the infantry is absent.

The Malenkov commission was based on the reports by the General Staff's representative with the Western Front, Colonel Nekrasov, and the chiefs of the Front's

OPERATION BAGRATION: AN INCOMPLETE TRUTH

and armies' special sections. For example, on 31 October 1943 Nekrasov reported on the 31st Army's unsuccessful offensive on Orsha, the preparation and realization of which was overseen personally by Sokolovskii. It is not accidental that it was precisely this report that brought about the angry exclamations of the Front commander cited above. Here the poor intelligence activities were singled out in particular:

> Intelligence work by the combined-arms men and materiel of the enemy's front line and its outline, his fortification system and his organization of fire, as well as data from aerial reconnaissance, did not correspond to the actual main line of the enemy's defence, which, being well disguised, proved to be significantly further to the east than was indicated on the aerial reconnaissance map, where, according to these maps, there proved to be fake trenches, which were later discovered during the fighting. It is extremely typical that the false forward edge turned out to be not in front of, but behind the real one in the tactical depth of the enemy's defence.
>
> The 31st Army's intelligence section only knows the number of forces and the presence of the enemy's units directly along the front line; that is, the enemy's units in direct combat contact with our units along the front line along the army's front.
>
> The interrogation of prisoners is carried out by the divisions' and army's intelligence sections in a rote manner and according to the book. Attention is often not paid to questions of the tactical and operational influence of our forces on the enemy's troops – how does the enemy evaluate our tactical and operational methods, the strength of our rifle and machine-gun fire, the enemy's evaluation of our artillery fire, the strength of our infantry attacks, and the secrecy of our manoeuvre and operational preparation, and thus completely fails to take advantage of opportunities for correcting mistakes made along this or that line where our forces are conducting operations, or to evaluate the units' correct actions. This deprives us of the opportunity for commanders at all levels to draw conclusions and issue instructions issuing from shortcomings uncovered, on the basis of the battle already conducted.
>
> The army's intelligence organs at all levels do not conduct interrogations of the local population and does not have any agent data about the enemy, and thus the army staff and command only knows about the enemy's tactical depth through incomplete data from occasional prisoners.
>
> The reconnaissance in force conducted on 27–28.10.43 to determine the enemy's fire system was unsuccessful and essentially failed to carry out its assignment, because the reconnaissance detachments did not penetrate into the enemy's defence and the enemy repelled their attack with just the fire system located along the front line and did not employ his weapons in the defensive depth and did not reveal them, while prisoners captured by regimental intelligence revealed only the firing points along those sectors where they were defending and also failed to reveal the fire system in the depth of the enemy's defence.

WHY WAS THE WESTERN FRONT COMMAND REMOVED

The main conclusion drawn by the General Staff's representative was that 'the 31st Army's offensive operation of 29.10.43 was not prepared, was conducted by rote, without employing tactical and operational deceit and the exclusion of any surprise, and thus was completely unsuccessful'.

Reports from the special sections at all levels (they were renamed counterintelligence directorates and sections in 1943), which were summarized in a report by the chief of military counterintelligence, SMERSH, Abakumov, on 1 April 1944, painted most fully and critically the Western Front's situation. Viktor Semyonovich personally informed the Supreme Commander-in-Chief of the following:

> I report that that agent intelligence from the main administration of SMERSH and the Western Front's counterintelligence directorate has fixed a number of statements by generals and officers from the Red Army General Staff and the Western Front that the commander of the Western Front, General Sokolovskii, and his chief of staff, Lieutenant General Pokrovskii, are not exercising control over combat operations.
>
> For example, the chief of the Red Army General Staff's operational directorate, Lieutenant General Shimonaev, stated: 'The Western Front, beginning in 1942 and continuing until this day, expends two or three times the amount of munitions as the other Fronts, but the desired results are missing and do not exist [Zhukov commanded the Western Front for the greater part of 1942, and he was relieved by Konev at the end of August; both of them operated no better than Sokolovskii in 1943–4, B.S.].
>
> For example, during February of this year the Western Front expended 1,300 rail cars of ammunition and failed to achieve the desired success, while at the same time the First Ukrainian Front expended only 560 cars and the Second Ukrainian Front 370 cars, while at the same time achieving great successes.
>
> During 20 days in March the Western Front expended 1,050 rail cars of shells and also enjoyed no success.
>
> This speaks to the unserious and unthinking attitude of the Front command, and most of all Sokolovskii and Pokrovskii, toward the preparation and conduct of operations. Sokolovskii and Pokrovskii poorly organize intelligence and thus lack a clear understanding of the enemy – as to the number of his military-engineering fortifications, when this is very important for choosing the place for breaking through the enemy's defence.
>
> Moreover, the Front command is not capable of organizing a breakthrough and securing its success.

Lieutenant Colonel Lobanov, the assistant for the Western Direction in the General Staff's operational section, said:

> Sokolovskii and Pokrovskii prepare the operations with insufficient fullness and, what is most important, do not control and do not check the course of the subunits' preparation for the fighting, as a result of which units and formations go into battle under circumstances of cooperation that have not been clearly worked out.

OPERATION BAGRATION: AN INCOMPLETE TRUTH

>The majority of the operations conducted by the Western Front are prepared in haste, are lacking in secrecy measures, and by rote, which is why the enemy is ready beforehand to meet our attacking units.
>
>Intelligence is conducted without clear aims and does not yield complete data on the enemy. The cooperation of the troops directly on the battlefield is poorly organized. The artillery preparation is conducted by rote, which gives the enemy the opportunity to take countermeasures and almost always preserve his personnel.
>
>Our forces' shock core, as a result of the enemy's countermeasures, is diffused in repelling his small counter-attacks. Under the cover of this, the enemy carries out regrouping along the threatened sector.

Major General Ryzhkov, the assistant chief of the Red Army General Staff's operational section, said to a small group of officers concerning the situation with the Western Front:

>Sokolovskii and his staff do not secure the secrecy of troop concentration in offensive operations, thus there was no surprise attack, because the enemy guessed our command's plan beforehand.
>
>This was the case in the conduct of all the operations by the Western Front, with the exception of an operation which was commanded by Bagramyan [this refers to the Gorodok offensive operation, which was conducted jointly with General I.Kh. Bagramyan's First Baltic Front and the Western Front; during the operation's course Gorodok and another 2,622 inhabited locales were liberated, B.S.].
>
>Pokrovskii, as the chief of staff, works poorly. He never really knew the situation at the front and does not know it now. Thus it is hardly surprising why our leading workers say: 'No matter what you say, it's useless to speak'. The senior assistant to the chief of the Red Army General Staff's western direction, Colonel CHUVILEV, stated: 'The Western Front's headquarters is ill-assorted as to its composition and training. There are a lot of people there who should have been removed a long time ago from the headquarters because they are useless. One can feel the conceit in the headquarters, while control over execution is organized poorly. Sokolovskii does not meet the modern requirements of a Front commander.

The senior assistant for the same Direction, Lieutenant Colonel Alekseev, said: 'At the least failures on the Western Front, the headquarters intentionally raises the enemy's strength. There always exist great exaggerations of reality in conversations with Front commander Sokolovskii.'

A similar opinion on this question was also expressed by the senior assistant of the General Staff's Western Direction, Lieutenant Colonel Medvedev and the General Staff officer with the Western Front, Colonel Serebryakov:

>According to agent intelligence, received from the Western Front's SMERSH directorate, Pokrovskii and the chief of the Front's

intelligence section, Colonel Il'nitskii, exaggerate the strength of the enemy facing the Western Front. By making use of these data, the Front's military council explains, among other reasons, their failures at the front.

For example, for a long time in 1943 the enemy's 1st Panzer Division, although unconfirmed and ultimately not confirmed [from January through May 1943 this division was in the West and from July through October in the Balkans, and only in November did it arrive on the Eastern Front, but in Army Group South, and not Army Group Centre, B.S.] was counted among the Spas–Demensk group of forces.

The 104th Infantry Division was also counted, also without foundation, as being with the enemy's Zhizdra group of forces.

From August until October 1943 the 96th Infantry Division, as well as the 104th, 179th, 236th, and 239th Infantry Divisions, were counted in the enemy's same Spas–Demensk group of forces, without a sufficient basis, of which, it transpired that not a single one of these was confirmed [there was no 104th Infantry Division in the Wehrmacht at all, while the 104th Jäger Division was in the Balkans; the 179th and 236th Infantry Divisions simply did not exist; the 239th Infantry Division was broken up as early as January 1942; the 96th Infantry Division was operating in 1943, first as part of Army Group North, and then as part of Army Group South, which was renamed in April 1944 Army Group North Ukraine and having no relationship at all to Army Group Centre, which was facing the Western Front, B.S.]

During the fighting in the summer of 1943 many of the German divisions facing the Western Front were defeated and broken up and their remnants sent to reinforce other formations. Despite this, the chief of the Front's intelligence section, Colonel Il'nitskii, did not write them off and these divisions were portrayed for a long time as being in the first line of the German defence.

Such are the facts of eye-wash in evaluating the enemy's forces being done by Il'nitskii, as instructed by Pokrovskii.

The striving to exaggerate the enemy's forces along this sector of the front can be explained by Pokrovskii's desire to insure himself against unpleasantness in the event of our forces' unsuccessful actions, as well as to get the justification for demanding additional troops from the *Stavka* of the Supreme High Command.

One should note that typically information from the Front's intelligence section sent to the Red Army General Staff, if they indicate an increase in enemy strength facing the Front, are signed by Pokrovskii without correction. If these reports contain evidence about a reduction in enemy forces, then Pokrovskii usually crosses out these data.

The deputy chief of the Front's intelligence section, Lieutenant Colonel Dyrin, once asked Il'nitskii why he exaggerates data on the enemy, to which Il'nitskii replied: 'Just try writing off one division, and Pokrovskii and the Front commander will relieve you. To write off enemy divisions from the Front is to not receive extra divisions from the *Stavka* for the Front.'

Data from the intelligence section as to the enemy's intention to fall back from the positions occupied by him is crossed out by Pokrovskii. For example, in the early days of February of this year, the intelligence section's information department presented verified data about the enemy's evacuation of his rear units from Vitebsk. Pokrovskii crossed out these data from the report. These data were later confirmed in full. The chief of the Red Army General Staff's intelligence directorate, comrade Kuznetsov, having received material from us as to the unfavourable situation in the Western Front's intelligence section, sent in January of this year a commission under the leadership of Lieutenant General Vavilov, in which Major Krylovskii also served. The commission unearthed significant shocking things in the work of the intelligence section and evidence of exaggerating the strength of the enemy facing the Western Front. Il'nitskii, with Pokrovskii's knowledge, took measures so as to compromise this commission and even accused Krylovskii that while he was with the Western Front, instead of work, he was systematically drunk. In this way Pokrovskii and Il'nitskii managed to fix it so that the necessary measures were not taken by the Western Front's military council against the outrages uncovered.

It is also known that besides Pokrovskii, Il'nitskii enjoys a great amount of support on the part of Sokolovskii.

The chiefs of the axes in the Western Front staff's operational section, Colonel Dyukov and Lieutenant Colonel Sever, the assistant chiefs of the Front staff's operational section, Major Boiko and Major Chekrenev, the senior assistants of the chief of the operational group, Lieutenant Colonel Obalenskii and Lieutenant Colonel Protasov, also speak of the unsatisfactory command of combat operations on the part of the Western Front's chief of staff, Pokrovskii.

On 25 March of this year the fortified area sector chief of the Western Front's staff, Colonel Tyoplykh, in reporting to Pokrovskii on the serious shortcomings during the March offensive by units of the 31st Army, pointed out that due to poor organization during the artillery preparation, the rocket-powered artillery fired a salvo on its own infantry, as a result of which units of the 352nd Rifle Division suffered heavy losses. Pokrovskii replied that he knew nothing and simultaneously asked Tyoplykh not to tell anyone about this, adding: 'Is it worth our while to show such big figures? We should not do this. If they should ask, then we'll tell them.'

As agent intelligence from the Western Front's headquarters reports, on the first day of the fighting, which began on 3 February along the Vitebsk axis, the initial success was not developed only because the divisional and corps reserves, as well as regimental reserves, were not committed into the fighting in a timely manner. This enabled the enemy to recover and to put himself in order and then defeat our attacking forces in detail.

WHY WAS THE WESTERN FRONT COMMAND REMOVED

Besides this, there was no coordination between corps and divisions. During the conduct of the March (from 23 through 28 March of this year) operation along the Vitebsk axis, according to data from our agent intelligence, because of the loss of the factor of surprise and the poor coordination between the combat arms, as well as the secrecy of its planning, this operation was also bungled.

In ten days of fighting in February of this year units of the 33rd and 39th Armies suffered losses of more than 28,000 men, and in March of this year the 33rd Army alone lost 8,000 in three days of fighting. In all of the combat operations Sokolovskii, while at the auxiliary command post, decided all matters on his own, without informing anyone of the decisions taken. For example, the commander of the Front's armoured forces, Hero of the Soviet Union Lieutenant General Rodin, stated: 'Sokolovskii's sitting out in the auxiliary command post, where there is no one from the Front staff's operational section except Colonel Veniyaminov, who serves as his adjutant. One does not feel Sokolovskii's leadership of the staff workers subordinated to him. He is connected to the army commanders over the high-frequency telephone and issues all commands orally. No one knows what the operational section of the Front's staff is doing.' Lieutenant General Vinogradov, the chief of the Western Front rear, said: 'Nothing goes right for us and will probably not go right, because Sokolovskii may not be a bad chief of staff, but he's not a commander.'

The chief of the operational section of the staff of the Front's armoured forces, Lieutenant Colonel Lazutin, said: 'Sokolovskii is dry and coarse with his subordinates. He passes on his coarseness to the army commanders, who, according to his example, never speak quietly in conversations with corps and division commanders and do not give sensible instructions, but while threatening to shoot them proposes controlling the fighting on the forward line.'

Colonel Veniyaminov, the Front deputy chief of staff for auxiliary command posts, stated: 'Sokolovskii's going to break his neck on these operations. He doesn't consider anyone else's opinion and considers everyone else useless.'

The chief of the replacement section of the Front's headquarters, Colonel Mikhlin, in a conversation with officers, in evaluating the operation conducted in February of this year, stated: 'The Western Front ground up all of its reserves in 1943. During the first 20 days of January of this year during the operation conducted around Orsha [the city, B.S.], we lost 50,000 men without achieving any kind of success.'

The commander of the 65th Rifle Corps, Major General Revyakin, stated: 'We still haven't learned how to fight and we fight by rote, and the German already knows this, draws his conclusions and organizes his defence as needs be.'

There are similar statements on the part of a number of other commanders. The member of the Western Front's military council, Lieutenant General Mekhlis, in a conversation with the chief of the counterintelligence directorate, Lieutenant General Zelyonyi, said that he can't understand Sokolovskii, who is closed off and dissatisfied with certain people in the Red Army General Staff, calling them idlers, and sometimes makes ironic comments about some orders and sometimes criticizes them.

OPERATION BAGRATION: AN INCOMPLETE TRUTH

Further on comrade Mekhlis stated that he was surprised why Sokolovskii supports such untalented people as Pokrovskii (the Front chief of staff), Kamera (the chief of the Front's artillery) and Gordov (a former army commander)'.

The SMERSH organs, just like the General Staff officers attached to the headquarters of the front and armies, were only responsible for reporting as precisely as possible to the higher authorities how events were developing, for the course and outcome of which they bore absolutely no responsibility. I understand that army commanders and political workers had no great love for the secret police and General Staff officers. It's not enough that they are not responsible for anything, but that at any moment they could write up a report-denunciation in which nothing would remain of the castles in the air erected in the generals' and colonels' reports.

As opposed to widespread opinion, all of the members of the military councils were very careful in their criticisms of the army and Front commands, insofar as they were fully responsible for the success or failure of the operations conducted. Even Mekhlis, whose name scared nervous commanders, did not play any kind of significant role in Sokolovskii's fall. For example, on 7 April 1944 Lev Zakharovich wrote to Malenkov:

> I'm sending you four documents directed against the mixing up of uniforms in hospitals, as well as bedding in the laundry detachments [Mekhlis had spoken on this matter as early as 1940 at a meeting of the higher command element on the results of the war with Finland, B.S.]. The mixing up of uniforms causes a great deal of dissatisfaction among the wounded and facilitates the growth of theft and abuses. I reported to Comrade Mikoyan [the chairman of the Committee on the Red Army's Food and Materiel Supply, B.S.], who spoke with comrade Khrulyov [the deputy defence minister responsible for troop supply, B.S.] and received permission to carry it out. This is now being carried out in practice. The problem is a general one for the entire Red Army.

Mekhlis also wrote about shortcomings in the food supply for the Western Front, about the poor condition of hospitals and other economic disorders, but did not touch upon questions of military operations and operational command.

Among the other documents of Georgii Malenkov's commission there was attached to the report one highly curious anonymous complaint, addressed to Stalin as well as to the commander of the Western Front, Sokolovskii, the representative of the *Stavka*, Chief Artillery Marshal Voronov, and the member of the military council, Mekhlis. The latter gave it to Malenkov. Judging by the text, the author was one of the regimental commanders. He expressed what had long been troubling him, although not always in agreement with Russian grammar:

> This letter is a cry from the soul from a troubled heart and I ask you, comrade Stalin, not to judge me harshly for this.
>
> A situation has arisen at the Western Front in the form of a real persecution and pursuit of the commanders of units and formations. There is absolutely no faith in the commanders. In the units and formations the

main honcho, so to speak, the czar and god, is the representative from counterintelligence. They do whatever they want and often completely undermine the authority of the unit or formation commander. On the basis of their unfounded denunciations, they harass and pursue and call you a crook, thief and scoundrel and they believe everything they do and believe the commanders in nothing.

If a unit commander has imposed a punishment on someone, then the perpetrator looks for protection from counterintelligence and the latter demands an accounting from the commander as to why a punishment was imposed and gives it to understand that the punishment may not be imposed, or lessened.

It's clear that they follow a commander and his every step. If a commander has summoned someone, then upon leaving the commander he turns to counterintelligence, where he is subjected to questioning: why was he summoned and what did they talk about. If a commander ate an extra piece of bread or an extra gram of sugar, then a big stink is made of this.

They have deprived the commander of all of his rights and initiative. A commander cannot make a decision without the agreement by a representative from counterintelligence. They have taken women from the commanders and each counterintelligence official has one or two. They frighten you with Mekhlis at every step, and now the commanders' mood is a very unenviable one, although the majority of them have been defending the motherland, not sparing their lives and has from four to eight medals.

Why is this so? Have we really returned to 1937–38, because it is painful and insulting.

I am not signing this, for I know that if I sign then I will surely suffer, and this is the real state of affairs.

The unknown fighter for the army commanders' 'sexual equality' with the SMERSH operatives was right in many ways. The representatives from military counterintelligence were by no means angels (we will become further acquainted with their works) and, bad or not, friendly relations with the commanders and political workers undoubtedly influenced the content and tone of their reports. However, their fantasies were highly limited by the fact that some of their colleagues might write the truth and then the one who embellishes reality would get it in the neck. The same was fair as regards the General Staff officers. Thus, on the whole, these two categories of reports yielded a picture of combat operations and the state of the army rear close to the truth.

The army commanders were a match for the Front commander. Among the materials of the Malenkov commission there is an order by the commander of the 33rd Army, Colonel General Vasilii Gordov of 4 September 1943 to the commander of the 173rd Rifle Division, Colonel Zaitsev, a copy of which was forwarded to the commanders of the 1311th, 1313th and 1315th Rifle Regiments, Lieutenant Colonels Milovanov and Sizov and Major Guslitser. This order was issued before the star-crossed offensive operations against Orsha and Vitebsk had begun. Vasilii Nikolaevich demanded that his subordinates break through the enemy's defence with all means, including some quite exotic ones:

> The division continues to stand in place on the second day, while being faced with small groups of enemy automatic riflemen. Your personal assurances to me (3.9) to carry out the assigned task proved to be the latest deception. This criminal standing in place and the elation of small groups of enemy automatic riflemen [the general has a remarkable style – in this case he probably had in mind that the German automatic riflemen were elated by the consciousness that they were holding up an entire Soviet division!, B.S.] is taking place because neither you, as a division commander, nor your regimental commanders understand or obviously do not wish to organize the battle. Do you really not understand that the enemy cannot put up any kind of resistance to your division, given the terrain conditions, nor does he have the capability for this. If you had taken the situation into account and organized the battle, if only in small groups (which in these conditions is very important), you would have long ago smoked out the small groups of automatic riflemen and enriched yourself with prisoners and would have long ago completed your mission of reaching the line Mishutkovo–Zapol'ye.
>
> I demand:
>
> Organize the battle in accordance with the instructions personally issued by me on 3.9.
>
> Place the entire complement of officers in the combat formations for the purpose of getting through the woods in a skirmish line, having appointed small detachments for flushing out the automatic riflemen from their nests. I am sending to you a group of officers who will assist you in arousing people and pushing them forward.
>
> The division's mission by the close of 4.9 must be accomplished no matter what the cost. Your failure to accomplish the mission puts your neighbours to the right and left in a difficult condition. It is better that you be killed today than not carry out your assignment. Understand that the interests of our arms demand this.

One feels that the film *Chapaev* had made an indelible impression on Gordov, particularly the 'psychological' attack by the officer companies. And, to judge by the quote, *The Lay of Igor*'s *Host* was also well known to him.

However, the members of the commission did not appreciate the general's devotion to the classics and in their report devoted to him, who had already been removed from command of the 33rd Army, a special section – 'On the Situation in the 33rd Army Under the Command of Colonel General Gordov', full of annihilating criticism:

> The 33rd Army occupied a central place in many of the Western Front's operations and significant reinforcements were attached to it, and the Front command allotted a good deal of attention to the army and considered army commander Gordov the best army commander.

However, the facts show the opposite. Nowhere was the battle so poorly organized as in Gordov's army. Instead of carefully preparing the operation and organizing the battle and instead of the correct employment of artillery, Gordov sought to break through the enemy's defence by manpower alone. Testimony to this are the losses suffered by the army. The overall number of losses suffered by the 33rd Army comes to more than 50 per cent of the losses for the entire front.

In defiance of the *Stavka*'s instructions which forbid the employment in the fighting of special subunits as common infantry, Gordov often committed scouts, chemical troops and engineers into the fighting.

Among the more serious of Gordov's faults is when Gordov dispatched a division's entire officer element on a mission. In his order of 4 September 1943, addressed to the commander of the 173rd Rifle Division, Colonel Zaitsev, and the regimental commanders Lieutenant Colonel Milovanov, Lieutenant Colonel Sizov, and Major Guslitser, Gordov demanded: 'Place the entire complement of officers in the combat formations for the purpose of getting through the woods, appointing small detachments for flushing out the automatic riflemen from their nests'. Gordov later wrote in the order: 'It is better that you be killed today than not carry out your assignment' [nevertheless, he did not move into the attack and undoubtedly was not prepared to die, B.S.]. On 4 September 1943 Gordov ordered the chief of staff of the 70th Rifle Corps, Major General Ikonnikov, 'to immediately dispatch the entire corps headquarters into the fighting. Leave only the chief of the operational section at headquarters'.

Such inadmissible actions by Gordov resulted in the disorganization of the command of the battle and to unjustified losses among the officers. For the last half year the 33rd Army under Gorodov's command has lost four division commanders killed and wounded and eight deputy division commanders and division chiefs of staff, 38 regimental commanders and their deputies and 174 battalion commanders.

Gordov criminally violates Stalin's order on resorting to executions of commanders without a trial and investigation. For example, according to a 6 March order by Gordov, Major Trofimov was executed without a trial and investigation, supposedly for avoiding battle. Actually, as was established by an investigation, Major Trofimov was not guilty. During combat activities command on Gordov's part came down to cursing and insults. Gordov often resorted to threats of execution directed at his subordinates. Such was the case with the commander of the 277th Rifle Division, Major General Gladyshev, and the commander of the 45th Rifle Corps, Major General Poplavskii. According to a statement by a number of commanders who worked with Gordov, the inhumane attitude toward people and complete hysteria had so overstrained them that there were instances when the commanders were unable to command their formations and units. The Front command passed over all of these disgraceful episodes in Gordov's actions and did not correct him and continued to consider him the best army commander.[14]

OPERATION BAGRATION: AN INCOMPLETE TRUTH

The commander of the Western Front, General Sokolovskii, was deprived of his position for 'the unsatisfactory leadership of the Front'. Lieutenant General N.A. Bulganin also came in for it and ceased to be a member of the Western Front military council as early as 15 December 1943. He was censured in an order by the *Stavka* of the Supreme High Command of 12 April 1944, 'because he, as a member of the Western Front's military council for a long time, did not report to the *Stavka* on the presence of major shortcomings at the Front'. The latter marks the end of the quoted section. The censure did not interfere with Nikolai Aleksandrovich becoming as early as 12 May a member of the military council of the First Belorussian Front, to which the main part of the forces of the former Western Front were transferred. Sokolovskii was removed by the same order from the post of commander of the Western Front as 'failing to cope with the Front command' and they appointed him chief of staff of the First Ukrainian Front. They warned Lieutenant General Pokrovskii that 'if he does not correct his mistakes, then he will be demoted in rank and position'. They removed Colonel General of Artillery I.P. Kamera from the post of chief of the Western Front's artillery and placed him at the disposal of commander of the Red Army's artillery. He received no more appointments and before long retired due to illness. Colonel Ya.T. Il'nitskii was removed from the position of chief of the Western Front's intelligence section, reduced in rank to a lieutenant colonel and was placed at the disposal of the General Staff's intelligence directorate. In June–September he was the deputy commander and chief of staff of a number of rifle divisions with the Second and Third Baltic Fronts. In September 1944 Yakov Timofeevich was awarded the Order of the Patriotic War First Class and restored to the rank of colonel. He ended the war as chief of staff of the 6th Guards Army's 2nd Guards Rifle Corps. They warned Colonel General V.N. Gordov, who was removed from the command of the 33rd Army, that 'if he repeats the mistakes committed by him in the 33rd Army, then he will be reduced in rank and position'. Vasilii Nikolaevich got off lightly then. On 2 April 1944 he was appointed commander of the First Ukrainian Front's 3rd Guards Army, with which he took part in a number of operations during the war's final year, including the Berlin and Prague operations. On 6 April 1945 V.N. Gordov was awarded the title of Hero of the Soviet Union for the skilful leadership of his troops and his bravery and heroism. He was doomed by incautious conversations with his fellow officers and wife in December 1946, in which he sharply criticized Stalin and the situation in the country and which were recorded by MGB listening devices. He was arrested in January 1947, and on 24 August 1950 was executed and rehabilitated in 1956. But his death was not linked to Gordov's failures in 1943–4.

In their report, the members of the Malenkov commission also proposed censuring Mekhlis (probably guided by the principle that the informer gets it first), for not earlier reporting on the shortcomings in the organization of the offensives. But Stalin chose not to follow this principle and considered that Lev Zakharovich had reported everything correctly and on time. He appointed him a member of the military council of yet another Front, which was formed in place of the Western Front – the Second Belorussian Front. Mekhlis began his debut address there before the command-political leaders with a declaration that the decision by the *Stavka* VGK and the State Defence Committee on the Western Front command 'reveals with Stalinist frankness the flawed style in the control of troops and operations', and that 'the Western Front command did not like to uncover mistakes and covered them up'. He offered a highly negative description of the Western Front's artillery chief, Colonel General of Artillery I.P. Kamera, and the commander of the 33rd Army, Colonel General V.N. Gordov: 'Their style of work is to ignore the staff. Blabbing and revealing secrets over the telephone', and 'hatred for the political officers and *Chekists*'.[15] According to an order of 12 April 1944 Ivan Pavlovich Kamera was removed from his post, after which he was sent into retirement due to his health (he was seriously ill). They transferred Vasilii Nikolaevich Gordov to the First Ukrainian Front, where he headed the 3rd Guards Army.

Marshal G.K. Zhukov asserted that in the *Stavka*'s decision of 12 April 1944 'the rout of the group of German forces in Belorussia was established as one of the most important tasks for the summer of 1944. It was necessary beforehand to carry out a number of major attacks along other directions in order to pull the maximum number of German strategic reserves from the area of Belorussia.'[16]

In March 1944 the Third Belorussian Front's 31st Army carried out an unsuccessful operation to capture Orsha. L.N. Rabichev, a platoon commander in the 31st Army, described this in his memoirs, erroneously placing the time of action in May instead of March:

> The artillery preparation began on the morning of 19 May and the shells exploded in the Germans' trenches and dugouts and reduced them to rubble. Our bombers bombed the enemy's fortifications from the air.
>
> Our Il-2 dive bombers, in groups of six, flew over one behind the other. But something strange was happening to them: when they would fly up to the third line of the German defence, carry out their mission and sought to turn around, nothing came of this and, one after the other, they blew up and fell to the ground. One out of six returned. As early as the artillery preparation we emerged from our underground refuge, stood up straight on a height and in consternation observed these disastrous air attacks.
>
> Our infantry went into the attack after two hours. We ran through the first two lines and went to ground near the third and could no longer get on our feet. The Germans' guns and machine guns began to go to work, but by no means from those positions which our air force had bombed. A terrible crossfire opened up from the Germans' machine gun and mortar positions, which had not suffered at all. There was the appearance of the German bombers and the death of thousands of our infantrymen who were trying to get back to their assembly positions. And on the communications lines, on the ground, in the trenches, in the headquarters dugouts, and in the air, from our doomed aircraft there could be heard the desperate cursing which confused all orders and which was mixed with the nervous yelling of staff telephone operators.
>
> The offensive collapsed completely. There were thousands of killed. Wounded soldiers crawled back to their assembly areas. The Germans did not launch a counteroffensive. Our knocked-out tanks and self-propelled guns burned out before my eyes. Then for eight nights our tank and motorized infantry divisions [he means corps, B.S.] slowly moved along the Minsk highway and country roads. On 29 May our troops' offensive once again collapsed. We did not advance beyond the Germans' third line of fortifications and suffered enormous losses.

OPERATION BAGRATION: AN INCOMPLETE TRUTH

> The next day they read before the assembled troops a terrible letter from the *Stavka* of the supreme high command, addressed to the commander of the Third Belorussian Front, General Chernyakhovskii [he was then a colonel general, B.S.], that the Third Belorussian Front had not justified the faith of the party and the people and was obliged to expiate its guilt before the Motherland with blood.[17]

We're actually speaking here of the *Stavka* VGK order of 12 April 1944, according to which General Sokolovskii was removed from the command of the Western Front and a number of other generals received reprimands or were transferred to other posts. Because of the failure of the 31 March offensive against Orsha, the commander of the 31st Army, Lieutenant General V.A. Gluzdovskii, was removed from his position on 27 May 1944 and sent to the *Stavka* reserve. This move saved him from the hail of awards that fell upon the generals and troop commanders during the course of Operation 'Bagration'.

Three months later the 31st and 11th Guards Armies, which attacked Orsha on 22 June on the first day of 'Bagration', like in March were unsuccessful and fell back to their assembly areas. But by this time Army Group Centre had almost no aircraft remaining with which to oppose the Soviet offensive. Besides this, much larger forces were now thrown against Orsha. Besides the 31st Army, the troops of the 11th Guards and 5th Armies were now outflanking Orsha from the north. On 27 June Orsha was liberated.

Chapter 2

The *Poles'ye* Tragedy

In order to understand why Soviet partisans and Red Army soldiers were often so cruel to German prisoners taken in the course of Operation 'Bagration', I will put forth only one document concerning the conduct of punitive operations by the Germans and their collaborators in Belorussia. The population of the partisan-held areas was subjected to terrible repressions on the part of the Germans and their accomplices – punitive units made up of Soviet citizens. The sadistic tendencies of their participants were on full display during these acts of intimidation. Here is just one document, compiled on 1 September by the inhabitants of the Lel'chitsy area of Belorussia's Poles'ye Oblast', under the chairmanship of the secretary of the underground regional party committee, Roman Luk'yanovich Lin, entitled 'On All of the German-Fascist Crimes Conducted by the Punitive Expedition from 25 June through 20 August of This Year'. It was published in abbreviated form by the partisan press. The full text of the document reads:

> On direct orders of the ruling clique of Fascist Germany, headed by the cannibal Hitler, a punitive expedition consisting of the Eighth Army [this is an obvious mistake, as the German Eighth Army was at this time operating as part of Army Group South in the Khar'kov area and, moreover, it had only been formed on the basis of operational group 'Kempf' on 16 August 1943, B.S.] was sent to our area, numbering 50,000 bandits [the size of the punitive expedition was overstated by several times. In reality, it probably did not exceed 1,000 men, B.S.], which arrived in the area on 25 June and left on 20 August. All of the facts speak to a previously thought-out plan for the wholesale extermination of the peaceful inhabitants of the Poles'ye Oblast'. This bloody plan for destroying completely innocent old men, women and defenceless children is being carried out by the Hitlerite band of cutthroats and sadists. Upon breaking into the villages, the Hitlerites burned everything to the ground, killed old men, women and children, raped women and underage girls and carried out brutal and bloody reprisals. They blasphemed Christian churches and their servants. Entire hordes hunted for both people and animals. They killed and drove off livestock and destroyed sown areas for the purpose of leaving the population (which was hiding in the forests) without food. Of 62 inhabited areas, all were burned, while 22 inhabited areas (including the regional centre of Lel'chitsy were burned down for a second time. 103 men were killed and tortured, as were 105 women and 105 children. In all, this amounted

OPERATION BAGRATION: AN INCOMPLETE TRUTH

to 313 people. 532 people were driven off [to Germany, B.S.], 1,522 homesteads and 111 state and collective farm buildings were burned. 187 horses, 1,217 cattle, 69 calves, 1,508 sheep, and 480 pigs were driven off . . .

Further on specific facts of brutality by various villages were put forward:

The village of Zaberzhnitsa, of the Sinitsko-Pol'skii village council: 1) Yevdokiya Ivanovna Doroshuk, 60 years of age, was bestially tortured: her breasts were cut off, her eyes put out and her ears cut off; 2) Antonina Ivanovna Levkovskaya, 34 years of age, was bestially tortured: her arms and feet were dislocated and then she was killed; 3) Malan'ya Baranovskaya, 72 years of age, had her breasts cut off, her eyes put out, her arms dislocated and her skull fractured; 4) Yelena Levskovskaya, a 75-year-old woman, was discovered in a well, blindfolded.

The village of Buinovichi, from the same village council: Anna Ivanovna Malets, a 17-year-old girl, was raped by a group of Hitlerites, after which she was cut up into pieces while still alive; 2) Miron Alekseevich Malets, 32 years old, was placed on the ground and a fire lit around him, and after his hair and skin were burned he was killed. A church was defiled in Buinovichi: the windows were broken and equipment was broken [here one can feel the style of a party bureaucrat, as church belongings are referred to, production-style, as 'equipment', B.S.], the floor was blown up and turned into a toilet. All of the church books and records were tossed about and torn up.

The village of Krupka, of the Buinovichi village council. Ivan Mishura, an 83-year-old man was thrown into the flames of his burning hut while still alive. Mariya Stepanovna Korbut, 32 years of age, was raped by a group of Hitlerites in front of her mother. Mariya Markovna Obykhod was raped by a group of Hitlerites, after which her arms were dislocated and she was beaten until she lost consciousness, and then killed. Mariya Mishura, an 83-year-old woman, was raped by the fascists.

The village of Berestyanyi Zavod, of the Buinovichi village council. Iosif Antonovich Akulich, an 82-year-old man. His arms and legs were dislocated, his eyes put out, his teeth knocked out, and his skull split. Following prolonged tortures, the old man died. Antonina Grigor'evna Akulich, a 20-year-old girl, was raped by the fascists and died under lengthy torture, with her breasts cut off and her arms and legs dislocated.

The village of Zarubany, of the Buinovichi village council. Mikhail Samuilovich Shcherbachenya. His three children were brutally murdered: they cut off their heads and their arms were dislocated. Grigorii Savanovich. His boy was brutally tortured: his arms were broken and his stomach cut open. The village of Voronov, of the Grebenev village council. Serafima Grigor'evna Navmerzhitskaya was thrown into a fire alive, with her child, Ul'yana. Ul'yana Grigor'evna Navmerzhitskaya, 32 years old, was thrown alive into a fire with her children, Dunya, Marfa and Ivan.

THE *POLES'YE* TRAGEDY

The village of Ol'khovaya, of the Grebenev village council. Vladimir Markovich Bezmen, 28 years old, was brutally tortured: he was hanged by his arms for several hours; they put needles under his fingernails and dislocated his arms and legs. These torments continued for a day and a half. The Germans sought to get information from him about the partisans, but got nothing. The torments continued in front of his fellow villagers. His courage and self-control during these tortures amazed his fellow countrymen and enraged the fascists. At the end he said that 'The Soviet people will settle accounts with you' (the fascists), after which he was killed.

The village of Sinitskoe Pole, of the same village council. Maksim Vas'kovskii, 50 years old and an invalid without legs. The torments continued an entire day and his arms and legs were dislocated and his eyes put out. The fascists attempted to get information about the partisans, but achieved nothing. Khatimiya Filintsova, an 80-year-old woman, had her eyes put out and arms and legs dislocated. She died after lengthy torture. Akulina Troshko, 55 years old, was brutally tortured. The fascists tried to find out where her partisan son and the partisans were, but found out nothing.

The village of Chemernaya, of the Lel'chitsy village council. Marina Burnich was cut to pieces while still alive. Vasilii Voronich. The fascists beat him with their rifle butts, cut him with knives and then shot him.

The village of Dubrova, of the Lel'chitsy village council. Mariya Vasil'evna Kolos, 47 years old, and her daughters Praskov'ya and Anastasiya, each 12 years old (twins), her eight year old daughter Ol'ga and two-year-old son Adam, were stabbed with bayonets and placed on a wagon, where they gradually died. They wounded her five-year-old daughter Anna and threw her on the wagon with her dying relatives, on whose corpses she also died. Afanasii Stepanovich Kolos, 35 years old, his 32-year-old wife Varya, his 75-year-old mother Varvara, and children Yevdokiya, nine years, seven-year-old Ol'ga, three-year-old Pavel, and his 12-year-old niece Lida, were thrown alive into a fire. Sil'vester Nikitich Shchukolovich, 87 years old, and Yevdokiya Ivanovna Ostapovich, 80 years old, were brutally tortured.

The village of Liplyany, of the Lel'chitsy village soviet. The fascists stabbed Vasili Vasil'evich Khalyava, 52 years old, and a 20-year-old girl, Ol'ga Yevseevna Los' and removed their skin and then threw them alive into a fire. The Hitlerites beat with rifle butts 75-year-old Mitrofan Feodos'evich Pavlechko until he died. In this village a lousy fascist went into the church with his hat on and with a cigarette in his mouth. He found a priest's garments and tried to force the old men who had been driven inside to pray for him. The old men refused. The drunken barbarian began to shoot at the old men and then closed the door and set fire to the church and people.

The village of Lel'chitsy. 40-year-old Maksim Aleksandrovich Zhurovich, his wife and six children were brutally tortured and thrown into a fire. 43-year-old Semyon Aleksandrovich Podol'skii, his wife and six children, 43-year-old Vasilii Sapozhnikov, his wife and five children, 36-year-old Dunya Larionovna Zhurovich, and her three-year-old child were driven into a barn and burned alive. 73-year-old Afanasii Fillipovich Voronovich and 78-year-old Khristina Voronovich were cut up while alive and had their stomachs sutured and had the skin from their scalps removed and were thrown into a fire.

The village of Chiyane, of the Lil'chitsky village soviet. 73-year-old Prokhor Sachko was stabbed with bayonets and then killed. 47-year-old Matryonya Ivanovna Zhurovich, Yakov Iosovich Voronovich, and three children, had their stomachs cut open, heads cut off and were thrown into a fire.

The village of Staryi Fol'vark. 70-year-old Varvara Ivanovna Lisitskaya. The fascists tied her hair to a pine tree, pulled out her hair along with the skin and tore open her mouth and, following all of these torments, cut off her head. 77-year-old Anton Yul'yanovich Kotinskii and 19-year-old Fyodor Andreevich Grintsevich were thrown into a fire while still alive.

The village of Buda Lel'chitskaya. The fascists subjected 75-year-old Yelizaveta Vikent'evna Khomutovskaya to cruel torture, after which they threw her while alive into a burning house. They stabbed 24-year-old Anastasiya Nazarovna Leshchinskaya with bayonets and then gradually (over a small fire) burned her alive. They shot 60-year-old Vasilii Konstantinovich Tushinskii in the arms and legs and fractured his skull, after which they killed him. The fascists tortured 30-year-old Ul'yana Martynovna Dashkeevich and her 12-year-old son Aleksandr, broke their arms and legs and tormented them for a long time and then shot them.

The village of Glushkovichi, of the same village council. They cut off the ears of 45-year-old Grigorii Yefremovich Shved, plus his fingers and toes, cut up his back with a knife, cut out his tongue, and then threw him into a fire while still alive. They cut the body of 52-year-old Moisei Stepanovich Radilovets with knives, after which they hanged him. They cut off the nose of, ears and sexual organs of 45-year-old Makar Ivanovich Akulich, cut his body with a knife, and burnt him up after prolonged torture. They tore out the hair of 39-year-old Vasilii Mikhailovich Burim, broke his arms and legs and shot up his body, and he died under torture. They cut 45-year-old Feodosiya Grigor'evna Gapanovich's body with knives, beat her with rocks and sticks and then buried her alive. The Hitlerites raped 22-year-old Praskov'ya Makarovna Burim and 22-year-old Teklya Yevdokimovna Burim, after which they placed them on stakes and shot them.

The village of Kartynichi, of the same village council. The fascists buried alive 20-year-old Mariya Petrovna German and her two-year-old baby. Twenty-eight people were buried alive in the village of Kartynichi.

The village of Osenskoe, of the Kartynichi village council. 48-year-old Dmitrii Yul'yanovich Rafalovich was beaten with rifle butts until he died. 8-year-old Vladimir Dmitrievich Rafalovich was brutally tortured.

THE *POLES'YE* TRAGEDY

The village of Ostrozhanka from the same village council. 24-year-old Aksin'ya Grigor'evna Vysotskaya was raped by a group of fascists and afterwards killed. 60-year-old Grigorii Il'ich Vysotskii was brutally tortured. They tormented 50-year-old Mark Yeliseevich Lesenya and then forced him to dig his own grave. 30-year-old Grigorii Semyonovich Nered was forced by the Hitlerites to carry them across a river. He was then brutally tortured.

The village of Stodolochi of the same village soviet. 40-year-old Praskov'ya Krupnik was raped by a group of eight fascists in front of her children and fellow villagers. 13-year-old Feodosiya Ivanovna Zhoglo was raped by a group of fascists (seven men) in front of her grandmother. 13-year-old Anna Zhoglo was raped by a group of fascists in front of her mother. 59-year-old Dmitrii Fomich Shur was brutally tortured; they shot him in the arms, beat him and forced him to dig his own grave. 17-year-old Aleksandra Dmitrievna Shur was beaten for an entire week and the fascists demanded information about her three partisan brothers, but learned nothing.

Note: the document indicates the crimes of one expedition. Aside from this, since the beginning of the German occupation about 7,500 peaceful inhabitants have been shot in the Lel'chitsy area.[1]

Judging by the names and surnames, only a minority of those who became victims of the punitive expeditions in the Lel'chitsy area could have been Jews. The majority were subjected to agonizing deaths for real or imagined contacts with the partisans, or simply because they ran afoul at the wrong time of people whom it would be difficult to call people.

It's possible that this document, which was intended for publication, contains some propagandistic exaggerations, but it's hard to doubt that in the main what was communicated corresponds to reality. Similar atrocities by Nazi punitive expeditions contained a significant portion of collaborators, which to a large degree explains the murders and cruel treatment of German prisoners on the part of the partisans and Red Army troops, as well as the cruel settling of accounts with collaborationists and their families during Operation 'Bagration'.

Chapter 3

The Belorussian Partisan Movement through the Eyes of a Cadre *Chekist*

But the Soviet partisans in Belorussia were also by no means angels and their anger at times rained down upon not only the Germans and collaborators. This is proven by the following document, which we present in abbreviated form: 'The Commission on the History of the Fatherland War under the Central Committee of the Communist Party (Bolsheviks) of Belorussia'. This is a stenographic account of a conversation with Lieutenant Colonel of State Security, Hero of the Soviet Union comrade Kirill Prokof'evich Orlovskii.

The conversation was conducted by senior academic associate, comrade I.K. Kireev. Stenographer Z.A. Berezhkovskaya took it down.

24 September 1943.

I, Orlovskii, Kirill Prokof'evich, was born in 1895 in the village of Myshkovichi, in the Kirov District of the Mogilev Oblast' in the Belorussian Soviet Socialist Republic. I have a mid-level education and a higher party education (I completed the Communist Higher Educational Establishment of the Peoples of the West). I have been the organizer of red-partisan detachments and diversionary groups in the USSR, Spain and China. I have been a member of the All-Union Communist Party (Bolsheviks) since 1918. I am a lieutenant colonel of state security in the Red Army. I served in the Red Army from 1918 through 1920. In 1920 I completed the First Moscow Infantry Courses for the Command Element. I was awarded the title of Hero of the Soviet Union for active combat work in the rear of the German occupation forces in the Baranovichi and Pinsk oblasts of the BSSR.

In 1932, for active combat work in the rear of the White Poles I was awarded by the government of the BSSR the order of the Labor Red Banner of the BSSR. In 1937 I was awarded the Order of Lenin for combat work in the rear of Franco's army and in 1943 awarded the Hero of the Soviet Union.

In my eight-year combat and intelligence work in the enemy rear I have clandestinely crossed the front line and the state boundary with a group of armed soldiers more than 70 times.

THE BELORUSSIAN PARTISAN MOVEMENT

Under my leadership, several tens of thousands of officers, landowners, gendarmes, and policemen have been killed, while at the same time losing only six men killed amongst my comrades and several men wounded . . .

The comrades of the following honorary detachments have been: Kirov – comrade Botin; Sverdlov – comrade Khaletskii, and; Beria – myself . . .

A little something about the Kirov detachment. I organized the Kirov detachment exclusively from Jews who had escaped being shot by the Hitlerites. I knew that I was facing ungodly difficulties, but I did not fear these difficulties and did this only because all the partisan detachments and formations in the Baranovichi and Pinsk oblasts had turned these people down. There were instances in which they were killed. For example, the 'partisan' anti-Semites from Tsygankov's detachment killed 11 Jews, the peasants of the village of Radzhalovichi, in the Pinsk Oblast', killed 17 Jews, and the 'partisans' in the Shchors detachment killed seven Jews.

When I first came to these people, I found them unarmed, barefoot and hungry. They declared to me that 'We want to avenge ourselves on Hitler, but we lack the opportunity'.

After this I spared neither energy nor time in order to teach these people the tactics of partisan warfare against our common inveterate enemy. And I must say that my work was not in vain. It seems that these former speculators, petty tradesmen and craftsmen, and others – these people, desiring to revenge themselves on the German monsters for the people's blood that has been spilled, under my leadership in 2.5 months have carried out no less than 15 combat operations, while daily destroying the enemy's telegraph and telephone communications, killing Hitlerites, policemen and traitors to our motherland. They gradually became not only disciplined, but also brave, both in carrying out diversions and in night marches from one area to another. Alongside diversionary, organizational and intelligence work I have been daily conducting a ruthless struggle with bandit attitudes toward the local population on the part of certain bandit 'partisan' groups in the Baranovichi and Pinsk oblasts. I could not but devote time to this matter, because in each village there were incidences of drunkenness, marauding, raping women, murder and the torching of farmsteads and villages on the part of the bandit groups, which, under the guise of partisans, systematically terrorized the local population and in this manner compromised the people's avengers – the partisans, and frightened and repulsed the peasants from helping the partisans in their struggle.

I can cite a few facts:

By order of the commander of a partisan group, the former prisoner of war and son of a *kulak* and native of the Kalinin Oblast', Andrei Leont'ev, in March 1943 the village of Novoselki, Gantsevichi area, Pinsk Oblast' (150 homes) was burned down only because there were 10–15 men in the village from the so-called 'self-defence' forces [members of a self-defence detachment organized by order of the Germans, B.S.].

OPERATION BAGRATION: AN INCOMPLETE TRUTH

As a result of such a bandit act, half of the male population of the village has gone over to the Germans.

The independent partisan groups of Semyonov and Pugachev and others were systematically drunk and shot, robbed and raped women in the territory of the Lyakhovichi and Kletsk districts of the Baranovichi Oblast'.

Therefore the bandits guilty in this matter were shot at my demand in June 1943.

The local Belorussian population, seeing in the Beria detachment its defenders, not only against the German occupiers, but also bandit elements who hide in the forests under the guise of partisans, were quite content with this.

The Belorussian population is rendering all kinds of assistance to the partisans and, most of all; about half of the grown male population in the Minsk and Pinsk oblasts has joined the partisans. Of course, there's a black sheep in every family and there are traitors among the population. They account for no more than 2–3 per cent. During this time I saw quite a large number of Latvians, residents of the Kuban' area and others serving in the punitive expeditions, who waged a ruthless war against the Belorussian partisans.

I'll cite one such fact. At the end of June 1943 the security detail along the Baranovichi–Minsk railway, made up of Austrians, was removed as unreliable and replaced by Ukrainians and residents of the Kuban'.

At present the Germans are flirting with the Belorussian population of western Belorussia and treating them better than the population of the eastern Belorussian oblasts. Quite a large number of newspapers in the Belorussian, German and Polish languages are being published. The newspapers propagandize the population that the Germans have given them a good life, have eliminated the collective farms and divided up the land, but not a word is said in the papers about how for two years not even two rail cars of manufactured goods and essential products have been delivered to Belorussia.

The local population and the partisan detachments are forced to put into food a solution extracted from artificial fertilizer.[1]

Chapter 4

The Prelude to 'Bagration'

In his Directive No. 51, entitled 'Preparation for a War on Two Fronts', which was issued on 3 November 1943 and prepared by Colonel General Alfred Jodl, the chief of the OKW (Wehrmacht high command) operations section, Hitler declared his intention to shift the focus of his main forces from the Eastern to the Western Front:

> The danger in the East remains, but now an even greater danger is arising in the West: an Anglo-American landing! In the East the enormous expanse of territory enables us to lose positions of even greater extent without fatal consequences for the German nervous system. But in the West everything is different! If the enemy here manages to penetrate our defence along a broad front, then the consequences of this will immediately be felt and they will be unforeseeable. Therefore I can no longer take responsibility for the fact that the West is being weakened in favour of another theatre of operations. Thus I have decided to strengthen the power of our defence, especially there, from which we will begin the bombardment of England. For it is there that the enemy must launch and will launch his attack, and it is there that, if this is not all disinformation, that the decisive battle against the landing will take place.[1]

In this directive, Hitler also demanded: 'Not one unit or formation stationed in the West or in Denmark is to be removed for employment on other fronts without my permission, nor even a single panzer, anti-tank subunit or assault gun unit that are being formed in the West.'

The following was demanded of the Luftwaffe:

> Taking into account the new, overall situation, it is necessary to strengthen the offensive and defensive capabilities of our air formations stationed in the West and in Denmark. At the same time, we should make preparations for freeing up and employing in the West and in Denmark, for defensive purposes, all of the available and useful air units and self-propelled national anti-aircraft means from schools and training subunits located on German territory . . . As concerns aviation, I demand that all forces be denuded from lesser-threatened areas to be set aside, without any other considerations.[2]

Thus from this moment the main forces of the German panzer arm and Luftwaffe were to be transferred to the West, which included weakening the Eastern Front.

OPERATION BAGRATION: AN INCOMPLETE TRUTH

The Wehrmacht high command was particularly fearful of an offensive on the Western Front, as this could very quickly expose the 'industrial heart of Germany' – the Ruhr – to an attack. In the East there still remained sufficient space for retreating to the borders of Romania, Poland and East Prussia. German forces and their allies still blockaded Leningrad and were holding the main part of Belorussia, the Ukrainian right bank, and the Crimea.

By the beginning of May 1944 the situation for Germany on the Eastern Front was significantly worse. Soviet forces had reached the borders of Romania and the 1939 south-eastern border of Poland, and had crossed them in places. The Crimea had been lost and the blockade of Leningrad lifted, while the forces of Army Group North had been pushed back to the Narva and Velikaya rivers. The Red Army posed a realistic threat to the Romanian oil fields, which were of critical importance to Germany. Nonetheless, the Western Front remained a priority concern for the German command, all the more so as up until June 1944 the German forces had almost always managed to break out of the 'cauldrons' and rescue the majority of their personnel, although at the loss of heavy equipment and the vehicle park.

On 5 May 1944 Jodl approached the Reich Cabinet: 'I await this battle [the Allied landing in the West, B.S.] with complete confidence. A victory in a defensive battle will change the military-political situation from top to bottom, because a landing operation of such scope, which has been preparing for many years, cannot be repeated so simply, putting aside the political consequences in England and America [in the event of the landing's failure, B.S.].'[3] It's not known whether Jodl himself believed in the possibility of defeating an Allied landing. But, in any event, he wanted to raise the ministers' spirits.

From the end of May 1944 the Germans expected a major Soviet offensive which, as they understood it, must be coordinated with the Allies' grand landing in France. On 29 May the commander of the German Fourth Army, Colonel General Gotthard Heinrici, wrote his children: 'There's no fighting in our sector. As before, we expect an offensive on Mogilev. The enemy is concentrating his forces in this area. But he is not yet ready to launch an attack. As a result of this, I would like to hope that the [Allied] landing will be delayed a while for the time being.' On 3 June Heinrici was forced to go on extended leave due to his coming down with hepatitis, so he played no part in the rout of the Fourth Army during the course of Operation 'Bagration' and the cup passed from his lips. He was replaced as chief of the Fourth Army by General of Infantry Kurt von Tippelskirch, who was fated to taste the bitterness of defeat.[4]

In May 1944 one of the Wehrmacht's elite divisions, the 6th Panzer, which had lost almost all of its tanks in breaking out of the encirclement of the German First Panzer Army and in the subsequent fighting to stabilize Army Group North Ukraine's front, had been withdrawn to north-western Germany for refitting.[5] Other elite divisions – the *Grossdeutschland* Panzergrenadier Division (actually, a panzer division), the SS *Totenkopf* Division, and the 24th and 11th Panzer Divisions – which took part in the counteroffensive in Romania, were also undergoing refitting. The 11th Panzer Division was sent to France, but was only able to enter the fighting there in August 1944. This counteroffensive, which ended on 6 June, was completely successful. The Soviet bridgeheads over the Dnestr River were destroyed and two Soviet armies, the 5th Shock and 8th Guards, were routed. Thus it seemed as though the immediate threat to the oilfields in Ploesti had been removed. However, this success had been purchased at a heavy price in the form of the exhaustion of several panzer divisions. In the same way the Wehrmacht's successful operations in the Kovel' area had led to the exhaustion of two divisions – the 4th Panzer and SS *Wiking* Divisions – which had to be sent away for refitting. As a result, by the start of 'Bagration' these divisions could be employed neither on the Normandy front, nor on the Eastern Front.

In the opinion of the German military historian Karl-Heinz Frieser:

> From the spring of 1944 Hitler and the Wehrmacht's higher headquarters awaited the invasion with increasing impatience. Their interest was concentrated exclusively on the Western Front. As a result of the shifting of strategic priorities, the Eastern Front now became to be viewed as a secondary theatre of military operations, while the threat on the part of the Red Army's increasingly superior forces was disastrously underestimated. The plan was to chiefly reinforce the Western Front with recently reinforced formations and newly-produced weapons, particularly tanks.[6]

In our opinion, this did not mean that the *Führer* did not pay any attention to the Eastern Front. But the threat from the West was viewed as more dangerous than the threat from the East, insofar as the French or Belgian coastline, where the Western Allies were supposed to land in the immediate future, were much closer to Germany's vital centres than the existing line of the Eastern Front. Frieser also notes that 'However, in this regard Hitler was not entirely consistent in the distribution of forces needed for this strategy. In the first half of 1944 a number of formations, which had originally been designated for the Western Front, were sent to the East or to Italy, in order to assist in coping with the repeated crises along these fronts.' But the Eastern Front was transformed into a 'poor relation' in regards to the supply of weapons, ammunition and fuel. It was planned to meet the Allied offensive with counterblows, while in the East they were to limit themselves to a stubborn defence and the employment of fortresses. It was clear that the weak divisions on the Eastern Front would not be able to hold off the Red Army's pressure for long and that they should be reinforced as quickly as possible by divisions freed up from the Western Front.[7] In an OKW memorandum of 14 April 1944 it was maintained that 'The high command, being fully aware of the crisis situation in the East, has decided to take an extremely profound risk before history and the nation'. Only 53 per cent of the Wehrmacht's ground forces were stationed on the endless expanses of the Eastern Front. By 14 April 1944, of 341 division-size formations of the ground forces and SS, only 131 divisions were located in the West and Italy, or 38.4 per cent of the overall number, but in a corresponding OKW memorandum all of the formations in Germany were considered to be part of the Eastern Front, when in reality many of them, following the landing in Normandy, were sent to the Western Front. The OKW maintained that at that moment, that is by the middle of April, only 41 divisions among those considered outside the confines of the Eastern Front possessed sufficient combat capability to successfully conduct operations on the Eastern Front. However, many of the Eastern Front's divisions, following the heavy fighting in the first half of 1944, were in no better condition than the divisions of limited capability in other theatres.[8]

Hitler hoped only to relatively quickly inflict defeat on the Allied landing forces, after which he would transfer 30–35 divisions from the Western Front to the Eastern

Front. In any event, on 22 January 1944 he spoke about this to his close friend, ambassador Walther Hewel, the Ministry of Foreign Affairs' communications officer with the *Führer*'s headquarters.[9] It's difficult to say whether Hitler believed in the possibility of so completely defeating the Allied landing force that it would be possible to remove at least 30 divisions from the Western Front. And it could take more than a month to transfer such a number of divisions from France to the Eastern Front, and during that time the Red Army might manage to advance far to the west and reach the borders of Germany. It would take no less than three weeks to transfer 5–6 panzer divisions that could slow down a Soviet offensive through counterblows. And this does not take into account the time necessary for reinforcing them with equipment. Even given the most favourable outcome of the fighting in Normandy for the Germans, the losses in tanks and assault guns would still have been significant.

It's doubtful that Hitler believed that they would manage to so decisively defeat the Allies in the West so that he could manage to transfer 30–35 divisions to the Eastern Front. After all, for this it would be necessary to completely destroy 15–20 American and British divisions (Allied divisions were superior in strength to German ones); that is, to create a 'cauldron' on the scale of Stalingrad. However, taking into account the Western Allies' overwhelming superiority, particularly in the air, even if it had been possible to create such a 'cauldron' by some sort of miracle, then the Wehrmacht would certainly not have been capable of eliminating it. The Allies would have organized an 'air bridge' to the surrounded forces and would then have broken through the ring. It's most likely that the tale of the 30–35 divisions was necessary for Hitler to calm his entourage, including the generals. The most that the *Führer* could have hoped for would be to remove 5–6 mobile divisions (of these, no less than three panzer divisions) from the Western Front and send them east, in order to cover the retreat of Army Groups Centre and North Ukraine into Poland and to hold the front in Romania. But this variation also proved to be incapable of realization.

Nevertheless, up until 6 June 1944 Hitler continued to hope that they could maintain a sufficiently powerful mobile reserve on the Eastern Front with whose assistance they would be able to, if not repulse the expected Soviet general offensive, then at least seriously slow it down. The II SS Panzer Corps, comprising two elite panzer divisions, still remained on the Eastern Front in a reserve capacity. Aside from this, in the beginning of June another two panzer divisions, including an elite panzer training division, were being hurriedly transferred to the Eastern Front. Four panzer divisions, including three elite ones, were a serious shock force, capable of inflicting heavy losses on the attacking Soviet forces. However, the first day of the Allied landing in Normandy had already shown that its scale was such that it was necessary to throw all possible forces against it. Thus a panzer training division and 9th Panzer Division were deployed to Normandy, and on 9 June the SS Panzer Corps was sent there from the Eastern Front. After this Army Group Centre was doomed to destruction, regardless of where the Red Army might launch its main attack – in the Kovel' area or along the entire perimeter of the 'Belorussian balcony'.

In the summer of 1943 about 80 per cent of the Germans' armoured might was located on the Eastern Front. In the summer of 1944 the picture was different. A little more than half of the Germans' tank strength remained on the Eastern Front, if one judges by the number of divisions. If one excludes from the calculation those panzer divisions which were formally assigned to the Eastern Front, but which were actually located in Germany or in Poland for refitting, as well as taking into account the divisions' level of materiel supply, then less than half of all German tanks and assault guns were on the Eastern Front. From 1943 the Western Front had priority concerning personnel, armament and equipment reinforcements. Thus by the summer of 1944 the Western Front's panzer divisions were far more fully outfitted with armoured equipment and motor transport that the ones on the Eastern Front, many of which were still in the rear undergoing refitting by the start of Operation 'Bagration'.

The greater part of the Luftwaffe also had to combat the Western Allies in 1944. In the late spring of 1944, immediately prior to the landing in Normandy, Anglo-American airpower had reduced the production of oil by 40 per cent in Romania and the production of synthetic fuel in Germany by 90 per cent. Oil supplies in Germany remained significant, but the Germans nevertheless had to cut the consumption of fuel for training and to reduce the volume of automobile supply. A quarter of all German artillery production was for anti-aircraft artillery and ammunition for it. In April and May 1944 alone the Reich's anti-aircraft aviation lost 100 per cent of its average monthly strength in planes and 40 per cent of its average monthly strength in pilots in battles with the US Army Air Force. As a result of this, Germany was forced to concentrate its main fighter forces in the West and even before the summer campaign of 1944 the Red Army had gained air superiority on the Eastern Front.[10]

At the end of the first week in April the heads of the American and British military missions in Moscow, Major General John R. Deane and Lieutenant General Montague B. Burroughs, informed the deputy chief of the Red Army General Staff, General A.I. Antonov, that Operation 'Overlord' would begin on 31 May (the start of the operation might be moved forward or backward due to weather conditions). On 23 April Antonov replied to Deane that the General Staff was 'satisfied' with the date for beginning 'Overlord' and that the Red Army would begin its offensive simultaneously.[11]

In the middle of May 1944 the chief of the section 'Foreign Armies East', Major General Reinhard Gehlen, presented a report by an agent, according to which a meeting took place in the *Stavka* at the end of March, chaired by Stalin, during which two plans for a future offensive were discussed: the first called for carrying out the main attack in the Kovel'–L'vov area, with a movement toward Warsaw (with a simultaneous Polish uprising in the German rear), and the second an offensive to the Baltic coast along with a supporting attack in the south. According to the agent's report, Stalin finally chose the second variation, which also included a Polish uprising.[12] This was actually the future 'Bagration'. As one can see, the planned Polish uprising in Warsaw would make sense only with the approach of the Red Army. It follows that the variant chosen by Stalin assumed the movement of Soviet forces on Warsaw from the east and, on the other hand, a movement to the Baltic also assumed arriving at the borders of East Prussia.

A supporting attack in the south clearly assumed an offensive, not in Romania, but along the L'vov–Sandomierz direction, which really could have directly facilitated 'Bagration'. Thus the report by the unknown agent corresponded to the truth. If Hitler read it then he should have reached the conclusion that the main Soviet offensive was planned against Army Group Centre. However, the timely concentration of the German Eastern Front's meagre tank reserves on the 'Belorussian balcony' might well have prompted Stalin to return to the first variant of an offensive from Kovel' to Warsaw, which was the most dangerous one for the Germans.

OPERATION BAGRATION: AN INCOMPLETE TRUTH

The variant which called for an offensive in the Kovel'–L'vov area was actually proposed by the commander of the First Belorussian Front, K.K. Rokossovskii, on 3 April 1944, but was rejected by the *Stavka*. Rokossovskii believed that the optimum solution, which would deprive the enemy of a breathing spell, would be to rout him in the area of Minsk, Baranovichi, Slonim, Brest, Kovel', Luninets and Bobruisk and arriving at the line Minsk–Slonim–Brest–the Western Bug River, which would cut all of the main lateral railways and highways in the German rear. Konstantin Konstantinovich planned a two-stage operation. At first four armies from the First Belorussian Front's left wing would attack from the south and seize positions along the eastern bank of the Western Bug River along the sector from Brest to Vladimir-Volynskii. The second stage foresaw an offensive by all of the Front's forces to rout the enemy's Bobruisk and Minsk groups of forces. Then the Front's left-flank armies were to launch a second attack from the Brest area in the direction of Kobrin, Slonim and Stolbtsy, into the rear of the Belorussian group of forces. Simultaneously, the Front's right-flank armies would launch a second attack from the area of Rogachev and Zhlobin on Bobruisk and Minsk. Rokossovskii supposed that approximately 30 days would be required to carry out this plan, taking into account the time needed for regroupings. The Rokossovskii plan required the strengthening of the Front's left wing with one or two tank armies, but it was rejected.[13]

Thus as early as the beginning of May 1944 the German command knew that the Soviet *Stavka* had rejected an attack through Kovel', but nevertheless held a group of tank divisions there, fearful that an attack might still be launched here, insofar as there were sufficient forces for such an operation along the First Belorussian Front's left wing and the First Ukrainian Front.

On 3 May Gehlen reported that there were 39 Soviet tank corps (106 formations) on the Soviet side of the front. One thousand two hundred tanks were arrayed against Army Group South Ukraine, 500 against Army Group North Ukraine, 423 against Army Group North, and only approximately 91 tanks against Army Group Centre. In all, the Red Army had 2,214 tanks at the front. Within less than four weeks this number increased to 2,437 tanks and to more than 3,400 within another month, at which time the overall number of Soviet tanks, including reserves, would amount to 8,117. Radio silence by the enemy was also pointed out, particularly in the south. The German command was increasingly inclined to the idea that the main Soviet summer offensive would take place in the Kovel'–L'vov area, although it allowed that it might follow north of the Pripyat' Marshes. Moreover, the Allies' headquarters and the Red Army's General Staff were spreading disinformation regarding a joint operation, 'Bodyguard', supposedly being prepared by the Red Army and the Allies against the Norwegian coast (with a simultaneous ground offensive on Petsamo) and Romania.[14]

Overall control of forces during Operation 'Bagration' was to be exercised by Stalin, on the Soviet side, and Hitler on the German. Both dictators appointed as commanders in the zone of Operation 'Bagration', those generals whom they fully trusted and whom they considered to be talented leaders. Stalin entrusted the coordination of the actions of four Fronts to two marshals – his deputy as Supreme Commander-in-Chief, Georgii Konstantinovich Zhukov, and the chief of the General Staff, Aleksandr Mikhailovich Vasilevskii. Zhukov had conducted the successful counteroffensive around Moscow, which halted the blitzkrieg, and Vasilevskii had controlled the

THE PRELUDE TO 'BAGRATION'

Stalingrad counteroffensive. Both had controlled operations by Soviet forces during the Battle of Kursk. In 1944, before 'Bagration', Zhukov had managed to carry out the coordination of operations by the First and Second Ukrainian Fronts in the Korsun–Shevchenkovskii operation. As a result, two German army corps had ended up being surrounded, but were able to break out of the encirclement, although they lost almost all their heavy weapons and equipment. Then, following the wounding of N.F. Vatutin, Georgii Konstantinovich took over the command of the First Ukrainian Front and carried out the Proskurov–Chernovtsy operation, during which Soviet forces reached the foothills of the Carpathian Mountains and encircled the German First Panzer Army, which, however, was able to break out of the ring, while again losing the greater part of its armoured equipment. Now, in Belorussia, Zhukov calculated not only encircling major enemy forces, but to deprive them of the opportunity of breaking out of the encirclement. In the first half of 1944 Vasilevskii coordinated operations for liberating the Ukrainian right bank and the Crimea, during which a large amount of territory was liberated, but he was unable to destroy major enemy groups of forces. Even the major part of the German-Romanian forces in the Crimea was quite successfully evacuated. Aleksandr Mikhailovich calculated that in Belorussia the enemy would not escape complete defeat.

General Konstantin Konstantinovich Rokossovskii commanded the First Belorussian Front. He had earlier managed to show himself in commanding an army during the Battle of Smolensk and the Battle of Moscow and had commanded the Don Front in the Battle of Stalingrad and the Central Front in the Battle of Kursk. Konstantin Konstantinovich commanded the First Belorussian Front in the first half of 1944 and in February conducted the not overly successful Rogachev–Zhlobin operation, during which he managed to liberate Rogachev, but the attempt by the Soviet 3rd Army to attack Bobruisk was repelled by the Germans. Now Rokossovskii was counting on encircling and routing the enemy in the Bobruisk area through a two-pronged turning movement.

The Second Belorussian Front, which was fated to play a supporting role in Operation 'Bagration', was commanded by Colonel General Georgii Fyodorovich Zakharov. He had taken part in the Battle of Moscow, as chief of staff of the Bryansk Front and deputy commander of the Western Front. Zakharov also took part in the Battle of the Caucasus and in the Battle of Stalingrad, as the deputy commander and chief of staff of a number of Fronts. As commander of the 2nd Guards Army, Georgii Fyodorovich took part in the liberation of the Crimea in the spring of 1944 and it was his army that played the main role in the liberation of the peninsula. Zakharov commanded a Front in 'Bagration' for the first time and hoped to show himself at his best. This is how Marshal A.I. Yeremenko described G.F. Zakharov: 'Zakharov's head is pretty good and he's a man of great will and demanding commander, but is terribly rude, and I would even say a petty tyrant. Without looking into matters appropriately, he can yell at a man and even beat him.'[15] By the way, Zhukov enjoyed the same reputation, the same as the commander of the neighbouring front, I.D. Chernyakhovskii; just like Yeremenko himself, who could beat some of his subordinate generals in the heat of the moment.

In general, instances of using one's fists and arbitrary behaviour among the Red Army's higher command element was widespread, including while conducting Operation 'Bagration'. Here is an amazing document, a directive issued on 27 May 1944 by the First Belorussian Front's military council, in connection with outrageous instances of arbitrary behaviour by commanders at all levels, which had led to tragic consequences:

> The commander of our Front's 12th Division, Colonel Gavilevskii, during the recent fighting and without a substantial investigation of the matter, executed battalion commander, Major Durnov, without trial. During the war Major Durnov had been awarded the Order of Suvorov 3rd Class, the Order of the Red Banner, and the Order of the Red Star, and was described as a brave and intelligent officer. This shameful incident for the Front is not the only one. The Front's military council has decisively condemned Gavlievskii's actions and turned him over to be tried by a military tribunal. Some officers, even among the higher command element, still do not understand that by an unauthorized execution, arbitrary behaviour and the flouting of the law they do not strengthen discipline among the troops, but quite the opposite, they undermine it, and that such actions do not raise the commander's authority in the eyes of his subordinates, but rather undermine his authority and discredit and shame the commanders who allow such things.
>
> It is also completely inadmissible that higher commanders in the armies, formations and units struggle insufficiently against acts of arbitrary punishment and do not prevent such occurrences.
>
> Party and political organs in the units, formations and armies also do not wage a campaign against these shameful phenomena.
>
> The Front's military council demands that all generals, officers and political workers eliminate instances of unauthorized executions without trial and other acts of arbitrary behaviour in relations between military personnel.
>
> The military councils and formation and unit commanders are to explain and demand of officers the strict observation of the tenets of manuals regarding a commander's service relations with his subordinates.
>
> To remind officers and commanders of units that the employment of weapons is allowed only in extreme cases, as called for by the defence minister's Order No. 227 [strictly speaking, this order did not discuss very exactly the circumstances under which a commander might employ his weapon against subordinates; it was only maintained: 'Panic mongers and cowards should be exterminated on the spot. From now on the demand of not a step back without orders from a higher command must be an iron law of discipline for each commander, Red Army soldier and political worker. Company, battalion, regimental and division commanders, the corresponding commissars and political workers who retreat from their combat position without orders from above are traitors to the Motherland. Such commanders and political workers must be treated as traitors to the Motherland', B.S.], only in a difficult combat situation and only for the purpose of guaranteeing and forcing them to carry out the combat assignment.
>
> The commanders and political organs, while not leaving a single instance of unauthorized execution without a careful investigation and

preventing these acts in every way, are to immediately report them to the Front'ss military council.

The Front procurator is to direct the work of the military prosecutors toward uprooting incidents of arbitrary behaviour among the troops and bringing the guilty parties to trial.

The directive was followed by a special letter by the member of the First Belorussian Front's military council, N.A. Bulganin, on unauthorized executions, addressed to G.M. Malenkov. It was noted that '... the military prosecutor's office has gathered data on acts of unauthorized executions at the front. It has been established that during the period from 1 January 1944 there have been 30 instances of unauthorized executions, of which there was one in the 30th Army, four in the 70th Army, five in the 47th Army, six in the 48th Army, six in the 65th Army, and eight in the 69th Army.'

The facts were as follows:

1. On 6 April 1944 the commander of the 498th Rifle Regiment's 2nd Rifle Battalion, Major Durnov, was executed at the observation post of Colonel Gavilevskii's 132nd Division under the following circumstances:

    On 6.IV.44 the 498th Rifle Regiment's 2nd Rifle Battalion was occupying defensive positions. Its neighbours were: the 498th Rifle Regiment's 1st Rifle Battalion to the right, and the 712th Rifle Regiment's 1st Rifle Battalion to the left. At 1630 on 6.IV the enemy, following an artillery preparation, attacked along the sector of the 498th Rifle Regiment's first battalion and the 712th Rifle Regiment's first battalion. As a result of the attack, both battalions were thrown out of their positions and began to fall back in disorder; as regards the 498th Rifle Regiment's 2nd Battalion, which was commanded by Major Durnov, the latter firmly maintained its line. All attacks along this battalion's sector were beaten back. Lacking communications with the regiment and neighbours for an hour and a half, and thus not knowing the situation, Major Durnov made the decision to personally go to the regiment's command post in order to learn the situation and make a report. The battalion command appointed his deputy Major Sorokin, in his place. The enemy, having taken advantage of the retreat by the first battalion of the 498th Rifle Regiment and the first battalion of the 712th Rifle Regiment, which were covering the flanks of the 2nd Battalion, upon Durnov's departure because he did not know the situation, cut the battalion off from the regiment's and divisions' remaining forces, as a result of which Durnov was unable to return to his battalion.

    At 1900 the chief of division intelligence, Major Skvortsov, informed by radio the division commander, Gavilevskii, the situation, while also informing him that the 2nd Battalion was encircled and that the battalion commander, Major Durnov, was with the 1st Battalion.

    Colonel Galievskii, not knowing the reasons for Major Durnov being with the 1st Battalion, ordered Major Skvortsov by radio to execute Major Durnov for cowardice and panic mongering. But because Major Durnov was at the regimental commander's command post, Skvortsov did not carry out the order of the division commander, about which he reported to Colonel Gavilevskii.

Gavilevskii passed on his order to shoot Major Durnov to the regimental commander, Chizhevskii.

Regimental commander Chizhevskii did not carry out this order and sent Major Durnov to the division.

Major Durnov arrived at the division around 2000 and tried to report on the situation to division commander Gavilevskii and asked him to investigate it. Gavilevskii refused to listen to Major Durnov's report and ordered the sergeant of the command platoon, Kharlov, and also his adjutant, Senior Lieutenant Telegin, to execute Durnov. Durnov was shot.

Before his execution Major Durnov asked that his medals be removed. Durnov had been awarded three orders: the Red Star, the Red Banner and the Order of Suvorov, 3rd class. However, this request was refused.

Division commander Gavilevskii has been removed from command by the military council and turned over for trial.

2. On 3 April of this year Junior Lieutenant Sviridenko, the commander of a platoon of anti-tank weapons in the 339th Independent Anti-Tank Battalion, while at his firing position, organized a drinking bout with his subordinates. The enemy fired on the combat formation with artillery during the drinking bout.

Junior Lieutenant Sviridenko ordered Corporal Ivanov, who was taking part in the drinking, to take up his firing position. Ivanov, being drunk, was not in a condition to carry out Sviridenko's order. Then Sviridenko shot him.

By verdict of a military tribunal, Sviridenko was sentenced to eight years of deprivation of freedom with an annotation to article 28 of the criminal code; that is, to be sent to a punishment unit.

3. On the night of 12 April of this year Private Kadzhiev, from the 2nd Company of the 1st Rifle Battalion/ 110th Guards Rifle Regiment/38th Guards Rifle Division was found sleeping at his post. The company commander, Lieutenant Kubyshko, upon learning of this, summoned Kadzhiev and, upon determining that Kadzhiev had actually been asleep at his post, made the decision to shoot Kadzhiev before the troops and carried out this decision then and there.

By verdict of a military tribunal, Kubyshko was sentenced to seven years of deprivation of freedom with an annotation to article 28 of the criminal code; that is, to be sent to a punishment unit.

4. On 3 April the first sergeant of an administrative platoon of the 2nd Battalion/113th Guards Rifle Regiment/38th Guards Rifle Division, Demidkin, while on his way to the front line, discovered along a forest path a soldier with a bandaged head who was resting. Demidkin decided to check to see if the soldier was really wounded. When the soldier

removed the bandage from his head, Demidkin determined that there was no head wound at all. Demidkin immediately shot this soldier.

By verdict of a military tribunal, Demidkin was sentenced to eight years of deprivation of freedom with an annotation to article 28 of the criminal code; that is, to be sent to a punishment unit.

5. On 15 April of this year signals personnel from the 1st Rifle Battalion/1297th Rifle Regiment/160th Rifle Division, under the command of the deputy communications platoon commander Kozlov, were working on laying down a telephone line. Kozlov was feeling sick and left for a farmstead to rest, leaving his subordinates to work. Senior Lieutenant Tatarintsev, the assistant battalion commander, arrived and discovered Kozlov asleep and began to beat him, and then killed Kozlov with a shot from his pistol.

Tatarintsev was drunk.

Tatarintsev has been turned over to a military tribunal.

6. On 8 January of this year the assistant to the chief of staff of the 4th Independent Rifle Battalion/115th Independent Rifle Brigade, Senior Lieutenant Smurnikov, received an order from the brigade chief of staff, Major Shekhter, to determine why supplies were not being delivered to the 1st Rifle Company. Smurnikov left for the battalion rear and determined that First Sergeant Bochkarev, of the 1st Company, had gotten drunk and fallen asleep in his overhead cover, which is why the delivery of munitions had not been organized. Smurnikov summoned Bochkarev and shot him with his pistol.

Smurnikov has been turned over for trial.

7. On 1 February of this year the deputy commander of the 4th Rifle Division's 220th Rifle Regiment for political affairs, Major Grishchenko, killed the first sergeant of the 101st Rifle Regiment's 2nd Battalion, Bannykh, with two pistol shots. Grishchenko was drunk. While setting up the regimental headquarters, he had several times chased Bannykh out of one building after another. When Bannykh came for his things, Grishchenko cursed him out and pushed him into the vestibule, and then took a pistol from his orderly and killed Bannykh with two shots.

Grishchenko has been condemned.

8. On 5 February of this year the deputy commander of the 2nd Battalion/471st Rifle Regiment/73rd Rifle Division, Senior Lieutenant Moisa, on orders from the battalion commander, Senior Lieutenant Sadykov, shot on the battlefield the seriously wounded commander of the regiment's 4th Company, Lieutenant Shevchenko, who was suspected of cowardice. An investigation determined that Shevchenko had in no way manifested cowardice.

Sadykov has been condemned.

9. On 6 February of this year the commander of the 307th Rifle Division, Major General Yenshin, personally shot the acting chief of artillery of the 1019th Rifle Regiment, Captain Barankov, at his observation post. Yenshin has been administratively punished by the army's military council.

10. In February and March of this year there were three incidences of the unlawful execution in the 188th Independent Punishment Company of Red Army soldiers by the company commander, Lieutenant Kashtanov. The three soldiers were shot because they had fallen behind the company during the march to their assembly area.

   Kashtanov has been turned over to a military tribunal.

11. On 9 January the assistant to the chief of the 1st section of the headquarters of the 60th Sevsk Rifle Division, Major Demchenko, shot the commander of the 2nd Mortar Company/2nd Rifle Battalion/1481st Rifle Regiment, Senior Lieutenant Kuts. The circumstances of the execution are as follows. Kuts, being extremely drunk, reported to the regimental commander, Major Sheptev, for orders. Instead of removing him from the command of the company, he was ordered to leave for his subunit for carrying out his combat assignment. But instead of commanding the fire from his mortar batteries, Kuts ended up in the woods in the rear of his company's combat formation and failed to control the fighting. Major Demchenko discovered him in the woods. Having gotten in contact with the commander of the 60th Rifle Division, Colonel Bogoyavlenskii, Major Demchenko reported to him on Kuts's behaviour, Colonel Bogoyavlenskii issued the order to execute Kuts. The latter was shot.

12. On 21 January of this year the commander of the 218th Rifle Division's 372nd Rifle Regiment, Lieutenant Colonel Ryabov, shot the commander of the 2nd Battalion's Machine Gun Company, Lieutenant Mitrofanov. When Lieutenant Colonel Ryabov arrived at the company to check the subunit's combat readiness, he found the soldiers, including Mitrofanov, asleep, and there was no combat security, the machine guns were not being guarded, and the platoon commanders not at their posts. Ryabov tried to wake Mitrofanov up, but the latter did not get up. Ryabov shot Mitrofanov with two shots at point blank range [it would seem that the lieutenant colonel could not even be bothered to wake his victim up, B.S.].

   On 22 January Ryabov himself was severely wounded and evacuated to the rear by plane.

   The facts laid out here show that arbitrariness and unlawful executions are widespread. For the purpose of waging a decisive struggle against these shameful facts, the Front's military council has issued the attached directive. The armies' political organs and members of the military councils have been correspondingly oriented to prevent these shameful incidents.

What is striking is the high concentration of unlawful executions in the punishment units – three of 30 victims out of the entire First Belorussian Front were executed in a single company.

Generals did not end up in punishment units and they were shot extremely rarely, and then almost exclusively in 1941. Misdemeanours for which lieutenants and captains went straight to a punishment battalion were often forgiven them for their past services. Here is another unlawful execution that had an entirely different outcome than the ones listed above, only because a general figured here, and one who was under the protection of Georgii Zhukov himself. The chief of the Red Army's Personnel Administration, Colonel General F.I. Golikov, wrote in this regard to the secretary of the CPSU Central Committee, G.M. Malenkov, on 30 April 1944: 'Marshal of the Soviet Union, comrade Zhukov (coded telegram no. 117396, 30 April 1944), reported to comrade Stalin on the personal execution by the commander of the 18th Rifle Corps, Major General Afonin, of the commander of the 237th Rifle Division's intelligence section, Major Andreev. I am presenting to you a copy of my report to comrade Stalin on this matter.'

Malenkov had informed Stalin a day earlier, on 29 April:

> Marshal Zhukov has reported to you on the personal execution by the commander of the 18th Rifle Corps, Major General Afonin, of the chief of the 237th Rifle Division's intelligence section, Major Andreev.
>
> Despite the fact that this unlawful execution was carried out on 12 April of this year, the report was made only on 28 April; that is, 16 days later.
>
> Despite the entreaties of Marshal Zhukov not to turn Afonin over to the judgment of a military tribunal and to limit itself to measures of social and party influence, I implore you to turn Afonin over for trial.
>
> If, in contravention of all the manuals and orders by the Supreme Command and the principles of the Red Army, General Afonin believes that it is allowed to strike a Soviet officer, then he is hardly able to believe that each Red Army officer (all the more, a combat officer) will remain within the confines of discipline, so shamelessly and easily violated by the general himself, after such a physical and moral insult.
>
> Moreover, following the murder of Andreev, one can hardly believe General Afonin's reference that he tried to strike him back and behaved impudently. As regards General Afonin's positive traits, due to which Marshal Zhukov asks that we not judge the latter, Colonel General Chernyakhovskii gave me the following appraisal (orally) of Afonin the other day: a lightweight and conceited lord, intolerant in his treatment of people; he does not know the artillery and is incapable of organizing cooperation on the battlefield; he does not study, is a braggart and loves the loud phrase.
>
> Comrade Chernyakhovskii (in his own words) gave his opinion of Afonin personally to Marshal Zhukov.
>
> Afonin worked for Marshal Zhukov as a messenger at the beginning of 1943 and in the headquarters of his group at Khalkhin-Gol.[16]

It's of interest that in his memoirs Zhukov characterized Afonin quite differently. In recalling the fighting at Khalkhin-Gol, he wrote:

> Before dawn on 3 July [1939, B.S.] the senior adviser to the Mongolian army, Colonel I.M. Afonin, left for Bain-Tsagan Mountain in order to check on the defence by the Mongolian 6th Cavalry Division, and quite

unexpectedly discovered there Japanese troops who had secretly crossed over the Khalkhin-Gol River under the cover of night and attacked elements of the 6th Mongolian Cavalry Division. They, taking advantage of their superiority in numbers, captured Bain-Tsagan Mountain and the adjacent area before dawn on 3 July. The Mongolian 6th Cavalry Division fell back to the north-western sectors of Bain-Tsagan Mountain.

Upon evaluating the danger of the new situation, Ivan Mikhailovich Afonin immediately arrived at the command post of the Soviet forces . . . and reported on the new situation at Bain-Tsagan Mountain. It was clear that because of the disorganized withdrawal by the Mongolian 6th Cavalry Division there was no one in the area to contest the advance of the Japanese group of forces for launching an attack in the flank and rear of our main force.

Here Ivan Mikhailovich is portrayed as a smart commander, capable of correctly evaluating a situation. And don't think that this lightweight and conceited man, although incapable of organizing the control of troops, could not strike and shoot a subordinate.

The picture of the incident is cleared up in Golikov's letter. Afonin hit Andreev for some reason and the major gave as good as he got. Here the valorous general, who evidently understood that he could not beat the healthy intelligence officer one-on-one, grabbed his revolver and shot the uppity man on the spot.

And the highly-regarded combat officer got off scot free. Nobody turned Ivan Mikhailovich over for trial. He ended the war as commander of the 18th Guards Rifle Corps on the Fourth Ukrainian Front, in Prague, was promoted to Lieutenant General, and on 24 June 1945, among the best generals, took part in the victory parade in Moscow, where he led the 2nd Ukrainian Regiment. It's possible that Zhukov also interceded for Afonin because not long before this, on the First Ukrainian Front in March 1944, where he took over following Vatutin's wounding, he encountered the same sort of incident which, fortunately, did not end so tragically. The chief of the Front's engineer troops, Lieutenant General of Engineer Troops Boris Vasil'evich Blagoslavov (1901–79), recalled how Zhukov, having just taken over command, gathered the commanders at night for a meeting. There, on the basis of short reports, he was ready to recommend some for citations, to remove others from their positions, to turn others over to the courts, and others to simply shoot. At the same time, the marshal made use of untranslatable Russian phrases and addressed everyone exclusively as 'thou', although he had not previously drunk to friendship with anyone. Zhukov immediately took a dislike to Blagoslavov. When the general requested that Zhukov not subject him to cursing and threats, the marshal grabbed his Mauser. In reply, Blagoslavov grabbed his Luger (both preferred captured weapons). An awkward pause ensued. Blagoslavov reminded Zhukov that he was waiting for his shot. This was not just a general, but a general of engineers, a man far more educated than an average infantry general, and with a well-developed sense of his own dignity. But there was no duel. Zhukov understood that they would not pat him on the head for the summary execution of such a high-ranking general. After all, this was not just some commander of a regiment, or even of a division. Georgii Konstantinovich put his Mauser back in the holster and promised that he would get even with Blagoslavov.[17] However, Zhukov's reach did not extend to the uppity general, possibly the only one in the Red Army (others had silently

THE PRELUDE TO 'BAGRATION'

put up with more than this). Evidently, his power did not extend to the lawless removal from their posts of army commanders and their corresponding ranks at Front level. Blagoslavov successfully ended the war at his former post with the Second Belorussian Front, with Rokossovskii, with whom he had excellent relations. As for the lower ranks, such as Major Andreev, such 'physical resistance to evil' usually ended in death.

In general, scenes with Marshal Zhukov versus General Blagoslavov, or General Afonin versus Major Andreev, remind one not even of a so-so Western, but of a typical shootout in a bandit hideout, where the chiefs, in the role of which we have Zhukov and Afonin, maintain their power over their underlings – subordinate officers and generals. And over all the Red Army soldiers, officers, generals, and marshals stood the big chief – Stalin. The generals who commanded corps and above, as well as the marshals, were afraid of him because only the 'father of the peoples' could order their execution, demote them or put them in prison (the generals were not sent to the punishment battalions, fearing that they would be captured or go over to the enemy). The officers and major generals who commanded divisions were not afraid of Stalin and sincerely loved him and sometimes appealed to him and his actual party deputy, Malenkov, with complaints of being oppressed and being treated unfairly by the higher-ranking officers and, at time, in the form of denunciations against these officers. On the other hand, the officers were afraid of and often hated their immediate superiors – from company commander to Front commander, each of which at any moment could shoot them or send them to a punishment battalion. At the same time, of course, a threat on the part of one's own battalion commander was far more real than that of a far-off army commander, and even more so a Front commander and they stood little chance of being struck by them. As regards their soldiers, platoon commanders and, to a certain degree, company commanders, had to be more careful and not shoot them or send them to the punishment battalions without good reason, otherwise one could easily get a bullet in the back during a battle from the condemned one's comrades. The exception, as we have seen, was only the punishment units and subunits, where the permanent (officer) element would shoot the rotating element (punishment troops) with pleasure. They would die tomorrow in battle in any event, while officers did not go into battle with the punishment troops, but remained in the rear in the capacity of blocking detachments. In usual units the soldiers were not shot by their immediate superiors, but by higher-ranking ones, beginning at battalion headquarters level or blocking detachments and headquarters companies made up of NKVD troops. They were not threatened with a bullet in the back. They also shot soldiers from the rear elements in order to raise the spirits of those going to the front.

Ivan Danilovich Chernyakhovskii commanded the Third Belorussian Front. He began the Great Patriotic War as the commander of a tank division. From July 1942 Chernyakhovskii commanded the 60th Army, with which he successfully operated in the Voronezh–Kastornoe operation, the Battle of Kursk and in forcing the Dnepr. In March-April 1944, prior to Chernyakhovskii's departure, the army's forces were unable to take the 'fortress' of Ternopol', which had a very small garrison and no fortifications. However, the delay at Ternopol' did not keep Stalin from appointing Chernyakhovskii in April the commander of the Third Belorussian Front, which was to play an important role in Operation 'Bagration'.

General Ivan Khristoforovich Bagramyan commanded the First Baltic Front. His career during the Great Patriotic War had both its ups and its downs. Ivan

Khristoforovich began the war as a colonel and chief of the operational section of the South-western Front's headquarters. Bagramyan managed to break out of the Kiev 'cauldron' in the autumn of 1941. At the end of 1941 Ivan Khristoforovich planned the successful offensive against Rostov-on-Don. But they made him the 'scapegoat' for the Khar'kov 'cauldron' of May 1942, reducing him in rank from the post of chief of staff of the South-western Direction to that of chief of staff of the 28th Army. Bagramyan nearly once again became the 'scapegoat' at his new post for the army's abandoning Rossosh' without a fight, but thanks to Zhukov's intercession in July 1942 Ivan Khristoforovich became commander of the 16th Army (later the 11th Guards Army). He successfully commanded during the Battle of Kursk and as early as November 1943 became commander of the First Baltic Front. In February–March 1944 Bagramyan took part in the failed Vitebsk operation, during which he was unable to take the city. Now he hoped to extract his revenge.

One may say that Stalin's choice proved quite fortunate. Although Zakharov and Chernyakhovskii had no prior experience of commanding Fronts, both successfully coped with their tasks during Operation 'Bagration', the same as the more experienced Bagramyan. Stalin correctly considered Rokossovskii, Zhukov and Vasilevskii his best commanders, and they did not let him down on this occasion. One might say that neither the *Stavka* representatives nor the Front commanders made any mistakes during the course of Operation 'Bagration'. If there were any kind of mistakes, then they were at the level of army commander.

On the German side, Army Group Centre was commanded from 12 October 1943 by General Field Marshal Ernst Busch. During the Polish campaign he commanded the army corps that took Cracow. During the French campaign of 1940 Busch commanded the Sixteenth Army that captured Verdun. According to Plan 'Barbarossa', Busch's army attacked toward Leningrad and in 1942 it defended the Demyansk bridgehead, the Kholm area and Staraya Russa. On 1 February 1943 Busch was promoted to field marshal for his successes in defensive fighting. In commanding Army Group Centre, he successfully repulsed all of the offensive operations by the forces of the Western, Kalinin and Second Belorussian Fronts up until May 1944. In the two and a half years preceding 'Bagration' Busch carried out successful defensive operations in conditions of positional warfare against an enemy significantly superior to the German forces in men and materiel. Only this time the Soviet superiority was particularly great, while Army Group Centre had been weakened by the removal of panzer divisions and the lessening of air support. There was also the negative factor that Busch suffered from heart disease and at times it was difficult for him to command his forces. The illness also served as the formal excuse for relieving him from the post of commander of Army Group Centre and his dispatch to the commander reserve. Busch remained there until 20 March 1945, when he was appointed commander of German forces in the north-west (Schleswig-Holstein, Magdeburg, the Netherlands), consisting of the First Parachute and Twenty-Fifth Armies, which successfully held out until almost the very end of the war. It was at this post that Busch subordinated to himself the remnants of Army Group Vistula and, with the permission of Grand Admiral Karl Dönitz, capitulated to British forces on 4 May 1945. He died from heart failure on 17 July 1945 in a British prisoner of war camp in Aldershot (county of Hampshire) at the age of 60. Busch did not have time to leave any memoirs and did not keep a diary. Thus even now there is no monographic biography of the field marshal. This circumstance enabled the German generals who wrote memoirs to lay the main part of the blame on Busch for the Wehrmacht's defeat in Belorussia. However, an objective analysis shows that Busch did not commit any fundamental mistakes during the battle in June 1944 and any of his alternative actions would have led to the same or even greater rout of Army Group Centre.

Since 5 October 1941 the German Third Panzer Army had been commanded by Colonel General Georg Hans Reinhardt. He commanded the 4th Panzer Division during the Polish campaign and during the French campaign of 1940, the Balkan campaign of 1941 and Operation 'Barbarossa' he commanded the XLI Panzer Corps. During the fighting around Sedan his corps carried out the crossing through the Ardennes and reached the sea at Abbeville. During Operation 'Barbarossa' the XLI Panzer Corps routed the 12th Mechanized Corps in the fighting around Raseiniai. Reinhardt, as head of the Third Panzer Army, took part in the offensive on Moscow, but during the Red Army's counteroffensive he was forced to fall back to the Velikie Luki area. Then Reinhardt's army conducted defensive battles north of Smolensk, gradually falling back to the west. In June 1944 he was defending in the Vitebsk area. Thus Reinhardt, although he had experience in offensive fighting as head of a panzer corps and panzer army, had waged only defensive battles in the year and a half preceding 'Bagration', and in June 1944 his panzer army had no armoured formations at all.

From 16 August 1944 Reinhardt headed Army Group Centre and remained at this post until 27 January 1945, when he was removed and dispatched to the commander reserve for his defeat during the East Prussian operation. In June 1945 he was arrested by the American occupation authorities. In 1948 he was sentenced to 15 years in prison for carrying out 'scorched earth' tactics and repressions against civilians during the conduct of anti-partisan operations. In 1952 he was freed for reasons of health. From 1954 Reinhardt was the president of the Society of Military Science (*Gesellschaft fur Wehrkunde*), and on 24 November 1962 was awarded the commander's cross of the Order 'For Services to the German Federal Republic'. Georg Hans Reinhardt died on 23 November 1963 in Tegernsee (Bavaria) at the age of 76. He did not keep a diary and left no memoirs.

General of Infantry Kurt von Tippelskirch took over command of the Fourth Army on 4 June in place of the sick Gotthard Heinrici. In November 1938 he had been appointed chief of the Army General Staff's intelligence section. From January 1941 Tippelskirch was the commander of the 30th Infantry Division, which took part in Operation 'Barbarossa' as part of Army Group North. In August 1942 he was appointed advisor to the command of the Italian Eighth Army along the Don and from December 1942 he was the actual commander of this army. From February 1943 Tippelskirch commanded the Fourth Army's XII Army Corps, which was defending in the area of Bryansk and Mogilev. Thus Tippelskirch had experience in positional warfare for a year and a half, as well as the not too successful experience of manoeuvre defence with the Italian Eighth Army. However, he would have to rely only on positional defence in repelling the forthcoming Soviet offensive, because in June 1944 the Fourth Army had no tank formations. We should note that by the beginning of Operation 'Bagration' Tippelskirch had been in command of the army for only 18 days. Nonetheless, Hitler considered all of his actions to be correct, because he awarded Tippelskirch with the Oak Leaves to the Knight's Cross for the fighting in Belorussia. On 18 July 1944 Tippelskirch, of whose army there remained by this time only a headquarters, was involved in a plane crash, was severely injured and did not return to active duty until October. On 31 October

OPERATION BAGRATION: AN INCOMPLETE TRUTH

1944 he was appointed commander of the First Army in Lorraine, and in February 1945 commander of the Fourteenth Army in Italy. On 27 April 1945 Tippelskirch became commander of the Twenty-First Army in Mecklenburg and Brandenburg. On 29 April he was appointed the last commander of Army Group Vistula, and on 2 May he capitulated in the Ludwigslust area to American forces. In 1951 Tippelskirch wrote *The History of the Second World War*, in which he devoted a great deal of attention to the summer battle of 1944 in Belorussia, which included relying on his own recollections. He was also one of the editors and authors of the collection entitled *The Results of the Second World War*, which was published in 1953. Kurt von Tippelskirch died on 10 May 1957 in Luneburg (Lower Saxony) at the age of 65.

From 20 May 1944 the German Ninth Army was commanded by General of Infantry Hans Jordan. He had been only a regimental commander during the Polish and French campaigns. It was only in December 1941 that Jordan became the commander of the 7th Infantry Division during the Battle of Moscow. In November 1942 he headed the VI Army Corps defending in the Rzhev area. I should note that like Tippelskirch, Jordan had only a month's experience of commanding an army before the start of 'Bagration', while there were no active combat activities in his army's sector. As early as 27 June 1944 he was removed from the post of army commander, including for the unsuccessful employment of the 20th Panzer Division, and was assigned to the commander reserve. In August 1944 Jordan was dispatched to northern Italy to oversee the construction of a defensive line in the foothills of the Alps, and from March 1945 commanded the Tyrol Army, which took no part in the fighting. On 8 May 1945 Jordan capitulated to the Anglo-American forces. Hans Jordan died on 20 April 1975 in Munich (Bavaria) at the age of 82. He left behind no memoirs or diaries.

From 4 February 1943 the Second Army was commanded by Colonel General Walter Weiss, who in the Polish and French campaigns had commanded an infantry regiment. In Operation 'Barbarossa' he commanded the 26th Infantry Division as part of Army Group Centre. From 1 July 1942 Weiss headed the XXVII Army Corps. During the entire period of Weiss's command of the Second Army it was engaged only in defensive fighting. From 12 March through 8 April 1945 Weiss commanded Army Group North in East Prussia, and was then evacuated to northern Germany, where he surrendered to the Americans. Walter Weiss died on 21 December 1967 in Ascheffenburg (Bavaria) at the age of 77. He too did not keep a diary and left no memoirs.

Thus before the beginning of the operation two out of four army commanders in Army Group Centre lacked experience in commanding an army, and it was precisely against these armies that the Soviet forces launched their main attack. In the case of one of the commanders (Jordan) the choice proved to be unlucky, but one should not say that this had significance for the rout of Army Group Centre. Tippelskirch quite successfully pulled back his army from the Dnepr to the Berezina, which made it possible to save at least a small part of it.

For the sake of comparison, let's examine which generals Hitler entrusted to repel the Allied landing in Normandy. The commander-in-chief of German forces in the West was General Field Marshal Gerd von Rundstedt. During the Polish campaign he had commanded Army Group South and during the French campaign of 1940 Army Group A, which played the main role in encircling the Anglo-French troops in Belgium and north-eastern France. In Operation 'Barbarossa' Rundstedt commanded Army Group South. Following the abandonment of Rostov-on-Don by the Germans on 28 November

THE PRELUDE TO 'BAGRATION'

1941 Rundstedt was removed from his position; although Hitler later recognized the correctness of the move and that a retreat to the Mius was the only correct decision. Following some leave, in March 1942 Rundstedt was appointed commander-in-chief in the West. Of course, he knew the western theatre of operations well. However, a negative factor was that Rundstedt commanded troops which in the two years and three months before the landing in Normandy had hardly been engaged in combat. He insisted that the panzer divisions should be located in the rear areas, so that they could be rapidly dispatched to any sector where the Allies might land. On 1 July 1944 Hitler replaced Rundstedt with Field Marshal Gunther von Kluge, who, however, as a participant in the 20 July plot, committed suicide as early as 19 August having learned that he would inevitably be found out. Following this Rundstedt was returned on 5 September to the post of commander in the West, replacing Field Marshal Walter Model, who had managed to command for only 18 days. Rundstedt was removed from his post on 18 March 1945, following the capture of the bridge over the Rhine at Remagen by the Allies. On 1 May 1945 he surrendered to American forces. Gerd von Rundstedt died on 24 February 1953 in Hanover (Lower Saxony) at the age of 77.

In January 1944 Field Marshal Erwin Rommel was appointed to command Army Group B, which included German forces in northern France. In the French campaign of 1940 he had commanded the 7th Panzer Division, and then from February 1941 through March 1943 he quite successfully commanded Italo-German forces in North Africa. However, being appointed on 15 July 1943 commander of Army Group B in northern Italy, he did not particularly distinguish himself in opposing the Allied landing in mainland Italy. In France, Rommel, as opposed to Rundstedt, believed that the German panzer divisions should be located along the coastline, immediately beyond the reach of Allied naval artillery. Such a deployment would put the German tanks under naval artillery fire and strikes from Anglo-American aviation from the start of the attack and, besides this, would make the transfer of tank units from the non-threatened sectors of the coast more difficult. On 17 July 1944, as the result of an Allied air attack on Rommel's car, the field marshal was seriously wounded in the head. Following the failure of the 20 July plot it was found that Rommel had taken part. On 14 October 1944 he was given the choice: take poison or be hanged by a verdict of the People's Court. Rommel chose the former. This took place in Herringen (Baden-Wurttemberg). Rommel was 52 years of age.

It has to be admitted that Hitler's choice of higher commanders for leading the repulsion of the landing in Normandy was not the most successful. Rundstedt had no experience in waging defensive battles, and he had not conducted any combat operations during the two years before the landing. Rommel had experience in conducting manoeuvre operations involving relatively small mobile forces, but lacked experience in conducting positional warfare along an Army Group front with counterblows by mobile reserves. Field Marshal Erich von Manstein and Field Marshal Ewald von Kleist, who had been dispatched by Hitler to the commander reserve in April 1944, would have been much better in the role of commander-in-chief of the Western Front and commander of Army Group B. Both field marshals had extensive experience in waging defensive fighting on the Eastern Front in 1943–4, when positional defence was combined with counterblows by mobile reserves. However, both Manstein and Kleist had the habit of often arguing with Hitler and upholding their point of view, and the *Führer* preferred to get rid of talented but willful commanders.

OPERATION BAGRATION: AN INCOMPLETE TRUTH

It would have been very difficult to replace Luftwaffe Field Marshal Alfred Kesselring, whom many experts rightfully consider to be the Third Reich's best commander, in his post as commander-in-chief in Italy, taking into account both his successful defensive operations in this theatre and his long-standing relations with Mussolini and the Italian politicians and military men. But it's possible that it would nevertheless have been worth it to appoint Kesselring as commander-in-chief of the Western Front, subordinating the Luftwaffe and *Kriegsmarine* to him (Rundstedt had no such powers). After all, the outcome of the war would be decided at that moment in the West, and not in Italy. Kesselring had great experience in organizing cooperation between the ground forces and the Luftwaffe in North Africa and Italy, while similar cooperation during the battle in Normandy among the Germans was not at the highest level. It's possible that Kesselring could have done more and, in any event, would have avoided the disaster at Falaise.

If one takes the commanders of the German armies in northern France, then this was also not an ideal situation. From 19 November 1943 the commander of Panzer Group West was General of Cavalry Baron Leo Geyer von Schweppenburg, who had commanded the 3rd Panzer Division during the Polish campaign and distinguished himself in the capture of Chelmno. During the French campaign he was the commander of the XXIV Army Corps. By the start of Operation 'Barbarossa' this corps had been motorized. With it Geyer von Schweppenburg operated successfully as part of the Second Panzer Group in Belorussia and played an important role in the creation of the Bryansk 'cauldron'. In July 1942 he commanded the XL Panzer Corps attacking in the Caucasus, but he was removed from his post at the end of September, when Hitler came to understand that the offensive into the Caucasus would not achieve its main goal – Baku. Geyer von Schweppenburg was dispatched to the commander reserve, where he remained until the spring of 1943. Rundstedt, with Hitler's approval, ordered him to begin the formation of a tank group in the West. In November 1943 this group was named Panzer Group West. Among Geyer von Schweppenburg's shortcomings was the lack of experience in commanding a panzer army in combat conditions and the absence of experience in combat operations for almost two years before the Allied landing in Normandy. On 10 June 1944 British aircraft bombed the headquarters of Panzer Group West in La Caine and Geyer von Schweppenburg was seriously wounded. On 2 July he was removed from his post for proposing to abandon Caen. After this and until the end of the war he served in the Armoured Inspectorate under Guderian. In 1947 Geyer von Schweppenburg was released from American captivity and later played an active role in the creation of the Bundeswehr. He also wrote a number of volumes of memoirs. Geyer von Schweppenburg passed away on 27 January 1974, at the age of 87, in Irschenhausen (Bavaria).

The German Seventh Army in Normandy had been commanded since 27 August 1939 by Colonel General Friedrich Dollman. During the French campaign this army had captured Alsace and Lorraine, while operating along a secondary axis. Following this Dollman took no part in combat operations all the way up to the landing in Normandy. On 28 June 1944, not long after the Seventh Army was forced to abandon Cherbourg, Friedrich Dollman died as the result of a heart attack at the age of 62. Among Dollman's obvious shortcomings was his limited combat experience and poor health.

Also stationed in Normandy was the German Fifteenth Army, which since August 1943 had been under the command of Colonel General Hans von Salmuth. He was chief of staff of Army Group North during the Polish campaign, and during the French campaign of 1940 he was chief of staff of Army Group B. In Operation 'Barbarossa' von Salmuth headed the Eleventh Army's XXX Army Corps and took part in the fighting in the Crimea. Then, from April 1942 and up until June 1943 he quite successfully commanded the Seventeenth, Second and Fourth Armies. Von Salmuth was removed from the post of commander of the Fifteenth Army at the end of August 1944 for the Falaise disaster and remained in the commander reserve until the end of the war. He ended up in American captivity and in 1948 he was found guilty of war crimes and crimes against humanity and sentenced to 20 years confinement. Von Salmuth was freed in 1953. He died on 1 January 1962 in Heidelburg (Baden Württemberg) at the age of 73. Out of the three army commanders in Normandy, von Salmuth was the only one who possessed sufficient combat experience at army-commander level. The tense situation on the Eastern Front prevented Hitler from transferring other experienced commanders to the West.

The section 'Foreign Armies East' considered two variants of a possible future Soviet offensive – the Balkan (south-western) and Baltic (north-western). It was assumed that the Red Army might launch its main attack along the front of Army Group North Ukraine, between the Pripyat Marshes and the Carpathian Mountains, where there were no significant natural obstacles, and then turn either to the north-west and the border of East Prussia, cutting off Army Group Centre in the 'Belorussian balcony' and Army Group North in the Baltic States, and then launching an attack through the Hungarian plain against Romania and its oil fields. For this reason, the main German armoured reserves on the Eastern Front were concentrated in Army Group North Ukraine.[18] Moreover, a significant number of armoured and panzergrenadier divisions remained with Army Group South Ukraine. But these had been exhausted during the course of the heavy fighting in April-May 1944. They did not transfer them to either Germany or the West for reconstitution and employment against the Allied landing, because this was difficult to carry out due to geographical conditions. It was much simpler to transfer armoured divisions to the West from the central and northern sectors of the Eastern Front. But they did not hasten to reinforce Army Group South Ukraine's divisions with armoured equipment, insofar as the Western Front had priority. Thus Army Group North Ukraine was stronger in tanks and assault guns than Army Group South Ukraine.

At first German intelligence believed that the Balkan variant was more likely, but at the beginning of summer, upon taking into account the concentration of Soviet forces against the 'Belorussian balcony', it inclined toward the Baltic variant. Particularly worrisome was the Kovel' area, where during the spring offensive a large number of Soviet forces had been concentrated and from where lay the shortest route to Warsaw.[19]

On 21 April 1944 the commander of Army Group Centre, Field Marshal Busch, warned the OKW about the growing threat to his rear: 'At the present time a major concentration of forces is taking place in the Kovel' area. One may assume that the Russian command intends to launch an attack against Army Group Centre through Brest and Warsaw in the direction of Königsberg and Danzig. The first stage of this operation will probably be to reach the line L'vov–Lublin–Brest, and the second an advance to the Baltic.' On the whole, in his opinion, the Soviet command had 'very broad operational goals'. The German command took into account the fact that Soviet forces would have to cover 700km from Vitebsk to the Vistula over wooded and swampy terrain, when the distance from Kovel' to Warsaw was a mere 200km, and over terrain much more suitable for an offensive.[20]

In the words of the American historian Paul Adair, the people who knew Busch assumed that although he had his qualities as a leader, he owed his rise to his strong ties to the Nazi Party. Colonel Peter von der Greben, who at the time was the Ia officer (the chief of the operational section) on Busch's staff, said: 'I was present at some discussions during which he sought to talk Hitler out of a specific course of action. If he was unsuccessful, then he considered it his duty to carry out the decision. He often told me: "Greben, I'm a soldier. I have learned to obey". Then, against all common sense, he would carry out the order.'[21]

Busch had actually never been a member of the Nazi Party. During the 1938 conflict between Hitler and Field Marshal Werner von Blomberg and Colonel General Werner Fritsch, Busch was on Hitler's side, although the majority of generals acted the same way and by no means did all of them have such as successful career as Busch.

On 12 May Gehlen reported that although the main offensive would take place in the south, an additional offensive would occur in the area of Army Group Centre, in the direction of Brest and Lublin. The OKH (army supreme command), in order to ward this off, planned to launch a preventive attack with the help of the LVI Panzer Corps. The corps had been removed from Army Group Centre into the Army Group North Ukraine reserve. At the end of May there appeared signs that part of the Soviet armoured park had moved to the north. Although General P.A. Rotmistrov, the commander of the 5th Guards Tank Army, had been spotted in the Smolensk area by a Russian prisoner of war, no tanks had been noted, nor was there any assurance that his army had moved to an area directed against Army Group Centre. Nonetheless, there were clear signs of the concentration of Soviet forces in Army Group Centre's area, insofar as rail movement along this direction had intensified. Interrogations of prisoners of war and deserters told the same story. At the end of May and beginning of June the intelligence of Army Group Centre's four armies had uncovered the reinforcement of Soviet forces. The LVI Panzer Corps' pre-emptive attack was called off, although the corps remained with Army Group North Ukraine.[22]

The German Second Army's headquarters was inclined to believe that the Soviet offensive would most likely be launched against the neighbouring Ninth Army's formations in the Bobruisk area, and not along its own front. The German Third Panzer Army expected a Soviet offensive in the area of the Vitebsk salient, although not a frontal attack but along the salient's flanks. The Fourth Army expected the main Soviet attack in the area of the Moscow–Minsk highway. As late as 17 June there were no doubts within the army's headquarters that a Soviet offensive would be launched within the next few days. In the same way the headquarters of the Ninth Army did not doubt the immediacy of a Soviet attack. In a report on the enemy's intentions of 17 June, it noted: 'The situation along the army's front has radically changed in a short time. While the distribution of the enemy's forces near the front remains unchanged, a major regrouping of forces in depth along the entire sector of the army's front is taking place.' At the same time, the Ninth Army's headquarters had noticed the first signs of the forthcoming Soviet offensive as early as 3 June. Soviet reinforcements had arrived before 15 June, which the Ninth Army's headquarters calculated at 10–15 rifle divisions and 1–2 tank corps. The Ninth Army's intelligence assumed that additional reinforcements had also arrived, although they had not been fixed by observers, because the heavy forests over large areas 'makes observation of the enemy's situation almost impossible'. The Ninth Army's headquarters assumed that the enemy would attempt to split the army's front 'by several major attacks, independent of each other, with a subsequent offensive against Bobruisk and Minsk and the conduct of a broad-ranging offensive'. The Ninth Army's headquarters had also received information that Zhukov and Rokossovskii would coordinate the offensive, which was considered a sign that it was precisely here that the main attack would occur. The Ninth Army's headquarters came to the conclusion that the Soviet command had temporarily decided to forego the realization of the south-western offensive variant against L'vov and the Balkans in favour of 'reconquering Belorussia' and that the enemy's main forces would undoubtedly be concentrated along Army Group Centre's front. On 22 June, when the stunning and major Soviet offensive began, the German Ninth Army remained practically unharmed. Nonetheless, in its war diary there is the notation that, in the words of Bundeswehr Lieutenant General Gerd Niepold, predicted the inevitable catastrophe 'in an almost prophetic way'. The notation maintained that 'The Ninth Army is on the eve of a new and great battle, the scale and length of which can only be guessed at. One thing is clear, however: during the last few weeks and days the enemy has concentrated enormous forces along the army's front and the staff is convinced that this concentration has put into the shade even the concentration of enemy forces against the northern wing of Army Group North Ukraine.'

The first defensive belt along the Bobruisk axis was the 'Loewen' line along the western banks of the Drut', Dnepr and Ptich' rivers. It consisted of a main line of resistance and a line of artillery cover, which began directly in front of the division artillery's positions. In each line there were two series of fully-outfitted trenches, with connecting trenches, foxholes for individual riflemen, machine gun nests, artillery observation posts for 2–3 men, and shelters for 4–6 soldiers. Obstacles of 1–2 layers of barbed wire lay before the first line.

The 'Nessel', 'Aster' and 'Bruchenkopf' lines defended the approaches to Bobruisk from the east, and 'Paula', 'Barbara' and 'Bieber' from the south, with work on the 'Munna' line ongoing. They consisted of 1–2 trench lines, although far from being fully fitted out. Three defensive rings had been built immediately around Bobruisk along the eastern bank of the Berezina River, with five along the western bank. Bobruisk had been declared a fortress city, although it had no forts nor other fort-like fortifications, nor even pillboxes. The historical Bobruisk fortress, which was built in 1810–36, was here. However, it had been disarmed in 1897. Its bastions were worn down and had been partially destroyed.

Bobruisk was defended along a 192km front by two corps of the German Ninth Army, consisting of the 6th, 35th, 36th, 45th, 129th, 134th, 296th, and 383rd Infantry Divisions, with the 707th Infantry and 20th Panzer Divisions in reserve. There was an average of 48 armed men per kilometre of front. Overall, the infantry divisions disposed of 73 assault guns and 58 tank destroyers. Along with the 505th Heavy Panzer Battalion, there were 93 tanks and 28 tank destroyers in reserve. The majority of divisions were not up to authorized strength. Only the 35th and 129th Infantry Divisions managed to fall back to the west before the formation of the 'cauldron', while only the 20th Panzer Division managed to break out of the 'cauldron', while preserving more than half of its rank and file. At the same time, however, it lost a third of its rank and file and almost all of its armoured equipment.[23]

OPERATION BAGRATION: AN INCOMPLETE TRUTH

Thus, tactically speaking, the Soviet offensive was not a surprise for any of Army Group Centre's armies. These armies' headquarters, just like the headquarters of Army Group Centre itself assumed that the offensive would begin on 22 June, on the third anniversary of the attack on the USSR. And they were not wrong. It was precisely on 22 June that they carried out a reconnaissance in force along the majority of Soviet fronts during Operation 'Bagration'. Moreover, the growing activity of the surviving Soviet partisans in Belorussia pointed to the approach of the Soviet offensive. The main question was whether Army Group Centre would receive sufficient mobile reserves for repelling the expected Soviet offensive.[24]

Army Group Centre's headquarters, as opposed to the headquarters of its subordinate armies, was more optimistic and up to 14 June assumed that the Soviet offensive along its front would only be a supporting one. But on 14 June 'the systematic strengthening' of the enemy's forces was noted in the Army Group war diary. On that day a meeting of the Eastern Front army and Army Group chiefs of staff was held. At this meeting the chief of staff of Army Group Centre, Lieutenant General Hans Krebs, concluded that the enemy offensive would be directed against both flanks of Army Group Centre. During the meeting it transpired that only along Army Group Centre's front were there unambiguous signs of a nearly-completed regrouping of the enemy's forces before the offensive. This was not the case in any of the other Army Groups, even in Army Group North Ukraine. As K.H. Frieser notes, 'The meeting would have been the proper moment for reacting to the danger – there still remained eight days before the major offensive expected on 22 June, but there was not even the slightest sign that the Army Group Centre chief of staff had managed to arouse any alarm in the hearts of the other conference participants. Instead of this, he gave way and accepted the assurances that the 20th Panzer Division (a quite weak one) would be transferred to him.'[25] Here, however, the question arises as to what Krebs could have done to convince the acting chief of the Army General Staff, Lieutenant General Adolf Heusinger, and the other Army Group chiefs of staff that Army Group Centre needed immediate assistance. By this time the Allied landing in Normandy had taken place and it had already become clear that the Germans would not be able to inflict a serious defeat on it. Quite the opposite, the German forces in the West were barely holding against the pressure of the British, American and Canadian armies and it was clear that in the foreseeable future the Western Front would not be able to spare any forces for the East. They even had to immediately transfer the SS II Panzer Corps, which was in the Eastern Front reserve in the Kovel' area, to Normandy. Heusinger transferred the 20th Panzer Division from the Army Group North Ukraine reserve to Army Group Centre. After this there remained another two panzer divisions there – the 4th and 5th. But it would have been too risky to leave Model's Army Group completely without a mobile reserve. After all, Army Group North Ukraine was also faced with the same superior Soviet forces, ready for an offensive. And it would have cost Stalin nothing to issue an order to the First Ukrainian Front and the left wing of the First Belorussian Front to begin a simultaneous offensive upon the start of Operation 'Bagration', which would have created a fatal threat for Busch's Army Group of a breakthrough by Soviet forces through Kovel' toward Lublin and Warsaw. Thus at best it would have been possible to transfer one more panzer division from Model to Busch. They could have risked it and transferred before the beginning of the Soviet offensive to Army Group Centre another quite weak division – the 12th Panzer – the only mobile reserve of Colonel General

THE PRELUDE TO 'BAGRATION'

Georg Lindemann's Army Group North. Again, this would have involved the risk that the Soviet forces might begin an offensive against Army Group North, along the front of which they also enjoyed an overwhelming numerical advantage. But even if we could imagine Heusinger and Hitler risking the transfer of another two panzer divisions – one from Model and another from Lindemann, then this, in the best case, would not have altered the fate of Army Group Centre in the slightest, and might have even changed it for the worse. Busch had stationed the single panzer division – the 20th – which had been transferred to him before the offensive in the reserve of the Ninth Army, which was defending Bobruisk. There is no doubt that had he received one panzer division from Model, that he would have transferred it to the Fourth Army, which was defending Minsk and Mogilev, and he would have dispatched the 12th Panzer Division to the Third Panzer Army, which was defending Vitebsk. But, taking into account the overwhelming Soviet superiority in tanks, artillery and aviation, these divisions might have been able to slow the enemy offensive for 1–2 days and no more. As it transpired, all of the above-named panzer divisions – the 4th, 5th and 12th – had been transferred to Army Group Centre at the end of June and beginning of July. If two of them had been, like the 20th Panzer Division, bled white as early as 'Bagration's' early battles, they would not have been able to fight along the Berezina. So, by maintaining Army Group North Ukraine's and North's reserves, it's possible that the OKH had already written off Army Group Centre and spared forces for the subsequent fighting. The fact that the 20th Panzer Division was dispatched namely to Bobruisk was probably determined by the fact that that the main road to Minsk lay through Bobruisk and it had to be held first of all. Hitler categorically forbade a withdrawal by the forces of Army Group Centre, demanding from them that they 'hold their lines under any and all circumstances', but did not send any reserves.[26]

The concentration of artillery along the assumed breakthrough sectors and the regrouping of Soviet aviation were signs of an imminent Soviet offensive along Army Group Centre's front. On 29 May 1944 438 German planes in Army Group Centre's sector were opposed by no less than 3,495 Soviet planes, as determined by German intelligence. By 19 June the number of Soviet aircraft had risen to 4,500. In the opinion of K.H. Frieser, 'the situation literally called for immediate action to prevent the looming disaster'.[27] But he does not explain exactly what actions should have been taken. Actually, neither on 19 June nor even 29 May were any strategic solutions possible for the German side.

On 30 May Stalin approved the final plan for Operation 'Bagration', which it was planned to begin on 19–20 June. A breakthrough of the enemy's defences was to take place simultaneously along six sectors. The encirclement and destruction of Army Group Centre's flank groups of forces in the area of Vitebsk and Bobruisk was to be followed by the development of the offensive along the Kaunas, Minsk and Brest axes in order to arrive at the line Daugavpils–Kovno (Kaunas)–Bialystok–Brest–Lublin. Then the forces of the First Baltic Front were to attack toward Königsberg, with part of its forces on Siauliai, the forces of the Third Belorussian Front toward Allenstein, and the forces of the First Belorussian Front on Warsaw.[28]

Only a deep withdrawal to the approximate line of the Western Bug River would have saved Army Group Centre. At the same time, this would have required the withdrawal of Army Group North to the line of the Western Dvina River and Army Group North Ukraine to the line of the San River, because following a deep withdrawal by Army

Group Centre it would have become impossible to defend their previous positions. At the same time, during such a withdrawal it would be necessary to simultaneously transfer forces from the Eastern to the Western Front and prepare a new defensive line in the East as early as the beginning of May. The withdrawal would have been completed approximately by the middle of June. Even if the withdrawal had been carried out very successfully and the Soviet forces had been unable to either encircle or capture any significant enemy groups of forces during the pursuit, the expenditures for the German side would nevertheless have proved to be excessively great. After the German forces left Estonia, it is unlikely that Finland would have continued the war, and most likely following the Allied landing in Normandy would have concluded an armistice without waiting for the Soviet offensive along the Karelian Isthmus. Then as early as the middle of June the Soviet forces in Karelia would have been freed up and could have been transferred for operations against Germany. The main thing is that, even given a withdrawal to the line Western Dvina–Western Bug–San rivers, the Red Army's overwhelming superiority in men and materiel would not have gone away. Soviet forces would have suffered far fewer losses during a pursuit than they actually suffered during Operation 'Bagration', the L'vov–Sandomierz operation and the fighting in Karelia and the Baltic States. And it would have come to a situation in which the Red Army would have stood on the same line as early as the middle of June that it actually reached at the end of July, and along the lower course of the Western Dvina in the middle of September. At the same time, there was no guarantee that they could manage to hold the line indicated. After all, the correlation of forces along the front of Army Groups Centre and North Ukraine would have remained the same as it was on 22 June, before the start of Operation 'Bagration'. The Soviet superiority in artillery and tanks might even have grown, taking into account the inevitable equipment losses while withdrawing and the reinforcement of the Soviet forces with new tanks and guns. Thus the most probable development of events would have been a rapid breakthrough of the German defences along the Western Bug and San rivers and the Soviet forces' arrival at the Vistula within no later than a month; that is, as early as the middle of July. Moreover, Army Group Centre would still have been routed and Hitler was absolutely indifferent as to whether this occurred on the Berezina or the Western Bug. Moreover, given such a scenario, it is unlikely that the Germans could have launched powerful counterblows against Soviet forces along the Vistula. It's more likely that they would have been forced to abandon Warsaw and retreat as far as the pre-war fortifications in the Oder River area. Naturally, such a prospect appealed neither to Hitler, nor the OKW nor the OKH. Thus there is no information that they considered the variant of withdrawing Army Group Centre in May-June 1944. Hitler and his generals evidently assumed that the losses from such a decision would prove to be greater than the possible advantages.

Given the absence of strategic opportunities to ward off the disaster, the German command was able to undertake only elementary measures – to remove the main mass of its forces from the first line of defence and to leave only observers there, in order to minimize losses during the Soviet artillery preparation. In the last evaluation of the situation before the start of 'Bagration', which was carried out by Army Group Centre's intelligence section (IC) on 19 June, it was stated: 'The picture has changed significantly . . . since 2 June. Up until now we have forecast a local offensive . . . for the purpose of an operational encirclement. Events along the Army Group's eastern front after this date indicate . . . the enemy's more far-reaching intentions.' The intelligence section now suspected that the enemy was preparing 'to break through the front and destroy the salient [the 'Belorussian balcony', B.S.] by means of a simultaneous offensive at several points'.[29] All of these forecasts were accurate, but there were not sufficient forces to oppose to the Soviet plans, neither with the Army Group Centre command, nor with the OKH, nor the OKW. Regarding the report of 19 June, Frieser notes that:

> If the report on the enemy's situation had concluded with this phrase, then the higher headquarters would have been forced to react. It's typical of the lack of consistency in the headquarters of Army Group Centre that this alarming predication was immediately softened in the next phrase by a statement that the disposition of the Red Army's forces 'does not enable us to draw a conclusion as to whether the enemy has a more ambitious goal, such as Minsk'. Thus the operational conclusions enumerated above collapsed like a house of cards.

Here we should note that the higher German headquarters, given all the will in the world, were not able to help Army Group Centre with anything, all the more so, three days before the assumed start of the Soviet offensive. The summary conclusion, that it was unclear whether the enemy would attack further on Minsk (evidently following his arrival at the Berezina), in no way cancels the preceding conclusions. It's simply that Busch and his staff were not sure whether the Soviet command would continue the offensive beyond the Berezina, or would prefer to attack along Army Group North Ukraine's front in order to outflank the remaining German forces in Belorussia from the rear.

In Frieser's opinion,

> the mistaken interpretation of the situation by the Army Group Centre command seems all the more incomprehensible in the light of the annotations made by the intelligence section on the situation maps. These annotations, while taking into account the large number of identified Soviet divisions, reveal a very alarming scenario. Most of all there is the undoubtedly high concentration of forces along the flanks of the Belorussian salient around Vitebsk and Bobruisk; that is, namely where the main breakthroughs took place. A great deal of imagination is not required in order to see that the shock groups would link up in depth in the Minsk area. An evaluation of the situation maps as regards the Soviet reinforcements that continued to arrive shows the dynamism of the development of events in time, which was unprecedented for the Russian campaign. Thus it is incomprehensible why the Army Group Centre headquarters underestimated the threat to such an extent.[30]

Strictly speaking, the Soviet shock wedges did not link up in Minsk, but to the east of the city, where the largest 'cauldron', in terms of size and number of troops encircled, formed in Army Group Centre's area of operations. Nor was Busch sure whether or not Minsk was the target of the Soviet forces, or whether they were preparing to rout Army Group Centre's main forces east of the Belorussian capital by cutting off the 'Belorussian balcony' along the shortest route, along the Sluch' and Berezina rivers, and then toward Polotsk. In reality a middle variant was realized, when the encirclement ring around the German forces closed between the Berezina and Minsk.

Having discovered quite accurately the Soviet forces' first echelon, Army Group Centre's intelligence section, however, lacked sufficient information regarding the enemy's second echelons and his tank reserves. Nor was anything known about the transfer of the 5th Guards Tank Army to the Smolensk area. But even without this, the concentration of Soviet forces was impressive. When on 22 June 1941 Operation 'Barbarossa' began, the entire German army in the east disposed of only 7,000 artillery pieces. On 22 June 1944 the Soviet command had concentrated against Army Group Centre alone 45,000 guns and mortars, of which 24,383 tubes were employed during the first phase of Operation 'Bagration'.[31]

At the end of May Army Group Centre's intelligence had accurately surmised that the blow would be launched in the second half of June. The intelligence section of the Ninth Army's headquarters maintained that this would be the main offensive and not just a local attack. The concentration in Belorussia since the beginning of May of an additional 1,850 combat aircraft and the growth in the number of newly-discovered artillery batteries was proof of this. For example, the Third Panzer Army noted an increase in the number of artillery batteries in its sector since the beginning of April to the middle of June from 243 to 340. This had been established with the aid of aerial reconnaissance. On the eve of the Soviet offensive Army Group Centre's intelligence had uncovered 140 of 168 Soviet rifle divisions, but only three tank corps. Actually, there were eight tank and mechanized corps and two cavalry corps. The highest German estimate of Soviet tank strength was 1,800 tanks, although the figure was actually more than two times this amount. The presence of the 5th Guards Tank Army was not discovered, nor was the presence of several other major field forces, including the 6th Guards Army in the Vitebsk area.[32]

The selection of the correct grouping of forces on the Eastern Front in the summer of 1944 was also made more difficult for the German command by the circumstance that the Soviet superiority in forces was so great that the Red Army command could organize a simultaneous offensive against three Army Groups. The 'Foreign Armies East' section at first assumed that the main attack would be launched either against Army Group North Ukraine or against Army Group South Ukraine. But as early as May the concentration of Soviet forces along Army Group Centre's front began to be observed. In an appreciation of the situation on 13 June, Reinhard Gehlen noted that the enemy 'is planning to go over from holding attacks to an offensive operation along the Gomel'–Smolensk axis, aimed, in the final analysis, at Minsk'. 'Foreign Armies East' explained that the Red Army was preparing to unleash independent 'mobile armoured groups', which were designated for deep blows. In an appreciation of the enemy's intentions on 13 June, Gehlen predicted that the Soviet operations would develop in two stages. At first powerful attacks would be launched against the flanks of Army Group Centre and Army Group South Ukraine, in order to deceive the German command as to the area of the main attack and force it to remove reserves from the area between the Carpathians and Kovel'. As soon as the centre was weakened in favour of the flanks, the main offensive against Army Group North Ukraine would begin. The OKH chief of staff, Colonel General Kurt Zeitzler, agreed with this estimate. Hitler and the OKW also assumed that the main attack would come along Army Group North Ukraine's front, particularly along its left flank in the Kovel' area.[33]

THE PRELUDE TO 'BAGRATION'

The Luftwaffe's aerial reconnaissance in the East was poor due to the shortage of fuel and the transfer of the greater part of its reconnaissance aircraft to the West, and the powerful Soviet anti-aircraft defence, which made intelligence-gathering in the depth behind the front lines very difficult. On 26 June 1944 the commander of Army Group North, Colonel General Georg Lindemann, wrote indignantly to the commander of the First Air Fleet, Aviation General Kurt Pflugbeil, that the Soviets had pulled 37 rifle divisions, eight tank formations and one artillery division from his Army Group's front 'without any kind of information on that score on the part of aerial reconnaissance'. Moreover, the Soviet formations tried to observe radio silence and the density of the Soviet forces around the 'Belorussian balcony' was so great that the German reconnaissance groups had no opportunity to penetrate into the depths of Soviet territory and observe their second echelons.[34]

On 23 June Busch transferred his single 501st Heavy Panzer Battalion to the Orsha area, where the 14th and 256th Infantry and 78th Assault Divisions were fighting. At the beginning of June the 501st Battalion was forced to hand over nine of its Tigers to the 509th Heavy Panzer Battalion in Army Group North Ukraine and was left with only 20 vehicles. Aside from the 509th Battalion, Army Group Centre disposed of the 505th, 506th and 507th Heavy Panzer Battalions. Following the fighting along the Berezina there remained only six combat-ready Tigers in the 501st Battalion. On 4 July the 501st Battalion received five new Tigers, while a few tanks were repaired. The battalion fought in the Minsk area. The last two of the 25 Tigers were blown up near Molodechno on 5 July, after their fuel ran out.[35]

This is how Marshal G.K. Zhukov described the Belorussian operation during a conversation with the writer Simonov in 1965:

> If you take, for example, the situation as it had developed before our offensive in Belorussia in the summer of 1944, then it was sufficient to look at a map in order that it become fully clear: that we had to launch our attacks precisely along those axes from which we later did launch them, that we were in a condition to create the Belorussian cauldron and that this would ultimately end in a breakthrough 300–400km wide, with which the Germans had nothing to close.
>
> The Germans could foresee this. The logic of events and elementary military literacy suggested the necessity of pulling out their forces from the future cauldron, to shorten and consolidate their front and to create operational reserves behind the front – in a word, do what is necessary in such cases. But the Germans did not do this and as a result were routed in the Belorussian operation. But subsequently, when they were in a very serious situation, when they had nothing with which to close the 400km breach, one must give them their due and admit that they found a bold and correct way out of the situation. Instead of attempting to close all of this enormous breach by extending themselves in a line, they began by concentrating a shock group of forces and launched a meeting attack against us in the centre of this empty space. They tied us down and forced us into extended fighting and thus halted our offensive. In the meantime, they began to build a new defensive line and, thanks to this unexpected and bold attack, they managed to do this to a significant

degree. One must recognize the decision following the rout in the Belorussian cauldron as bold and wise.[36]

By a 'bold and wise attack' Zhukov, by all appearances, meant the meeting engagement between General Karl Decker's 5th Panzer Division, which had been transferred from the area south of Kovel', and units of the Soviet 5th Guards Tank Army, which took place on 28 June, the last day of Busch's command of Army Group Centre. So this attack was still carrying out Busch's plan and not Model's. But the German 5th Panzer Division had no other tasks but to hold, as much as possible, the 5th Guards Tank Army's advance. During this battle P.A. Rotmistrov's army suffered heavy losses and its advance was halted for a day, but it is hardly fair to attach any kind of decisive significance to this battle. It's possible that Zhukov was exaggerating the Germans' mobile reserves on the Eastern Front and that he took the 5th Panzer Division's local attack for the start of a large counteroffensive.

The Army Group Centre staff proposed two solutions which, as they believed, could ease the repulse of the Soviet offensive. The 'small solution' consisted of withdrawing the Fourth Army behind the Dnepr, along the western bank of which the 'Bear Line' was being constructed. It would close up with the 'Tiger Line' north of Orsha, which had been prepared by the Third Panzer Army and which stretched as far as the Western Dvina. Besides shortening the front line by 80km, this would also have led to abandoning the Vitebsk salient, which was threatened with encirclement.

The 'large solution' called for a withdrawal behind the Berezina, which Busch and his subordinates considered the most expedient solution from the operational point of view, insofar as it would result in a more significant shortening of the front line. With the silent consent of the Army Group staff, its subordinate armies had prepared along the Berezina the 'Beaver Line', which lay along the western bank from Bobruisk to Polotsk. The timely withdrawal to this position by troops not yet exhausted in heavy fighting was also expedient in light of the intense partisan activity in the woods to the east of the Berezina. The most significant advantage of the 'large solution' was the fact that as a result of it the length of the front would be reduced by approximately 250km, which would allow them to free up additional reserves and to form a reserve army behind the northern flank of Army Group Centre.

Colonel General Alfred Jodl, the chief of the OKW operations section, had proposed an even more radical solution at the beginning of 1944 – in light of the necessity of transferring major reserves to the West for repelling the inevitable Allied invasion of France: to carry out a withdrawal to the shortest line on the Eastern Front, which would stretch from Odessa to Riga. This would have freed up an additional 20 divisions which could have been employed both for counterblows in the East and for repelling the Allies in the West. Hitler rejected Jodl's plan in the same way he rejected on 20 May Busch's plan for withdrawing to the Dnepr or the Berezina.[37]

One must say that Hitler was right in both decisions, according to the principle of choosing the lesser of two evils. Jodl's plan could have been carried out in February or March, before the start of the spring thaw, or during the second half of May and the first half of June, after the spring thaw. In both cases they would have had to abandon Estonia, part of Latvia and Lithuania, almost all of Belorussia, all of eastern Ukraine and the Crimea. If Jodl's plan had been carried out before the thaw, then as early as the middle of March the Red Army would have reached the line Odessa–Dnestr–

THE PRELUDE TO 'BAGRATION'

Ternopol'–Kovel–Brest–the Western Dvina, which it actually reached only from April through October 1944. At the same time, the 20 divisions, which they would have managed to free up, would in any event, as the further development of events showed, have been dispatched to the West, in order to repulse the Allied invasion of France and their offensive in Italy. The Red Army would not have suffered those losses which it actually incurred while breaking through the German defences. It goes without saying that in the event of the Germans abandoning Estonia as early as March, Finland would have left the war several months earlier than was actually the case and this would have additionally freed up no less than 20 Soviet divisions. And when Soviet forces resumed the offensive in the second half of April and in May, the Germans would not have been able to hold them and, as early as May, before the Allied landing in Normandy, Soviet forces would have ended up along the Vistula. They could have put off carrying Jodl's plan to the time following the thaw. Then Odessa would already have been lost along the southern and south-western directions and, taking into account the Soviet forces' actual advance, the Germans would have been forced no later than the middle of June to fall back even further to the west of the line proposed by Jodl, probably as far as L'vov and Rava-Russkaya. And, once again, they would not have been able to hold this line and the Soviet forces, continuing their pursuit without an operational pause, could have as early as the end of July ended up along the Vistula. And if the Red Army had begun a simultaneous major offensive in Romania, then they would have taken the latter out of the war by approximately this time. Thus Jodl's plan could not save the Wehrmacht and would only have hurried its defeat along the Eastern Front. In the same way Busch's plan, both in its large and small variants, would not have yielded the Germans any advantages, even given a maximum withdrawal to the Berezina, and under attack by Soviet aviation. It's probable that if the Germans had begun an immediate withdrawal, on 20 May, then by the middle of June they would have succeeded in falling back as far as the Berezina. But at the same time the Soviet forces would not have suffered those losses which they actually did in breaking through the German defence in the last ten days of June and the beginning of July and could have set about breaking through the new defensive line following a pursuit and would probably have broken through it. Even according to official and highly understated Soviet (Russian) data, the First Baltic and Second and Third Belorussian Fronts lost more than 19,600 men killed and more than 74,600 wounded and missing in action between 22 and 30 June 1944. During the period from 24 June through 4 July the First Belorussian Front's right-wing armies lost more than 50,000 men, including 9,160 killed.[38] Total losses for the beginning stage of the operation exceeded 144,000 men. According to official and similarly understated data, Soviet forces lost 765,815 men during all of Operation 'Bagration', which lasted from 22 June through 29 August.[39] Losses during the first stage of the fighting amounted to about 18.8 per cent, while at the same time the period from 22 through 30 June accounted for only 13 per cent of the operation's duration, while at the same time the First Belorussian Front's left wing engaged in very little fighting.

On 28 June, the day he left his post as commander of Army Group Centre, Busch, even taking into account the reinforcements being sent to him and the Soviet losses, which made the correlation of forces along the Berezina approximately what it had been at the start of the Soviet offensive on 22 June, no longer hoped to hold neither the line of the Berezina, nor Minsk, from which he hurriedly moved his headquarters to Lida. In the same way Walter Model, who replaced Busch on 29 June, did not attempt to hold these lines. Thus Busch's plan would not have saved the Germans. Hitler understood this and was able to fully convince Busch, who agreed with his thesis: 'The word "withdrawal" no longer exists'. The task of Army Group Centre was only to defend for as long as possible, while holding the existing front and inflicting the heaviest losses possible on the attacking Soviet forces, but without hope of receiving any kind of significant reinforcements during the first days of the Soviet offensive.

On 8 March 1944 Hitler, instead of accepting Jodl's plan, issued an order on creating and holding 'fortresses'. The Army Group Centre command objected to the creation of too large a number of 'fortresses' in Belorussia, because it would have had to allot six divisions for the Bobruisk, Mogilev and Orsha garrisons alone, and three divisions for defending Vitebsk. Aside from this, there were not enough construction materials or engineer units for building fortified positions in the 'fortresses'. But on 20 May Busch was forced to agree to the fortress concept.

Colonel General Georg Hans Reinhardt, the commander of the Third Panzer Army, insisted on abandoning the Vitebsk salient, which was tying down five of his divisions, and a withdrawal to the fortified 'Tiger' position to the west of the city, but did not receive permission. Busch repeated the argument that the Vitebsk salient was tying down 30–40 Soviet divisions.[40]

In reality, the First Baltic Front's 43rd Army (nine rifle divisions, one fortified area, one tank corps, two tank brigades, one tank regiment and two self-propelled artillery regiments), the First Baltic Front's 6th Guards Army (nine rifle divisions, two tank brigades, three tank regiments and two self-propelled artillery regiments), the Third Belorussian Front's 39th Army (seven rifle divisions, one tank brigade and two self-propelled artillery regiments) and the Third Belorussian Front's 5th Army (nine rifle divisions, one fortified area, a tank brigade and three self-propelled artillery regiments) were concentrated against the Vitebsk salient.[41] Taken together, this accounted for 38.5 divisions, which practically coincided with Hitler's and Busch's calculations.

If the Germans had begun to pull back their forces from the Vitebsk salient as early as the beginning of the Soviet offensive, then the Soviet forces would probably have taken up the pursuit and would most likely have encircled a part of the retreating German forces. But given the timely withdrawal from the 'Vitebsk cauldron', more Germans would have been able to break out than was actually the case.

On 2 April 1944 Stalin, in the name of the *Stavka*, issued this directive to the First Baltic Front:

1. To go over to the defensive with the forces of three armies within the confines of the front and securely hold the present lines.
2. The 11th Guards Army, consisting of nine guards divisions and two independent rifle divisions, is to be put into the Front reserve in the area to the south-west of Nevel' and to be brought up to strength during April, employing front resources and 15,000 reinforcements being prepared for the 11th Guards Army from the *Stavka*'s resources. Aside from this, there should be five–six rifle divisions in the reserves of the armies along the front line.

    The 11th Guards Army is to be operationally employed only with the permission of the *Stavka*.[42]

THE PRELUDE TO 'BAGRATION'

On that same day Stalin signed a similar directive concerning the Belorussian Fronts:

1. The forces of the Second Belorussian Front are to no later than 5 April transfer to the First Belorussian Front the following: the 61st Army, consisting of the 9th Guards and 89th Corps headquarters and nine rifle divisions; the 70th Army, consisting of the 114th and 96th Corps headquarters and four rifle divisions; the 47th Army, consisting of the 77th and 125th Corps headquarters and nine rifle divisions; the 2nd and 7th Guards Cavalry Corps, consisting of six cavalry divisions; the 69th Army (25th, 61st and 91st Corps headquarters, nine rifle divisions), which is arriving from the *Stavka* reserve, and: the 6th Air Army (336th Fighter, 3rd Guards Assault and 242nd Night Bomber Divisions).

    These forces are to be transferred with all their reinforcement units, army rear units and establishments and supplies on hand.

2. By 5 April the chief of the General Staff is to determine the composition of the Second Belorussian Front's front rear units and establishments to be transferred, first of all, to the First Belorussian Front and, secondly, to be sent to the *Stavka* reserve.
3. By 2400 on 5 April the commander of the First Belorussian Front is to transfer to the Western Front the 10th Army, consisting of the 38th and 70th Corps headquarters and six rifle divisions, and the 50th Army, consisting of the 19th and 121st Corps headquarters and seven rifle divisions.

    The enumerated armies are to be transferred with all their army reinforcement units, rear units and establishments and supplies on hand . . .

6. The Belorussian Front is to have its headquarters in the area of Ovruch and an auxiliary headquarters in the Sarny area.
7. The headquarters of the Second Ukrainian Front and the 6th Air Army is to be transferred to the *Stavka* reserve in the Zhitomir area by 20 April.
8. By 5 April the commander of the First Belorussian Front is to present in code his views on the further operational employment of the Belorussian Front's forces in their new makeup.[43]

On 3 April Stalin issued an order for inspecting the Western Front staff's work:

To entrust an extraordinary commission, consisting of [State Defence Committee] member, comrade Malenkov (chairman), Colonel General Shcherbakov, Lieutenant General Kuznetsov, Colonel General Shtemenko, and Lieutenant General Shimonaev, to inspect in 4–5 days the work of the Western Front's staff on the basis of documents furnished by the General Staff, and to report its conclusions to the *Stavka* of the Supreme High Command.[44]

On 19 April there followed directives ordering the Third and Second Belorussian Fronts to go over to the defensive.[45]

OPERATION BAGRATION: AN INCOMPLETE TRUTH

Then the Red Army's relations with the Polish Home Army were finally defined. As early as 26 March Stalin, in a directive to the commander of the Second Belorussian Front, Colonel General Pavel Alekseevich Kurochkin, ordered the following:

1. Inform the Polish partisan division's command that its joint operations with the Red Army are desirable only under conditions of its complete subordination in all instances to the Red Army command in the person of the Second Belorussian Front command. There can be no division of authority in military affairs. The division may maintain communications with whomever it likes, with Sosnkowski or anyone else, but in its operations it must be subordinated to the Red Army's orders if it truly wants to operate jointly with the Red Army against the German aggressors.
2. Should the Polish partisan division accept this condition, then it must be supplied by the Red Army command with everything necessary for fighting. The division must be concentrated in one area and employed for carrying out combat assignments along one of the sectors of the front.
3. Should the Polish partisan division command refuse to accept these conditions, its joint operations with the Red Army, as well as its materiel supply on our part, is considered inadmissible.
4. The *Stavka* is to be regularly informed of the results of the negotiations and the Polish partisans in general.[46]

But on 20 April Stalin issued a directive to the commander of the First Belorussian Front, General Konstantin Konstantinovich Rokossovskii, that he was not to have any kind of dealings with the Home Army's troops:

According to data received at the centre, Oliwa and his officers are suspicious personages who maintain contact with the Germans. There is a real danger than they will inform the German command as to the location and operations of our forces. In connection with this, the *Stavka* of the Supreme High Command orders you to break off any kind of dealings with General Sosnkowski's underground detachments. Corresponding Front orders are to be sent to all the armies.[47]

And on 16 May there followed a directive to the commander of the First Belorussian Front: 'Poles from the Polish partisan divisions who come over to our side are to be dispatched to the disposal of the commander of the Polish 1st Army, comrade Berling, who, following a vetting, is to concentrate the Poles among the Polish 1st Army's reserve units.'[48]

On 3 May there followed a directive on removing the 5th Guards Tank Army, which was to take part in Operation 'Bagration', from the Second Ukrainian Front by 6 May. The directive pointed out that the commander of the Second Ukrainian Front should subsequently employ the 5th Guards Tank Army for reinforcing the Front's right wing.[49] However, this was done only for the purpose of masking their true intentions. As early as 6 May there followed a directive for the Second Ukrainian Front to go over

THE PRELUDE TO 'BAGRATION'

to a rigid defence and to prepare for renewing the offensive no later than 25 May.[50] On the same day the same sort of directive was issued to the Third Ukrainian Front.[51] But in a 26 May directive the beginning of the Second and Third Ukrainian Fronts' offensive was shifted to an unspecified date, 'until the *Stavka*'s special instructions'.[52]

On 9 May a directive was issued for the transfer of the Polish 1st Army's 8th Guards Tank Corps to the First Belorussian Front.[53] This is how the group of forces for 'Bagration' was created.

By 14 May the elaboration of the plan for the Belorussian strategic offensive operation was basically completed. All of the Fronts' designs had been collapsed into a unified plan and put into order in the form of a short text and maps. The text was written by hand by the chief of the General Staff's operational directorate, Lieutenant General A.A. Gryzlov. On 20 May General A.I. Antonov signed the text and presented it to Stalin.[54] The plan called for the following:

> The First Baltic Front is to break through the enemy's defence northwest of Vitebsk, to force the Western Dvina River and, covering itself from the direction of Polotsk, launch its main attack in the general direction of Lepel', Dokshitsy and Molodechno. Part of its forces is to attack on Senno and, in conjunction with the Third Belorussian Front, is to destroy the enemy's Vitebsk group of forces.
>
> During the first stage it is to force the Western Dvina River and reach the line Ulla River–Senno.
>
> During the second stage it is to capture the Glubokoe–Dokshitsy–Begoml' area.
>
> During the third stage it is to capture the Vileika–Molodechno area.
>
> The operation's overall depth is 250km and its length is 45–50 days.
>
> The Third Belorussian Front is to break through the enemy's defence south-east of Vitebsk and launch its main attack in the general direction of Senno, Borisov and Minsk.
>
> During the first stage, in conjunction with the First Baltic Front's right left wing, it is to destroy the enemy's Vitebsk group of forces and reach the front Senno–Orsha.
>
> During the second stage it is to reach the Berezina River and capture Borisov.
>
> During the third stage, in conjunction with the Second Belorussian Front, it is to capture the Minsk area, launching its attack from the north.
>
> The operation's overall depth is 250km and its length is 45–50 days.
>
> The Second Belorussian Front is to break through the enemy's defence north-west of Novyi Bykhov and launch its main attack along the western bank of the Dnepr River toward Mogilev. It is to subsequently develop the offensive in the direction of Berezino and Minsk.
>
> A supporting attack is to be launched from the area north of Chausy toward Mogilev.
>
> During the first stage it is to eliminate the enemy bridgehead along the eastern bank of the Dnepr and capture Mogilev.
>
> During the second stage it is to reach the Berezina River along the Berezino–Svisloch' sector.

During the third stage, in conjunction with the Third and First Belorussian Fronts, it is to capture the Minsk area, launching an attack from the east.

The operation's overall depth is 200–250km and its length is 40–50 days.

The First Belorussian Front is to break through the enemy's defence along two sectors – north of Rogachev and along the front Mormal'–Ozarichi, launching an attack in the general direction of Bobruisk. It is to subsequently develop the offensive to outflank Minsk from the south, with part of its forces directed at Slutsk.

During the first stage it is to capture the Bobruisk area.

During the second stage it is to reach the line Minsk–Stolbtsy–Starobino.

The operation's overall depth is 200–250km and its length is 40–50 days.

The beginning of the operation is set for 15–20 June 1944.[55]

On 27 May there followed a directive for the removal from the front line of the First Baltic Front's 6th Guards Army, which had just been transferred from the Second Baltic Front.[56] This was done in order to reinforce it and for its subsequent participation in Operation 'Bagration'. On that same day an order was issued by the people's commissar of defence for reinforcing the First Baltic and First and Second Belorussian Fronts with a number of aviation formations, and that their transfer was to be completed before 10 June.[57]

On 31 May the First, Second and Third Belorussian and First Baltic Fronts received their directives for conducting Operation 'Bagration'. All of these directives had been signed by Stalin and Zhukov. The First Belorussian Front was ordered to do the following:

1. To prepare and conduct an operation for the purpose of routing the enemy's Bobruisk group of forces and reach with its main forces the Osipovichi–Pukhovichi–Slutsk area, for which it is to break through the enemy's defence, launching two attacks: one with the forces of the 3rd and 48th Armies from the Rogachev area in the general direction of Bobruisk and Osipovichi, and the other with the forces of the 65th and 28th Armies from the area of the lower course of the Berezina River–Ozarichi in the general direction of Porogi station and Slutsk.

    The immediate task is to defeat the enemy's Bobruisk group of forces and capture the Bobruisk–Glusha–Glusk area, while part of its forces is to assist the forces of the Second Belorussian Front in defeating the enemy's Mogilev group of forces. It is to subsequently develop the offensive for the purpose of reaching the Pukhovichi–Slutsk–Osipovichi area.

2. The mobile forces (cavalry and tanks) are to be employed for developing the success following the breakthrough.

3. To establish from 2400 on 10.06.1944 the following boundary line between the First and Second Belorussian Fronts : as far as Chigirinka

THE PRELUDE TO 'BAGRATION'

as before, and then Svisloch'–Pukhovichi (all locales are for the First Belorussian Front inclusively).

The Second Belorussian Front was ordered to do the following:

1. To prepare and conduct an operation with the goal of, in conjunction, with the Third Belorussian Front's left wing and the First Belorussian Front's right wing, to defeat the enemy's Mogilev group of forces and reach the Berezina River, for which it is to break through the enemy's defence with the forces of no less than 11–12 rifle divisions and reinforcements, launching one general attack from the area Dribin–Dednya–Ryasna in the general direction of Mogilev and Belynichi.

   The immediate task is to reach the Dnepr River and seize a bridgehead along its western bank. It is to subsequently force the Dnepr River and capture Mogilev with its main forces and to develop the offensive in the general direction of Berezino and Smilovichi.
2. To establish from 2400 on 10.06.1944 the following boundaries with the Third Belorussian Front: as far as Zubov as before, then Krucha–Ozdyatichi–Smolevichi–Minsk (all locales for the Third Belorussian Front inclusively); and with the First Belorussian Front, as far as Chigirinka as before, then Svisloch'–Pukhovichi (both locales for the First Belorussian Front inclusively).

The Third Belorussian Front was ordered to do the following:

1. To prepare and conduct an operation with the goal of, in conjunction with the left wing of the First Baltic Front and the Second Belorussian Front, defeating the enemy's Vitebsk–Orsha group of forces and reach the Berezina River, for which two attacks are to be launched:
   a) one attack with the forces of the 39th and 5th Armies from the area to the west of Liozno in the general direction of Bogushevskoe and Senno; part of this group of forces is to attack to the north-west, outflanking Vitebsk from the south-west, for the purpose of, in conjunction with the First Baltic Front's left wing, defeating the enemy's Vitebsk group of forces and capturing the city of Vitebsk;
   b) another attack with the forces of the 11th Guards and 31st Armies along the Minsk highway in the general direction of Borisov; part of this group of forces is to capture Orsha by an attack from the north.
2. The Front's immediate task is to capture the line Senno–Orsha. It is to subsequently develop the offensive on Borisov with the mission of, in conjunction with the Second Belorussian Front, defeating the enemy's Borisov group of forces and reaching the western bank of the Berezina River in the Borisov area.
3. Mobile forces (cavalry and tanks) are to be employed for developing the success following the breakthrough in the general direction of Borisov.

4. To establish from 2400 on 10.06.1944 the following boundary lines with the First Baltic Front: as far as Vitebsk as before, then Chashniki–Begoml'–Dolginov (all locales for the First Baltic Front inclusively); with the Second Belorussian Front: as far as Zubov as before, then Krucha–Ozdyatichi–Smolevichi–Minsk (all locales for the Third Belorussian Front inclusively).

The First Baltic Front was ordered to do the following:

1. To prepare and conduct an operation with the goal of, in conjunction with the Third Belorussian Front, defeating the enemy's Vitebsk–Lepel' group of forces and reaching the southern bank of the Western Dvina River in the Chashniki–Lepel' area, for which the forces of the 6th Guards and 43rd Armies are to break through the enemy defence in the area south-west of Gorodok, by launching one general attack in the direction of Beshenkovichi and Chashniki. The immediate objective is to force the Western Dvina River and capture the Beshenkovichi area. Part of your forces, in conjunction with the Third Belorussian Front's right wing, is to defeat the enemy's Vitebsk group of forces and capture the city of Vitebsk. The Front is to subsequently develop the offensive in the general direction of Lepel', while firmly securing the Front'ss main group of forces from the Polotsk axis.
2. To establish from 2400 on 10.06.1944 the following boundary between the First Baltic and Third Belorussian Fronts: as far as Vitebsk as before, then Chashniki–Begoml'–Dolginov (all locales for the First Baltic Front inclusively).[58]

In order to distract the Germans' attention from the Soviet forces' main operation, a 16 June directive ordered the First Ukrainian and Second and Third Baltic Fronts to do the following: '1. To organize and conduct during 20–23.06.1944 a reconnaissance in force along a number of sectors of the front in strength from a reinforced company to a reinforced battalion. In the event of the detachments' successful actions, you are to have prepared reserves for developing and consolidating the success for the purpose of improving your position.'[59]

The situation was viewed as follows from the German side. Kurt Tippelskirch, the former commander of the Fourth Army, maintained:

Army Group Centre, following the transfer of one corps to the Fourth Panzer Army in the Kovel' area, in which a large part of its tanks and a significant number of troops were located since the lifting of the blockade of the city, disposed for defense only 38 divisions to defend its 1,100km front, of which 34 were employed. Only three infantry divisions, including one which was hardly fit for combat, and one panzer division, were in the reserve. Because the enemy, in all likelihood, intended to attack all of the Group's armies simultaneously, with the exception, perhaps, of the Second Army, the Army Group command could not count on, as had been the case the previous winter, by means of rapidly transferring divisions from the sectors of the front not under attack, of organizing a reliable defence along the threatened areas. Over the course of a number of months the army commanders had unsuccessfully appealed to the Army Group command, and the latter to Hitler, to shorten the length of the front. From the autumn of 1943 the Fourth Army had outfitted a defensive line along the Dnepr, whose steep western bank was unfit for tanks along a significant distance between Bykhov and Orsha. Moreover, against Hitler's will and with the silent consent of the Army Group command, the outfitting of yet another line along the Berezina had been proceeding for a number of months. The evacuation of the existing bridgehead along the Dnepr would have rendered the army's front nearly invulnerable and would have simultaneously resulted in the economizing of no small number of forces. Even more efficacious would have been a well-prepared withdrawal of forces immediately before the start of the Russian offensive to the line Bobruisk–Polotsk, thanks to which there would have been created a straight and significantly shortened front and the deployment of the enemy's forces would immediately have been deprived of any effect.

Field Marshal Busch, the commander of Army Group Centre, was unable to maintain his point of view against Hitler. The attempt undertaken by him as early as the end of May to point out the lack of correspondence between the length of the front line and the number of forces and to bring about a change in the Army Group's task, which obliged it to hold and defend the line held, ran into harsh resistance. Hitler cynically asked Busch whether or not he belonged to that group of generals who constantly look over their shoulders. After this, Busch submitted to Hitler's will and set about carrying out the latter's order to throw all his forces into outfitting the forward lines. Busch, evidently not wishing to get involved in more unpleasantness, did not renew any more attempts to achieve another decision, until by the middle of June the scale of the enemy's preparations along the Army Group's front had become clear. Nevertheless, it's unlikely that the Army Group command assumed that the enemy would undertake an offensive here with major forces and with such broad goals as it transpired several days later and therefore its chances for defending had obviously been overestimated. The last bit of uncertainty regarding the time for the beginning of the offensive cleared up on 20 June, when major sabotage operations along the Pinsk–Luninets, Borisov–Orsha and Molodechno–Polotsk rail lines; that is, along Army Group Centre's communications, were carried out by partisans.[60]

Chapter 5

The Rout

The overall strength of Army Group Centre as of 1 June 1944 was a little more than 849,000 men, while the strength of its divisions and other combat units was only 486,493 men. The difference of 363,000 men is due to counting the workers in the military administration in the occupied territories, German security units, men from the Reich Labour Service and the Todt military construction organization, the 390th Field Training Division, and 103,000 personnel from anti-partisan detachments and security units formed from the local population. Moreover, the 363,000 figure included people on leave or commandeered to other units outside Army Group Centre, as well as wounded, sick and missing in action and not yet removed from their units' rolls. For example, in the Fourth Army as of 1 June there were 18,069 men absent or otherwise assigned, as well as 7,500 wounded and sick in hospitals. If one excludes the 70,099 men in the Second Army, which was not subjected to attack during the first stage of Operation 'Bagration', then the strength of the divisions and other combat units falls to 336,573 men. Army Group Centre's combat strength amounted to only 236,772 men and, not counting the Second Army, to 166,673 men.[1]

On 1 June 1944, of the 4,740 tanks and assault guns on the Eastern Front, Army Group Centre disposed of only 11 per cent – 553 armoured vehicles, including 480 Stug III assault guns. The Fourth Army had 246 assault guns and 40 tanks, including 29 Tigers. There were also a couple of hundred tank destroyers, including Hornisse 88mm self-propelled guns.[2] Soviet forces along the 'Bagration' front disposed of 2,715 tanks and 1,355 self-propelled guns, not counting the forces of the First Belorussian Front's left wing.[3]

There was little in the way of armoured equipment in Army Group Centre. The Third Panzer Army disposed of 76 assault guns. In all, there were 377 assault guns in the Third Panzer, Fourth and Ninth Armies out of 452 in the Army Group as a whole. The 20th Panzer Division, which had been transferred to Army Group Centre not long before the beginning of the Soviet offensive, had only 56 tanks, while the Army Group had only a total of 118 tanks, the remaining 62 being in the Fourth Army as part of the 18th and 25th Panzergrenadier Divisions and the 505th Heavy Panzer Battalion.[4] The number of tanks in Busch's Army Group corresponded to the strength of two Soviet tank brigades. Army Group Centre had 602 combat aircraft and 3,236 guns (including 2,589 along the front during the first stage of Operation 'Bagration'. There was a shortage of machine guns and artillery ammunition, while the Soviet artillery felt no such shortage.[5]

Moreover, Army Group Centre's divisions were poorly motorized and were forced to rely predominantly on horse transport, mainly due to a shortage of fuel. They were forced to employ horses even in the panzergrenadier divisions. They had only 120 motor vehicles left in each of the 18th and 25th Panzergrenadier Divisions. About 60,000 horses were employed in the Third Panzer Army. Railway transport was made more difficult due to partisan attacks. As K.H. Frieser notes, 'In the summer of 1944 it was already normal to see the Wehrmacht's troops marching on foot, accompanied by horse-drawn carts and pursued by Red Army soldiers on tanks and trucks'.[6]

Of the Sixth Air Fleet's 920 aircraft, only 604 were combat-ready by the start of the Soviet offensive. Moreover, the IV Air Corps' long-range bombers were also being used in the interests of the other Army Groups. Of 44 strategic reconnaissance aircraft, only 21 were combat-ready, of 99 tactical aircraft only 69, of 104 day fighters only 61, of 43 night fighters only 30, of 115 ground-attack aircraft and dive bombers only 53, and of 434 bombers only 286.[7]

According to other data, the Sixth Air Fleet, which was covering Army Group Centre, had 839 combat aircraft, probably without counting long-range bombers. By 22 June it disposed of only 40 combat-ready fighters. There were 312 bombers, mostly He 111s and a small number of Ju 88s. The air fleet also disposed of 106 Ju 87 dive bombers and Fw 190 fighter-bombers.[8] In the beginning of June the Sixth Air Fleet had only 43 strategic reconnaissance aircraft, of which only 26 were combat-ready. This made it difficult for the Luftwaffe to carry out aerial reconnaissance along Army Group Centre's sector.[9]

During the first days of Operation 'Bagration' the Luftwaffe could employ only 61 day fighters against 6,334 Soviet aircraft. Major General Paul Schurmann, the commander of the 25th Panzergrenadier Division, which managed to break out of the cauldron east of Minsk, reported on the 'absolutely monstrous number of enemy attack aircraft and the complete absence of our aviation'.[10]

Army Group Centre's combat composition was as follows. The Third Panzer Army included the IX, LIII and VI Army Corps. The IX Corps contained the 252nd Infantry Division, Corps Group D, and the 246th Infantry Division. The LIII Corps included the 4th and 6th Luftwaffe Field Divisions and the 206th Infantry Division. The VI Corps included the 197th, 299th and 256th Infantry Divisions. The 95th Infantry Division was in the Third Panzer Army's reserve and the 201st Security Division was operating in the army's rear area.

The Fourth Army included the XXVII Army, XXXIX Panzer and XII Army Corps. The XXVII Army Corps included the 78th Assault Division, the 25th Panzergrenadier Division and the 260th Infantry Division. The XXXIX Panzer Corps included the 110th, 337th and 12th Infantry Divisions. The XII Army Corps included the 31st Infantry Division, the 18th Panzergrenadier Division and the 267th and 57th Infantry Divisions. The 286th Security Division operated in the Fourth Army's rear area.

The Ninth Army included the XXXV Army, XLI Panzer and LV Army Corps. The XXXV Corps included the 134th, 296th, and 6th Infantry Divisions. The XLI Panzer Corps included the 383rd, 45th, 36th, and 35th Infantry Divisions. The LV Corps included the 129th, 292nd and 102nd Infantry Divisions. The 707th Infantry Division was in the Ninth Army's reserve.

The Second Army included the XXIII, XX and VIII Army Corps. The XXIII Corps included the 7th Infantry and 203rd Security Divisions. The XX Corps included Corps Group E, which consisted of the 3rd Cavalry Brigade and the 5th Light Infantry Division. The VIII Corps included the 211th Infantry Division and the Hungarian

12th Reserve Division. The Hungarian 1st Cavalry Division was in the Second Army's reserve. The Hungarian forces' combat effectiveness was rated as low by the German command. The chief of staff of the German XXIII Army Corps, Lieutenant Colonel Gerhard Rempel, requested on 14 July 1944 that the headquarters of the Second Army remove the Hungarian cavalry division from its combat positions: 'The corps demands that the Hungarian cavalry division be pulled out. It's better to employ the Hungarians for your needs. No help at all is better than the Hungarians. Each time the Hungarians are at the front they attract the Russians like a magnet. It there's no one there, the enemy will most likely not dare to move into the breach than when there are Hungarians there.' He was seconded by the commander of the XXIII Corps, General of Engineer Troops Otto Tiemann: 'The Hungarians blew up a bridge. I request that you remove them as soon as possible from the area of combat operations.'[11]

The 221st, 52nd and 391st Security Divisions and the 390th Field Training Division were subordinated to the Wehrmacht command *Weiss Ruthenia*.

The 20th Panzer and 14th Infantry Divisions were in the Army Group Centre reserve. Besides this, units of the *Feldherrnhalle* Panzergrenadier Division, which was in the OKH reserve, were in the rear of Army Group Centre.[12] Army Group Centre had almost no mobile formations and was not in a position to launch even local counter-attacks. All of the most powerful German divisions had been concentrated for repelling the Allied landing in Normandy, which had begun on 6 June 1944. The Wehrmacht had no strategic reserves at its disposal whatsoever. By stretching the definition, one may include as such the *Totenkopf* and *Wiking* SS Panzer Divisions, the 6th Panzer Division, and the *Grossdeutschland* Panzergrenadier (actually, panzer) Division, which were undergoing refitting. These were all elite divisions, but due to the heavy, although successful, fighting that had continued for several weeks before this on the Eastern Front, they had suffered heavy losses, particularly in armoured equipment, and by the start of the major Soviet operation of 1944 – Operation 'Bagration' – they had not regained their combat capability. They would subsequently be employed along Operation 'Bagration's' front, but only during its second phase during the second half of July.

The German historian Karl-Heinz Frieser believes that the best strategy for Army Group Centre would have been a withdrawal, under the cover of rearguards, which would hold the enemy along the lines of the rivers flowing north and south, but Hitler forbade such a withdrawal.[13] However, it should be pointed out that this thesis, while correct from the point of view of military theory, was completely inapplicable in practice in the specific conditions of the summer of 1944 in Belorussia. While not even speaking of the Soviet forces' overwhelming superiority in men and material, even more important was that the Soviet forces were colossally superior to Army Group Centre in mobility. During the first phase of Operation 'Bagration' all of the German mobile formations (minus the Second Army) along the front came down to the 20th Panzer Division and units of the *Feldherrenhalle* Panzergrenadier Division against which the Soviet forces had five tank corps, two mechanized corps, 16 independent tank brigades, including the Polish 1st, and an independent mechanized brigade. This entire enormous motorized armada would have easily cut the retreating Germans' path of withdrawal before they had arrived at their designated defensive lines. And the rearguard divisions, with a front significantly greater than 30km per division, could not have held off the attackers for long. As a result, numerous 'cauldrons' would have formed in any event and Army Group Centre's irreparable losses, given such a strategy, would likely not have been less than what actually happened. Moreover, Soviet losses, given such a strategy, would have been significantly less than was actually the case, insofar as the majority of Soviet corps and divisions would have been in pursuit of the enemy. And by the time the remnants of Army Group Centre had fallen back to the Vistula and the East Prussian frontier, the correlation of forces for the Germans would have been even less favourable than was actually the case during Operation 'Bagration'. Thus in the final analysis, Hitler proved to be right in forbidding a withdrawal.

On the Soviet side of the Soviet-German front, which stretched some 4,500km, on 1 June 1944 the active army numbered 11 Fronts, 55 combined-arms armies, five tank armies and 12 air armies, three fleets, 435 rifle divisions, ten airborne divisions, 18 cavalry divisions, nine rifle brigades, four ski brigades, 22 fortified areas, 16 tank and six mechanized corps, 33 independent tank brigades, one independent mechanized brigade, one independent motorized rifle brigade, three self-propelled artillery brigades, 59 independent tank regiments, 72 self-propelled artillery regiments, six motorcycle regiments, one independent tank battalion, six independent armoured battalions, four independent motorcycle battalions, one special-designation motorized battalion, 11 independent aerosleigh battalions, 41 independent armoured train battalions, 16 artillery breakthrough divisions, six artillery divisions, 13 independent artillery brigades, 82 independent artillery regiments, seven independent artillery battalions, 35 anti-tank artillery brigades, 101 independent anti-tank artillery regiments, one anti-tank artillery battalion, eight independent mortar brigades, 91 independent mortar regiments, five guards mortar divisions, 13 independent guards mortar brigades, 90 guards mortar regiments, 16 bomber divisions, 17 long-range air divisions, five mixed air divisions, 26 assault air divisions, 34 fighter divisions, 11 night bomber divisions, three independent assault air regiments, six independent fighter regiments, 12 air reconnaissance regiments, nine fire-correction air reconnaissance regiments, two independent night-bomber regiments, 72 engineer brigades, eight pontoon-bridge brigades, five pontoon-bridge regiments, 79 engineer battalions, 43 pontoon-bridge battalions, 27 independent flamethrower battalions, and 19 independent flamethrower companies. Ground air defence included 46 anti-aircraft divisions, 121 anti-aircraft regiments, which were not organized into divisions, and 64 independent anti-aircraft battalions. In all, the active army included 6,600,000 men, about 98,000 guns and mortars, 7,800 tanks and self-propelled guns, and 13,400 combat aircraft. The *Stavka* reserve included the headquarters of the Fourth Ukrainian Front, two combined-arms, one tank and one air armies, 20 rifle and three cavalry divisions, eight tank and seven mechanized corps, eight independent tank regiments, three self-propelled artillery regiments, four motorcycle regiments, one independent tank battalion, one independent armoured battalion, two independent armoured train battalions, one artillery breakthrough division, one artillery division, 11 independent artillery brigades, five independent artillery regiments, two independent artillery battalions, five anti-tank artillery brigades, five independent anti-tank artillery regiments, one mortar brigade, four independent mortar regiments, one independent guards mortar brigade, eight guards mortar regiments, three independent guards mortar battalions, two bomber divisions, seven attack air divisions, 12 fighter divisions, three engineer brigades, five anti-aircraft artillery divisions, and 15 anti-aircraft artillery regiments, numbering about 650,000 men, 9,500 guns and mortars, 2,000 tanks and self-propelled guns, and 3,000 aircraft.[14] This does not include reinforcements on the march, rear units and combat-ready formations being formed in the internal military districts and inactive fronts. Among the military districts the most powerful one was the Moscow Military District, which included three rifle and four airborne divisions, three fortified areas, five independent tank brigades, one independent mechanized brigade, three self-propelled artillery brigades, 22 independent tank regiments, 25 self-propelled artillery regiments, one self-propelled artillery battalion, eight independent special-designation motorized battalions, one independent armoured train battalion, 11 independent artillery brigades, one independent artillery regiment, six independent artillery battalions, four anti-tank artillery brigades, two independent anti-tank artillery regiments, two independent mortar brigades, one Guards mortar division (under strength, a headquarters and the 1st Guards Mortar Brigade), six Guards mortar regiments, one independent Guards mortar battalion, four engineer brigades, five engineer battalions, two pontoon-bridge battalions, two bomber divisions, two assault air divisions, one fighter division, two special-designation air divisions, three reconnaissance regiments, six anti-aircraft divisions, one anti-aircraft artillery regiment, and five independent anti-aircraft battalions. The two special-designation air divisions, among other things, shipped arms and ammunition to the partisans and took a very active part in preparing Operation 'Bagration'.

Of the active army's 445 rifle and airborne divisions, 144 divisions, or 32.4 per cent, took part in Operation 'Bagration', as did two rifle brigades out of 13 (15.4 per cent) and six fortified areas out of 22 (27.3 per cent). Of 18 cavalry divisions, six (33.3 per cent) took part in 'Bagration'. One cannot speak of any sort of concentration according to the number of rifle formations. There was no less infantry among the remaining eight Fronts. As to tanks, a concentration was also not felt by 1 June and could not be noticed by German intelligence. Of the 16 tank and six mechanized corps, three (13.6 per cent) were with the four Fronts in 'Bagration', as were only nine (27.3 per cent) of 33 independent tank brigades and 12 (20.3 per cent) of the 59 independent tank regiments. The single independent tank battalion in the active army was also there, but it made no difference. It makes no sense to examine the concentration of aviation by 1 June, insofar as aircraft could be relocated along a different direction in a matter of days before an offensive.

On 1 July the situation was already different. Of the 452 rifle and airborne divisions in the active army, 172 (38.1 per cent) were along 'Bagration's' fronts, as were two (16.7 per cent) of the 12 rifle and ski brigades, and 6 (28.6 per cent) of 21 fortified areas. Even more impressive was the growth of the number of mobile formations for the operation. Of 21 cavalry divisions, 12 (57.1 per cent) took part in 'Bagration', as did ten tank and two mechanized (41.4 per cent) of 21 tank and eight mechanized corps, 15 (44.1 per cent) of 34 independent tank brigades, 27 (37.5 per cent) of 72 independent tank regiments (these were usually attached to rifle formations, thus their number is closer to the share of rifle troops), and four (57.1 per cent) of seven independent special-designation motorized battalions. The single independent tank battalion and single mechanized brigade also fought in 'Bagration'. The majority of tank and mechanized formations were transferred to the 'Bagration' front after 10 June, or, as was the case with the 5th Guards Tank Army, they arrived after the start of the operation. Due to the fact that the tank formations taking part in 'Bagration' were outfitted with armoured equipment to a much greater degree in comparison with the other Fronts and the rifle formations had been reinforced to a much greater degree with troops, the concentration of men and materiel was even greater than one can judge by the number of formations.

Naturally, it was difficult for German intelligence to make any judgment as to the level of strength of these or other Soviet rifle divisions and tank brigades.

According to V.O. Daines's calculations, 36.3 per cent of personnel, 37.1 per cent of guns and mortars, 73.2 per cent of tanks and self-propelled guns, and 41 per cent of all aviation assets of the active army were concentrated along the four Fronts that occupied a 1,100km-long sector (24.4 per cent) of the overall length of the Soviet-German front). By 20 June a group of forces had been deployed that numbered more than 2,400,000 men, 36,400 guns and mortars, 5,200 tanks and self-propelled guns, and 5,300 aircraft. Besides this, it was planned to bring in 1,007 long-range aircraft and 500 fighters from the National Air Defence Forces.[15] The extremely high percentage of tanks and self-propelled gun indicate that the tank and mechanized formations along the other sectors of the Soviet-German front were far from their required strengths in armoured equipment.

Only six men knew the plan for 'Bagration' in its full detail: I.V. Stalin, the deputy supreme commander-in-chief, G.K. Zhukov, the chief of the General Staff, A.M. Vasilevskii, the deputy chief of the General Staff, A.I. Antonov, the chief of the General Staff's operational section, S.M. Shtemenko, and the deputy chief of the General Staff's operational section, A.A. Gryzlov.[16] Nevertheless, as early as the beginning of May German intelligence had been informed of the early variation of 'Bagration', a variant that subsequently did not undergo significant changes. Thus Hitler knew that there would be no attack on Kovel', at least at the early stage of the Soviet offensive against Army Group Centre. However, the panzer divisions were nonetheless left with Army Group North Ukraine. It's possible that Hitler decided to sacrifice the infantry divisions of Busch's Army Group in the hope that they would manage to delay the Russians' advance and inflict maximum losses on them. Then, with the aid of the panzer divisions from Model's Army Group that were not subjected to the first destructive attacks, the *Führer* probably was preparing to recreate the front west of its previous position, but he did not know exactly where.

All of the partisan detachments and underground organizations received a radiogram from the chief of the partisan movement's staff, P.Z. Kalinin: 'Prepare to begin a partisan rail war on the night of 19/20 June'. Each detachment was assigned tasks: which railway sector was to be put out of action and how many rails were to be destroyed.[17] However, the partisan attacks proved less effective than had been expected. From the middle of May 1944 Army Group Centre's rear units carried out a series of anti-partisan operations and were able to defeat the partisans' main forces, inflicting heavy losses on them and pushing them back from the front line. Moreover, the Germans intercepted the order for the start of the 'rail war' and were able to defuse a significant number of the partisans' mines. Nonetheless, movement was paralyzed along certain sectors for several hours, and up to a day along several others.[18]

The German Third Panzer Army was attacked on 22 June, the Fourth Army on 23 June, and the Ninth Army on 24 June. The plan was to pull the German reserves to the area of the first attack and thus make the breakthrough easier along the Fourth and Ninth Armies' fronts. But it appears that the Soviet command overestimated Army Group Centre's reserves. In any event, its single serious reserve – the 20th Panzer Division – remained in the Bobruisk area. Busch evidently did not doubt that there would be no less powerful attacks along the Fourth and Ninth Armies' fronts and did not move von Kessel's panzer troops to the north. Had the Soviet offensive begun simultaneously along the three German armies' front, then the Soviet command would have won an extra 1–2 days for developing the offensive on Bobruisk, Mogilev and Minsk. According to German estimates, the attacking Soviet units outnumbered the defenders by 10:1.[19]

Reinhardt, the commander of the Third Panzer Army, considered the Vitebsk salient a trap and wanted to pull his forces out of there as soon as possible, but Hitler demanded that the 'fortress' be defended to the last. As Reinhardt foresaw, the Soviet forces carried out a two-pronged envelopment of Vitebsk. The front was broken through in as little as two days. As early as 22 June Reinhardt had received permission to pull back his units defending along the army's left flank. But only Hitler could authorize a withdrawal from Vitebsk, and not Busch. On 24 June there still existed a corridor along which the LIII Corps could have retreated from Vitebsk. On that morning the chief of the OKH General Staff, Colonel General Kurt Zeitzler, arrived at the headquarters of Army Group Centre. Busch explained to him that it was impossible to hold the front and insistently demanded that Vitebsk be abandoned and that they fall back to the 'Tiger Line'. Zeitzler flew directly from Minsk to Hitler at Berchtesgaden. Zeitzler called Reinhardt at 1520 Berlin time. The latter insisted that the last moment had come to carry out a successful breakout from Vitebsk. But Hitler did not give his permission. Within several minutes, following the conversation with Zeitzler, Reinhardt received a radio report that the Soviet forces had cut the last passable road and had nearly closed the ring around Vitebsk. As a result, Hitler gave his permission for a breakout by all of the LIII Corps' divisions, except for the 206th Infantry Division, which was to remain and defend Vitebsk, which was clearly a hopeless task. Busch unsuccessfully sought to convince Hitler to authorize a breakout by all the divisions, but the *Führer* insisted that Vitebsk should be held to the last due to 'political considerations'. He hoped that the city could be held for 6–7 days, which was clearly an extremely optimistic forecast.[20] To be sure, not so long ago the Ternopol' garrison, which consisted of only a reinforced motorized-infantry regiment, had held out for a month against Soviet forces that outnumbered it by several times. But then the Red Army did not have such an overwhelming superiority in artillery, tanks and aircraft. The Ternopol' garrison had a significant supply of ammunition. Besides this, munitions were delivered to Ternopol' by an 'air bridge'. A powerful group of forces also attempted to relieve Ternopol', a fact which distracted a significant part of the Soviet forces from storming the city. None of these conditions was at hand in Vitebsk. The garrison had almost no munitions and the Soviet Air Force's overwhelming superiority excluded the organization of an 'air bridge'. Also, neither the defeated Third Panzer Army nor all of Army Group Centre disposed of forces to attempt a relief of Vitebsk. Thus if the 206th Infantry Division had remained in Vitebsk, it could hardly have held out more than a day. But on 25 June Hitler confirmed that the 206th Division must hold on in Vitebsk until it could be freed by a relief attack. This order caused indignation in Army Group Centre's headquarters, where they fully understood that Hitler was openly lying about the possible relief of Vitebsk. General of Infantry Friedrich Gollwitzer, the commander of the LIII Corps, considered that he was no longer bound by Hitler's order and ordered all his divisions, including the 206th, to try and break out, and communicated this to Army Group headquarters. Several attempts were made on 25 and 26 June to break out of Vitebsk. The encirclement ring had grown tighter. If authorization for a withdrawal from Vitebsk had been issued as late as 23 June, a breakout might have been more successful. Early in the morning of 27 June the remnants of the LIII Corps undertook a last attempt at a breakout with the desperation of the doomed. They sent their final radiogram at 0345 on the morning of 27 June from a location 13km to the south-west of Vitebsk. It read: 'A night breakout with the personal participation of the corps commander has begun successfully.' But, according to Soviet data, of the LIII Corps' 28,000 personnel, 10,000 were captured and nearly all the rest perished in the forests and swamps. Only a very few elements were able to make it to German lines, which on 27 June were already 80km from Vitebsk.[21] According to Gollwitzer's memoirs, only 5,000 men perished from his corps, while 22,000 were captured.[22]

The Soviet forces attacked through the nearly 100km breach in the centre of the German Third Panzer Army's front, meeting almost no resistance. The VI Army Corps was pushed back so far to the south that it was incorporated into the Fourth Army. Only the IX Army Corps along the left flank, consisting of two divisions, which were joined by various rear and security units, as well as the remnants of some combat units, remained under the command of the Third Panzer Army's headquarters. Only 70 guns remained with the Third Panzer Army. Because of Hitler's order, the 252nd Infantry Division was unable to fall back behind the Ulla River in time. The retreat turned into an unorganized rout, during which many soldiers had to swim across the river. Reinhardt wrote in his final report that 'Almost all of the orders which the army's headquarters received in those days had to be marked as "too late".' This was caused not only by the Soviet forces' headlong offensive, but also by the fact that each withdrawal order had to be coordinated not only with the Army Group headquarters, but with Hitler personally. The indignant Reinhardt put in a request to be relieved, but Busch, who supported the decision by the commander of the Third Panzer Army to fall back with delaying rearguard fighting, turned it down. A gap of 10km opened up between the Third Panzer Army and Army Group North, which threatened its left flank with encirclement.[23]

On 29 June they transferred the 100th Rifle Corps (21st Guards, 28th and 200th Rifle Divisions) from the Second Baltic Front to the First Baltic Front. Even earlier, on 26 June, the transfer of the headquarters of the 14th Rifle Corps and the 378th, 239th and 311th Rifle Divisions from the Third Baltic Front to the First Baltic Front had begun. On 27 June Bagramyan's Front was reinforced with the 2nd Guards Army, which by 7 July was supposed to arrive in the Vitebsk area.[24]

It was planned to encircle and destroy the enemy's Polotsk group of forces through concentric attacks from the north-east and south-west, while simultaneously developing the offensive to the west in the direction of Usachi, Glubokoe and Kozyany. On 29 June formations of the 4th Shock and 6th Guards Armies began the offensive on Polotsk. Stalin was dissatisfied with the First Baltic Front's slow advance on Polotsk. In Bagramyan's words, the Supreme Commander-in-Chief maintained in the conversation:

> I understand the situation that has arisen in the Polotsk area. Taking into account the important operational significance of this major defensive hub for covering the Riga axis, the Hitlerite command will hang on strongly to Polotsk. Unfortunately, Yeremenko is still not ready to go over to the offensive and this has enabled the enemy to significantly reinforce the Polotsk group of forces. In spite of all this, you must adopt the most decisive measures to throw the Germans out of Polotsk as quickly as possible. Otherwise, you may miss the chance and the enemy

will be able to slow down the offensive by the Front's main forces along the Kaunas axis, which is important for us. I have given orders to reinforce the Fourth Shock Army with a rifle corps. I wish you success.[25]

Buoyed up by Stalin's words, Bagramyan threw all of his forces against Polotsk. On the night of 2/3 July units of the 4th Shock Army's 23rd Guards Rifle Corps reached the Western Dvina and seized bridgeheads. On the morning of 4 July Polotsk had been cleared of Germans, who however had managed to avoid being encircled, insofar as the 4th Shock Army's formations were late in cutting the path of retreat of the 81st, 290th and 24th Infantry Divisions, which had fallen back to the north-west without major losses. With the fall of Polotsk, the conditions had been created for a deep envelopment of Army Group North's right wing.[26]

A similarly disastrous situation had arisen along the front of General Kurt Tippelskirch's Fourth Army, particularly along its left flank near Orsha. The army's XXVII Army Corps was attacked by three Soviet armies. There also opened up a gap between the German Third Panzer and Fourth Armies. The 2nd Guards Tank Corps, Lieutenant General N.S. Oslikovskii's cavalry-mechanized group and P.A. Rotmistrov's 5th Guards Tank Army poured into the breach. The Fourth Army's right flank, along with the XII Army Corps, was also hanging in the air, because the neighbouring German Ninth Army's positions had been penetrated near Rogachev. In the centre of the Fourth Army's positions the XXXIX Panzer Corps had only four weak infantry divisions, but, nonetheless, during the Soviets' reconnaissance in force of 22 June the corps captured 181 prisoners, as opposed to the Soviets taking only 11 prisoners.[27] Before long the Second Belorussian Front broke through its positions and reached the Dnepr to the north of Mogilev. A single German battalion often had to fight against one or two Soviet divisions. In order to save themselves, they had to fall back to their rear positions as quickly as possible.

On 24 June the German XXVII Army Corps was still holding a strong position to the east of Orsha, where the 78th Assault Division, with 31 assault guns, and the 25th Panzergrenadier Division, with 45 assault guns, was fighting against overwhelmingly superior Soviet forces. But when the 78th Division was attacked by two Soviet divisions and pushed back to the north-west of Orsha, its commander, General Traut, who had been appointed commander of 'Fortress Orsha', discovered that he had no forces at all for the defence of the 'fortress' and requested permission for a withdrawal from Orsha, but on 27 June Hitler confirmed the order to defend Orsha as a fortress, which Traut was nevertheless unable to carry out.[28] His 78th Assault Division was stronger than a regular infantry division, with 5,700 bayonets versus 3,000 in regular infantry divisions, 46 light and 55 heavy guns and 31 assault guns, as well as 18 Nashorn 88mm self-propelled anti-tank guns.[29]

In a report on the operations of the German Fourth Army during Operation 'Bagration', the following was noted:

> The Fourth Army's chief of staff laid open the reasons behind the enemy's stunning successes during the first two days of fighting as early as 23.6 in a report to the Army Group headquarters, mentioning a number of factors. First of all, the active nature of the enemy's artillery, the amount of munitions spent and the length of the hurricane of fire was

THE ROUT

significantly greater than in previous battles. The enemy's coordination of artillery fire has become more manoeuvrable, and more attention was paid to suppressing the German artillery than was previously the case.[30]

Here the matter was not so much in the more effective suppression of the German artillery by the Soviet side, as the fact that in comparison with the end of 1943 and beginning of 1944 the Soviet numerical advantage had grown not only in artillery, but in men and tanks, and also in aviation. As a result, along Army Group Centre's front the Germans had to attempt to suppress with artillery and mortar fire a significantly greater number of targets than before with the same amount of artillery, which led to a much more rapid expenditure of munitions and, accordingly, to the necessity of falling back and even abandoning those guns without ammunition, if they were late in evacuating them. Besides this, due to the almost complete lack of fighters, the Luftwaffe was forced to reduce the number of bombing and strafing sorties, while the artillery had to take on part of these targets, which further reduced its capabilities. As of 26 December 1943 Army Group Centre included the 4th, 5th and 16th Panzer Divisions, as well as combat groups from the 12th and 20th Panzer Divisions, but by the start of 'Bagration' there remained only the 20th Panzer Division, which sharply limited the opportunities for launching counterblows.[31]

On the evening of 24 June Busch requested that Hitler authorize a withdrawal by the Army Group along the entire front. On the following day the field marshal, on his own authority, authorized the withdrawal of two divisions. After this, Tippelskirch made the decision to pull back the entire Fourth Army to an intermediate position in front of the Dnepr. Busch, upon learning of this, would have ordered the troops to return to their former positions, but there was no longer any one to carry out the order. Tippelskirch only ordered his troops 'to remain along those sectors of the front which have not yet been subjected to attack . . . until they are attacked and thrown back by the enemy's overwhelming forces'. In reality, this meant permission to continue the retreat along all of the sectors of the army's front. On the evening of 25 June Hitler authorized the withdrawal requested by Tippelskirch.

On 26 June Busch landed at Berchtesgaden in order to explain to Hitler just how dangerous Army Group Centre's situation was. But the latter demanded that the 'fortresses' of Mogilev and Orsha be held. However, Hitler's orders to 'firmly hold the occupied positions' no longer corresponded to the situation, because Soviet forces had crossed the Dnepr, pre-empting the retreating Germans. Along the Fourth Army's flanks Soviet tank formations had advanced far to the west. The race to the Berezina had begun. However, German forces behind the Berezina had already been surrounded by the First and Third Belorussian Fronts. Hitler nevertheless demanded that Orsha and Mogilev hold out, at least for a couple of days. But when this order reached the Fourth Army, both 'fortresses' were already in Soviet hands.[32]

It was noted in the XXXIX Panzer Corps' war diary for 25 June:

> The rout of individual formations by overwhelming enemy forces exerting powerful pressure has led to a situation in which the soldiers leave the battlefield for the rear over and over without the commander's order. The corps commander orders us to act in such cases with extreme harshness, so that everyone, down to the last man, operates with a

weapon in his hands. The crews of all the heavy weapons which are no longer operable are to be gathered up and used as infantry.[33]

The storming of Orsha began at 1820 on 26 June, following a 90-minute artillery preparation. The 84th Guards Rifle Division attacked from the west and north-west, and the 16th Guards Rifle Division from the north. The 20th Artillery Division, from the High Command Reserve, a tank and self-propelled artillery group with the 345th Heavy Self-Propelled Artillery Regiment, the 517th Independent Flamethrower Tank Regiment, the 35th Guards Tank Regiment, with Iosif Stalin tanks, a tank and self-propelled gun group with the 63rd Guards Tank Regiment, with KV tanks, and the 348th Heavy Self-Propelled Artillery Regiment supported them. By 0100 Orsha had been completely liberated. As was noted in the 11th Guards Army's war diary, 'the success of the fighting was facilitated by the fact that the enemy was defending [Orsha] with units, the majority of which had already been defeated in the preceding fighting, and which were falling back and did not have sufficient time for organizing the city's defence'. On 27 August the commander of the 25th Panzergrenadier Division, General Schurmann, shortly after coming out of the encirclement, testified that on 27 June he met with Traut, who had been appointed commandant of Orsha, and had the following conversation with him:

> General Traut reported that he had abandoned Orsha with the permission of the XXVII Army Corps command. The reasons were as follows: according to the *Führer*'s well-known instructions for the commandants of fortresses, he, in his capacity as commandant, 'must have sufficient time' so as to distribute his troops along their defensive positions. But he had no time and there was no opportunity of occupying defensive positions, insofar as the enemy had entered the city from the north and north-west before the 78th Division's units. Bitter street fighting broke out and General Traut finally requested permission to abandon Orsha, and it was granted by the XXVII Army Corps command.

In a report written by a staff officer from the 78th Division who had gotten out of the encirclement, it was stated: 'On 26.6 the division's combat group was located in Orsha, while the supply trains were already west of the city. On 26.6 the enemy launched an enveloping attack against Orsha from the north and south. Lieutenant General Traut's combat group, which was located in Orsha, defended the city until it received orders to retreat.'

Major General A.S. Burdeinyi's 2nd Guards Tank Corps seized the important road junction of Starosel'ye, cutting off the XXVII Army Corps' withdrawal route. The Germans unsuccessfully sought to break out through Starosel'ye. In captivity, Traut testified:

> The agreement between the division commander and the commander of the 25th Panzergrenadier Division, which was moving ahead, to leave behind all unnecessary transport (vehicles) and to take only what was necessary, did not yield the desired result. The slowed-down crossing of too large a vehicle park most irresponsibly delayed the crossing by

THE ROUT

combat-effective units not only here, but at other crossings. Despite this, no one was able to take up the matter of freeing the units from their unnecessary ballast with sufficient energy.[34]

As we shall see, in Bobruisk General Hoffmeister did undertake such a radical step.

In the German Fourth Army's war diary for 26 June, they wrote: 'The Chief Quartermaster has been informed that supply of the XXVII and VI Army Corps, as well as the 110th Infantry Division, is possible only by air'.[35]

The low offensive speed of the 11th Guards and 31st Armies along the Moscow–Minsk highway resulted in a situation in which the commitment of the 5th Guards Tank Army was delayed and was carried out along the 5th Army's sector.

On 24 June the German Ninth Army's positions in the Bobruisk area were subjected to an intensive artillery bombardment and attacks by ground-attack aviation. Twenty-seven Soviet rifle battalions and 15 engineer companies fought against three German infantry battalions along the XXXV Army Corps' 5km front. The breakthrough of the front was inevitable. On the first day two Soviet armies carried out a breakthrough 30km in breadth and 10km in depth along the XLI Panzer Corps' front in the Parichi area. In the evening, with the commitment of the 1st Guards Tank Corps, the depth of the breakthrough increased to 20km. On 25 June the cavalry-mechanized group entered the breach. The 707th Infantry Division, which was also known as the 707th Security Division, numbered only about 4,300 men at the start of the Soviet offensive; that is, it was not larger than a Soviet rifle brigade. During the period from 2–13 June 1944 the division's units, which included the 747th Grenadier Regiment, took part in Operation '*Pfingstrose*' against Soviet partisans. This operation was described as follows in the Ninth Army's combat journal: 'Unfortunately, the last major operation ('*Pfingstrose*') against bands in the area between the inhabited locales of Mar'ina Gorka, Osipovichi, Starye Dorogi, Shatsk, and Slutsk, did not achieve the expected success: the bands' losses did not correspond to the employment of our own forces'.

Following the conclusion of '*Pfingstrose*', the 707th Division was stationed in the Bobruisk area. On 17–18 June the division's headquarters, the 747th Grenadier Regiment, the 707th Signals Battalion and the 707th Anti-Tank Company arrived in the Ugly–Stasevka area 20km to the south of Bobruisk, and the 727th Grenadier Regiment concentrated in the Khomichi area, 33km north-east of Bobruisk. The division's artillery battalion was attached to the XXXV Army Corps to cover the Bobruisk–Starushki rail line. Insofar as the Fourth Army's 57th Infantry Division had pulled back three battalions from the front along the boundary with the Ninth Army, on 18 June the 727th Grenadier Regiment received orders to move north, to the Osovniki–Lake Krushinovka area. Due to the start of the Soviet offensive, on the evening of 23 June the 747th Grenadier Regiment received orders to move to the Knyshevichi area, behind the 53rd Infantry Division's rear positions.

On the night of 24 June Soviet aviation launched an attack against the 707th Division's artillery and positions. Then, following a 45-minute artillery preparation, six Soviet divisions, along with 150 tanks, attacked the 134th Infantry Division's positions. At the same time, two of the 5th Rifle Division's regiments launched an attack in the Fourth Army's sector, against the 1st and 2nd companies of the 57th Infantry Division's 164th Grenadier Regiment and broke through the front between the villages of Lozki and Rekta and capturing light howitzers from the 157th Artillery Regiment's 8th and 9th Batteries.

OPERATION BAGRATION: AN INCOMPLETE TRUTH

In the Ozerany area the 250th Rifle Division attacked in several places and broke through the defence of the 446th Grenadier Regiment's 1st Battalion. The Germans held the northern part of Ozerany, but the 446th Grenadier Regiment was cut off from the 134th Infantry Division's main forces. On the morning of 24 June units of the Soviet 323rd Rifle Division attacked Height 148.0 and broke through the defence of the 439th Grenadier Regiment's 1st Battalion. The commander of the 134th Division, Lieutenant General Ernst Phillip, committed a fusilier battalion and the 1134th Assault Gun Company into the fighting, but the counter-attack was beaten back thanks to the commitment on the Soviet side of the 223rd Independent Tank Regiment and the 1812th Self-Propelled Artillery Regiment. At the same time, the 348th Rifle Division, supported by the 40th Tank Regiment (21 T-34s with mine rollers), the 36th Tank Regiment (KV tanks, self-propelled guns, and SU-152s), as well as the 8th Self-Propelled Artillery Brigade's 2nd Battalion (21 SU-76s), attacked the positions of the 439th Grenadier Regiment's 2nd Battalion from the area of Bol'shaya Konoplitsa. Thirty Soviet tanks were destroyed before lunch, according to German estimates. After lunch the Soviets committed into the fighting the 63rd Tank Battalion and a battalion of automatic riflemen from the 108th Tank Brigade (21 T-34s), which attacked south of Height 147.1. In the evening the 40th Tank Regiment reported the loss of 13 tanks, while the 108th Tank Brigade lost 14 T-34s burned and four T-34s knocked out, and the 36th Tank Regiment lost three KV tanks and one SU-152, while the 8th Self-Propelled Artillery Brigade reported the loss of several SU-76s. The majority of the knocked-out vehicles remained in the depth of the German positions.

As a rule, in those places where the Soviet tanks and self-propelled guns ran into German armoured units they suffered heavy losses and were not able to fully break through the enemy defence. Corporal Franz Waldner, a gunner with the 665th Anti-Tank Battalion's 2nd Battery, was credited with 17 destroyed Soviet tanks, and Lieutenant Daum, from the 244th Assault Gun Brigade, claimed to have destroyed nine Soviet tanks. The 244th Brigade's irreparable losses totalled four assault guns. The companies in the 439th Grenadier Regiment's 2nd Battalion numbered 50 men each. At 0330 units of the 108th and 120th Guards Rifle Divisions, supported by the 510th Flamethrower Tank Regiment (21 T-34 flamethrower tanks), the 340th Guards Heavy Self-Propelled Artillery Regiment (21 SU-152s) and the 8th Self-Propelled Artillery Brigade's 1st Battalion (21 SU-76s) attacked the positions of the 445th Grenadier Regiment's 1st Battalion in the area of the Tikhnichi State Farm and the village of Velichev, but captured only part of the first trench. At the same time, the 510th Tank Regiment lost one T-34 irreparably; the 340th Guards Heavy Self-Propelled Artillery Regiment lost one SU-152, while the losses of the 8th Self-Propelled Artillery Brigade's 1st Battalion are unknown. Units of the 108th Guards Rifle Division broke through the enemy's positions along the southern flank of the 439th Grenadier Regiment's 2nd Battalion, but the companies of the 130th Grenadier Regiment's 1st Battalion managed to localize the breakthrough.

As early as around 0500 the 707th Division's 727th Grenadier Regiment received orders to carry out a counter-attack along the 446th Regiment's sector. Soviet units had cut off the 446th Regiment west of Ozerany, but a messenger on a motorcycle was able to get through to a company of the 727th Regiment's 3rd Battalion near Lake Krushinovka. The battalion counter-attacked to the south and lost two men killed and

THE ROUT

one wounded from air attacks, but at about 1100 its offensive was beaten back by a counter-attack by major Soviet forces. The Germans lost 35 men killed and wounded. They managed to halt the Soviet troops in the area of the village of Bol'shaya Lyada. It was here that the headquarters and 9th Company linked up with the battalion's main forces at around 1900.

At 0905 the 134th Infantry Division's chief of staff, Lieutenant Colonel Degen, issued an order to the 727th Regiment (minus the 3rd Battalion) to carry out a counter-attack north of Lake Krushinovka in the direction of the village of Lozka and the Drut' River. At around 1400 the regiment's forward detachments reached the corduroyed road, where they got into a fight with Soviet units, which had managed by 1900 to occupy positions in a glade 1,800m east of height 155.1. The 57th Division's shock group, which consisted of the remnants of the 164th Regiment's 1st Battalion, four companies from the 157th Reserve Battalion and two engineer companies from the 157th Regiment, reinforced by six assault guns from the 157th Engineer Battalion, captured the village of Lipki. They recaptured the howitzers from the 1157th Artillery Regiment's 8th and 9th batteries, which had been lost on the morning of 24 June.

The counter-attack by Colonel Demme's panzer group, which consisted of the headquarters and 2nd Battalion of the 59th Panzergrenadier Regiment and part of the 21st Panzer Battalion's panzer company, halted the Soviet forces' advance to the north-west in the Staiki–Seliba (Felikspol'ye) area.

During the day of 24 June the commander of the 707th Division (Major General Gustav Gihr, received orders from Ninth Army headquarters to concentrate the division in the Starosel'ye–Kirov area in order to straddle the Bobruisk–Mogilev road. The 747th Regiment, which had just arrived at Knyshevichi, 50km south of Bobruisk, had to be quickly transferred by motor transport to the area north of Cherebomirka, 45km north-east of Bobruisk. The regrouping had to be carried out mostly at night, due to the activity of Soviet aviation. On the morning of 25 June the 747th Regiment relieved Colonel Demme's panzer group south of Buda. During the counter-attack the regiment was able to take back Felikspol'ye, but in the evening, due to the critical situation along the 134th Division's sector, they had to halt the attack. The division's 727th Regiment attacked with varying success, but at 1100 was forced to halt, when Soviet units, supported by tanks, broke through the 446th Regiment's defence and got as far as Lake Krushinovka. During the counter-attacks the 727th Regiment lost no less than 13 men killed and 32 wounded, having killed 28 and captured two soldiers from the 186th Rifle Division. By 1600 the 727th Regiment had to fall back and take up defensive positions 2km west of height 155.1. On the night of 25/26 June the regiment, with the exception of the 3rd Battalion, with which it had no communications, occupied positions in the Zabudnyanka farms–Novoe Zalitvin'ye area, on orders from the headquarters of the 707th Division. The 3rd Battalion of the 727th Regiment included the 134th Division's 439th Grenadier Regiment. It was supported by the 1st Company of the 20th Panzer Division's 21st Panzer Battalion. By 1200 on 25 June the 439th Regiment's defence had been penetrated by the 223rd Rifle Division's infantry, supported by the 223rd Independent Tank Regiment and the 9th Tank Corps' 95th and 108th Tank Brigades. Part of the 446th Regiment's 1st Battalion had been encircled in the ruins of the village of Ozerany. The 727th Regiment's 3rd Battalion repelled an attack by the 323rd Rifle Division. The German armoured units that were supporting it reported destroying 25–28 Soviet tanks and self-propelled guns. The 108th Tank Brigade reported on that day to have lost 13 tanks destroyed and eight damaged.

OPERATION BAGRATION: AN INCOMPLETE TRUTH

At 1500 Soviet troops broke into the rear positions of the 727th Regiment's 3rd Battalion on the eastern outskirts of the village of Bol'shaya Lyada and reached the area of the battalion's headquarters. Counter-attacks by the 11th and 12th Companies and the battalion headquarters threw the enemy back to the edge of the village. But new Soviet units got around the 3rd Battalion's left flank. The battalion commander, Captain Weindel, was forced to pull it back 800m to the west in the direction of Malaya Krushinovka. Meanwhile, tanks from the 1st Company of the 21st Panzer Battalion and the 1st Battalion of the 36th Artillery Regiment from the high command reserve, and assault guns from the 224th Assault Gun Brigade were pulled back toward Bobruisk on orders from the headquarters of the XXXV Army Corps. The 3rd Battalion was forced to fall back toward Malaya Krushinovka with heavy losses, where it managed to beat back a Soviet frontal attack. On the night of 26 June the 3rd Battalion made a fighting withdrawal to a position along the western bank of the Dobritsa River in the area of the village of Dobrotin. By this time it had lost its combat effectiveness due to heavy casualties.

By the morning of 26 June the 747th Grenadier Regiment had taken up defensive positions along the 'Habicht' and 'Nessel' lines. At about 1100 a Soviet battalion, supported by tanks, attacked the 727th Regiment's rear positions from the south in the area of the Novoe Zalitvin'ye–Buda road. Simultaneously there followed a frontal attack. The Germans had to fall back to the 'Aster' line, where the 727th Regiment was supposed to occupy positions east of Beresnevka and the 747th Regiment east of the Bobruisk–Mogilev road. But they were unable to carry out the withdrawal. The 727th Regiment's transport was cut off and suffered heavy losses from aviation and tanks. Both battalions of the 747th Regiment were cut off and its headquarters column was routed by Soviet tanks. The 727th Regiment's headquarters also lost control over its units and individual groups began to fall back to the west. The 727th Regiment's 2nd Battalion was encircled and began to try and break out to the west, but was routed. On 26 June the German defence along the Bobruisk axis collapsed. The remnants of the 707th and 134th Divisions sought to gather in the area of the inhabited locales of Vyzhary, Ala and Vilenka. They were led by the commander of the 747th Regiment, Colonel Schwandtner.

On the evening of 26 June the headquarters of the 707th Division, the majority of the administrative and quartermaster sections, a motorized signals battalion, the 657th Reserve Battalion, part of an anti-tank company, the transport of the 727th Regiment's 2nd Battalion, and the transport of all the 747th Regiment's subunits gathered in the woods west of Kazulichi. General Gihr ordered them to fall back to the western bank of the Berezina. Despite the opposition of Soviet aviation, the crossing was carried out more or less successfully. But Soviet forces had already broken through to the western bank from the south. A large part of the transport was lost. On the morning of 27 June General Gustav Gihr, with part of the division's staff, rode into Bobruisk, which was before long completely surrounded. Gihr was appointed to command the 383rd Infantry Division, the former commander of which, Edmund Hoffmeister, had been appointed commander of the XLI Panzer Corps.

On the night of 28/29 June the Germans were able to break out of Bobruisk, but on 30 June they were once again surrounded in the Oktyabr'–Svisloch' area. Only a few were able to break out from here. On 7 July General Gihr was captured. Almost all of the officers of the 707th Division's headquarters perished or were captured. The headquarters was destroyed on the evening of 30 June in the Oktyabr' area. On this same day Captain Weindel perished during an attack on Soviet positions in the area of the railway north of Oktyabr'. Only one officer and 20 men from the 727th Regiment's 3rd Battalion managed to break out. Only two officers and 15 men from the 707th Medical Company managed to break out of the encirclement.

The remnants of two battalions from the 747th Regiment were able to cross to the western bank of the Susha River. But all those who remained were subsequently killed or captured. The only one to make it back to the German lines was the commander of the 5th Company, Captain Erich Brendal, who was captured twice and escaped both times and, on 14 August, having covered over 700km, safely crossed the front line to the south of Lake Vigra.

Only five officers, two clerks and 126 soldiers were able to save themselves in Schwandtner's combat group. Six light howitzers, more than 300 soldiers and more than four officers from the 657th Artillery Regiment's 1st Battalion survived. Two officers, 45 men and one anti-tank gun remained of the 707th Anti-Tank Regiment. A reserve battalion, which had been created from the 727th Grenadier Regiment's surviving personnel, numbered eight officers, 62 NCOs and 224 privates, and about 250 men from the 747th Regiment's analogous reserve battalion.[36] In all, there remained in the 707th Division no more than 1,000 men out of 4,300 at the start of Operation 'Bagration'.

On 24 June the 20th Panzer Division was dispatched to the Ninth Army's northern flank. But on the night of 25 June it was thrown into the fighting around Bobruisk. However, as early as nightfall on 25 June it had to carry out a 100km march back to the south. But by midday on 25 June it was already too late to attack. The division's 40 combat-ready tanks were a drop in the ocean in comparison with the Soviet tank armada. On 25 June the division destroyed 40 Soviet tanks. The following entry appeared in the German Ninth Army's combat journal for 25 June: 'Insofar as the Army Group did not send us reinforcements, the Ninth Army is also not in a condition to halt the breakthrough, while the 20th Panzer Division must continue its offensive. This offensive is encountering a swamp and, at least one tank corps, so it no longer has any chance of success.'

On that same day the commander of the Ninth Army, General Hans Jordan, wrote in his military diary:

> The Ninth Army's headquarters is fully aware of the disastrous consequences of all these orders. It can accept them only to that degree in which, having responsibly elaborated his opposing point of view, the field commander is obliged to carry out his superior's orders, even if they contradict his own convictions. Nonetheless, this is a bitter pill that must be swallowed, when you feel that behind the Army Group's instructions, which so completely ignore your own insistent proposals, and behind the replies issued by the field marshal and his chief of staff, there are no visible signs that the commander is manifesting any kind of purposeful will to do everything possible beside carrying out orders, the bases for which have long since been destroyed by events.

On the morning of 26 June it had become clear that the 20th Panzer Division could do nothing to the south of Bobruisk and it was ordered to pull out of the fighting and cover the south-western approaches to the city. But Soviet tanks had destroyed the bridge along the direct route and the division had to make a broad hook through the automobile bridge over the Berezina in the suburb of Titovka. Half of the division managed to cross before the tanks of the Soviet 9th Tank Corps, which had arrived from Mogilev, seized the bridge.

The First Belorussian Front's 1st Tank Corps was encircling Bobruisk from the west while advancing to the north-west, and Lieutenant General I.A. Pliev's cavalry-mechanized group had cut off the Bobruisk group of forces from Baranovichi.[37]

The 20th Panzer Division was able to destroy 213 Soviet tanks in the Bobruisk area in a few days, but this did almost nothing to reduce the Red Army's overwhelming superiority in armoured equipment. K.H. Frieser calls the dispatch of the 20th Panzer Division from one flank of the Ninth Army to the other 'senseless', insofar as

> its deployment along the northern flank took place too late, but its surprise transfer to the southern flank was an even greater mistake, because it must not arrive there too late. As a result, the division was unable to achieve anything on any sector of the front. But even an attack by the division's 40 tanks at a better time and place could not halt, of course, about 900 tanks and self-propelled guns or so which Rokossovskii had deployed along the Ninth Army's front.[38]

But here one must add the proviso that whether the 20th Panzer Division destroyed 213 Soviet tanks along the Ninth Army's northern or southern flank made no real difference, because neither could have halted the Soviet offensive. Thus one should not speak here of any serious mistake on Jordan's part, although, of course, the expenditure of fuel on a useless 200km march was a perceptible negative act. But in any event, it's doubtful that the division's 40 combat-ready tanks, given the existing amount of munitions, could have destroyed a large number of Soviet tanks and it made no difference whether it did this on the northern or southern flank, or a day earlier or later. However, it is likely that the very fact of such heavy losses in the Soviet tank formations rendered the subsequent breakout from the Bobruisk 'cauldron' easier.

The 20th Panzer Division's report stated:

> On the night of 26/27 June units of the 6th, 36th, 45th, and 383rd Divisions gathered behind the division along the Zhlobin highway. The 20th Panzer Division, with the 1st Battalion of the 112th Panzergrenadier Regiment and the 1st Battalion of the 59th Panzergrenadier Regiment, took up defences with its front facing north and north-east against Titovka and the Rogachev highway. It was planned to attack on the morning of 27.6 with all available forces and clear a path into Bobruisk along a wooden bridge. However, by the morning of 27.6 the enemy had significantly strengthened his forces near Titovka and the Rogachev highway. 25–30 enemy tanks were initially discovered occupying very favourable firing positions. Moreover, the enemy had already managed to bring up infantry. A panzer battalion was pushed forward, as well as a battalion of anti-tank troops from the 383rd Infantry Division, to crush the enemy's resistance. The panzergrenadier battalions attacked

the enemy tanks with the aid of personnel anti-tank weapons. 18–20 enemy tanks were destroyed, while, however, we suffered significant losses in men and tanks. When the impression had been created that the main mass of the enemy tanks had been destroyed or knocked out, at 1130 the 21st Panzer Battalion, supported by a battalion on armoured personnel carriers, began an attack along both sides of the highway in the direction of Titovka.

The forward units managed to reach the fork in the Bobruisk–Mogilev and Bobruisk–Rogachev roads. However, subsequent fighting against the enemy's arriving fresh forces entailed such losses that we were unable to capture the wooden bridge on the road to Bobruisk. The 383rd Infantry Division's grenadiers, who were later relieved by the panzergrenadiers of the 20th Panzer Division, were able to throw back the enemy infantry in a swamp south of Titovka and to capture the rail bridge. The shortage of ammunition, particularly for the artillery, was becoming quite evident. Besides this, after midday waves of enemy attack aircraft attacked a large gathering of equipment along both sides of the Zhlobin highway.

While the main mass of the 20th Panzer Division was engaged in fighting, the 45th Infantry Division, which was defending with its front facing the south-east, was unable to withstand the enemy's pressure. The enemy's tanks broke into the retreating infantry's ranks and transport, completely mixing them up. In this situation it was necessary to adopt a new decision. In agreement with the commander of the 36th Infantry Division, an order was issued to abandon all horse-drawn transport with the onset of darkness and to dispatch the motorized equipment of the 36th Infantry Division, and then of the 20th Panzer Division, along the railway bridge. At the same time, the panzer group, by putting all its forces into the fighting, was to clear a path to Bobruisk for itself along the wooden bridge. There was practically no artillery support for this operation, because our munitions were almost all expended. However, there was no other way out of the situation at hand.

The corresponding movements began; however, the infantry divisions' transport, which under attack by attack aircraft and the enemy, who was pressing the 45th Infantry Division from the south, got on the railway embankment and ended up blocking it completely. The path along the embankment was blocked by burning equipment. The last hope for an orderly fulfilment of the order and the preservation of the remaining motorized equipment disappeared after the 134th Infantry Division, in the east, began withdrawing. Thus any kind of flank protection disappeared and the combat formations of the 20th Panzer Division and the 36th Infantry Division, which were engaged in fighting, became disorderly. The 1A (the chief of the operational section of the division's headquarters) explained that the 134th Infantry Division's withdrawal was due to the fact that the division commander, General Philipp had shot himself. There remained only the possibility that by abandoning and destroying all the equipment the personnel could be pulled back along the railway bridge. The panzer subunits fighting around Titovka became victims of this battle, with rare exceptions, not having received support from Bobruisk. The main part of the division's elements that broke through along the railway bridge was gathered and put into order in Bobruisk, in the building of the former rear area.

A report on the activities of the 383rd Infantry Division, which took part in the breakout attempt, adds to the description of events by the 20th Panzer Division's headquarters:

> At 0400 the 532nd Grenadier Regiment was located south-east of the fork in the road in Titovka, having collided with an enemy screen. The regimental commander, Colonel Juttner, who was at the 20th Panzer Division's command post (in the woods south-east of Titovka), found out that an attack had begun against the enemy's strongpoint of Titovka. By 0600, however, the failure of this offensive was becoming known, insofar as the enemy, in force, was occupying the commanding heights which were primarily north of Titovka, from which there opened excellent opportunities for firing. For this reason, Colonel Juttner requested permission to join the attack along with his regiment. The commander of the 20th Panzer Division, Lieutenant General von Kessel, agreed. The 532nd Grenadier Regiment was to occupy the commanding heights and thus create the prerequisites for the 20th Panzer Division's attack. While the 532nd Grenadier Regiment was concentrating in its jumping-off positions, at 1000 at the command post of the 20th Panzer Division, in the presence of the commander of the XXXV Army Corps, General von Lützow, as well as the commanders of the 36th Infantry Division (Lieutenant General Conrady) and the 20th Panzer Division, orders were issued. At the same time, the commander of the 20th Panzer Division's 112th Panzer Regiment reported that the fork in the road near Titovka can be seized only if the infantry is able to destroy or drive away the enemy tanks in Titovka, which, on the other hand, can knock out our tanks without any particular difficulty. This was the basis of the attack plan, which called for the seizure of the inhabited locale of Titovka by infantry, with a subsequent panzer attack against the enemy elements occupying positions north of Titovka. While the conference was going on, it became known that the front west of Rogachev had been pulled back to Ola as the result of strong enemy pressure.
>
> At 1100 the 532nd Grenadier Regiment, supported by the 383rd Artillery Regiment's 2nd and 4th battalions, under the command of Major Klassen and Major Holtzammer, as well as light and heavy infantry weapons from the 532nd Grenadier Regiment's 13th Company, went over to the offensive. The anti-tank platoon of the 532nd Grenadier Regiment's 14th Company knocked out four T-34s hiding in the hollows in the southern part of Titovka. The 532nd Grenadier Regiment's 2nd Battalion broke through to the height 1km north of Titovka, while

destroying the enemy. The 3rd Battalion was attacking to the west and toward the centre of Titovka. 20 minutes following the start of the infantry attack, the 20th Panzer Division began an attack on Bobruisk in a long armoured column. The attack failed. The enemy, who had been constantly strengthening his forces since yesterday, brought up heavy weaponry and fired with tanks and anti-tank guns on the 20th Panzer Division's tanks from the height north-west of Titovka and Selenka, throwing them back again and again. Nor was the 532nd Grenadier Regiment in a condition to throw the enemy from his commanding positions. One may consider the attack on Titovka during the second half of the day as unsuccessful.[39]

On 27 June Hitler removed the commander of the Ninth Army, General of Infantry Hans Jordan, from his post and replaced him with General of Panzer Troops Nikolaus von Vormann. Jordan suffered, among other things, for the irrational trip along the front line which he forced the 20th Panzer Division to undertake. According to Tippelskirch, 'The insufficiently rapid employment of the 20th Panzer Division – the army's sole reserve – which, however, even being theoretically correct, could not have changed the Ninth Army's fate, led to the removal of the army commander, General Jordan, who was replaced by General von Vormann'.[40] On that same day the XXXV Army and XL Panzer Corps were almost completely surrounded in the Bobruisk area and at 0900 received permission to break out toward Osipovichi, to which there remained a narrow corridor. The 20th Panzer Division was supposed to support the breakout. But as early as 0915 there arrived Hitler's order revoking the breakout and obliging the Ninth Army's divisions to defend Bobruisk. Part of the formations fell back into the city, while others continued to prepare to break out. At about 1600 a new order arrived from Army Group headquarters authorizing a breakout to the north-west. The Ninth Army's chief of staff called what was going on a 'madhouse', insofar as the new order practically completely repeated that which had been received at 0900. But by 1600 two Soviet tank corps had already cut the corridor. At the same time, the 383rd Infantry Division was to nevertheless remain to defend Bobruisk and thus was doomed to certain death. However, insofar as several breakout attempts had failed, there remained in the Bobruisk 'cauldron' several divisions with an overall strength of 70,000 men. Breakout attempts to the north were halted by the actions of Soviet attack aviation of the 16th Air Army, which had 526 aircraft. The Ninth Army's LV Army Corps, which avoided being surrounded, was transferred to the Second Army.[41]

On 23 June the 5th Guards Tank Army numbered 294 T-34s, 22 IS-2s, 63 Shermans, 38 Valentines, 23 SU-152s, 42 SU-85s, 42 SU-76s, eight SU-57s and 3,606 combat troops (soldiers from the motorized rifle companies). In all, Rotmistrov's army numbered 23,999 men. The army was supposed to attack north of Orsha along the Moscow–Minsk highway, liberate Borisov and prevent the remnants of the enemy's Orsha group of forces from crossing the Berezina. The 5th Guards Tank Army included Major General Yevgenii Fominykh's 29th Tank Corps and Major General Ivan Vovchenko's 3rd Guards Tank Corps. Vovchenko's corps was to launch its main attack along the highway along the route Smolyany–Tolochin–Bobr–Novyi Borisov. The 29th Tank Corps was to attack to the right along the route Obol'tsy–Obchuga–Igrushki–Kostritsa–Staryi Borisov. The 3rd Guards Tank Corps included 125 T-34s,

43 Shermans, 38 Valentines, 23 SU-152s, 21 SU-85s, 20 SU-76s and 2,200 combat troops. The 29th Tank Corps included 169 T-34s, 22 IS-2s (IS-122), 10 Shermans, 38 Valentines, 23 SU-152s, 21 SU-85s, 22 SU-76s, and 1,159 combat troops. The 8th Independent Guards Motorcycle Regiment had ten Shermans, 13 MZA (small anti-aircraft artillery) armoured cars, eight SU-57s, 235 motorcycles and 247 combat troops. The German 505th Heavy Panzer Battalion, under Captain Werner von Beschwitz, with 29 Tigers (20 of which were combat ready), was stationed in the Krupki–Bobr area. The battalion began its movement from Army Group North Ukraine to Army Group Centre on 24 June. The 505th Battalion was supposed to hold the Minsk–Orsha highway open for the withdrawal of the Orsha group of forces and to hold the bridges over the Berezina near Borisov.

The offensive by Rotmistrov's army began at 1000 on 25 June. Having crushed the resistance by units of the German 256th and 299th infantry divisions, the Soviet tank troops rapidly advanced. But on 26 June they encountered fierce resistance. Fominykh's corps attacked on Tolochin and captured the village of Obol'tsy, but was halted near Obchuga by an impassable wooded and marshy sector of terrain. And then a German motorized column, which had been routed by aviation, blocked the way along the highway west of Obol'tsy. The corps' 25th and 32nd Tank Brigades had to make a detour in order to reach Obchuga.

Vovchenko's corps defeated the German 286th Security Division's rearguards and broke into the village of Smolyany, thus cutting the Orsha–Lepel' railway, and in the evening occupied the important transportation centre of Tolochin. Its main forces cut the Moscow–Minsk highway and the Orsha–Borisov road. The 3rd Guards Tank Corps' losses for the first two days of the offensive were not heavy: 70 men killed, 90 wounded and 18 tanks, two guns, ten vehicles, three armoured personnel carriers, and eight motorcycles.

On 27 June units of the 3rd Guards Tank Corps' 3rd Guards Tank Brigade and the 2nd Guards Motorized Rifle Brigade reached the Bobr River, where units of the German 286th and 299th Divisions had taken up the defensive along previously prepared positions. The Soviet tank troops were unable to force the river and lost three tanks. Companies from a motorized battalion of automatic riflemen, under Captain Leonid Yerofeevskikh, forced the Bobr under air cover. By 1630 they had broken into the western outskirts of Bobr. The Germans fell back to the woods north-west of the village and with heavy fire prevented the Soviet tanks from forcing the river. Meanwhile, Lieutenant Colonel Sergei Shpol'berg's 1st Independent Guards Motorcycle Regiment, forced the Orsha–Minsk road in the Tolochin area and moved to the south along the left bank of the Drut' River. During the offensive Rotmistrov's tank troops had taken a rich haul of captured equipment – 150 motor vehicles and 230 tons of fuel. North of the highway, units of the 29th Tank Corps captured Osinovka, but were halted along the line Lyada–Ostrovno by two Tigers, under Lieutenant Grewen. In all, according to German data, on 27 June the 505th Battalion's panzer troops destroyed 16 Soviet tanks.

By the morning of 28 June the 3rd Guards Tank Corps' tank troops had seized the villages of Krupki and Sheiki and the town of Bobr, but the crossing over the Bobr in the Krupki area had been destroyed. By the close of 28 June 115 T-34s, 33 Shermans, 35 Valentines and 63 self-propelled guns remained in line as opposed to 125 T-34s, 43 Shermans, 38 Valentines and 66 self-propelled guns before the start of the offensive. The corps' losses for 28 June were 80 killed and 100 wounded, while 20 tanks had been burned and another 11 knocked out. The 505th Battalion of Tigers claimed to have knocked out 34 Soviet tanks on 27 and 28 June. The German 638th French Infantry Regiment, to which the 505th Battalion was attached, estimated Soviet loses for 27–28 June at 40 tanks, of which 26 were due to the Tigers. The 638th Regiment's losses amounted to 41 men killed and 24 wounded. On 28 June units of the 29th Tank Corps captured the village of Igrushki and reached the line Luzha–Loshantsy. Near Igrushki Fominykh's tank troops ran into a reconnaissance detachment from the 5th Panzer Division. Its 89th Engineer and 5th Reconnaissance Battalions were the first to reach Borisov. The 5th Panzer Division numbered about 14,000 personnel and 55 Panzer IVs and 70 Panthers.

Troops from the 13th Panzergrenadier Regiment's 2nd Battalion, under Captain Ulrich Kopp, and Panthers from the 31st Panzer Regiment's 1st Battalion, under Major Hubert Feldtkeller, were the first to enter the fighting. On this day they, along with the 505th Battalion, destroyed six Soviet tanks. Meanwhile, units of Vovchenko's corps forced the Muzhanka River and captured the village of Loshnitsa. In the fighting on 29 June the corps lost 15 tanks (5 irreparably) and 91 soldiers (25 killed). The 505th Battalion claimed 21 Soviet tanks while losing three Tigers irreparably.

Matters went more successfully along the 29th Tank Corps' front. The 31st Tank Brigade's motorized rifle battalion, under Captain Kuz'ma Sokolov, forced the Berezina in the area of the Vesyolov State Farm. But the Germans blew up the bridge, thus closing the route for the tanks. The 1st Guards Motorcycle Regiment reached the Berezina in the Chernevka–Murovo area, having liberated Chernevka. A group of soldiers under Captain Vasilii Avramenko captured a bridge, cleared the approaches to it of mines, took up an all-round defence and awaited the arrival of the tanks and self-propelled guns.

On 30 June the 3rd Guards and 29th Tank Corps suffered heavy losses in fighting along the Berezina: 38 tanks were burned and another 25 knocked out. The 3rd Guards Tank Corps was pretty worn down: 22 T-34s, 19 Shermans, 16 Valentines and 57 self-propelled guns remained in line. On the night of 30 June/1 July, when construction of the bridge was completed, tanks and self-propelled guns crossed into Borisov. On 1 July Borisov was liberated by the 5th Guards Tank Army, supported by units of the 11th Army's 5th and 83rd Guards Rifle Divisions. By the morning of 2 July Rotmistrov's army had irreparably lost 143 tanks and self-propelled guns. More than 60 vehicles had been damaged. Vovchenko's corps alone lost 170 soldiers and officers killed. According to German data, during six days of fighting, from 27 June through 2 July, the 5th Panzer Division and the 505th Panzer Battalion destroyed 295 tanks and self-propelled guns. They kept the Orsha–Minsk highway open for four days, which enabled the remnants of the Orsha group of forces to fall back to the west. From 27 through 30 June the 505th Battalion lost nine Tigers, while destroying, according to its own reports, more than 70 Soviet tanks and self-propelled guns.[42]

The German 5th Panzer Division and the 505th Panzer Battalion fell back to the north-west of Minsk. From 1 through 6 July the battalion fought at Molodechno. On 7 July Soviet forces cut the battalion off, which forced the Germans to blow up 12 damaged Tigers and to retreat further to the north-west with the remaining eight vehicles. On 9 July the remnants of the panzer battalion arrived in Grodno, more than 200km from Minsk, after which it was sent to Germany to be outfitted with King Tigers.

OPERATION BAGRATION: AN INCOMPLETE TRUTH

In all, during the course of Operation 'Bagration' the 505th Battalion irreparably lost 21 Tigers, while having destroyed, according to German estimates, 128 Soviet armoured vehicles.[43] From 11 through 20 July the 5th Panzer Division lost three officers wounded and two soldiers killed, 31 soldiers wounded, and 23 missing in action. The division also fought against Lieutenant General N.S. Oslikovskii's cavalry-mechanized group, which consisted of the 3rd Guards Mechanized and 3rd Guards Cavalry Corps. The mechanized corps alone lost 40 tanks irreparably.[44] From the end of June to the end of July the 5th Panzer Division, according to its likely inflated estimates, destroyed 486 tanks, 11 self-propelled guns, 119 anti-tank guns and 100 trucks.[45]

The 507th Heavy Panzer Battalion left Army Group North Ukraine for Army Group Centre as early as 22 June, as soon as the Soviet reconnaissance in force along the front of Busch's Army Group became known, but changed its destination several times along the way because of the Soviet offensive, and detrained in Baranovichi only on 2 July, after the road to Minsk had been cut. Up to 10 July the battalion was fighting in the Baranovichi and Slonim areas. Following the Soviet forces' seizure of Vilnius and Lida, the 507th Battalion fell back by 20 July along the Narew River as far as Treszczotki. It lost irreparably ten Tigers, while another Tiger was blown up by its own crew. The battalion delayed the Soviet offensive for seven days.

On 28 June the *Stavka* issued a directive on the capture of Minsk. The Second Belorussian Front was ordered 'no later than 30.06–1.07 to force the Berezina River and, while bypassing the enemy's strongpoints along the way, to develop a vigorous offensive in the general direction of Minsk, as you have already been directed by comrade Zharov [Zhukov, B.S.]. No later than 7–8.07, in coordination with the 3rd Belorussian Front's left wing and the First Belorussian Front's right wing, capture the city of Minsk and reach the western bank of the Svisloch' River.' The Third Belorussian Front was to 'force the Berezina River from the march and, while bypassing the enemy's strongpoints along the way, to develop a vigorous offensive on Minsk and to occupy Molodechno with its right wing'. At the same time, it was noted that 'The *Stavka* is dissatisfied with the slow and indecisive actions by the 5th Guards Tank Army and attributes this to its poor handling by comrade Rotmistrov. The *Stavka* demands vigorous and decisive actions from the 5th Guards Tank Army that correspond to the situation that has arisen at the front.' The *Stavka* also ordered: 'To demand from the infantry the necessary exertion of strength so that it, insofar as possible, not fall behind the tank and cavalry formations operating ahead of it.'[46]

On 29 June the Third Belorussian Front's headquarters ordered the 5th Guards Tank Army: 'The enemy, who has been routed in the preceding fighting, is attempting to delay our advance with the remnants of worn-out formations. The situation greatly favours the vigorous actions of the mobile forces. There is the distinct possibility in the immediate future of inflicting a final defeat on the enemy and capturing the city of Minsk.' P.A. Rotmistrov was ordered to force the Berezina River no later than 30 June and to capture Minsk 'by the close of 2.7.44'.[47]

The *Stavka*'s plans for liberating Minsk were more than fulfilled by five days, while Rotmistrov was late by one day versus the deadline set for him by Chernyakhovskii, because Soviet forces entered Minsk, which had been abandoned by the Germans, on 3 July.

On 29 June the Minsk operation began to capture the city and destroy the formations of the German Fourth Army that had been encircled east of it. The First

THE ROUT

Belorussian Front's right wing and the Second and Third Belorussian Fronts took part in the operation. Lieutenant General Dietrich von Saucken's combat group (5th Panzer Division, a battalion of Tiger tanks, an engineer training battalion and police companies), the 78th Assault and 286th Security Divisions, and combat groups from the 3rd Panzer Army's 95th, 14th, 299th and 260th Infantry Divisions faced Chernyakhovskii's Front. Zakharov's Front faced the German Fourth Army's main forces, while its task was to tie down the enemy until the neighbouring Fronts could cut off its avenue of retreat.

Units of five infantry (14th, 12th, 337th, 57th, and 260th) divisions and one security (286th) division from the Ninth Army held defensive positions along the Minsk axis, and the remnants of four infantry (36th, 35th, 296th, and 283rd) divisions and the 20th Panzer Division were along a sector from Grodzyanka to Zhernovka. Units of the 12th Panzer Division, which had arrived from Riga, and the remnants of the 134th, 383rd, 45th, 6th, and 707th Infantry Divisions were consolidating along the line Zhernovka–Vesyolovo. The scattered units of the 35th Infantry and 20th Panzer Divisions were along the Baranovichi axis. The 170th Infantry Division was being transferred from Army Group Centre to the Minsk area.[48]

Model was not counting on holding the line of the Berezina, but hoped to retain Minsk and the crossing at Borisov, until the Fourth Army's divisions encircled to the east could cross the Berezina and pass through Minsk. But these tasks could not be fulfilled.

The Soviet plan called for an attack by the Third Belorussian Front's left wing and part of the First Belorussian Front's right wing along converging axes on Minsk in order to complete the encirclement and then, in conjunction with the Second Belorussian Front, to destroy the German Fourth Army's main forces. A forward detachment from the 3rd Guards Mechanized Corps' 35th Guards Tank Brigade, along with elements of Lieutenant General N.I. Krylov's 5th Army from the Third Belorussian Front, captured a bridge over the Berezina in the Brody area. Units of the 3rd Guards Cavalry Corps, having repulsed counter-attacks by the enemy's 5th Panzer Division, seized a bridge in the Studenka area. The commander of the Fourth Army, General of Infantry von Tippelskirch, pulled back his headquarters to the rear, having turned over command of the encircled troops to the commander of the XII Army Corps, Lieutenant General Vincenz Müller, who before long ended up with them in Soviet captivity. Tippelskirch, according to Müller, on 1 July declared to him the following:

> The Russians are approaching Borisov. The situation along the Ninth Army's sector is unclear. In general, my place is here, but the chief of staff has convinced me that we can help the Fourth Army only by abandoning the area of direct combat operations. According to some, still unconfirmed, data from the Army Group headquarters, the 5th Panzer Division is coming to our assistance. I authorize you to issue all necessary orders for the army in case communications should be cut. The Fourth Army's immediate task is to further retreat to reach the area 50–60km south of Minsk.

'It's already clear that this is a serious defeat, although it consequences are difficult to foresee', Tippelskirch added. 'The only thing remaining is to attempt to bring out as many people as possible from the encirclement.'[49]

OPERATION BAGRATION: AN INCOMPLETE TRUTH

As early as 8 July Müller preferred to surrender. He recalled:

> On 5 July we sent our final radiogram to the rear: 'At least drop maps of the terrain from a plane, or have you already written us off?' There was no reply.
>
> The situation had become completely hopeless. On 7 July I approached the officers and soldiers with a proposal to cease the pointless resistance and to enter into negotiations with the Russians for capitulation. However, everyone insisted on making new attempts to break through the encirclement ring.
>
> Each day of further fighting cost us senseless casualties. Thus at about four o'clock on the morning of 8 July 1944, accompanied by an officer and a bugler, I left our position on horseback and headed blindly toward the Russians, orienting ourselves by their artillery fire. We ran into the headquarters security unit of a major artillery formation; I was taken immediately to one of the senior Soviet officers. I told him about the situation in the cauldron and declared that I want to issue orders to cease resistance, but no longer possessed the means to transmit this order to my subordinates. The Soviet commander expressed his readiness to assist me in this matter. I then dictated to one of the German prisoners an order to cease resistance, which was written out on the spot on a German typewriter. This order was then copied and dropped from Soviet light aircraft over German troop concentrations inside the cauldron. I decided upon this step also because, foreseeing my inevitable capture, did not want to abandon my officers and soldiers to the vicissitudes of fate.[50]

Müller subsequently cooperated with the National Committee of 'Free Germany' and occupied high-ranking posts in the East German army, but he committed suicide on 12 May 1961.

Tippelskirch recalled these events as follows:

> The fate of the Ninth and Fourth Armies was decided in the beginning of July. At that time, when at least parts of the Ninth Army's forces (altogether about 15,000 men), lacking heavy weapons and artillery, had managed to link up with a panzer division, which had been sent to meet us in the area north-east of Slutsk, and with whose weak forces the Fourth Army command hoped to cover the withdrawal of its corps to the Berezina, were retreating more under the enemy's attacks along the flanks. West of the Berezina the enemy had launched attacks to the north from the Bobruisk area and to the south through Borisov, the retention of which, following the pullout of the 5th Panzer Division, proved to be impossible. In order not to lose the last remnants of the troops and to not completely open the road to Minsk, the Fourth Army had to fall back from the Berezina.
>
> Meanwhile, the Russians continued to push their wedges deeper along the Slutsk and Molodechno axes. On 2 July the southern wedge reached the Minsk–Baranovichi railway near Stolbtsy, while the northern

one was approaching Molodechno and Smorgon'. On the following day the Russians broke through the weak screens still facing them along the roads leading to Borisov and Berezino to Minsk and broke into the city, which as a 'fortress' was well supplied with everything necessary, but which, however, due to the absence of any kind of sufficient forces, could not actually hold out any longer.[51]

I should note that Hitler did not consider Tippelskirch, who had been seriously injured in a plane crash on 18 July, a coward and did not place the blame for the Fourth Army's defeat on him and on 30 July 1944 awarded him the Oakleaves to the Knight's Cross. It follows that the *Führer* believed that the evacuation of the Fourth Army's headquarters out of the nearly-closed cauldron was sensible.

During the day on 1 July units of the 5th Guards Tank Army were completing their crossing of the Berezina. On that day these units had 307 tanks in line and 24 under repair, while before the start of the operation Rotmistrov's army numbered 417 tanks. Of the 3rd Guards Tank Corps' 21 SU-85s there remained two. At the same time there were no losses among the 23 SU-152s.[52]

The 5th Guards Tank Army claimed to have destroyed 139 tanks (including 24 Tigers), 25 self-propelled guns, 204 armoured personnel carriers, 104 guns, seven aircraft and 2,799 vehicles with freight. According to the army staff's report, another 2,070 vehicles had been captured.

The 5th Guards Tank Army's losses suffered in the fighting, primarily against the 5th Panzer Division and the 505th Panzer Battalion during the period from 23 June through 6 July, proved to be quite significant. One hundred and nine T-34s, nine Valentines, 32 Shermans, six SU-85s, two SU-76s, six SU-M-10s and eight SU-57s were irreparably lost, for a total of 150 tanks and 22 self-propelled guns. Seventy-nine T-34s, 20 Valentines, 12 Shermans, one IS-122, 12 SU-152s, 11 SU-85s, seven SU-76s, 12 SU-57s and one SU-M-10 were undergoing repairs, for a total of 112 tanks and 43 self-propelled guns. On 7 July there remained 69 T-34s, 12 Valentines, 11 Shermans, ten SU-152s, 21 SU-85s, 13 SU-76s and 14 SU-M-10s in line, for a total of 92 tanks and 58 self-propelled guns. The 2nd Guards Tank Corps suffered irreparable losses of 63 T-34s, three SU-85s and four SU-76s. Sixty-two T-34s, three SU-85s and four SU-76s had been knocked out. During the period from 23 June through 8 July the 3rd Guards Mechanized Corps suffered irreparable losses of 21 Shermans, 13 Valentines, seven SU-76s, and four SU-85s. Another 30 tanks and self-propelled guns had been knocked out. In all, during the fighting against the German 5th Panzer Division and the 505th Panzer Battalion the 5th Guards Tank Army, the 2nd Guards Tank and 3rd Guards Mechanized Corps lost irreparably 247 tanks and 40 self-propelled guns, while another 254 tanks and self-propelled guns had been damaged.[53]

Field Marshal Busch was removed from his post on 28 June. Post-war German historians, as well as German generals who, as opposed to him, had the good fortune to leave their memoirs, strongly criticize the field marshal for supposedly unthinkingly passing along Hitler's orders to 'hold fast'.[54] However, if one objectively approaches an evaluation of Busch's actions during the first week of Operation 'Bagration', then one must admit that he simply had no alternative. The field marshal understood perfectly well that a positional defence with such weak forces could not withstand a Soviet attack. A sufficiently large number of mobile formations were required for a mobile defence, but at the start of Operation 'Bagration' Busch disposed of only one such formation – the 20th Panzer Division, which according to its amount of armoured equipment was no stronger than a Soviet tank brigade. Other mobile formations were transferred to Army Group Centre only on the eve of or on the day of Busch's departure. He had time to employ for a mobile defence the 20th and 5th Panzer Divisions, which achieved some local successes, but they were not enough to halt the Soviet offensive. The irrational employment of the 20th Panzer Division was on the conscience of the commander of the Ninth Army, Jordan. The only thing Busch could order was to demand of the encircled infantry formations to hold to the last man, in order to win time for transferring the mobile reserves. In conditions in which the Soviet forces significantly outnumbered Army Group Centre in mobility, a breakthrough out of the 'cauldron' essentially meant a breakthrough into another 'cauldron', only one of larger size. The losses of the German troops would have been the same as during the defence of the 'fortresses', while the Soviet troops' losses were greater than during German breakouts from the encirclement. On the other hand, for the overwhelming majority of German troops and officers, these rationalistic considerations meant nothing. They understood only one thing well. If one remains to defend 'fortresses' to the last bullet and shell, then this meant sure death or capture. A breakout offered at least some chances of salvation. The German generals understood their subordinates' feelings and were thus inclined to authorize a breakout even when the higher headquarters forbade it. Otherwise, there existed the real danger that the soldiers and officers would cease carrying out the generals' orders.

On 28 June Field Marshal Walter Model replaced Busch as head of Army Group Centre. By the evening of this day Soviet forces operating against the Army Group had advanced 150km along a 400km front. Almost all of the Army Group's divisions had either been encircled or were under the threat of encirclement. For the time being, only the relatively weak Second Belorussian Front was making a frontal attack against the Fourth Army, but the *Stavka*'s plan called for its encirclement by the First and Third Belorussian Fronts' mobile forces. Following the encirclement of the Third Panzer Army's divisions in Vitebsk, and those of the Ninth Army in Bobruisk, the First and Third Belorussian Fronts' mobile formations turned toward Minsk. The German Fourth Army's withdrawal route from the Drut' to the Berezina could be cut in the near future, not to mention that the enemy was threatening in to occupy Minsk, 150km west of the front line. The trap had already slammed shut for the Ninth Army, although there remained a chance to break through the comparatively weak Soviet screen in the north. The Ninth Army's headquarters had quite clearly predicted all the Soviets' future encirclement manoeuvres even before the start of their offensive, while the 'Foreign Armies East' section had also predicted this. The forcing of the Berezina and the capture of Minsk were to become the second phase of Operation 'Bagration', while the seizure of the transportation hubs of Molodechno and Baranovichi the third phase. If these hubs were to be captured, then Army Group Centre's path of retreat to the west would be cut off. The Army Group's immediate withdrawal was necessary. However, on 29 June Hitler issued Order No. 8, which demanded that 'not a single inch of territory be abandoned without a fight'. According to this order, a defensive line Lake Chernovo–Berezino–Lake Lukoml'skoe as far as the Third Panzer Army's present positions should run to the east of Minsk, in the centre of the developing Minsk 'cauldron'. But by that time this line had already been overcome in several places by Soviet troops. The 5th Panzer Division from Army Group North Ukraine and the 12th Panzer Division from Army Group North were transferred to Army Group Centre.[55]

According to K. Tippelskirch,

> Of the three panzer divisions that arrived initially, two were sent to the Slutsk area with the task, in conjunction with the two infantry divisions following behind them, of clearing the enemy out of this area and holding it and, besides this, to help break out of encirclement the corps of the Ninth Army that were attempting to break out north-west of Bobruisk to the west. On 28 June the 5th Panzer Division, which had prevented the enemy's crossing over the Berezina in the Borisov area, arrived in the sector between the adjacent flanks of the Fourth and Third Panzer Armies. However, within the following days a new danger began to emerge for Army Group Centre that scattered all hopes of creating a new defence along the line Slutsk–Minsk–Polotsk. The Russians disposed of sufficient forces and space for operational manoeuvre and were able to, along with the planned encirclement and destruction of the Ninth and Fourth Armies, assign themselves broader goals. Their intention, in all likelihood, was to move from Slutsk to Baranovichi and through Lepel' on Molodechno, thus preventing the formation of a new German defence north and south of Minsk. The Army Group command's main efforts were now directed toward eliminating this new threat. The situation could be corrected only by committing into the depth of the defended area the weak reserve forces and the arriving reinforcements, which, however, meant the forced abandonment to their fate of both armies encircled in the centre, which, as it followed, would be left to fend for themselves. The Ninth Army's encircled units were breaking out too slowly. The Fourth Army command, having gathered everything possible, attempted to hold near Berezino, as well as to the north and south of the town, the crossings over the Berezina and to secure them along the flanks. As before, three of the army's corps were east of the river and were having trouble fending off the enemy energetically pressing from the front and along the flanks, and against the partisans, while overcoming the impassable swamps, which excluded any kind of freedom of movement. The endless flow of heavy artillery equipment, anti-aircraft batteries and all sorts of vehicles advanced with great effort along the heavily rutted but single road possible for retreat, which crossed the Berezina River near Berezino. In the same way the shortage of fuel prevented us from transferring so much as a single division by vehicle from Army Group North Ukraine's front.[56]

The following was entered on this day in the Ninth Army's war diary: 'The news of Field Marshal Model's arrival has been met with satisfaction and faith.'[57] Model continued to command Army Group North Ukraine, leaving his deputy Colonel General Joseph Harpe in his stead. It was thought that this would make it easier to transfer reinforcements from one Army Group to another.

OPERATION BAGRATION: AN INCOMPLETE TRUTH

At noon on 27 June the forward units of the 12th Panzer Division unloaded in the Mar'ina Gorka–Osipovichi area. The division numbered 11,600 men and 681 *Hilfswilligen* ('*Hiwis*) 'volunteer assistants', that is, Soviet citizens who served in the German in a non-combat capacity. The 29th Panzer Regiment's 2nd Battalion, with 35 Panzer IVs and nine Panzer IIIs (all with long guns) managed to arrive. At this time the 1st Battalion was in Putlos (Germany), where it was being rearmed with Panthers. There were four panzergrenadier battalions (one of them with armoured personnel carriers, and the remainder with trucks). The 2nd Panzer Artillery Regiment had 22 guns, including 12 Wespe self-propelled guns on Panzer II chassis. There was only a single company from an anti-tank battalion on hand. The remaining companies, along with a reconnaissance battalion, an anti-aircraft battalion and part of an engineer battalion, were in Germany or Courland. The division's first train, which arrived at Mar'ina Gorka, had been halted by a railway official who brought the news that the line ahead had been destroyed in order to prevent its use by the Soviets and that the unloading ramp was about to be blown up, so the division had to unload very quickly. The panzer company and two panzergrenadier companies were quickly off-loaded and sent to defend a height in the east. The 12th Panzer Division's chief of staff, Lieutenant Colonel Gerd Niepold, who had arrived at the Ninth Army's command post, was met there by the Ninth Army's chief of staff, Major General Helmut Stedke, his former tactics instructor at the General Staff course in Berlin in 1941. Stedke greeted him with the words 'Am I glad to see you! The Ninth Army no longer exists!' Niepold found out that its remnants were in a critical condition and surrounded in Bobruisk. The situation to the east of Bobruisk was chaotic. Units of two army corps were fighting on the eastern bank of the Berezina. They were connected to the city by only a narrow railway bridge. The 20th Panzer Division had lost the majority of its tanks in an attempt to win back the wooden road bridge. At first the Ninth Army had received orders from Busch to close the breach to the south of the city, and then a contradictory order to break out of the surrounded city. Hitler's later orders demanded that Bobruisk be held, but they were overruled before the first order had been received. Model's latest order read: 'New orders from the Army Group commander. The XLI Panzer and XXXV Corps are to break out to the line Osipovichi–Staryi Ostrov and there create a new defensive position. General Hamann and the 383rd Infantry Division must hold Bobruisk as a "fortress". Confirm execution.' This order to break out of the encircled city was actually the same as Busch's second order, but much irreplaceable time had been lost.

First of all, it was necessary to throw as many people as possible across the bridge to Bobruisk. Lieutenant Colonel Niepold recalled: 'Any semblance of order had ended. Transportation and guns were exploding everywhere. This was simply a disorderly column of people, moving along the railway bridge to Bobruisk. When the enemy started to rain shells and bombs down the chaos reached its apogee.' Attempts by units of the XXXV Army Corps to break out of the 'cauldron' ended in failure, and the corps commander, Lieutenant General Baron Kurt-Jurgen von Lützow, was captured and only freed in 1956.

The XLI Panzer Corps' breakout from Bobruisk, under the command of Lieutenant General Edmund Franz Hoffmeister, began at 2300 on 28 June. Three thousand five hundred seriously wounded men had to be left in the city at the mercy of the victors. The 20th Panzer Division's tank group was in the vanguard of the breakout. The rearguards

THE ROUT

abandoned the city at 0200. The tanks were able to break through the Soviet positions, but with the coming of dawn came under air attack and were then attacked by T-34s. The column broke up into a multiplicity of small groups trying to break out to the northwest. On 7 July the largest group, which was trying to break out under Hoffmeister, the commander of the 36th Infantry Division, Major General Alexander Conrady, and the commander of the 45th Infantry Division, Major General Joachim Engel, was captured by Soviet troops literally within a few kilometres from the positions of the German relief group, led by the 12th Panzer Division. Hoffmeister died in captivity in 1951 and Engel committed suicide in 1948 in the Grodno prison. Only Conrady lived to be freed in 1955.

Let's examine along with the Polish historian, Robert Wroblewski, the fate of still another German division destroyed during the course of Operation 'Bagration'. Major General Joachim Conrad Engel's 45th Infantry Division numbered 12,870 men. Its infantry units numbered 4,729 men, 2,378 of whom were in the reserve. There were 789 men along the front line, which came to 66 men per kilometre of front. There was an average of 120 men in the companies. The May reinforcement came to 394 men and the losses for May to 186 killed, wounded and missing. In May 99 Red Army soldiers were supposedly killed by the 45th Division's snipers. This figure has probably been exaggerated several times. The condition of the units' combat training was rated as excellent. The division's combat report noted: 'The units' combat spirit is very good'. The 45th Division was defending the 'Loewen' position, which ran along the swamps and a dense forest. It had two lines of trenches. Combat security posts, numbering five to ten men, were located at a distance of up to 3km in front of the main positions. They had time to build only 25 false positions with dummy guns and single wood and earthen dugouts in order to mask the artillery's firing positions.

On 17 June about 250 soldiers from the 17th Rifle Division's 1316th Rifle Regiment seized a bridgehead on Khalyun' Island. The German counter-attacks were not crowned with success. One NCO and two soldiers went missing and three soldiers were wounded in the 45th Infantry Division. On 18 June west of Khalyun' Island about 100 Red Army soldiers pushed the Germans' combat security back to the main position, but were then thrown back by a counter-attack. The Soviets were obviously striving to improve their position for a major offensive. By the evening of 19 June the Germans were able to throw the 1316th Rifle Regiment off Khalyun' Island, taking four soldiers and a lieutenant from the 17th Rifle Division prisoner. The bodies of 21 Red Army soldiers were found in the recaptured positions. During the period from 17 through 20 June the 45th Division captured four heavy and 13 light machine guns, 11 automatic rifles, 22 rifles, six light mortars, a radio transmitter, and a large quantity of ammunition in the fighting for Khalyun' Island. It was later learned that along the division's left flank units of the 96th Rifle Division had been relieved by units of the 17th Rifle Division. This also indicated a regrouping ahead of an offensive. On 20 June a company from the 1316th Rifle Regiment once again attacked Khalyun' Island, but was beaten back, losing more than 20 killed.

The Soviets carried out a reconnaissance in force along the right flank of the 45th Infantry Division and along the 'Krummau' position. On 20–22 June assault groups from the 338th and 350th Rifle Regiments unsuccessfully attacked the advanced positions of the 135th Regiment's 7th Company. A soldier from the 96th Rifle Division came over to the Germans and gave them valuable information.

OPERATION BAGRATION: AN INCOMPLETE TRUTH

The main offensive followed on 24 June. On the night of 23/24 June Soviet aviation bombed the area where the headquarters were located, and the supply routes and artillery positions in the rear of the 135th Regiment. At 0430 Soviet forces attacked the 135th Infantry Regiment's 2nd Battalion and the 45th Fusilier Battalion. According to a report by the 45th Division, the first wave of Soviet troops was dressed in German uniforms, but the Germans did not fall for this ruse. It's quite possible that this did not involve a ruse, but was the result of the Red Army's widespread use in 1943–5 of captured German clothing taken from storage depots. Sometimes the clothing was dyed and they put Soviet epaulets and other indications of rank on them. But the Germans focused first on all on the cut of the clothing and not the indications of rank, and thus they determined that the soldiers were trying to disguise themselves as Wehrmacht personnel. The 350th Rifle Regiment's 1st Battalion soon joined the attack and reached the forward trenches of the 13th Regiment's 7th and 9th companies along some sectors. The 135th Regiment's 3rd Battalion, which attacked along the 45th Fusilier Battalion's sector, and the 1316th Regiment's 3rd Battalion, reached the German positions in the area 1.5km west of the village of Gryada. But the Germans beat off the subsequent attacks and returned to their forward trenches with counter-attacks. Soviet losses amounted to 200 men killed and wounded. The 45th Infantry Division was not located along the axis of the First Belorussian Front's main attack, thus fewer Soviet troops attacked it than in the 134th Infantry Division's sector, where the Soviet 3rd Army was attacking, or of the 35th Infantry Division, where the 65th Army was attacking.

The 45th Infantry Division was forced to help its neighbours who had ended up in a much more difficult situation. The 99th Artillery Regiment's 1st Battalion, two batteries armed with six 150mm heavy field howitzers, was dispatched to the 134th Infantry Division to strengthen its defence in the Ozerany area. In exchange, the 98th Artillery Regiment's 1st Battalion of light howitzers returned from the 383rd Division to the 45th. Before the start of the main Soviet offensive on 25 June, Engel's division had 34 light 105mm howitzers and six heavy 150mm howitzers. General Hoffmeister's group, which consisted of the 45th, 383rd and 6th Infantry Divisions, had become the target of only a supporting attack, but its flanks had been deeply turned. On the night of 25 June two Red Army soldiers crossed the front line along the 45th Division's sector and informed them that an attack would be launched in the morning.

Two divisions from the Soviet 53rd Rifle Corps attacked the 45th Division's positions along the way to Khalyun' Island and west of the Long Woods and broke into the trenches in the first position. The 45th Fusilier Battalion repelled the attack on Khalyun', but lost the important height 1.5km to the west. Soviet troops, in the form of the 1314th and 1316th Rifle Regiments, suffered heavy losses. The 1316th Regiment's 3rd Battalion was unable to cut the road to Zamen' Rynya. On the other hand, on the left flank the 1314th Regiment's 2nd Battalion had crossed the swamps during the night and in the morning attacked the positions of the 45th Fusilier Battalion and the 135th Grenadier Regiment's 1st Battalion and as early as 0930 had occupied both trench lines. But they were unable to develop the success, despite the commitment into the fighting of the 3rd Battalion of the 1314th Regiment, due to the resistance of the German artillery. As a result of a counter-attack by the 135th Regiment's 1st Battalion and the 2nd Engineer Company the Soviet troops were thrown back to their

THE ROUT

initial position, leaving a lot of heavy weaponry on the battlefield. The 135th Grenadier Regiment repelled all attacks by the 96th Rifle Division.

However, the right flank of the neighbouring 36th Infantry Division was thrown back to Parichi, which threatened the rear of the 45th Division. Engel, by employing his last reserves, created a switch position along the eastern bank of the Berezina. As early as midday on 25 June, in accordance with an order by the Ninth Army's artillery command, the 98th Artillery Regiment's 1st Battalion was transferred to the XLI Panzer Corps. The 98th Artillery Regiment's 2nd Battalion was transferred to the 296th Infantry Division. Engel was left with only the 98th Artillery Regiment's 3rd Battalion, with 12 105mm light howitzers and the 99th Artillery Regiment's 3rd Battery, with six 150mm heavy field howitzers.

On the night of 25/26 June the 36th Division had to pull back its left flank to positions north of Skala, which also forced them to pull back the 45th Division's right flank to the 'Sau-Rigel' position, which stretched from the village of Bel'cho along the southern outskirts of the village of Dobrovol'shchina, south of Zamen' Rynya, and Height 133. On the evening of 25 June a general withdrawal by the German Ninth Army began. Due to the withdrawal of the left-flank 383rd Infantry Division, the 45th Division had to pull back its left flank and take up the defence along the 'Elch' position.

At around midday on 26 June the 45th Division received orders to occupy the defensive sector of the 383rd Division, which had to fall back toward Bobruisk. The 383rd Division left only the 533rd Grenadier Regiment, which consisted of the 533rd Regiment's 3rd Battalion and a composite battalion, to cover a nearly 15km sector of the 'Elch' line. The 533rd Regiment was subordinated to the 45th Division, but it was insufficient for a defence. Meanwhile, along the XLI Panzer Corps' front units of the Soviet 65th Army and the tanks of the 1st Guards Tank Corps had carried out an operational breakthrough and were headed directly toward Bobruisk. The 36th Infantry Division was pressed against the Berezina, while holding a bridgehead in Parichi. The 45th Division's right flank had been bared and it had to take up positions along the eastern bank of the Berezina. Two Soviet motor launches from the 2nd Armoured Launch Battalion's 4th Armoured Launch Detachment/1st Guards Brigade/Dnepr Military Flotilla, appeared near Bel'cho. A detachment from the 45th Division repelled the attack, damaging launch *BK-41*. Following an artillery preparation, cutters *BK-42*, *BK-43* and *BK-44* tried to seize the crossing at Parichi. *BK-44* was set on fire and *BK-43* was damaged. But *BK-42* was able to break through to the area of the bridge. *BK-43* joined it, along with three launches from the 3rd Guards Armoured Launch Detachment. At around 1400 Engel ordered the commander of an anti-tank company, Captain Enders, to dispatch a rapid-reaction detachment to the village of Gorki and for Captain Grul's 98th Reserve Battalion to take up positions along the sector Gorki–Bel'cho. The 36th Division's main forces managed to cross to the eastern bank, but part of its artillery and infantry remained along the western bank. The armoured launches *BK-14*, *BK-41*, *BK-42*, *BK-43* and *BK-44* had been seriously damaged. By 1730 on 26 June the last organized elements of the 36th Division, as well as a company of armoured personnel carriers from the 59th Panzergrenadier Regiment, which was evacuating the wounded, abandoned the bridgehead, after which the Germans blew up the bridge. In eliminating the Parichi bridgehead, the Soviet troops took 121 prisoners and four guns from the 36th Division, as well as one armoured personnel carrier from the 59th Panzergrenadier Regiment.

OPERATION BAGRATION: AN INCOMPLETE TRUTH

The units of the 36th Infantry and other divisions, which were falling back into Bobruisk, blocked the 45th Division's supply route. Nevertheless, it managed to repel all attacks (in all, the division's headquarters counted 26 Soviet attacks on 26 June).

The headquarters of the XXXV Army Corps ordered the withdrawal of the 45th Division to the 'Gorilla' positions, which lay along the line Gorki–Shchedrin'–Selishche. But on the evening of 26 June a new order sanctioned an even deeper withdrawal to the 'Bertha' ('Bruchenkopf') position, from the inhabited locale of Ugly to the Zhlobin–Bobruisk railway line in the area of the settlement of Oktyabr'. The right flank was covered all the way to Bobruisk by the swampy Berezina, whose bank was patrolled by reconnaissance detachments.

On 27 June the 96th Rifle Division, supported by the 231st Tank Regiment, broke through the 135th Grenadier Regiment's defence in the Malevo area. The German subunits fell back to the heights toward the positions of the artillery, which was able to repel an attack by 20 Soviet tanks.

At about 1200 on 27 June the commander of the XXXV Army Corps, General von Lützow, arrived at the 45th Division's command post. At that moment a radiogram arrived from Ninth Army headquarters addressed to him. He was asked whether he was preparing to break through to Bobruisk with his divisions in order to link up with the XLI Panzer Corps, in order to break out of the encirclement together, or did he intend to break out to the north to link up with the Fourth Army. Lützow chose the second option. It is possible that had he preferred the Bobruisk option, then the remnants of the XXXV Corps would have had a greater chance to break out of the encirclement by taking advantage of help from the 20th Panzer Division. But at that moment Lützow could not have known that the entire German Fourth Army would soon be encircled.

After midday the 96th Rifle Division launched an attack against the 135th Grenadier Regiment in the area of the Malevo–Telusha road. They managed to repel the attack, although the tanks from the Soviet 231st Tank Regiment, which broke through to the division's command post, had to be destroyed by *panzerfausts*, because all of the anti-tank guns had been put out of action.

At about 1500 Soviet troops attacked both flanks of Major Wolfsmaier's 533rd Regiment. The 102nd Rifle Division's 40th Rifle Regiment attacked south of the railway, supported by self-propelled guns from the 713th Self-Propelled Artillery Regiment, and south of Tazhilovichi by units of the 17th Rifle Division. The 533rd Regiment was partially surrounded. Soviet reconnaissance detachments reached the 45th Division's deep rear through the positions of the 6th Infantry Division in the area of the Zhlobin–Bobruisk railway east of Telusha. Composite detachments, taken from artillery elements, were created, including the 383rd Artillery Regiment's headquarters battery, and occupied switch positions. The division staff moved its command post to Dubrovka, which worsened communications with the division's units. Now communications were maintained only by radio or through orderlies.

Meanwhile, units of the 20th Panzer Division were attempting to punch through a corridor to Bobruisk. German columns had bunched up in the Telusha–Stupeni–Dubrovka area, awaiting the breakthrough by Kessel's division. At 1400 on 27 June they were discovered by Soviet aviation. The headquarters of the First Belorussian Front estimated the strength of these columns at 150 armoured vehicles, 1,000 guns, 6,000 automobiles, 400 tow tractors and a large number of horse-drawn transports. The scale of the amount of equipment piled up here was greatly exaggerated. It's unlikely that there was so much armoured equipment in the entire German Ninth Army, particularly as the 20th Panzer Division was already fighting and its tanks and assault guns could in no way have been in the traffic jam near Telusha. Nor were there that many artillery pieces, motor vehicles and tractors in the entire Ninth Army and only a small part of this equipment was caught up in the traffic jam. Rokossovskii ordered a bombing-strafing attack against the collection of enemy troops and transport. Beginning at 1715, 526 planes from the 16th Air Army attacked the enemy for an hour and a half. The 45th Anti-Tank Battalion's 2nd Anti-Aircraft Battery opened fire on the planes, but was quickly suppressed. Dozens of vehicles were destroyed and the horse-drawn transports suffered heavy losses. A large number of soldiers were killed and wounded, and part of the subunits was scattered.

Before the raid Lützow issued an order that all of the corps' units located along the western bank of the Berezina should try and break out to the north, to link up with the Fourth Army. However, at 1900, stunned by the bombing raid, units of the 45th Division could not withstand the Soviet attack. Its defence was penetrated. At that moment Engel understood that his soldiers would not have time to reach the Fourth Army's positions and would either be destroyed or captured by the pursuing Soviet troops. Thus at 2000, contrary to the corps commander's order, he issued orders through communications officers to the division's units to try and break through to Bobruisk, to link up with Hoffmeister's XLI Panzer Corps, but the order did not reach all elements. As Robert Wroblewski rightly notes, 'having issued this order, Engel thus saved part of the division'.[58] But part of the subunits, that did not receive the second order, was attempting, as before, to break through to the north. Other elements, which had not received any kind of orders, remained in place and were taken prisoner. Out of 12,870 men, 2,769, or 21.5 per cent, were saved. For all of Army Group Centre, if we count only destroyed divisions (not counting the 20th Panzer Division) and units subordinated to corps and armies, an average of 26.1 per cent (102,812 men) survived. So the fate of the 45th Division was by no means the happiest. If we exclude from our calculations the units subordinated to the corps and armies and security troops, where the chances of saving oneself were greater, because they were stationed farther from the front, then the average percentage of those saved comes to 24.5 per cent.[59]

By the evening of 28 June Engel had formed nine composite detachments from combat-capable soldiers: the first was the 130th Grenadier Regiment and the remnants of the 45th Fusilier Battalion, one battalion – for a total of 180 soldiers; the second was one battalion from the 133rd Grenadier Regiment, for a total of 180 soldiers; the third was a battalion from the 135th Grenadier Regiment, for a total of 180 soldiers; the fourth was a battalion from the 98th Artillery Regiment, for a total of 180 soldiers; the fifth was a company from the 81st Engineer Battalion, for a total of 80 men; the sixth was two companies from the 45th Anti-Tank Battalion, for a total of 140 soldiers; the seventh was two companies from the 65th Signals Battalion, for a total of 150 soldiers; the eighth was two medical service companies, for a total of 120 men, and; the ninth was two companies from the supply service, for a total of 120 soldiers. In all, there were 1,330 men.

The unarmed wounded and sick made up a separate march column. Those who could not walk had to be carried on carts. The breakout under General Hoffmeister's leadership was supposed to begin before midnight on 28 June, along a road west of the Berezina in a northerly direction. The 20th Panzer Division was in the lead as a panzer group, and behind it was a combat group from the 45th Infantry Division (2,500 soldiers), and then the 36th Infantry Division. The remnants of the 134th Division, which also included the remnants of the 707th, 6th and 296th Infantry Divisions were to move behind the 20th Panzer Division's right flank. The 383rd Infantry Division, along with a group headed by the commandant of Bobruisk, General Gamann, constituted the rearguard. The rearguard was to hold its positions until 0200. The panzer group began its attack at 2300 and seized the first line of Soviet trenches, and at 0130 broke through the defence of the 356th Rifle Division's 1183rd Rifle Regiment and reached Nazarovka. At 0330 the 45th Infantry Division's columns overcame the Soviet defence near Kur'yanchiki. Kessel's panzer troops reached the village of Luki, 3.2km north of which there was a bridge, in Shchatkovo, over which the Soviet 9th Tank Corps was crossing at this time. The 20th Panzer Division got into a fight with the Soviet 95th Tank Brigade.

The attack by the group breaking out of Bobruisk struck the front of Major General M.G. Makarov's 356th Rifle Division. At that moment it stood astride the road running from Bobruisk to the north. The formation was occupying defensive positions along quite a narrow front of only about 4km. The Germans' first attack was beaten back by artillery, with a total of 57 guns in the division firing over open sights (12 76mm divisional and nine 76mm regimental guns, as well as 36 45mm anti-tank guns).

At 0200 on 29 June, following a second and fiercer counter-attack, the Germans managed to penetrate into the defence of the 356th Rifle Division's 1181st and 1183rd Regiments at the cost of heavy losses. However, the attack was beaten back by massed artillery fire. As early as the morning of 29 June, at about 0800, there followed a third attempt at a breakthrough in which, according to Soviet estimates, approximately 10,000 men took part. This time the Germans managed to split the 356th Rifle Division's combat formations and immediately break through along two axes. According to Soviet data, the first group, which was smaller, broke through along the bank of the Berezina to the north. The larger group moved along the road to the village of Sychkovo. As regards the 356th Rifle Division's losses and missing in action, an explanatory note to a report on losses to the 65th Army's organizational-accounting and replenishment section noted the following:

> 1,208 men in the 356th Rifle Division. On 29 June 1944, while destroying the enemy's surrounded group of forces in the area of the city of Bobruisk, the enemy managed to penetrate the division's combat formations, as a result of which the division's rank and file was scattered. The division command took measures to gather and determine the exact fate of the missing in action, as a result of which it was determined that from 1 through 4 July 117 men were found dead, 166 wounded, while 377 men returned to their unit.

Thus the fate of 448 men missing in action was not cleared up. It is most likely that they perished, because the Germans breaking out of the 'cauldron' did not take prisoners.

In the 356th Rifle Division's report of 30 June it was pointed out that during the fighting of 28–29 June 1,785 men were killed, wounded and missing in action, according to unverified data. The commander of the 1183rd Rifle Regiment, Lieutenant Colonel Kovriga, the division artillery commander, Lieutenant Colonel Golovichev, and the chief of the operational section, Major Andreev, perished, while the commander of the 1181st Rifle Regiment, Lieutenant Colonel Danilov, and the division's communications chief, Lieutenant Colonel Ryzhikh, and others, were wounded.[60]

From 24 June through 1 July the 1st Guards Tank Corps lost 2,584 men, including 528 killed. The 9th Tank Corps lost 805 men during the same period. Losses for the entire 65th Army from 20 through 30 June 1944 were 10,369 men, including 1,544 killed and 1,269 missing. The 28th Army lost from 20 through 30 June 8,295 men, including 1,519 killed and 47 missing. From 1 through 30 June the First Belorussian Front's troops took 5,089 prisoners and the front staff estimated the enemy's losses in killed at 23,252 officers and men. 24 tanks and assault guns were captured and 104 tanks and 84 assault guns were destroyed. They were able to capture 3,877 trucks, with another 1,721 destroyed.[61] It's possible that the number of Germans killed is exaggerated. B.S. Bakharov's 9th Tank Corps lost 11 T-34s burned, 15 knocked out and one missing from 26 through 29 June, as well as two SU-76s and one SU-85 knocked out. The corps' personnel losses from 24 through 29 June were 241 killed, 563 wounded and 16 missing in action.[62]

At about 0530 on 29 June units of the 108th Tank Brigade launched an attack against the flanks of the German columns, forcing them to fall back to the woods northeast of Shchatkovo. After the Soviet tank troops left for the west, the Germans renewed their attacks and broke through near Lukov. A column from the 45th Division bypassed Shchatkovo from the south and continued its journey through Ponyushkevichi and Solomenka, where it collided with a column from the Soviet 286th Guards Mortar Battalion. At about 1800 a group from the 45th Division reached the Volchanka River and crossed to the opposite bank, where it halted and regrouped its detachments. At about 0100 on 29 June the lead panzer group threw back a Soviet combat screen in the area of the inhabited locale of Stolyary and reached the Oktyabr' (Yelizovo) worker's settlement, where the Soviet 210th Rifle Regiment was defending, supported by the 795th Artillery Regiment's 2nd Battalion and self-propelled guns. They repelled the first attack. But by 0700 groups from the 20th Panzer and 45th and 36th Divisions captured Oktyabr'. Then the 45th Division's combat groups, supported by the remnants of the 6th Infantry Division, managed to seize a railway bridge over the Berezina by a surprise attack.

In the first half of the day on 30 June a large part of Slobodka, which was being defended by the 250th Rifle Regiment, ended up in the hands of the Germans and they attempted to seize the bridge. They managed to do this with the support of assault guns. But the 250th Rifle Regiment and a battalion from the 601st Rifle Regiment, supported by the 1900th Self-Propelled Artillery Regiment, held on to Svisloch'.

By 1500 the Germans had lost the bridge over the Svisloch' and all of the bridges over the Berezina. By midday on 30 June the 45th Division's combat group had broken up into a multitude of small groups, the largest of which occupied positions in the area of the bridge before the village of Svisloch'. Engel and other generals hid in the woods to the west of Oktyabr'. During the night of 1 July the combat groups between Ustizh and Malinovka were able to force the Svisloch' across a temporary bridge and in the morning reached the positions of the German 12th Panzer Division near Barantsy.

At 2100 on 30 June the main group of the 383rd Division and groups of soldiers from other defeated divisions, mostly the 134th, 45th and 6th, began to move along the Svisloch' to Ustizh. Other groups joined them along the road. At about 0245 on

OPERATION BAGRATION: AN INCOMPLETE TRUTH

1 July the group, 3km from Ustizh, in the area of the Bekno woods, collided with the powerful defensive positions of the 8th Mechanized Brigade's 1st Battalion, which had been reinforced by several T-34s from the 23rd Tank Brigade. The Russians fired on the breakthrough column with machine guns and mortars.

The continuous attacks were beaten back each time by the Soviet units. The Germans' losses grew. They began to experience a shortage of officers, which the Soviet snipers hunted. Things came to the point where Captain Tekhaus, a doctor from the 1st Medical Company, who had been wounded in the chest, was forced to assume command over one of the combat groups.

At about 0700 on 1 July, following four hours of desperate attacks, the Germans broke through. A Soviet battalion was encircled and suffered heavy losses in killed and missing. Two tanks were destroyed by *panzerfausts* and a third was captured as a prize, after which the soldiers of the 383rd Anti-Tank Battalion put it into action.

Having broken through the Soviet positions, the commander of the 1st Medical Company, Major Dr. Herwig, with a small group of medics, gathered up the wounded and placed them on several trucks. Major Wurdach's group, with a Panzer IV, was in the rearguard and was transporting the wounded on several overloaded trucks and carts. Wurdach's group had a radio set, which was manned by Lieutenant Meyer from the 511th Army Signals Regiment.[63]

A motorized column, in which German generals were riding, ran into Soviet tanks in the Britsalovichi area. Their armoured personnel carrier was destroyed. Engel, Conrady and Hoffmeister sought to get out of the encirclement on foot. Engel did not find elements of the 12th Panzer Division and on 9 July 1944 he was captured by partisans, along with 13 other soldiers, in the Trostenets (Sloboda) area.

At about 0500 on 30 June Juttner's group reached the area of the village of Krasnoe. The detachment numbered more than 1,000 men and consisted of the headquarters of the 532nd Grenadier Regiment, the 92nd Reserve Panzer Battalion (Major Jung's 1st Battalion), Captain Golten's 2nd Battalion (the remnants of the 532nd Grenadier Regiment) and Lieutenant Newiger's 3rd Battalion (the remnants of the 531st Grenadier Regiment), and individual soldiers from other divisions. A 20mm anti-aircraft gun mounted on an Sd.Kfz.7 armoured personnel carrier and a platoon of light infantry weapons from the 531st Grenadier Regiment's 13th Company provided fire support.

The attacks on Krasnoe were unsuccessful, but Juttner was able to pull the group back to the east and hide it in a swamp. At about 2200 on 1 July it began to move in the direction of the Volchanka River, which the Germans forced by swimming. Not far from the village of Verbki Juttner's soldiers broke through a Soviet screen. By the morning of 2 July Juttner had 150 Germans and six *Hiwis*. At about 1200 in the woods south of Oktyabr', Juttner's group linked up with the group of Captain Grimsel, the commander of the 531st Grenadier Regiment's 3rd Battalion. Several other groups joined them and the strength of Juttner's group rose to 350 men. On 10 July it split up into several small groups. Grimsel, who was falling back to the west, was captured. On the morning of 10 August Colonel Juttner, after 44 days of wandering over 700km, along with Captain Golten and four other soldiers, reached the positions of the 376th Infantry Division (2nd Company/974th Grenadier Regiment) near Krypno.[64] This is how Juttner described in his diary the final day of his odyssey:

THE ROUT

At 0200 on 10.8 we approached this height in the hopes that this is our forward defensive line. From here and the projecting points to the north we are being fired on. We advance slowly. Our artillery is laying down a barrage directly behind us. The Russians are firing from mortars and anti-tank guns directly in front of us. We crawl along the small hollows in the earth. At 0300 we arrived at calling distance. Senior Corporal Senker shouts: 'Are there German soldiers here?' No one hears. We crawl further. Automatic rifle and machine gun fire with tracers passes directly over our heads. Both of us shout. Finally – 'Yes'. We shout: 'There are German soldiers here, don't shoot!' The reply: 'Keep lying down and approach one by one with your hands up, and throw down your weapons'. At 0330 we reached the forward German defensive line west of Radovo, held by the 2nd Battalion/974th Infantry Regiment/367th Infantry Division/LV Army Corps/Second Army. Our first question is: 'What has happened in the overall situation?' and did we keep track of time correctly; we were off by one day, but our watches never stopped and were a quarter of an hour late. They fed us a little bit at the company command post and then further on to the battalion command post. As soon as we got there the Russians' offensive began. We went further to the regimental command post, where we met the division commander. I reported on the return of the regiment's remnants. There was a bathhouse and a heartfelt welcome at the division command post. We were glad beyond expression. In the evening, at corps headquarters, we learn that Senior Lieutenant Runge, with two soldiers, one of whom was wounded not long before, had broken through the previous evening to the 12th Panzer Division in Knychin, while Senior Lieutenant Newiger and a soldier perished right in front of our positions. In the evening the LV Army Corps' front was broken through again, so it was actually the last moment for our return, because we had nothing to eat and were completely exhausted.[65]

In all, 1,500–1,600 soldiers and officers from the 45th Infantry Division, who were able to break out of the encirclement, gathered in Volkovysk. Several hundred wounded were sent to hospitals. The remnants of the division that retained their combat capability, consisting of 18 officers and 1,210 soldiers, with 67 motor vehicles and 200 horses, were evacuated to Dollersheim, and later to Linz.

During the following weeks small groups that emerged from the encirclement joined the division, including the 240-man group lead by Karl Kiral, an *oberfeldwebel* with the 133rd Grenadier Regiment, which was able to pass through the Soviet positions south of Minsk and link up with German troops.

The 45th Division's 130th Grenadier Regiment, which remained in the Ninth Army's reserve, took part in the fighting as part of the 134th Infantry Division on 24 June. Near Height 150.3 the 1st Battalion prevented a breakthrough by units of the 108th Rifle Division, which was attacking along the boundary between the 439th and 445th Grenadier Regiments, and part of the 2nd Battalion to the south of Verichev counter-attacked the attacking units of the 269th Rifle Division. On the morning of 25 June the 130th Regiment, together with the 58th Regiment's 3rd Battalion, attacked the Soviet bridgehead on the Dobritsa River in the Franlevo area, but only managed to narrow it. Then it had to repel an offensive by the 120th Guards Rifle Division.

On the morning of 26 June the 130th Regiment occupied defensive positions in the area of the village of Dvorets, along both sides of the Rogachev–Bobruisk road. Up until midday of 26 June the regiment was repelling massed Russian attacks; however, at around midday Soviet tanks managed to break through the defence along the regiment's left flank, as a result of which the regiment lost touch with the 58th Grenadier Regiment. At night the 130th Regiment fell back to the 'Bertha' ('Bruchenkopf') position along the western bank of the Ola River. On 27 June its remnants began to fall back to Bobruisk. The majority of the 130th Regiment's elements linked up with those breaking out to the north, toward the Fourth Army's positions. On the night of 28 June these elements were subjected to a powerful attack and were almost completely destroyed. Only those few who headed toward the railway bridge in Bobruisk were able to link up with the 45th Division's main forces and take part in the attempt to break out of the encirclement.

The 133rd Grenadier Regiment, under the command of Colonel Hans von Horn, was in the XXXV Army Corps reserve. On 25 June it also began to operate along the 134th Infantry Division's sector. It was supposed to recover the positions along the Drut' River with a counter-attack. The regiment took back Mortkovo and Falevichi, but was outflanked on both sides. It had to fall back and by the morning of 26 June occupied defensive positions along the western bank of the Dobysna River. At around midday on 27 June Soviet troops broke through the 134th Infantry Division's front and the 133th Regiment was encircled. In the twilight the regiment's remnants broke through Novo-Velichki to the Bobruisk–Mogilev road. Colonel von Horn was wounded and captured. A group of 300 soldiers reached the Berezina, where the majority of soldiers surrendered. Only a few dozen men were able to force the river. A small group of soldiers from the 133rd Regiment linked up with the retreating elements of the 134th Infantry Division and took off for Bobruisk, where it linked up with the remnants of the 45th Division.

The 1st Battalion of the 45th Division's 99th Artillery Regiment, with six 150mm howitzers, was subordinated to the 134th Division and completely destroyed north-east of Bobruisk. The 1st Battalion of the 45th Division's 98th Artillery Regiment, with six 105mm howitzers, was subordinated to the headquarters of the XLI Panzer Corps on 25 June and supported the counter-attacks by the 20th Panzer Division. On the evening of 26 June it fell back to the northern bank of the Berezina along the bridge in the Ugly–Stasevka area, but was destroyed in the fighting east of Bobruisk. The 98th Artillery Regiment's 2nd Battalion was subordinated to the 296th Infantry Division and on the night of 28 June the battalion was destroyed north of Volosovichi during an attempt to break out of the encirclement.

On 27 June a company from the 1045th Assault Gun Battalion, with ten Stug IVs, detrained at the Tal'ka railway station north-west of Osipovichi and was subordinated to the 12th Panzer Division. By 13 July, following heavy fighting against units of the Soviet 1st Guards Tank Corps, there remained only two combat-capable assault guns in the company. On 16 July the Second Army command reported to the Army Group Centre command that the company 'has not been defeated and disposes of 12 assault gun crews. In order to restore it to full combat capability, besides assault guns, it needs the following transportation equipment: four motorcycles, three light off-road automobiles, nine trucks with a capacity of three tons (not counting those received from the 20th Panzer Division), and one medium tractor'. On 28 July the company left for Mlawa.[66]

Of the German divisions that ended up in the Bobruisk 'cauldron', the most fortunate was Lieutenant General Mortimer von Kessel's 20th Panzer Division. By 14 June 1944 the division had only Major Paul Schultz's 21st Panzer Battalion. Missing were Major Hermann Felk's anti-tank battalion and Captain Wilhelm von Hanneken's reconnaissance battalion, which were in Germany, respectively in Melau (now Mlawa, in Poland) and Wildflecken for refitting. The division was missing 20 per cent of its 20mm anti-aircraft guns and among the available units and subunits they were short 429 soldiers and NCOs and 419 *Hiwis*.

On 15 June 1944 the 20th Panzer Division, according to R. Wroblewski's estimate, had 13 (six ready) Panzer III tanks, four (four ready) Panzer III flamethrower tanks, five (five ready) Panzer III artillery observation tanks, two (two ready) Panzer 38(t)s, 83 (78 ready) Panzer IVs, and two (one ready) ammunition delivery vehicles mounted on Panzer IV chassis, six (four ready) Panzer III command tanks, six Grille self-propelled guns, 11 (11 ready) Marder II tank destroyers, 17 (17 ready) Marder III tank destroyers, nine (eight ready) Hummel self-propelled guns, 12 (ten ready) Wespes, and 173 (147 ready) armoured personnel carriers of various types. Wroblewski believes that the 92nd Battalion's 3rd and 4th Anti-Tank Companies were at the division's disposal by the start of 'Bagration', although earlier he mentions that the entire anti-tank battalion was in Melau.[67] Further on in Wroblewski's book the above-named companies do not figure in any way, which enables us to assume that they remained at the firing range in Melau. To judge from everything, the Polish historian's attention was fixed on the 20th Panzer Division's authorized strength, when in practice many of its subunits were not outfitted with armoured equipment or took no part in the fighting in Belorussia. The 20th Panzer Division was concentrating in the area of the Bobruisk–Mogilev road, in territory embracing Titovka, Stupeni, Malinovka, Malye Bortniki, Zabel'ye, Khomichi, Kostrichi, Dubrovka and the eastern bank of the Berezina. By 21 June all 39 trains with combat units had arrived, as had seven of 24 trains with support services.

In the XLI Panzer Corps' sector intelligence had discovered 160 new Soviet batteries, so the Ninth Army command decided to immediately concentrate its reserves in this area. On the morning of 20 June the 92nd Panzer Artillery Regiment's 2nd Battalion headed here. It was to be located behind the 35th Infantry Division's positions.

At 0230 on 23 June a powerful artillery bombardment of the Ninth Army's positions began and in the morning there followed several Soviet attacks, which were beaten back. But this was only a reconnaissance in force. On the evening of 23 June the division received orders to immediately prepare a transport column for moving the 707th Infantry Division's 747th Grenadier Regiment to Knyshevichi. On the morning of 24 June this regiment arrived at Knyshevichi, 50km to the south of Bobruisk, where it was immediately loaded onto the 20th Panzer Division's trucks and sent north, to the area east of Cherebomirka and 45km north-east of Bobruisk.

At 0130 on 24 June Soviet aviation launched a bombing raid against the positions of the XXXV Army Corps. Following an artillery preparation, the Soviet 3rd Army began its offensive. The army's troops broke through the defence between Lozka and Rekta, advanced 10km and were threatening Cherebomirka. The latter was occupied by a reconnaissance group from the 20th Panzer Division. Busch believed that the division's main forces should be sent there, while Jordan believed that the threat to the XLI Panzer

Corps south of Bobruisk was the more serious one. At 1130 the Ninth Army's chief of staff, Major General Helmut Stedke, informed the 20th Panzer Division's chief of staff, Lieutenant Colonel Hans Shoneich, that during the second part of the day the division might be sent to the area south of Stasevka, 20km to the south of Bobruisk. But at around midday the headquarters of Army Group Centre ordered the division to carry out a counter-attack north-east of Bobruisk by Demme's panzer group, which consisted of the headquarters and 2nd Battalion of the 59th Panzergrenadier Regiment, part of the 21st Panzer Battalion and an artillery battery. The group's departure was delayed because of the poor roads and the combat groups of the other divisions began the counter-attack before its arrival. The 57th Infantry Division's combat group, which consisted of the remnants of the 164th Grenadier Regiment's 1st Battalion, four companies (minus the headquarters and the 5th Company) from the 157th Field Reserve Battalion, the 2nd and 3rd Engineer Companies from the 157th Engineer Battalion, and six assault guns from the 1157th Battalion captured the village of Lipki. The division's second combat group, which consisted of the 487th Grenadier Regiment's 1st Battalion and ten assault guns from the 1267th Battalion, occupied the village of Podsely. The 727th Grenadier Regiment attacked from the area north of Lake Krushinovka in the direction of the village of Lozka and the Drut' River. Colonel Demme threw the main forces of the 59th Panzergrenadier Regiment's 2nd Battalion against Staiki and Seliba (Felikspol'ye) and one of the battalion's companies against Nemki. Staiki was captured in the evening. By night the Germans had managed to recapture the 'Habicht' and 'Nessel' positions. At about 1430 the 20th Panzer Division received orders to move to the Bol'shaya Krushinovka area the 59th Panzergrenadier Regiment's 1st Battalion and the 21st Panzer Battalion's 1st Company. At 1600 the division's units reached Kapustino.

But in the evening the situation had become more difficult to the south of Bobruisk, where P.I. Batov's 65th Army, along with the 1st Guards Tank Corps, had broken through the defence along the boundary between the 35th and 36th Infantry Divisions. The Ninth Army's headquarters, with the permission of Field Marshal Busch, ordered the 20th Panzer Division to transfer forces to the south. The 1st Panzer Company was left to cover the Soviet breakthrough around Ozerany.

The road to the south along the eastern bank of the Berezina and the crossing in the Ugly–Stasevka area was being bombed by Soviet aviation. For this reason, elements of the 20th Panzer Division crossed to the western bank and moved to Glebovaya Rudnya and then on to Malimonovo. At 0600 General von Kessel, along with the division's staff, arrived at the headquarters of Helmut Weidling's XLI Panzer Corps in a wood 1km from Malimonovo. At the same time, units of the 15th Guards Tank Brigade passed through Protasy and were approaching Chernye Brody, while the 17th Guards Tank Brigade's tanks had captured Tumarovka and were within 2.5km of the XLI Panzer Corps' headquarters. Kessel received an order from the corps headquarters to attack Tumarovka, Kovshitsy II and Protasy with the 112th Panzergrenadier Regiment, and Knyshevichi and Slobodka with the panzer group and reach the line Romanishchi–Ugly. But units of the 747th Grenadier Regiment reached Colonel Demme's command post only at 0230 on 25 June. Relief came only at 0600 and Demme's group began a 100km march to the attack area to the south of Bobruisk. But the 69th Rifle Division's 303rd Rifle Regiment, supported by self-propelled guns, had captured Zabolot'ye, while a company of T-34s from the 251st Tank Battalion, carrying troops from the 120th Rifle

Regiment, captured Kovshitsy I. Thus the 21st Panzer Battalion's 4th Company had to defend the bridgehead near Knyshevichi.

Later Captain Rudolph Schumacher's 1st Company (59th Panzergrenadier Regiment), with tanks from the 21st Panzer Battalion's 3rd Company, arrived at Malimonovo. Aside from the attack on Tumarovka, it was supposed to clear Kovshitsy I and Zabolot'ye of Soviet forces.

The 112th Panzergrenadier Regiment's main forces, supported by the 92nd Panzer Artillery Regiment's 7th Battery, attacked Tumarovka at 1125. The first attack against the 17th Guards Tank Brigade and the 354th Guards Heavy Self-Propelled Artillery Regiment (SU-122s) and a battery from the 1296th Self-Propelled Artillery Regiment (SU-85s) proved unsuccessful. The second attack, supported by units of the 59th Panzergrenadier Regiment's 1st Company and tanks from the 21st Panzer Battalion's 3rd Company was also barren of results.

At 1130 on 25 June tanks from the 16th Guards Tank Brigade and the 44th Guards Rifle Division occupied Knyshevichi. The 118th Grenadier Regiment's 1st Battalion, part of the 1036th Assault Gun Battalion, and an anti-tank company which were defending the bridgehead, fell back to the northern bank of the Rudnyanka, to Height 145.5. At about 1345 units of the 16th Guards Tank Brigade and the 44th Guards Rifle Division crossed to the northern bank of the Rudnyanka, but were counter-attacked by the 21st Panzer Battalion's 4th Company, which burned up four T-34s without suffering any losses. By midday the main forces of Demme's group had already concentrated and had been reinforced by the 1st Battalion of the 45th Infantry Division's 98th Artillery Regiment. At about 1500 a company from the 59th Panzergrenadier Regiment's 1st Battalion and eight Panzer IV tanks from the 21st Panzer Battalion's 3rd Company captured Kovshitsy I, catching the enemy by surprise. At the crossing between Kovshitsy I and Zabolot'ye three T-34s, which were blocking the crossing, were destroyed. The 44th Guards Rifle Division, supported by tanks and self-propelled guns, captured Moiseevka, Zubrets and Maidanov. On the evening of 25 June the 303rd Rifle Regiment, reinforced by self-propelled guns from the 925th Self-Propelled Artillery Regiment (SU-76s) recaptured Kovshitsy I.

The 21st Panzer Battalion's 1st Company, under the command of Lieutenant Begeman, supported by the 224th Brigade's assault guns, repelled attacks by the Soviet 9th Tank Corps during the first half of the day in the area of Bol'shaya Lyada and reported destroying 25–28 Soviet tanks. These elements fell back to Bobruisk in the evening.

Before long, after midnight on 26 June, the 20th Panzer Division had completed its regrouping for a new attack on Tumarovka and Kovshitsy I. Now the panzer group's main forces attacked Tumarovka from the Malimonovo area shortly after midnight, while a panzergrenadier company and four tanks attacked Kovshitsy I. Three self-propelled guns from the 925th Self-Propelled Artillery Regiment were burned in Kovshitsy. At the height of the fighting air reconnaissance reported the discovery of 25 Soviet tanks from the 15th Guards Tank Brigade north of Borzha station, a mere 20km to the south of Bobruisk. Captain Buchmann's 92nd Engineer Battalion and the 92nd Artillery Regiment's 1st Battery were thrown against them, but tanks from the 15th Tank Brigade's 2nd and 3rd Tank Battalions and the 1st Guards Mechanized Brigade's 1st Battalion pre-empted the Germans and occupied Glebovaya Rudnya. At around 0430 a company from the 20th Panzer Division's security force, which was defending the crossing over the Berezina, blew up the bridge as soon as Soviet tanks appeared and fell back to the north and then, with the aid of 8–10 tanks attempted unsuccessfully to take back the crossing. Tanks from the 15th Guards Tank Brigade's 3rd Battalion moved north but fell into an ambush by the 743rd Anti-Tank Battalion's Marders which destroyed three T-34s. Another three T-34s blew up on mines.

On the morning of 26 June the 92nd Engineer Battalion and the 1st Battalion of the 92nd Artillery Regiment arrived in Prodvino and discovered that the bridge in Glebovaya Rudnya had been blown up. They set out for Bobruisk along the single available crossing near Ugly and Stasevka.

At 0900 on 26 June the 20th Panzer Division received orders to break off the attack and to immediately fall back and take up defensive positions along the southern outskirts of Bobruisk. Kessel believed that his forward units would reach Bobruisk during the second half of the day and the main forces at the beginning of night. His division reported destroying 60 Soviet tanks, including 25 in Tumarovka. The 17th Guards Tank Brigade reported the loss of ten tanks burned and 12 knocked out around Tumarovka. A battalion commander, Captain Sysoev, and another 16 officers perished. The 16th Guards Tank Brigade lost four tanks burned and five officers killed around Knyshevichi. The 251st Tank Regiment and the 925th Self-Propelled Artillery Regiment suffered the irreparable loss of three tanks and three self-propelled guns. The 1296th Self-Propelled Artillery Regiment lost one self-propelled gun irreparably, while another two self-propelled guns were damaged. There are no data for losses for the 344th and 345th Guards Heavy Self-Propelled Artillery Regiments. The 92nd Engineer Battalion, with the 92nd Artillery Regiment's 1st Battery, and the forward detachment of the division's headquarters, under Lieutenant Colonel Shoniech, and the 92nd Signals Battalion reached Bobruisk during the second part of the day on 26 June. The 21st Panzer Battalion's 1st Company and the 92nd Reserve Battalion were already there. A security company from the division's headquarters, along with several Panzer IVs from the 21st Panzer Battalion's 2nd Company, and Marder tank destroyers from the 743rd Anti-Tank Battalion, which was subordinated to the Ninth Army's headquarters, were also falling back there. The commander of the 92nd Artillery Regiment, Colonel Joachim-Heinrich Knoch, took over the command of all the division's units in Bobruisk. By the end of the day units of the 20th Panzer Division managed to repel the 15th Guards Tank Brigade's reconnaissance in force, destroying all six tanks.

At about 1700 a forward detachment from the 9th Tank Corps, which included six tanks from Captain Ivan Shevtsov's 142nd Tank Battalion, carrying a company of riflemen from the 95th Tank Brigade and seven self-propelled guns from the 1455th Self-Propelled Artillery Regiment, appeared in the Titovka area, where Captain Müller's 350th Security Battalion was defending. He destroyed one tank and one self-propelled gun and abandoned Titovka, but held on to the road bridge 2km from there.

On the evening of 26 June the 95th Tank Brigade, with the 9th Tank Corps' 1508th Self-Propelled Artillery Regiment, occupied Zelenka-1 and Zelenka-2, with its front facing west and south. The 195th Tank Battalion was located north of Zelenka-2; the 142nd Tank Battalion in Zelenka-2, with the 3rd Tank Battalion in Zelenka-1. The 95th Tank Brigade had 58 T-34s and the 1508th Self-Propelled Artillery Regiment had 20 SU-76s. The 108th Tank Brigade, along with the 8th Mechanized Brigade's 1st Battalion from the same corps, were occupying defensive positions along the southern

THE ROUT

and eastern outskirts of Titovka. The 257th Tank Battalion was along the southern outskirts of Titovka and the 3rd Tank Battalion near the creek 1.5km to the east of Titovka, while the 63rd Tank Battalion was along the eastern outskirts of Titovka. The brigade had 38 tanks (30 combat-ready). The 8th Mechanized Brigade, along with the 1455th Self-Propelled Artillery Regiment (20 SU-85s) occupied the Yasnyi Les–Dumanovshchina sector, blocking the Titovka–Startsy road. The 21st Panzer Battalion (minus its 1st Company), the 92nd Tank Artillery Regiment (minus its 1st Battery), the 59th and 112th Panzergrenadier Regiments, the 295th Anti-Aircraft Battalion, and part of the 20th Panzer Division's headquarters were cut off along the eastern bank of the Berezina.

By the morning of 26 June elements of the 36th Infantry Division had established a bridgehead around Parichi. At 0600 the Soviet 75th Guards Rifle Division, supported by the 1201st Rifle Regiment and the 261st Punishment Company, broke into Kozlovka and reached the southern outskirts of Parichi. The commander of the 36th Infantry Division, Major General Alexander Conrady, threw everything he had into a counter-attack, including a company of armoured personnel carriers from the 59th Panzergrenadier Regiment's 2nd Battalion. By 1000 the Germans had recaptured Kozlovka, thus securing their path of retreat. The last unit to cross was Captain Hans Lauer's 36th Fusilier Battalion, which was covering the crossing. At 1730 the bridge was blown up.

The 20th Panzer Division had to defeat the 9th Tank Corps and break through to Bobruisk along the bridge west of Titovka. On the night of 27 June a motorized group under Colonel Hitzeroth, consisting of the 112th Panzergrenadier Regiment's 1st Battalion and the 59th Panzergrenadier Regiment's 1st Battalion supported by some tanks from the 21st Panzer Battalion, reached the area south of Titovka. Kessel established his command post 5km to the south of Titovka. At 0600, before Demme's group was fully concentrated, there occurred the first attack on Titovka, which the Soviet forces repelled. But Demme's panzer troops then came up, as well as units of the 36th and 383rd Infantry Divisions. At about 1000 a conference, which included the commander of the XXXV Army Corps, General von Lützow and the commander of the 36th Infantry Division, General Conrady, was held at the 20th Panzer Division's headquarters. The commander of the 59th Panzergrenadier Regiment, Colonel Rudolph Demme, explained that the 118th and 532nd Grenadier Regiments must seize the crossroads in Titovka. Then the 20th Panzer Division would destroy the Soviet tanks and Titovka would be easily captured. While the conference was going on intelligence reported that the Russians had reached the area west of Rogachev and the Ola River. If the breakthrough was unsuccessful, then the German group of forces would be faced with the danger of encirclement.

The tanks attacked 20 minutes after the infantry. They managed to capture the crossroads near Titovka, but Soviet tanks and self-propelled guns continued to fire from Zelenka and from the heights north-west of Titovka. The Germans began to experience a shortage of munitions. A battery of 88mm guns, which was defending a bridge on the Bobruisk side, destroyed one Soviet tank, but this was the limit of its assistance.

At 1630 Soviet tanks and aircraft routed a column from the 134th Infantry Division. Nonetheless, at 1900 the remnants of the division attacked again and captured the Bobruisk–Rogachev road. A detachment, headed by the commander of the 134th Artillery Regiment, Colonel Otto Witte, reached the southern part of Titovka, where

Colonel Juttner's headquarters was located and he ordered them to move to the rail bridge.

On Colonel Demme's orders, the adjutant of the 59th Panzergrenadier Regiment, Captain Gerd Fricke, reached the headquarters of the 532nd Grenadier Regiment and transmitted to Juttner the order to fall back to Bobruisk along the railway bridge.

In the fighting for Titovka the 20th Panzer Division lost up to half of its armoured equipment. The Soviet 9th Tank Corps lost 32 T-34s and two self-propelled guns irreparably. On the evening of 27 June Kessel coordinated the nighttime retreat along the railway bridge with Conrady. The motorized columns of the 36th Infantry and 20th Panzer Divisions were to go first, and behind them the surviving detachments from other divisions. It was decided to abandon all horse-drawn transport. However, due to the growing chaos, there was no chance of evacuating the motorized columns. Thus it was decided to destroy the motor transport and part of the armoured equipment. Colonel Juttner's 532nd Grenadier Regiment, which had been pulled out of Titovka, covered the crossing.

At 0200 on 27 June the 1st Guards Corps' 16th Guards Tank Brigade, which had 44 combat-ready T-34s, captured the village of Pobokovichi, 6km south of the Bobruisk–Minsk rail line, from the march. At around 0300, without encountering any resistance, the brigade occupied the railway station of Miradino, where it captured a train with supplies and army stores of ammunition and fuel. At 0430 the brigade captured Sychkovo. A panzer group from the 20th Panzer Division, consisting of a panzer company and the 92nd Engineer Battalion's 3rd Company, attempted to recapture it, but fell back, having lost one tank.

At about 1600 on 27 June the 1st Guards Tank Corps set about storming Bobruisk. The 15th Guards Tank Brigade, following the occupation of Yelovniki, moved on Bobruisk. But, upon coming under fire from Lieutenant Berman's panzer company and the 244th Brigade's assault guns, supported by the 92nd Engineer Battalion and the 92nd Signals Battalion, the Soviet tanks and motorized riflemen suffered heavy losses and fell back. The 20th Panzer Division managed to hold the 'Westring II' position near the Ogorodnichi State Farm and Heights 171.4 and 170.2. The main forces of Captain Buchmann's 92nd Engineer Battalion arrived here in the evening. The 17th Guards Tank Brigade broke through the 'Westring II' defensive position around Polovets and continued the offensive along the southern edge of the airfield. In the area of the rampart in the eastern suburb of Bobruisk, Soviet tanks broke through as far as the position of a battery of 88mm anti-aircraft guns. Ten tanks were destroyed here, but the German gunners lost the majority of their guns.

At around 1600 a detachment from the 16th Guards Brigade, under the command of Captain Nikolai Izyumov, began fighting for the bridge in Shchatkovo and by 1900 had captured it at the cost of losing its commander, thus closing the encirclement around Bobruisk. During 27 June the 15th Guards Tank Brigade lost five tanks burned and five knocked out and 40 men killed and wounded, including ten officers. But it still had 40 combat-ready tanks. By 1600 the 16th Guards Tank Brigade had lost five T-34s burned and one knocked out and 110 killed and wounded, but still had 31 tanks in line. The 17th Guards Tank Brigade lost six T-34s burned and four knocked out and still retained 38 T-34s.

At 1745 on 27 June the Germans had in Bobruisk 15 tanks from the 20th Panzer Division and ten assault guns from the 244th Brigade. The evacuation to Bobruisk of units of the 20th Panzer Division and other elements of the Ninth Army along the railway bridge continued all night. During the first half of 28 June the surviving groups of other divisions tried to break into Bobruisk and were assisted by individual tanks from the 20th Panzer Division that had remained along the eastern bank. At 0400 on 28 June the 15th and 16th Guards Tank Brigades renewed the assault on Bobruisk. Units of the 20th Panzer Division repelled this attack. Several Soviet tanks broke into Bobruisk, but were cut off from their infantry and destroyed. On 28 June the 15th Guards Tank Brigade lost 12 tanks burned and nine knocked out and 80 men, including 13 officers (six killed and seven wounded). At 1800 there remained only 13 T-34s in the brigade. The brigade was able to advance only 300–400m toward the railway bridge. The 16th Guards Tank Brigade, which was attacking along the Berezina, was unable to break into the city and was limited to occupying the Ogorodnichi State Farm. The brigade lost 21 tanks and had only ten remaining in line. At 1400 the headquarters of the 1st Guards Tank Corps received orders to withdraw its units from Bobruisk and to dispatch them to Pukhovichi. By 1800 Soviet tanks had left Bobruisk. By 2000 on 29 June there remained only 17 combat-ready tanks in the 15th Guards Tank Brigade, out of 51 available before the start of the fighting for Bobruisk; 13 tanks out of 44 in the 16th Guards Tank Brigade; 36 out of 43 in the 17th Guards Tank Brigade; in the 1001st Self-Propelled Artillery Regiment ten SU-76s out of 18; and in the 1296th Self-Propelled Artillery Regiment 17 SU-85s out of 20. The 13th Motorcycle Battalion and the 422nd Signals Battalion lost no tanks and they retained nine and four T-34s, respectively. According to a report by the repair units, on 27–28 June the 16th Guards Tank Brigade lost 49 tanks destroyed and damaged and received 19 tanks following repairs. In all, during the fighting for Bobruisk, the 1st Guards Tank Corps lost 75 tanks and self-propelled guns irreparably. Subsequently, on 29–30 June the Germans trying to break out of Bobruisk destroyed a large number of tanks located in the repair subunits west of Bobruisk.

In Operational Report No. 223 of 28 June 1944, the chief of staff of the 15th Guards Tank Brigade, Lieutenant Colonel Yakushin, reported: 'the Germans, throwing away their equipment and weapons, began to surrender by the hundreds, as a result of which Senior Lieutenant Sharov's tank company alone captured 250 prisoners. However, due to the withdrawal of our infantry, the tanks' success was not consolidated and the prisoners were shot up by fire from our tanks' machine guns.' The number of prisoners shot was not indicated in this report. Part of them was probably shot and part of them ran away. One may assume that the Germans also did not take prisoners while breaking out of the encirclement.

On the night of 28 June Major Jung's 92nd Reserve Field Battalion, which was fighting separately from the 20th Panzer Division, fell back to the 'Westring I' position, which ran along the eastern edge of the camp east of Bobruisk, where the Ninth Army's command post had previously been located. At 0400 the 1st Guards Mechanized Brigade, supported by the 1001st Self-Propelled Artillery Regiment, attacked the battalion's positions and broke through them along the northern sector. The 1st Mechanized Brigade's 1st Battalion was able to break through to the northern part of the camp and the 2nd Battalion reached the western outskirts of the village of Kopitsy; the 3rd Battalion's attack was unsuccessful. The 92nd Reserve Battalion counter-attacked, supported from Kopitsy by 20mm anti-aircraft guns mounted on Sd.Kfz.10/4 armoured personnel carriers. The Soviet brigade fell back with heavy losses.

After midday on 28 June a conference attended by Generals Gamann, von Kessel, Conrady and Engel, was held in General Hoffmeister's headquarters. It was decided, in accordance with the order by the Ninth Army's headquarters, to conduct a breakout from the encirclement along the Berezina to the north-west. The offensive began at 2300. General Hoffmeister's combat group, consisting of the 20th Panzer Division, the headquarters of the XLI Panzer Corps and the remnants of the 45th, 134th, 707th, 6th, and 296th Infantry Divisions attacked along the right flank in the direction of Kur'yachiki, Nazarovka and Shchatkovo. General Conrady's combat group, consisting of the remnants of the 36th Infantry Division and composite detachments of army artillery and various rear services, reinforced by elements of the 244th Assault Gun Brigade, attacked along the left flank in the direction of the Ogorodnichi State Farm, Brusenka and Chernitsy. The rearguard was made up of the 383rd Infantry Division, reinforced by the commandant of the Bobruisk garrison.

At 0130 the 20th Panzer Division's panzer group broke through the left flank of the 356th Rifle Division's 1183rd Rifle Regiment and reached Nazarovka. The regimental commander, Colonel Kovriga, the regiment's political chief, Major Rozenshtein, and nearly the entire regimental headquarters, as well as the headquarters of the regiment's 2nd Battalion, perished. General Conrady's combat group, upon breaking through the defence along the boundary between the 1183rd and 1181st Rifle Regiments and having destroyed a battery from the 275th Anti-Tank Battalion, captured Yelovniki. Soviet reserves entered the fighting. The 129th Rifle Division, reinforced by the 1888th Self-Propelled Artillery Regiment, was defending the bridge in Shchatkovo and the approaches to it. The 457th Rifle Regiment was occupying defensive positions along the line Ponyushkevichi–Kamenitsa–Chernitsy, and the 518th Regiment along the line of the road junction 700m south of the villages of Voskhod–Yelovniki–the camp north-east of Yelovniki. The Germans' surprise attack forced the 518th Regiment to retreat to the line of the road junction 700m to the south of the villages of Voskhod, Pavly and Antonovka.

At dawn on 29 June the 20th Panzer Division's panzer group reached Luki and attacked a column from the 95th Tank Brigade, which had just crossed over. At about 0530 the 108th Tank Brigade's 63rd and 257th Battalions left Shchatkovo in the direction of Sychkovo to support this brigade. The brigade's third battalion was left to cover the bridgehead. Part of the German detachments fell back to the area south-east of Shchatkovo under the attack by Soviet tanks and a part scattered in the woods. The bridge in Shchatkovo was shot up by the Germans' 88mm anti-aircraft gun and damaged. The 45th Infantry Division's combat group broke through Soviet positions north of Luki and attacked Shchatkovo. Because Soviet units in Shchatkovo were tied down by the fighting, the main group of German forces attacking to the north-east broke through the positions of the 518th Rifle Regiment. The 457th Regiment, which was attempting to come to its assistance, was routed and fell back to the line Ponyushkevichi–the height 500m south-west of Shchatkovo. All of the German units in this area poured into the resulting gap, including a large motorized column and the headquarters of the XLI Panzer Corps. The Germans reached Verbki during the second half of the day.

Units of the 36th Infantry Division, having broken through the Brusenka–Voskhod line, reached Sychkovo as early as 0230 on 29 June. The 1st Guards Mechanized Brigade arrived there from the south, but Conrady's group, supported by several assault guns, threw the Soviet motorized infantry back and at 0400 broke into Sychkovo, having captured the road junction along the Minsk road and two T-34s as souvenirs. The

THE ROUT

group continued its movement along the road in the direction of the village of Boyary. In the Chernitsy and Kalinin Collective Farm area the vanguard of another German combat group defeated the Soviet 918th Artillery Regiment, which suffered heavy losses, while its 2nd Battalion was completely destroyed. The commander of the 356th Rifle Division, Major General Mikhail Grigor'evich Makarov, whose headquarters had broken out of an encirclement with much effort, ran as far as Osipovichi, which was 40km from its division's position. This did not interfere with him receiving thanks from the Supreme Commander-in-Chief. The division's artillery chief, Lieutenant Colonel Logachev, and the chief of the division's operational section, Major Andreev perished, and the division's signals chief Lieutenant Colonel Ryzhikh was wounded in this fighting. According to preliminary and highly understated data, on 29 June the 356th Rifle Division lost 1,785 men killed, wounded and missing. The Germans partially destroyed the 8th Mechanized Brigade's transport column. The fighting then continued with units from the 1st Guards Mechanized Brigade. The Germans allowed the 95th and 108th Tank Brigades' tanks to pass through their positions to the west and then Conrady's group occupied the village of Sychkovo, but was unable to advance further. At about 1200 on 29 June units of the 36th Infantry Division moved to the north-west, toward Verbki.

The rearguard, under the command of Colonel Juttner, held the northern part of Bobruisk until 1300, after which it moved out behind the main forces. Characteristically, on orders from Colonel Juttner, Captain Kern's battalion released 800 captured Soviet soldiers.[68] They did not shoot them, not only for humanitarian considerations, but also so as not to provoke Soviet reprisals against the numerous German prisoners taken during Operation 'Bagration'.

At 1500 on 29 June the main forces of the 20th Panzer Division and groups from the 36th Infantry Division began to gather in the Golynka area. At about 1700 German aerial reconnaissance reported: 'A German forward detachment, with six tanks and ten trucks, has been discovered between Svisloch' and Osipovichi. Infantry is bringing up the column's rear.' This was probably part of Lieutenant Begeman's group from various combat elements. Begeman fell in battle with the 9th Tank Corps' tanks in the village of Aseredok.

Major Bensin's and Colonel Juttner's regiments from the 383rd Infantry Division were surrounded in the area of Nazarovka and Kur'yanchiki. Major Otto Bensen perished, but 200 men from his regiment, headed by Captain Grimsel, were able to break out. On 30 June Major Jung's 92nd Field Reserve Battalion was completely destroyed in fighting near the village of Krasnoe. By the close of 29 June there were two tanks, 12 armoured personnel carriers and one Hummel self-propelled gun left in the 20th Panzer Division's panzer group.

At 2000 on 29 June Soviet units attacked from the south, from the direction of Krasnoe, German detachments located along the southern bank of the Volchanka. Following the retreat of Captain Scharf's covering group, the bridge over the Volchanka was blown up.

At about 2100 on 29 June Colonel Juttner's group sought to break out in the Nazarovka area. Ten half-track Sd.Kfz.7, armed with 20mm anti-aircraft guns and under the command of Lieutenant Kemper, from the 92nd Reserve Panzer Battalion, went ahead of the group. The Soviet position was penetrated. Juttner's group managed to establish radio contact with the division's headquarters, which ordered him to attempt a breakout in the direction of Vinogradovka, mistakenly believing that it had not yet been occupied by the Russians. The strength of Colonel Juttner's detachment had increased to 1,000 men by the addition of encircled soldiers hiding in the woods, although the majority of those who attached themselves to the group were without weapons. At about 2300 in the Vinogradovka area the group ran into Soviet units that immediately attacked the 532nd Grenadier Regiment's 3rd Battalion, supported by part of the 92nd Reserve Panzer Battalion. This enabled the group's main forces to bypass the Soviet positions from the south. Juttner's group then headed to Volchanka.

At about 2200 on 29 June Colonel Demme's panzer group and Lieutenant Colonel Landerer's group from the 118th Grenadier Regiment set out. Other detachments followed them, while the remnants of the 383rd Division carried out the role of rearguard. In Raksolyanka there were 400 wounded men, which had been left behind by the panzer group and the infantry divisions. They placed them on the 383rd Division's vehicles and horse carts, which began the march right before dawn on 30 June.

At about 2300 German reconnaissance ran into scouts from the Soviet 82nd Rifle Division to the south of the village of Chuch'ya, and at about 0100 a security detachment near Stolyarov, and threw it back.

The fresh Soviet 82nd Rifle Division occupied the area of Oktyabr' and Svisloch', as well as the 1900th Self-Propelled Artillery Regiment, which contained 20 SU-76 self-propelled guns.

The worker's settlement of Oktyabr' (Yelizovo) was being defended by the 210th Rifle Regiment, which had been reinforced by the 795th Artillery Regiment's 2nd Battalion, which beat off all attacks by Demme's group. Only a combat group from General Conrady's 36th Infantry Division was able to capture the settlement, and this took place only at 0700 on 30 June. The elements of some Soviet units, having thrown away their weapons, swam across the Berezina. But the 269th Rifle Division, reinforced by the 1901st Self-Propelled Artillery Regiment and part of the 95th Tank Brigade, were approaching Oktyabr' from the south and south-west. The Germans who were trying to break out from Oktyabr' had to cover 8km through the woods, bypass the village of Sloboda, and then force the Svisloch' River and reach the small town of Svisloch'. Combat groups from the 383rd Infantry Division occupied defensive positions between Chuch'ya and Oktyabr', facing west and south, while detachments from the 6th and 45th Infantry Divisions captured a railway bridge over the Berezina north of Oktyabr' in a surprise attack. At 0815 General Hoffmeister sent the following report to the Ninth Army's headquarters: 'The corps is breaking out with heavy losses . . . We urgently demand ammunition, fuel and provisions. What is the overall situation? This is important for the direction of the breakout.' At 1015 they replied from the Ninth Army headquarters: 'Indicate the place to drop supplies.' At 1156 they reported again: 'There are powerful enemy units in Osipovichi, with tanks. Forward units are attacking in the direction of Tal'ka and Lapichi. Our left flank is in Pogoreloe. There are probably only bandits in the area east and north of Pogoreloe. Attack toward Pogoreloe.'

The 210th Rifle Regiment, which was defending the area of Oktyabr' (Yelizovo), practically ceased to exist following a one-day battle. The Germans seized a large amount of weapons and ammunition and one combat-ready self-propelled gun in the 'Oktyabr'' glass factory.[69]

The Soviet 250th Rifle Regiment was defending Sloboda. It was covering the approaches to the wooden bridge over the Svisloch', beyond which lay the small town

THE ROUT

of Svisloch'. The 134th Infantry Division's combat groups had occupied a large part of Sloboda and had begun fighting for the bridge. They were supported by the 244th Brigade's assault guns and tanks from von Kessel's division. By midday the Germans had captured the crossing over the Svisloch' River. They later managed to capture a bridge over the Berezina in Svisloch'. But the town itself remained under Soviet control.

Following the capture of the bridge, Hoffmeister got in touch by radio with the headquarters of the 12th Panzer Division: 'The bridge over the Svisloch' is in our hands. There's a shortage of provisions, ammunition and fuel. Where's the breakthrough?' The headquarters of the 12th Panzer Division immediately replied: 'In the direction of Pogoreloe.'

The Soviet 82nd Rifle Division was bled white in this fighting. The division, having lost more than 50 officers killed alone, was sent to be reconstituted. At the end of July, following partial reinforcement, it took part in the storming of Czeremcha, where in a battle with the 5th SS Panzer Division *Wiking*, it also suffered losses, which this time entailed a reconstitution that lasted two months.[70] After midday on 30 June the Soviet 413th Rifle Division arrived and recaptured both bridges over the Berezina and broke into Oktyabr'. The German detachments managed to hold the bridge over the Svisloch' and the buildings along the southern outskirts of Oktyabr'. At 1355 Hoffmeister reported to the Ninth Army's headquarters: 'There was also heavy fighting today. The bridge at Svisloch' is in our hands, but the bridge over the Berezina is in enemy hands. There's a shortage of ammunition, medical dressings and provisions.' A reply at 1430 stated: 'The supply drop is west of Oktyabr'.' Hoffmeister replied: 'The group is advancing from Bobruisk without food, by a night march and with heavy fighting every day. Losses are more than 12,500 men. General Gamann perished [he actually did not die, but was captured and hanged in 1945 for war crimes, B.S.]. Many commanders and staff officers have died or gone missing.'

By 1500 the Germans had lost the bridge over the Svisloch', and then the small town of the same name, but had then completely occupied Oktyabr'. Hoffmeister reported the following to Ninth Army headquarters: 'As a result of enemy counter-attacks, the bridge over the Svisloch' has been lost. There's a repeat attack today. Supply drop in the Oktyabr' area.' The reply was Model's heartening telegram: 'The entire world is watching you. Not a single soldier can compare with you.' Hoffmeister ordered his forces to fall back to the north-west, bypassing Oktyabr'. Those on foot and the vehicles were to move by country roads on Lipen', while the motorized column with tanks and the headquarters were to move along the road in the direction of Britsalovichi. The motorized column was then supposed to turn north and cross the Svisloch' over the bridge in Lipen'. But the officers dispatched to deliver the order did not make it to all of the subunits. During the second half of the day 30 Luftwaffe aircraft dropped containers with supplies from a low altitude, thanks to which the majority of them fell among the surrounded Germans. The majority of the breakthrough's participants were south and south-west of the small town of Svisloch'. A motorized column was in Sheipichi, while the headquarters of the LXI Corps and the divisions were in the woods south of Oktyabr'.

During the second half of the day on 30 June 350 men, under the command of Lieutenant Rusch, from the 69th Artillery Regiment's 5th Battery, broke through to the 12th Panzer Division's position. This was the first group of surrounded troops to get out of the Bobruisk 'cauldron'.

OPERATION BAGRATION: AN INCOMPLETE TRUTH

Soviet forces began to squeeze the 'cauldron' on the evening of 30 June. After 1700 the 1901st Self-Propelled Artillery Regiment attacked the German rearguard near Chuch'ya, and the 95th Tank Brigade reached Sheipichi. At 1715 Hoffmeister's motorized column began its march. The 20th Panzer Division's panzer group, consisting of 6–8 armoured personnel carriers, one tractor and several tanks and assault guns, moved in front. All-terrain cars, amphibious vehicles and trucks with wounded moved with the column. Part of the subunits moved on foot. Units of von Kessel's 20th Panzer Division, the 244th Assault Gun Brigade, under Captain Rade, the remnants of the headquarters of the LXI Panzer Corps, and units of the commandant of Bobruisk, headed by Colonel Zerchold, the headquarters of the 383rd Infantry Division, with General Gihr, and the division doctor, Lieutenant Colonel Worgrimer, as well as elements of the 6th, 36th, and 45th Infantry Divisions, moved with the column. At around 1800 the column's last groups set out. As early as 1830 a rifle battalion from the 95th Tank Brigade captured Oktyabr'. The groups defending it, under the command of Lieutenant Colonel Lenderer from the 118th Grenadier Regiment and Captain Scharf from the 531st Grenadier Regiment's 1st Battalion, fell back by way of the woods to the north-west, while other detachments from the 36th and 383rd Infantry Divisions surrendered.

South-east of the Britsalovichi railway station, the Germans' motorized column ran into the 95th Tank Brigade's 142nd Tank Battalion (16 T-34s), units of the 216th Anti-Aircraft Artillery Regiment and several hundred partisans from the 211th K.K. Rokossovskii and 214th M.I. Kalinin detachments late in the evening of 30 June. An ambush of two tanks from the 108th Tank Brigade's 63rd Tank Battalion covered these positions from the south. Colonel Demme's panzer groups broke through the partisans' position, but the Soviet tanks shot up two armoured personnel carriers. Generals Hoffmeister, Conrady and Engel abandoned the knocked-out armoured personnel carriers and, with small groups of soldiers and officers, continued to move north. On 1 July Conrady was taken prisoner by elements of the 9th Tank Corps. Hoffmeister and Engel got as far as the village of Britsalovichi, where they ran into an ambush, from which they turned to the west and then to the north. But they did not reach the 12th Panzer Division's positions. Hoffmeister, along with General Gihr, was captured on 7 July, and Engel on 9 July. The majority of the armoured personnel carriers and the 20th Panzer Division's last tanks were destroyed. General von Kessel attempted to continue the attack, but it was unsuccessful.

The 95th Tank Brigade reported capturing 2,500 prisoners near Oktyabr' and Britsalovichi. The brigade lost two tanks irreparably, while the 108th Tank Brigade's 63rd Tank Battalion lost one tank.

Kessel, having gathered his division's forces together, began to bypass Britsalovichi from the east at about 2230. By morning the detachment had crossed the Osipovichi–Britsalovichi–Sloboda road and had reached the swampy woods south-east of the village of Lipen'. At about 0700 on 1 July Kessel's troops reached the bridge at Lipen' and heard the roar of tanks, although they could not be sure if they were theirs or Soviet. There were no Soviet forces on the bridge at Lipen'. During the crossing there arrived combat groups that had been trying to break out of the encirclement along the Svisloch', accompanied by one captured T-34, one Panzer IV and Lieutenant Meyer's radio set from the 511th Signals Regiment. At 0840 Kessel's group received a message from the 12th Panzer Division: 'Our panzers are in Prudishche. The direction of attack is through Svisloch' and Pogoreloe'. By 1200 on 1 July Kessel's group had completed the crossing and continued the march in the direction of Malinovka and Pogoreloe. An armoured personnel carrier and the captured T-34 were in the vanguard and behind them the commander of the 20th Panzer Division, together with the commander of the 59th Panzergrenadier Regiment and the remnants of their headquarters. Before long the vanguard met armoured personnel carriers from the 25th Panzergrenadier Regiment's (12th Panzer Division) 1st Battalion, which (minus one company) had been reinforced by the 29th Panzer Regiment's 6th Company, which had been called back from its positions late in the evening of 30 June and concentrated 3km north of Lapichi, in order to launch a relief attack toward Bobruisk. At about 0210 on 1 July it had attacked thorough Pogoreloe, in the direction of the small town of Svisloch'. By morning the 1st Battalion of the 25th Panzergrenadier Regiment had occupied Malinovka, Novaya Niva and reached Prudishche. At about 0800 the Soviet 250th Rifle Regiment, which had been reinforced with a self-propelled gun, attacked the 3rd Company, which was stationed forward, from three sides. The Germans were driven a few kilometres from Prudishche. But at this point they were helped by the encircled troops from Bobruisk. The first group that reached the 12th Panzer Division's positions numbered 5,000 men. Before long their strength grew to 15,000. By the close of 3 July 25,000 encircled men from the Bobruisk area and the 'cauldrons' from either side of the Berezina had reached the Ninth Army's positions.

Captain Rade, the commander of the 244th Assault Gun Brigade, gathered the remnants of the combat groups together and on the morning of 1 July attacked the Soviet positions. At first the breakthrough went well, but Rade's group, which Zerchold's group had joined, was nevertheless unable to reach the German positions.

From 5 July the 20th Panzer Division's detachments began to gather in Volkovysk. Two hundred and fifty men from the 92nd Artillery Regiment were dispatched to dig trenches. A combat group under Colonel Demme was formed on the basis of the 59th Panzergrenadier Regiment. A three-company grenadier battalion was formed, under the command of Major Heine, from the remnants of the 112th Panzergrenadier Regiment and the 59th Panzergrenadier Regiment's 1st Battalion. Demme's group included an engineer company under Lieutenant Karl-Heinz Shade, which was formed from the remnants of the 92nd Engineer Battalion, and a composite detachment under Lieutenant Plettner. In all, the group numbered 1,138 men – 33 officers, 167 NCOs and 938 privates, and disposed of four 75mm heavy anti-tank guns, one Grille self-propelled gun and two Panzer IV tanks. The 'Eigenlaub' group, consisting of 450 troops under the command of Lieutenant Resner, which had been formed from the 151st Reserve Training Battalion in Bialystok, was subordinated to the group. Major Heinz-Georg Lemm's 1st Battalion (27th Fusilier Regiment) from the 12th Infantry Division, which had come out of the encirclement around Mogilev and Minsk, was subordinated to Colonel Demme's group. On 9 July Colonel Demme's combat group reached the Zel'va area, where it was attached to the 12th Panzer Division. On 14 July, in order to reconstitute the 20th Panzer Division, it was decided to recall all of the division's units from the front and transfer them to Romania. On 19 July Demme's group was disbanded. Only Major Heine's battalion remained at the front.

On 11–12 July Major Baron Tilo von Werten, on orders from the General Inspector of Panzer Troops, conduced an inspection of the 20th Panzer Division's units, the result of which was the compilation of a memorandum on 13 July, according to which the division numbered 129 officers, 812 NCOs and 3,311 privates, or a total of 4,252 men, of which 1,138 – 33 officers, 167 NCOs and 938 privates – were at the front in Demme's combat group. According to an estimate by the division command, there were still about 2,000 men in Bialystok, Volkovysk, Brest and Warsaw, and in the Third Panzer and Fourth Armies' combat areas. The division had retained seven Panzer IV tanks, 24 armoured personnel carriers, one Wespe self-propelled gun, one Hummel self-propelled gun, two Grille self-propelled guns, one 150mm infantry gun, five 75mm anti-tank guns and 219 machine guns. The division also disposed of 440 trucks with an overall capacity of 700 tons and 183 specialized trucks, including 142 field kitchens, 15 weapons repair shops, 100 mobile repair trucks, and 26 other specialized vehicles, 178 cars, 175 motorcycles, 16 command cars, 22 Maultier halftrack trucks, 53 tracked tows, 479 horses and 211 horse-drawn carts. A significant part of the rear service elements had not been encircled around Bobruisk and had fallen back to the west behind the units of the Ninth, and then the Second and Fourth Armies. Also surviving was the 20th Panzer Division's replacement battalion (620 men), which had just arrived at the front. On 23 July it was transferred to reinforce the 5th Panzer Division. From 1 June through 1 August 1944 the 20th Panzer Division's losses were 4,482 men, of whom 174 were killed (including ten officers), 455 wounded (including 32 officers) and 3,853 missing (including 109 officers). This amounted to about a third of the division's personnel strength.

On 19 June Captain Hermann Felke's 92nd Anti-Tank Battalion received 21 new Jagdpanzer IVs and on 6 July was sent to the Eastern Front. The battalion arrived at the Second Army's LV Army Corps on 10 July and on the first day it prevented a breakthrough of the defence of the 36th Infantry Division's composite regiment. It covered the corps' retreat to Bialystok. During July the battalion lost four Jagdpanzers irreparably. On the morning of 13 August the battalion, along with nine anti-tank weapons, was transferred to the XX Army Corps. Five vehicles were undergoing minor repairs and three major repairs.[71]

General Kessel's 20th Panzer Division was the luckiest of all. It became the sole division of those which broke out of 'Bagration's' 'cauldrons' that was able to retain more than half of its personnel upon reaching the German positions. Kessel's panzer troops managed to capture several Soviet depots, as well as an SU-122, which was placed at the tail of the column. Rumours circulated among those surrounded that some columns had been met by guides in German uniform who had led them into partisan ambushes or to the Soviet troops' positions. It was suspected that these were deserters who were cooperating with the National Committee for a Free Germany. No documentary proof of such operations has been found. The second and third wave of encircled men, which sought to break out during the daylight hours of 29 June, were even less successful than the first wave. Almost all of those who sought to break out in these waves were killed or captured. Many of those wounded were killed.

On 29 June yet another panzergrenadier battalion from the 12th Panzer Division arrived at Mar'ina Gorka. It was immediately dispatched to occupy a position along the Svisloch' between Talka and Pogoreloe. The division's new units arrived on 29–30 June, while debates went on in the Ninth Army's headquarters as how to best employ the 12th Panzer Division for helping those who were breaking out of the Bobruisk 'cauldron'.

THE ROUT

At 1500 on 30 June the new commander of the Ninth Army, General von Vormann, spoke by telephone with the chief of staff of the 12th Panzer Division and enquired whether he believed that the division was capable of attacking in the direction of the town of Svisloch' in order to assist in the breakout. Niepold replied that the division could not give up on its attempts to interfere with the Russians' attempts to form bridgeheads along the western bank of the Svisloch'. Several minutes later General von Vormann telephoned with orders for the division to undertake an attack from Pogoreloe in the direction of Svisloch' to aid the encircled troops as early as possible on the following day, while leaving the division the right to determine those forces which it could spare for this purpose. All that could be allotted for the attack was a panzergrenadier battalion and a company of tanks under the command of Major Blanschub. Towards evening they were moved to the Lapichi area and supplied with fuel and ammunition. Having left in the dark, in order to cover the 35km through the woods along narrow trails, they met no resistance until they approached their goal, but before the head of the column reached the single bridge over the river in this sector, the Russians had created a major defensive position with no fewer than 15 heavy anti-tank guns along the far side of the bridge. When the lead vehicle began to cross the bridge it suffered a direct hit in one of its tracks. Bitter and disorganized fighting raged that morning. The Germans sought to clear the bridge, while the Russians counter-attacked with tanks and artillery. This interfered with the battalion reaching the main group of the XLI Panzer Corps, which was only a few kilometres behind the Soviet anti-tank positions. Only a few exhausted German soldiers were able to break out of the ring.[72]

The 12th Panzer Division was supposed to relieve the Ninth Army's encircled divisions. Hitler wanted to throw the 20th Panzer Division into the relief effort, but it was already in the Bobruisk 'cauldron'. The 12th Panzer Division was far from its established strength. It lacked a panzer reconnaissance battalion and a battalion of anti-aircraft artillery. The 12th Panzer Division had only one panzer battalion instead of the authorized two – the 29th Panzergrenadier Regiment's 2nd Panzer Battalion, with 44 tanks. As of 1 June the division had nine Panzer IIIs and 35 Panzer IVs, as well as two command tanks and 91 armoured personnel carriers.[73] The division's transfer from the Riga area had been slow. By the evening of 30 June only the 1st Battalion (minus one company) from the 25th Panzergrenadier Regiment, which had been reinforced with a panzer company with 12 tanks, was ready to take part in the relief of the Bobruisk 'cauldron'. Nevertheless, the attack, which was led by the battalion commander, Gustav-Adolf Blancbois, was crowned with success thanks to the element of surprise. The attack began at 0200 on 1 July under the cover of darkness, and the Soviet units were caught off guard. Blancbois's battalion, which was awarded the Knight's Cross for this breakthrough, attacked to the south-west toward Bobruisk from the Mar'ina Gorka area and was able to create a narrow corridor. The encircled units undertook a breakthrough to meet them and at about midday they linked up with the relief group in the Svisloch' area. Out of 70,000 encircled men, 35,000, who had abandoned almost all of their heavy weapons, broke out of the 'cauldron', although Soviet troops continued to press them, striving to cut off their path of retreat. In the end, only 25,000 men of those encircled in Bobruisk were able to reach the area south-west of Minsk. To this number must be added a certain number of wounded, whom they managed to evacuate from Bobruisk before the encirclement ring closed.[74] That such a large number of encircled troops were able to break out of the Bobruisk 'cauldron' and reach the German positions owes a great deal to the fact that the 20th Panzer Division was part of the Bobruisk group of forces.

A large group of the Bobruisk troops managed to cross further along the course of the river; the rear units of a battalion group saw in the twinkling midday haze a long column of exhausted men, dragging themselves along the road in the rear of their position. Major Blancbois dispatched an officer to the crossroads to lead them to the German positions. He told them: 'The 12th Panzer Division's panzergrenadier battalion is here to pull you out. This is 20km from the German lines. You have managed to get this far and you must cover the final part of the journey.' Major Blancbois recalled that people were in a terrible condition and were at the end of their strength. The partisan were constantly pursing them on the ground and fighters and attack aircraft were attacking them from the air. They were hungry and exhausted, with only stagnant swamp water to quench their thirst. Many had thrown away their boots in order to swim across the river and had wrapped their feet in rags and straw. The wounded hobbled on with the aid of sticks and crutches.

During the second half of the day the battalion was ordered to fall back, because it was needed elsewhere. But Major Blancbois refused to obey until the stream of Bobruisk 'survivors' ran dry. The battalion fell back at 1800, having placed the seriously wounded on its vehicles; they returned to the German positions after midnight. Estimates of the number of those who broke out of Bobruisk varies from 15,000–20,000 to as high as 35,000. This was the single successful operation to render assistance during the breakout from the 'cauldron'. One of the last groups to arrive was the 20th Panzer Division, commanded by General von Kessel, and several of his officers. He demanded a truck and returned east to search for other survivors from his division. The 12th Panzer Division's officers thought that they would never see him again.

The 12th Panzer Division faced one of the 1st Guards Tank Corps' tank brigades, while two other brigades were moving toward Mar'ina Gorkka through Tal'ka, to the south of Minsk. Major General Müller's divisions had to fall back rapidly, in order not to be surrounded to the east of Minsk. But Army Group Centre was more concerned by the major threat to the south-west of Minsk. Lieutenant General I.A. Pliev's cavalry-mechanized group was ordered to capture Baranovichi. In order to forestall this threat, Model decided to transfer the 12th Panzer Division to the west, in order to attempt to defend his communications lines leading to Minsk, but it was already too late. A battalion from the 5th Panzergrenadier Regiment carried out an exhausting 160km march in order to create a bridgehead near Brest. But the 1st Guards Cavalry Corps managed to seize the bridges over the Bug River before its arrival and the panzergrenadiers were unable to regain them.

On 2 July all units of the 12th Panzer Division received orders to fall back to Stolbtsy. By the evening of 3 July the division's forward units had arrived there. Orders were received to occupy and defend the crossroads near Stolbtsy and to establish contact with the 4th Panzer Division. The commander of the 12th Panzer Division, Major General Müller, and the chief of staff, Gerd Niepold, arrived at the command post of the 25th Panzergrenadier Regiment to plan the attack. Niepold recalled that the commanders' faces appeared tense, tired and depressed, insofar as they did not have great hopes for the success of the forthcoming attack. It was decided to attack with three panzergrenadier battalions in a row from Stolbtsy to the south-west, in order to capture the crossings over the Neman River. It was planned to begin the offensive at 0400 on

4 July. It was supposed to be supported by a panzer battalion and the division's artillery. Niepold had little faith in success and ordered his men to carry out a reconnaissance of the path of retreat to the north-east. All the remaining routes had already been cut by the attacking Soviet tanks.

The 12th and 4th Panzer Divisions' attacks were halted before long due to the significant Soviet superiority in men and tanks. At 0900 an order arrived from Ninth Army headquarters to cross the Neman along the pontoon bridge in Yeremichi, to the north of Stolbtsy. This bridge had been built after General von Kessel and the remnants of the 20th Panzer Division had broken through the partisans' positions along the southern extremity of the nearly impassable Nalibok Forest. The 12th Panzer Division's headquarters was very glad to hear that General von Kessel had returned.

The 12th Panzer Division set out for the north-west, defended from the rear by a battalion to the east of Stolbtsy and another battalion east of the Nalibok Forest. The division encountered numerous surviving groups from the Fourth and Ninth Armies, including a battalion from a fusilier regiment under the command of Major Lemm, which was retreating from Mogilev. The area was crawling with partisans, who had burned the wooden bridge over the Sula River. At that moment the 12th Panzer Division command was preparing to send engineers to construct an improvised bridge, when an officer on a motorcycle appeared from the nearby woods. He said that he was from the 20th Panzer Division and that General von Kessel had sent him to take them to the bridge in Yeremichi and that he knew the road. At first there was some doubt as to his identity; many assumed German officers were working for the Russians, directing columns into ambushes. But his papers proved to be in order and although he was unable to show the route on a map, the division headquarters decided to follow him. The column turned around, which was difficult to do with heavy tracked vehicles along the narrow path, and followed the motorcyclist to another bridge over the Sula. Although the road was a bad one and attacks by the partisans continued, the division's forward units crossed the Neman by 1700. On the following day, after midday, the rear elements and the rearguard crossed the river. On the other side they learned that they were to attack on the western bank to the south of the 28th Jäger Division. But the main thing was that the 12th Panzer Division had managed to break out of the threatening encirclement, although with heavy losses in men and materiel.[75]

The 5th Panzer Division, under Lieutenant General Karl Decker, which had been reinforced by von Saucken's group, was supposed to throw back the Soviet tank units in the Borisov area, which had been moving to the west through the 100km breach between the Third Panzer and Fourth Armies. Here were operating the 5th Guards Tank Army, the 2nd Guards Tank Corps and Lieutenant General N.S. Oslikovskii's cavalry-mechanized group (3rd Guards Cavalry and 3rd Guards Mechanized Corps), as well as several combined-arms armies along with attached mobile formations.

The German 5th Panzer Division had 55 Panzer IV tanks and 70 Panthers, and had also been reinforced by the 505th Heavy Panzer Battalion with its 20 Tigers. But its complement of panzergrenadiers was small. There was an average of 35 men each in the companies, against an authorized strength of 150 men. At 0100 on 25 June the division received orders to move toward Bobruisk. But during the movement the destination was changed to Borisov and Krupki, to the east of the Berezina. Numerous delays on the way were brought about by the destruction of the railway lines by partisans and attacks by low-flying attack aircraft. The first trains arrived at Borisov on 27 June.

OPERATION BAGRATION: AN INCOMPLETE TRUTH

The 89th Engineer Battalion, which had a great deal of combat experience, arrived first and took charge of the unloading of the division's trains, with the aid of the division's reconnaissance battalion, which arrived next. The division's command element had already arrived along the road, having received orders from the headquarters of Army Group Centre in Minsk. On 28 June the unloading had to be shifted there, because the constant air raids had made it impossible to detrain in Borisov. The 31st Panzer Regiment's Panthers had to go into battle against Soviet tanks directly from their rail cars, before they could be fully unloaded from the last train arriving in Borisov. The engineer battalion attempted to occupy positions along the highway to the east of Krupki, coming under the command of SS *Gruppenführer* Joachim von Gotberg. The latter managed to create a combat group out of two police regiments and several hastily gathered battalions. The 5th Panzer Division established its headquarters in Nemanitsa, 6km to the north-east of Borisov.

On 28 June the 5th Panzer Division, with a battalion of Panthers, repelled an attack by 50 Soviet tanks from the 5th Guards Tank Army's 29th Tank Corps. Units of the 14th Panzergrenadier Regiment and the 31st Panzer Regiment, which had just unloaded in Minsk, took up a blocking position near Logoisk on the morning of 29 June, in order to prevent a breakthrough toward Rudnya by the 3rd Guards Mechanized Corps from Oslikovskii's group. Five Soviet tanks were destroyed along this axis. On 30 June the bridges over the Berezina were blown up by engineers from the 89th Battalion after the withdrawal of the rearguards, although by no means were the remnants of the Fourth Army saved. They would fall into an even larger cauldron along the western bank of the Berezina.[76]

On 1 July the 2nd Guards Tank Corps, which had been attached to the 31st Army, received orders to force the Berezina to the south of Borisov and to attack toward Minsk through Zhodino. But they were unable to force the river from the march. Then the corps commander, General Burdeinyi, decided to undertake the crossing in the Chernyavka area, where the width of the Berezina did not exceed 100–110m. But a downpour, which hindered the tanks from approaching the riverbank, interfered with the forcing. The problem was solved with the construction of a floating bridge and the approaches to the river were covered by artillery and machine gun fire.

On 2 July the 5th Panzer Division had to withstand heavy fighting directly along three axes. Combat Group 1, which consisted of the 14th Panzergrenadier Regiment's 2nd Battalion and a field reserve battalion, as well as elements of the 31st Panzer Regiment and the 89th Engineer Battalion, fought along the Krasnoe–Molodechno position. Combat Group 2, which consisted of the 13th Panzergrenadier Regiment, the main part of the 89th Engineer Battalion, and elements of the 31st Panzer Regiment, repelled powerful tank and infantry attacks near Radoshkovichi. Combat Group 3, which consisted of the 14th Panzergrenadier Regiment's 1st Battalion, the 505th Heavy Panzer Battalion and several tanks from the 31st Panzer Battalion, was fighting for Logoisk. The division was forced to fight along the north-western, northern and north-eastern axes and the distance between its furthest combat groups exceeded 70km, which meant they could communicate only by radio. Thus the division headquarters had to be divided in two. The division chief of staff, Colonel Anton Detlow von Plato, with half of the headquarters personnel, was located north-west of Molodechno and controlled Group 1. Division commander Decker controlled the operations of Groups 2 and 3 with the other half.

THE ROUT

Combat Group 1 managed to recapture Molodechno, despite the nearly uninterrupted attacks from the air. Now the railway line from Vilnius was open again, and reinforcements could be moved along it. On 2 July elements of the 170th and 221st Infantry Divisions began to arrive, along with a battalion of assault guns. A path of retreat had also been opened for the troops fighting to the north of the Borisov–Minsk highway, because the dense Nalibok Forest hindered any major movement to the west.

On the night of 2 July, before the Germans abandoned Minsk, 15,000 military personnel from different units had gathered in the city, predominantly without weapons and demoralized, about 8,000 wounded and about 12,000 rear-area civilian personnel, and 96 trains. And it was only on this night that they received Hitler's agreement to evacuate 'Fortress Minsk', which there was simply no one to defend. The 5th Panzer Division was holding the corridor to the north-west, through Molodechno. The 24th Panzergrenadier Regiment was holding a blocking position east of Radkovichi, which enabled the division to carry out a regrouping under this defence, so as to counter-attack to the south-west. But it was cancelled due to a shortage of fuel.

During the course of six days, from 27 June through 2 July, according to A. Detlow von Plato's data, the 5th Panzer Division, along with the 505th Heavy Panzer Battalion, destroyed 295 Soviet tanks, chiefly thanks to the Tigers and Panthers which could hit the majority of Soviet tanks at a safe distance. The 5th Panzer Division's 77th Panzer Battalion intercepted a Soviet radiogram, which stated: 'Avoid contact with the 5th Panzer Division. Fall back, where it's possible.' Commenting on this radiogram, K.-H. Frieser notes: 'This communication filled the soldiers of the 5th Panzer Division with pride, but upon closer examination it showed that the Soviet tank commanders had drawn the correct lesson from the preceding battles. They avoided tactical collisions with German tanks that brought them nothing but heavy losses, and instead advanced into the depth as rapidly as they could for resolving operational tasks, just as the German tanks had operated in 1941.'[77]

One can understand the commander of the 5th Guards Tank Army, P.A. Rotmistrov. Defeated in the tank battles of January–February 1943 by Hermann Balck near Rostov-on-Don, and in July 1943 by Paul Hausser at Prokhorovka, Pavel Alekseevich had well learned that it would be best for his army not to meet up with large German panzer formations, and that it was wiser to operate against German infantry that was supported by only an insignificant number of tanks and self-propelled guns. In essence, this was the correct tactic, taking into account the sharply diverging level of training for the German and Soviet tank crews, as well as the qualitative superiority of the Tigers and Panthers over the majority of Soviet tanks. However, Stalin and the *Stavka* did not wish to recognize such tactics, because that would mean accepting the superiority of German tank formations over Soviet ones. And before long Rotmistrov was removed from command of the tank army and was no longer sent to the front.

But insofar as the Third Belorussian Front had 1,810 tanks and self-propelled guns, the losses sustained in the fighting against the 5th Panzer Division were significant, but not catastrophic. Now the Soviet tank commanders sought to avoid collisions with the German tanks, but sought to move forward as quickly as possible in order to cut off the retreating German infantry divisions. This essentially was the Soviet tactic during the second half of 1944 and in 1945. It was mainly anti-tank artillery and assault aviation that fought the enemy's tanks. And in those instances when they did not manage to avoid meeting German panzer and mechanized troops, the affair would at times end quite unhappily for the Soviet tank crews. For example, in October 1944 three German and one Hungarian panzer divisions and one-and-a-half panzergrenadier divisions routed a Soviet tank army and two cavalry-mechanized groups in the fighting around Debrecen, but because of a shortage of infantry divisions were unable to carry out a major operation to encircle the Second Ukrainian Front. And in March 1945 the SS Sixth Panzer Army, while falling back in the Lake Balaton area, inflicted a defeat on the Soviet 6th Guards Tank Army, although before this that same army under Sepp Dietrich was unable to break through the front being held by Soviet rifle divisions, reinforced by anti-tank and self-propelled artillery and tank brigades. As we will see subsequently, during the course of 'Bagration' the German panzer divisions more than once defeated the Soviet tank corps.

The 5th Panzer Division was able to halt the advance by the 5th Guards Tank Army in Borisov, although the Soviet tank formations were subsequently able to bypass the German bridgehead near Borisov from the north and south. On 1 July they crossed the Berezina near Studenka. Faced with being outflanked, the 5th Panzer Division was forced to fall back. The Soviet mobile units were attacking toward Molodechno and Baranovichi. The 5th Panzer Division fell back to the area to the west of Minsk and on 3 July the Soviet 5th Guards Tank Army entered Minsk from the north and linked up with the First Belorussian Front's 1st Guards Tank Corps.

On the night of 3 July the 5th Panzer Division received orders for a subsequent attack to the south, into the flank of the Soviet offensive from Minsk along the northern axis. However, the attacks by the 3rd Guards Cavalry and 3rd Guards Mechanized Corps from Oslikovskii's group, which were directed at cutting the road and rail communications between Smorgon' and Molodechno, were more dangerous, and so the division's order was changed to attack in the direction of the Smorgon' area to the north-west. It got out of the fighting near Radoshkovichi with difficulty and during the next few days it sought to delay through attacks the Soviet forces attacking toward Vilnius. The Germans attempted to establish a defence along the railway to the north-west as far as Vilnius and to reduce the gap between the remnants of the Third Panzer Army in the Polotsk area and units of the Fourth Army, which remained in the large 'cauldron' to the east of Minsk. The role of the 5th Panzer Division was to delay the Soviet offensive on Vilnius as long as possible. In the opinion of Paul Eder, who relied on an interview with A. Detlow von Plato, the Soviet superiority along the 5th Panzer Division's front at that moment was 20:1 in tanks, 35:1 in artillery and overwhelming in the air.[78]

This appears to be greatly exaggerated. Two tank corps from Rotmistrov's army were fighting against Decker's division, plus another two tank corps not part of the 5th Guards Tank Army, as well as a mechanized and cavalry corps from Oslikovskii's cavalry-mechanized group. If we allow that by the start of the fighting for Vilnius there remained in the order of 50–60 armoured vehicles available in Decker's division, then it is doubtful that in the Soviet corps there remained more than half of that armoured equipment with which they began Operation 'Bagration'; that is, around 600 tanks, which yields a superiority of 10–12 times, but not 20 times. Besides, the above-named Soviet corps were fighting not only against the 5th Panzer Division, but also against other German divisions, which disposed of a certain amount of assault guns and tank destroyers. By the close of 9 July the 5th Panzer Division had 25 combat-ready Panthers, 25 Panzer IVs and 15 Tigers, while by the close of 8 July there were only 12 Panthers, six Panzer IVs and an unknown number of Tigers. This was due to the Germans getting closer to their repair bases as they retreated. It's possible that the comparison was based on the absolute minimum amount of combat-ready equipment in the Wehrmacht's 5th Panzer Division during Operation 'Bagration'.[79]

On 1 July the *Stavka* issued a directive to transfer Lyudnikov's 39th Army (two corps, seven rifle divisions and reinforcement units) by the end of 3 July from the Third Belorussian Front to the First Baltic Front, by moving it in the Lepel' area.[80] It was aimed at Lithuania and the approaches to the border of East Prussia.

The German Fourth Army's retreat beyond the Berezina could be carried out only along the single Mogilev–Berezino–Minsk highway. Units from 13 divisions and numerous army rear elements had to cross over the only bridge at Berezino. As a result, the column of armoured equipment, artillery pieces, motor vehicles and carts on the approaches to the bridge extended for 60km. It was subjected to Soviet air attacks, while there were almost no German fighters in the air and there was very little anti-aircraft artillery. On the morning of 29 June the bridge was partially destroyed as the result of bombing. Repairing it took several hours and while the main bridge was being prepared the German engineers were able to lay down several temporary crossings and put a large number of ferries into operation. But the Soviet forces crossed the Berezina behind the northern and southern flanks of the German Fourth Army, taking it in a pincer movement, so that Tippelskirch's army was already threatened with a two-pronged turning movement on the river's western bank. On 1 July German forces reached Cherven', 40km south-west of Berezino.

In the Poplavy area a German combat group, under Captain Heinrich Haun, broke through the Soviet troops' combat formation and witnessed a horrible scene of crimes carried out by Soviet soldiers: 'Behind the position which we had overcome, a terrible picture arose before our eyes. A kilometre-long sector of the highway was covered with shot-up vehicles, crippled soldiers and the half-naked bodies of murdered Russian women.' In K.H. Frieser's opinion, 'The Red Army soldiers behaved with particular cruelty toward their fellow countrymen; that is, toward Russian militarized auxiliary forces and civilians who had attached themselves to the retreating German forces'. He later cites Haun's report: 'Their dead bodies lay on the road, disfigured and defiled.'[81] Similar reports reached the headquarters of the Fourth Army in large numbers. Here one should note that part of such crimes could have been carried out by partisans, who, like the Red Army soldiers, considered women who retreated with the Germans to be collaborators and dealt cruelly with them, which, of course, in no way justifies the criminals. These women, in particular, could have been the wives or children of village elders, policemen and other persons who collaborated with the occupation administration.

Eyewitness data proves that Soviet military personnel carried out crimes before they crossed the borders of the USSR. However, to judge from everything, the command element did not pay any attention to this then. In any event, there are no known documents where the Soviet commanders affixed similar excesses and punished their subordinates for them during the course of Operation 'Bagration'.

On 3 July Soviet forces liberated Minsk. Thanks to this, there arose an external encirclement front around the German Fourth Army, separated from the internal front by more than 60km. This distance subsequently grew to 150km. The German forces were able to break through the internal encirclement ring, but on 5 July were split up into three groups. The westernmost group, consisting of units of the 110th Infantry Division, was in Gatovo, facing the external encirclement front. The second group of forces had concentrated around a munitions depot in Dubniki, 15km east of Minsk. It consisted of three divisions. And the third group of six divisions was between Belaya Luzha and Pekalino, approximately 40km east of Minsk. On 5 July a conference of the commanders of two army corps and four divisions took place in this largest of the three 'cauldrons'. Insofar as almost no fuel remained, they had to blow up all of their armoured equipment, motor vehicles and artillery pieces. Ammunition had also been nearly completely expended, so that many had to fight without firearms. There was also practically no food. And the front continued to fall back to the west. Molodechno and Baranovichi, to which the encircled troops were trying to break through, were located 95km and 170km respectively, from the largest 'cauldron'. They decided at the conference that the XXVII Army Corps would attempt to break out to the south-west and the XII Army Corps to the north-west. But the attempted breakout was not successful due to the colossal Soviet superiority in firepower. Following this, it was proposed that each division attempt to break out on its own. On that day the last radiograms from the Fourth Army's headquarters were received by the corps headquarters. The final attempt at a breakout, now by individual divisions, began at 2230 on 5 July. The majority of the assault groups were able to make a clean breakthrough of the internal encirclement ring. The Soviet forces were caught off guard. But they were motorized and before long, together with the partisans, they were once again standing in the path of the groups trying to break out. The remnants of the XII Army Corps, together with groups that had attached themselves to it, were able to cross the Minsk highway and reach the German positions near Molodechno in scattered groups. Lieutenant General Vincenz Müller abandoned the units of his XII Corps and, together with his staff, voluntarily surrendered on 8 July along the Polevtsy–Minsk road.

'Bagration's' success was in many ways predetermined by the fact that the Soviet forces along the external encirclement front did not go over to the defensive, but continued to develop the offensive, which prevented the launching of a serious relief attack by the enemy, because the external encirclement front was always moving away from the 'cauldron'.[82]

The Pekalino group of forces began its breakthrough on the night of 6 July. It consisted of the 57th, 267th and 31st Infantry Divisions and the remnants of the 25th Panzergrenadier, 260th Infantry and 78th Assault Divisions. The commander of the XII Army Corps, Lieutenant General Vincenz Müller, and the commander of the XXVII Corps, General of Infantry Paul Volckers, had ended up in the encirclement. The breakout began following the above-mentioned conference of the corps and division commanders. There still remained 42 assault guns and 20 tank destroyers in the 25th Panzergrenadier Division. But there were only 5–10 rounds per gun, and it had not been possible to establish an air bridge. The nearest German positions were more than 100km to the west. Volckers proposed remaining in place and fighting to the last, because it was impossible to evacuate the approximately 5,000 wounded. It was decided to leave them with a letter calling on the Soviet command to treat them in accordance with the customs of war. It is unknown whether this had any effect. At 2359 on 5 July the 25th Panzergrenadier Division began its breakout in the direction of Dzerzhinsk, to the south-west of Minsk. Upon firing off their last rounds, the artillery men destroyed their guns. Three groups attacked head-on, accompanied by cries of 'Hurrah!' Despite

THE ROUT

the very heavy fire, Lieutenant General Paul Schurmann got out with his group after overcoming a Soviet battery, but there remained only 100 men out of 1,000. The Soviet forces counter-attacked and the groups were split up into small ones, which attempted to break through to the west. Evidently some of them were able to do so, because Schurmann was not captured, and the division was reconstituted in Germany later that same year.

General Trowitz's 57th Infantry Division attempted to break out that same evening, but almost immediately came under heavy fire. However, the division's columns maintained their cohesiveness and at dawn on 6 July they linked up with the remnants of the *Feldherrnhalle* Panzergrenadier Division. The commanders of the two divisions, Major General Adolf Trowitz and Major General Karl von Steinkeller, decided to operate together, in order to cross the Cherven'–Minsk road, which was being held by Soviet troops. The two divisions awaited the coming of night before moving out. *Feldherrnhalle* was scattered and the majority of its troops were captured. Upon crossing the road, the 57th Division, which still numbered 12,000–15,000 men, split up into smaller groups. The division commander's group, which was the last to cross the road, had two *Schwimmwagen* amphibious vehicles for transporting wounded. At dawn the group was in the centre of the Soviet positions and decided to await the coming of night, before once again moving out. They hid in a field of rye and the exhausted people fell asleep before early evening, when they were awakened by rifle and mortar fire. The small groups were captured, one after the other. Adolf Trowitz was captured on 7 July.

One of the surviving soldiers from the 78th Assault Division, Lieutenant General Hans von Traut described the breakout as follows:

> The troops lined up for the assault at 2300. Individual elements began to sing the *Deutschlandlied* [the 'German Song' – the German national anthem, B.S.]. The survivors will never forget that night. The burning villages, howitzer and rifle fire, muffled explosions, interspersed with thunderous cries and the singing of the attacking subunits. The enemy forces that sought to offer resistance were seized and once again surrounded. The breakout was a success . . .
>
> By dawn on 6 July the enemy's surrounded positions had been left behind. However, the scattered Russian units quickly regrouped. The enemy's motorized forces arrived. The larger breakout groups were soon attacked and once more encircled. The only chance was to break up into very small groups.

On 6 July General Traut was captured, as was the greater part of his division. Only a very few men were able to make it to the German lines.

On 5 July the commander of the 267th Infantry Division, Lieutenant General Otto Drescher, issued a bombastic order which stated:

> Soldiers of my victorious 267th Infantry Division. At the time when the enemy's penetration into Army Group Centre's sector made a withdrawal inevitable, on 3 and 4 July the enemy moved up powerful forces against the XII Corps. Our division operated in the corps' rearguard and successfully repulsed all attacks, enabling the other divisions to

safely withdraw. You, the soldiers of my division, have proven your valour and heroism in your fealty to the soldiers of the other divisions. During this fighting the enemy has managed to encircle our troops. This encirclement must be broken and we must break out to freedom and our motherland. If we want to once again see our homeland and our families, we must fight. I want to be sure that no one doubts that the path will be difficult and will demand great sacrifices. He who prefers the dishonourable fate of captivity will be subjected to the usual cruelty of the Bolshevik murderers. I do not doubt that your choice will not be difficult. Forward, comrades! Forward, into the decisive attack and we will return to our motherland!

Drescher closely studied the intelligence reports before the breakout and distributed large-scale topographic maps to the commanders. He also sought to destroy, without making any noise, the remaining guns without ammunition, the motor vehicles without fuel, and even the field kitchens, and formed a squadron from the artillery horses. All of the troops were broken up into combat groups and weapons were distributed equally among them.

The breakout was to be accomplished by three columns, with the goal of crossing the Orsha–Minsk railway and the highway running parallel to it. The left column was able to carry out this task, but with the arrival of Soviet tanks was forced to capitulate. Small remnants of this column continued to attempt to break out, but having nearly no ammunition, were destroyed or captured by two rifle companies supported by mortars.

The central column, which was personally led by Drescher, was not only able to force the railway and road, but advance sufficiently far on the first day to the north-west in the direction of Molodechno. Here it broke up into small groups, which found it easier to break out of the ring. Each group was led by a commander who was able to orient himself well in the terrain, and he was given a specific path to the north-west. Even the division chaplain led a group of 100 men. The majority of the groups subsequently broke up into smaller groups, either on their own or under enemy pressure. The majority of the groups attempting to break out were destroyed or captured. Drescher was killed by Red Army troops on 13 August 1944 along the Neman River, in a wood 3km from Merkine, Lithuania, 100km south-west of Vilnius.[83]

The most successful proved to be the column of Lieutenant General Schurmann's 25th Panzergrenadier Division, who was the first to leave the commanders' conference and was thus the first to begin the breakout. His group attempted to cross the Bobruisk–Minsk railway, which had already been captured by Soviet forces. He then unsuccessfully attempted to get through the other Soviet screens and decided to turn to the east and bypass Minsk from the north. He managed to do this and Schurmann was finally able to bring out his constantly fighting detachment, which ultimately numbered only 35 men, to the German positions to the north of Molodechno and to the south of Vilnius on 17 August. His group was the most numerous of those which made it to the German lines. Schurmann was hospitalized for several weeks with foot ulcers, nephritis and a bladder infection. The general was awarded the Knight's Cross for his 46-day march through the Soviet rear. The division's remnants were moved to Bavaria. The reconstituted division was then employed during the Germans' Ardennes offensive and in February 1945 was transferred to the Oder for the defence of Berlin. Schurmann survived the war. On 10 February 1945 he was transferred to the command reserve for reasons of health, and on 8 May 1945, while still in the command reserve, was captured by the Western Allies. Paul Schurmann died on 1 February 1978 in Wiesbaden (Hesse), at the age of 82.[84]

Units of the XXVII Army Corps, which were attempting to break out to the southwest, at first enjoyed success, but were later forced to attempt to break out through more and more blocking positions. It was easier for those German divisions which had been encircled in Gatovo and Dubniki, which were significantly closer to the front line. The remnants of the 110th Infantry Division were able to cross the Minsk–Dzerzhinsk railway, but on 9 July they fell into an ambush and were scattered 10km from it. The surviving soldiers and officers continued to try and break out to the west in small groups. The Soviet troops continued to oppose these groups as late as 13 July. The commander of the Second Belorussian Front, G.F. Zakharov, noted in an order of 7 July:

> The elimination of the enemy's encircled and scattered groups is proceeding unforgivably slowly and in a disorganized manner. As a result of the lack of initiative and indecisive activity of the commanders, the enemy is rushing from one side to another in search of a way out, and is attacking the headquarters of corps and armies, depots and automobile columns, thus disrupting the uninterrupted work of the rear and headquarters.

The commander of the Second Belorussian Front ordered the 49th and 50th Armies to allot five divisions for fighting the Fourth Army's encircled units. The Second Belorussian Front's 33rd Army and the Third Belorussian Front's 31st Army were also operating against them.[85] Nonetheless, small groups and individual German soldiers and officers attempted to reach the German positions, not wishing to surrender and fighting to the end. They made their way through forests and swamps, often eating only berries and mushrooms, as well as potatoes and vegetables from the peasants' garden plots. A very few of them managed to make it – mainly those whom the local inhabitants helped, especially in Lithuania, which was a big surprise for the Germans. However, often the peasants did not only not help the encircled Germans, but guided Soviet soldiers and partisans to them. As late as the middle of July the surrounded troops' chances of reaching the German positions were quite high, but later the front rolled rapidly to the west. Despite this, from 10 August to the end of October 1944 80 officers and 838 NCOs and enlisted men from the German Fourth Army crossed the front line. Many of them crossed the front line along the East Prussian border, nearly 400km away.[86]

On 4 July the headquarters of Army Group Centre reported to the OKH that 126 rifle divisions, 17 motorized brigades, six cavalry divisions and 45 tank brigade-strength formations were operating against it along the 350km breakthrough front, while the Army Group had only eight division-strength formations.[87] The same day the *Stavka* issued new directives to the Fronts taking part in Operation 'Bagration'. The Third Belorussian Front was ordered:

> Consisting of the 5th, 11th Guards, 31st, and 33rd Armies, the 5th Guards Tank Army, the 3rd Guards Mechanized, 2nd Guards Tank and 3rd

OPERATION BAGRATION: AN INCOMPLETE TRUTH

Guards Cavalry Corps, it is to develop the offensive, while launching the main attack in the general direction of Molodechno and Vilnius.

The immediate task of the Front's forces is to, not later than 10–12 July, capture Vilnius and Lida. It is to subsequently reach the Neman River and seize bridgeheads along its western bank.

To establish from 2400 on 4.07.1944 the following boundary lines: with the First Baltic Front, as before, as far as Konstantinove, and then Podbrodze–Podberez'e–Kaisiadorys–Mariompol (all locales are for the First Baltic Front inclusively); with the Second Belorussian Front, as before, as far as Minsk, and then Kamen'–Nikolaev– Dokudovo–Ostrino–Grodno (all locales for the Third Belorussian Front inclusively).

The First Belorussian Front was ordered:

1. The right wing of the First Belorussian Front, consisting of the 48th, 65th, 28th, and 61st Armies, the 9th Tank, 1st Guards Tank, 1st Mechanized, and 4th Guards Cavalry Corps, is to develop the offensive, while launching the main attack in the general direction of Baranovichi and Brest. The immediate objective is to capture [the area, B.S.] of Baranovichi and Luninets and, no later than 10–12.07.1944, to reach the line Slonim–Shara River–Pinsk. It is subsequently to capture Brest and reach the Western Bug River and capture bridgeheads along its western bank.
2. To establish from 2400 on 4.07.1944 the following boundary line with the Second Belorussian Front: as before, as far as Svisloch', and then Osipovichi–Belaya Luzha–Gorodeya–Molchad'–Zel'va–Svisloch'–Surazh (all locales except for Osipovichi, Gorodeya and Molchad' are for the Second Belorussian Front inclusively).

The First Baltic Front received the following task:

1. The First Baltic Front, consisting of the 6th Guards, 43rd, 2nd Guards, and 51st Armies, is to develop the offensive, while launching the main attack in the general direction of Svencionys and Kaunas. The immediate objective is to capture the line Dvinsk–Novye Svencionys–Podbrodze no later than 10–12 July. Subsequently, while securing itself from the north, it is to attack toward Kaunas, with part of its forces on Panyvezys and Siauliai.
2. To establish from 2400 on 4.07.1944 the following boundary line with the Third Belorussian Front: as before, as far as Konstantinove, and then Podbrodze–Podberez'e–Kaisiadorys–Mariompol (all locales for the First Baltic Front inclusively).

The Second Belorussian Front,

consisting of the 50th, 49th and 3rd Armies, is to develop the offensive, while launching the main attack in the direction of Novogrudok,

THE ROUT

Volkovysk and Bialystok. The immediate task is to capture the Novogrudok area by no later than 10–15 July and reach the Neman River and the Molchad' River. It is to subsequently capture Volkovysk and attack in the direction of Bialystok.

2. To establish from 2400 4.07.1944 the following boundary lines: with the Third Belorussian Front, as before, a far as Minsk, then Kamen'–Nikolaev–Dokudovo–Ostrino–Grodno (all locales for the Third Belorussian Front inclusively); with the First Belorussian Front, as before, as far as Svisloch', then Osipovichi–Belaya Luzha–Gorodeya–Molchad'–Zel'va–Svisloch'–Surazh (all locales, except Osipovichi, Gorodeya and Molchad' for the Second Belorussian Front inclusively).[88]

Also on 4 July, the 33rd Army, consisting of two corps, seven rifle divisions and reinforcement units, was transferred from the Second to the Third Belorussian Front, while the army was to be concentrated in the Smolevichi area by the close of 5 July. Also, on 4 July, the 3rd Army, consisting of three corps and nine rifle divisions, was transferred from the First to the Second Belorussian Front. The 4th Shock Army, consisting of three corps, ten rifle divisions, one fortified area and reinforcement units, was to be transferred from the First to the Second Baltic Front.[89]

From 1 July the 51st Army was to be transferred from the *Stavka* reserve to the First Baltic Front, and on 8 July the 2nd Guards Army was transferred from the Third Belorussian Front to the First Baltic Front. On 9 July A.M. Vasilevskii was entrusted with the coordination of the Third Belorussian, First and Second Baltic Fronts' operations.[90] On 15 July the 39th Army was transferred from the First Baltic to the Third Belorussian Front and the 3rd Guards Mechanized Corps just the opposite, from the Third Belorussian to the First Baltic Front.[91] The *Stavka* of the VGK decided to launch an attack in the Baltic area with the forces of the First Baltic and Third Belorussian Fronts, to liberate Latvia and Lithuania and to cut off Army Group Centre from East Prussia, followed by its defeat.

Thus as early as the beginning of July Stalin began to gradually shift 'Bagration's' centre of gravity to the Baltic and East Prussia. It's difficult to say whether or not this decision was the correct one and what motivated it. Stalin could not foresee then that the future uprising in Warsaw, which he expected, would not be under Moscow's control and would create a major political problem. Thus an offensive on Warsaw, both from Minsk and along the Kovel' axis, should have seemed preferable. Following the rout of the German Fourth and Ninth Armies the Germans had few forces here. On the other hand, the capture of Warsaw and the Red Army's forcing of the Vistula would inevitably have forced the Wehrmacht to fall back to the Oder, from which Berlin was a stone's throw away. In this situation, Hitler would probably have had to move divisions for the defence of Berlin from the Western Front, which was barely holding on. In this case, it is unlikely that the Germans could have managed to stabilize the front along the Siegfried Line, and then later to even organize a counteroffensive in the Ardennes. Given such a scenario, there was every possibility that the war could have concluded by the end of 1944. If, for example, the 51st and 2nd Guards Armies, the 5th Guards Tank Army and the 3rd Guards Mechanized Corps, had been thrown against Warsaw as early as 10–15 July, it is doubtful that the Germans, even with the aid of hastily-transferred panzer divisions, could have held on to the Polish capital. On the other hand, Army

OPERATION BAGRATION: AN INCOMPLETE TRUTH

Group North, which did not have a single panzer formation, was too weak to inflict a defeat on even one of the Baltic Fronts, even having been deprived of two armies and a mechanized corps. In the same way the weak German groups of forces defending around Vilnius and Kaunas would not have been able to do this. At the same time, from the point of view of the war's outcome, this direction remained very secondary throughout the entire war. From the point of view of military art, the offensive by the Fronts that had begun Operation 'Bagration', in two diverging directions: Warsaw–Berlin and the Baltic–East Prussia, should be recognized as a mistake. The concentration of men and materiel along the Warsaw direction would have hastened the end of the war. To all appearances, at the beginning of July Stalin, as well as Vasilevskii and Zhukov, seriously overestimated the degree of the Wehrmacht's defeat in Operation 'Bagration' and were calculating that due to the landing in Normandy Hitler had almost no reserves left. Stalin wanted to seize everything and right away, also because the end of the war was clearly approaching. Iosif Vissarionovich had designs to control not only Poland, but also the Baltic States, as well as a significant part of East Prussia, with Königsberg and Pillau. He clearly would not have cared for a situation where at the moment of Germany's capitulation the Baltic States and East Prussia would still be held by German troops. What if all of a sudden the Anglo-American forces, accompanied by the émigré governments of Lithuania, Latvia and Estonia, whose incorporation into the USSR in 1940 the Western powers had never recognized, had managed to land there? Moreover, they could have refused to turn over East Prussia and Königsberg to the USSR. Thus Stalin could have thought that he should at least insure himself, just in case. Despite all Operation 'Bagration's' impressive successes, on 6 July 1944 the *Stavka* issued a highly critical directive, 'On Improving Troop Control While Pursuing the Enemy', which dealt with the activities of the troops of the four Fronts participating in the operation:

> In developing the operation, and particularly while pursuing the retreating enemy, there are a number of significant shortcomings in troop control, the chief of which are:
>
> 1. The violation of the order on transferring headquarters and command posts, which should be moved only after the organization of communications with subordinate and higher headquarters at the new site. The consequence of the violation of this basic requirement is the loss of troop control and the headquarters' ignorance of the situation over a lengthy period of time. Radio communications equipment is being ignored. When wire communications is disrupted, radio, as a rule, is not employed. Communications with cavalry and tank formations is particularly bad.
> 2. The absence of organized leadership and headquarters command service while the troops pass through defiles and crossings, which leads to a mixing up of units, the accumulation of troops and the loss of time.
> 3. The distraction of the main forces for the resolution of secondary tasks, as a result of which the pace of the offensive is lowered. For

example, the army's main forces (3rd and 49th Armies) are engaged in eliminating the remaining individual enemy groups in the woods, and not special formations and units allocated for this purpose.
4. In a number of cases a successful advance leads to carelessness on the part of formation and headquarters commanders, which is expressed in the absence of reconnaissance and security, which enables the enemy to carry out sudden attacks on our troop columns.

The *Stavka* of the Supreme High Command orders the front and army commanders to adopt decisive measures for eliminating the enumerated shortcomings and that the measures adopted be reported to the General Staff.[92]

I should note that this directive was issued even before the rout on 8 July of F.N. Rudkin's 11th Tank Corps, during which many of the above-mentioned shortcomings revealed themselves. To our great regret, even after the issuance of 'On Improving Troop Control While Pursuing the Enemy', all of these shortcomings did not disappear, and they were not fixed at least before the end of Operation 'Bagration'. As before, commanders preferred to rely upon wire communications, and not radio, which told in a particularly negative fashion on the tank and mechanized units. Regulating movement remained a sore point up until the very end of the war and, given the presence of a narrow defile or a single road, as a rule, traffic jams would arise even in those cases when the enemy's air force was not operating. Intelligence during the offensive proved to be unsatisfactorily organized and often the attacking Soviet troops came under sudden attack by German tank formations, even during the Berlin operation.

On 14 July the 3rd Guards Cavalry Corps was transferred from the Third to the Second Belorussian Front. The following boundary line between the Third and Second Belorussian Front was established at the same time: 'as before, as far as Dokudovo, then Vasilishki–Nowy Dwor–Sopockin–the Augustow Canal as far as Augustow (all locales, except for Sopockin and Augustow are for the Third Belorussian Front inclusively)'.

'The commander of the Second Belorussian Front is responsible for the boundary.'[93] On that same day the 39th Army was transferred from the First Baltic to the Third Belorussian Front and – just the opposite – the 3rd Guards Mechanized Corps from the Third Belorussian to the First Baltic Front.[94]

On 14 July all three Belorussian Fronts and the First Ukrainian Front were issued a directive on disarming detachments subordinated to the Polish émigré government:

1. Do not enter into any kind of relations or agreements with these Polish detachments. Upon finding the rank and file of these detachments, immediately disarm them and dispatch them to specially organized collection points for verification.
2. In instances of resistance by Polish detachments, resort to armed force.
3. Report to the General Staff on the course of disarming the Polish detachments and the number of soldiers and officers gathered in the collection points.[95]

OPERATION BAGRATION: AN INCOMPLETE TRUTH

On 19 July the coordination of the First Ukrainian and the First and Second Belorussian Fronts was entrusted to Marshal Zhukov.[96] On this same day there followed a directive to the First Belorussian Front on the dispatch to the *Stavka* reserve of the 61st (following the capture of Kobrin) and the 70th (following the capture of Brest) Armies (overall, four corps, or ten rifle divisions).[97]

The First Belorussian Front's offensive developed particularly successfully where the Hungarian divisions were defending. In regard to this, the Second Army's chief of staff, von Tresckow, reported to the Army Group Centre headquarters: 'The Hungarians are broken, although some of them were good in the fighting.' And on 21 July the chief of staff of the XX Army Corps, Colonel Wagner, reported: 'Enormous chaos in the neighbouring sector. The Russians have broken through along the Hungarian divisions' sectors. The forward enemy units are in Stradecha, 7km to the south of the fortress belt [Brest-Litovsk, B.S.].'

On 20 July the commander of the German I Cavalry Corps, Harteneck, reported to the headquarters of the Second Army: 'The ammunition situation is very bad. We have ammunition only until midday.' It turned out that the army headquarters dispatched an ammunition train for Harteneck's corps in the wrong direction. The same thing happened to a train carrying fuel. The German supply system fell apart due to the rapid Soviet offensive.[98]

On 21 July Rokossovskii received a directive to capture Lublin: '1. Capture the city of Lublin no later than 26–27 July, for which you will employ first of all Bogdanov's 2nd Tank Army and Konstantinov's [V.V. Kryukov, B.S.] 7th Guards Cavalry Corps. The political situation and the interests of an independent and democratic Poland demand this.'[99]

As K.H. Frieser believes,

> there, where large Wehrmacht formations were captured as a single unit, following official negotiations to capitulate, Soviet officers mainly followed the norms of international law. Nevertheless, those who were unable to keep up with the convoy during their exhausting march to the transit camps were immediately shot. In any case, the wounded had almost no chance of survival. A particularly awful carnage was carried out by Soviet forces in the Bobruisk citadel, where about 5,000 wounded soldiers from the Ninth Army were killed. Those few survivors who managed to hide in the basements later told about this orgy of violence.[100]

As is known, surviving eyewitnesses have a tendency to exaggerate the number of victims. But some number of German wounded was probably killed in Bobruisk, but in all likelihood their number was less than 5,000 men.

The German soldiers knew of the widespread practice in the Red Army of reprisals against prisoners, for which the Red Army soldiers, with extremely rare exceptions, were not punished all the way to the end of the war. Thus the Germans tried not to surrender. Those of them who were captured, alone or in small groups, were completely at the mercy of the victors. The situation of the encircled Germans was exacerbated by the fact that they were hunted by partisans, who avenged the crimes carried out by SS police units and the Wehrmacht against the civilian population during anti-partisan operations, and more often than not did not take prisoners. Prisoners were often tortured before their death. The German legal expert, Rolf Hinze, himself a veteran of the war, who spoke with the few survivors, concluded that for the German soldiers who fell into the hands of the partisans, 'shooting must have been considered a less common but more pleasant way to die'.[101] One should note that often those who called themselves witnesses were actually relaying rumours that they had heard, in which the death of those Germans who fell into the partisans' hands could acquire fantastically sadistic details. At the same time, one should take into account the preceding cruel acts of the punitive expeditions, which often destroyed not only partisans, but also the civilian population of the partisan zones, while the partisans and members of the underground were often tortured before being executed. To be sure, this was done not so much by the Germans themselves, but by their underlings from among the collaborationists. The paradox lies in the fact that the majority of German police units, security divisions and detachments of collaborationists located in the rear, including the infamous 'Kaminskii Brigade' (29th SS RONA Division), managed to retreat and avoid encirclement, while the overwhelming majority of those who were captured by the partisans were those German soldiers and officers who had never taken part in punitive operations. It's impossible to say just how many German prisoners died at the hands of the partisans. This could have been hundreds or a few thousand soldiers and officers. And the Soviet tank and mechanized units, which were vigorously moving to the west, had no means of escorting prisoners to the rear and often preferred to shoot them or crush them under the tracks of their tanks.

One captured Soviet senior lieutenant stated:

> To the east of Minsk I saw two columns of German prisoners of war, approximately 400 to 600 men, marching in the direction of Moscow. The majority of the prisoners were barefoot. Despite the heat, they were not allowed to drink water from the local streams during the march, so they drank dirty water from puddles. He who staggered was beaten, and if a prisoner fell they shot him. Once I saw executed German prisoners lying in a row in a roadside ditch. They had asked for bread when they passed through any kind of town, but the civilians did not dare to give them any. I saw a German senior lieutenant sitting on the edge of a trench. He was wearing his military tunic with chevrons on his shoulders and awards for heroism, but he had no pants and was barefoot. The guards had taken the best clothes from the prisoners so as to trade them for alcohol among the civilians.[102]

In Hitler's words, 'When Field Marshal Model arrived Army Group Centre was nothing more than an empty space'. On 2 July Model evacuated Minsk and pulled back the 5th and 12th Panzer Divisions for the defence of Molodechno and Baranovichi. The remnants of the Third Panzer Army were isolated along the northern flank. It was separated from the other armies of Army Group Centre by a gap of 60km. There yawned a hole in the Eastern Front, as the Fourth Army had been almost completely destroyed and there was no continuous front line. On the right flank the Ninth Army's surviving formations were transferred to the Second Army on 3 July. The latter was tied down by the enormous forces of the First Belorussian Front's left flank, which was preparing to attack Army Group Centre's southern flank in the Kovel' area. Model believed that he had to repel the attack by 116 Soviet rifle divisions, six cavalry divisions, 16 motorized rifle brigades, and 42 tank brigades, with eight exhausted divisions.[103]

Actually, as of 1 July 1944 the First Baltic Front had 46 rifle divisions, one rifle brigade, one fortified area, eight tank brigades, one motorized rifle brigade and one mechanized brigade. The Third Belorussian Front had 26 rifle divisions, three cavalry divisions, one fortified area, 14 tank brigades, three mechanized brigades, and three motorized rifle brigades. The Second Belorussian Front had 23 rifle divisions and four tank brigades. The First Belorussian Front's right wing disposed of 45 rifle divisions, one rifle brigade, nine cavalry divisions, one self-propelled artillery brigade, 13 tank brigades, four motorized rifle brigades and three mechanized brigades. All of this did not take into account the large number of independent tank and self-propelled artillery regiments.[104] In all, this yielded 117 rifle divisions, one rifle brigade, two fortified areas, 12 cavalry divisions, 37 tank and self-propelled artillery brigades, and 15 motorized rifle and mechanized brigades. Overall, Model was not wrong. Six extra tank brigades could easily be written off as independent tank or artillery regiments, and there was even twice as much cavalry as that estimated by German intelligence. To be sure, the Soviet divisions were no less run down than the German ones; moreover, part of the formations had to be thrown into the fight against the encircled German groups of forces. At various times 30–40 rifle divisions and NKVD troops for rear-area security could have been detached for these purposes. The Soviet offensive was also slowing down due to the Germans destroying the railways during their retreat, which had also suffered from the partisans' 'rail war'. Nevertheless, the Soviet superiority was overwhelming.

So why was this superiority not realized? It's possible that the reason lies in the fact that the Soviet command did not expect such a rapid and complete success and did not possess a ready plan for developing the operations. It is not excluded that the *Stavka* and the Front commands, as usual, exaggerated the Germans' capabilities, including the presence of mobile reserves, and operated with excessive caution.

On 30 June the German army General Staff came to the conclusion that Army Group Centre 'can no longer put up anything against the enemy armies except for regiments and battalions'. On 6 July Army Group Centre's headquarters reported that along its 430km front there yawned a breach of 150km that was unoccupied by German troops. K.H. Frieser maintains:

> However, Field Marshal Model nevertheless managed to stabilize the situation. His recipe for success was quite simple: insofar as he was too weak to defend, he decided to attack. Model did not even attempt to create a positional defensive front in accordance with Hitler's concepts, but deployed his few forces for mobile combat. By employing his newly-arrived armoured reserves, he unexpectedly attacked the enemy forces that were far out in front, at the tip of their spearheads. After Model took over command of Army Group Centre the Red Army created no more 'cauldrons' worthy of mention.[105]

THE ROUT

Further on, Frieser, in support of this idea, puts forward G.K. Zhukov's opinion:

> While observing and analysing the actions of the German forces then and that of their high command in this operation, we were, to tell the truth, amazed at their obviously incorrect actions which doomed their forces to a disastrous end. Instead of a rapid withdrawal to their rear positions and the dispatch of powerful groups of forces to their flanks, which were threatened by Soviet shock groups, the German troops got bogged down in extended frontal battles east, south-east and north-east of Minsk.[106]

Here the German historian cites Zhukov's evaluation of the subsequent actions of the Army Group Centre command:

> I must nevertheless say that in this extremely complex situation the Army Group Centre command found the correct means of operation. Due to the fact that the Germans did not have a continuous defensive front and that it was impossible to create one given the absence of the necessary forces, the German command decided to delay our troops' offensive chiefly through counter-attacks. Troops transferred from Germany and from other sectors of the Soviet-German front deployed for defence under the cover of these attacks.[107]

Frieser also praises Model for the fact that he did not follow Hitler's orders, while presenting the latter with a *fait accompli*.[108] But here it is necessary to object that Busch began to employ the exact same method, using for this purpose his sole mobile reserve, the 20th Panzer Division, and also, on the final day of his command of Army Group Centre, the 5th Panzer Division, which had arrived from Army Group North Ukraine. As one may conclude from the above-cited conversation between Zhukov and Simonov, it was precisely these counter-attacks that made such a powerful impression on Georgii Konstantinovich. There's no doubt that if Busch had remained at his post he would have continued the very same tactic of short counterblows, under the cover of which he would have sought to create a new front. The fact is that Busch had almost no panzer divisions, while they appeared under Model. The German generals Kurt von Tippelskirch and Edgar von Butlar believed that one of the reasons that Model was appointed to command two Army Groups simultaneously was that in this case he could independently dispatch reserves from Army Group North Ukraine to Army Group Centre, without wasting time on coordinating this action.[109] And one cannot say that while Model was in command of Army Group Centre that there were no 'cauldrons' worthy of the name. One such 'cauldron' appeared, although not along Army Group Centre's front, but along the front of Army Group North Ukraine, which Model continued to command in tandem. We are speaking here of the Brody 'cauldron', in which four German divisions ended up and 17,000 prisoners were taken. It's possible that if Model had been running only Army Group North Ukraine, then this encirclement could have been avoided. It's most likely that if Busch had remained in command of Army Group Centre, then the course of operations would not have been worse for the Germans.

OPERATION BAGRATION: AN INCOMPLETE TRUTH

The German 5th Panzer Division was facing an enemy which was superior to it in tanks by a factor of 20, and 25 times in artillery, while Soviet tactical aviation had air superiority. But the division managed to launch surprise attacks against the attacking Soviet forces and to rapidly avoid pursuit, acting according to the 'hit and run' principle. According to German estimates, from 27 June through 9 July the 5th Panzer Division destroyed 486 tanks, 11 self-propelled guns, 119 anti-tank guns and 100 trucks. The German tank commanders took advantage of the fact that many Soviet commanders did not know how to rapidly react to surprise attacks.[110] The fact that the 5th Guards Tank Army was commanded by Marshal P.A. Rotmistrov, who was far from being the best tank army commander and who had been twice subjected to harsh criticism by the supreme commander-in-chief for his actions during the Belorussian operation, also played into the Germans' hands, and on 8 August 1944 he was finally removed from the command of the army and dispatched to Moscow as deputy commander of the Red Army's armoured forces. Pavel Alekseevich took no further part in combat operations. It is possible that had there been in Rotmistrov's place the best Soviet tank army commander, M.Ye. Katukov, then they would have managed to develop the success of Operation 'Bagration's' opening phase to a much greater degree and to seize Warsaw from the march and to advance to the Oder.

On 7 July Hitler ordered the following: 'In light of its operational importance, the fortress of Vilnius is not to fall into enemy hands for any reason.' He hoped to gather four panzer divisions for an offensive on Vilnius in order to restore contact with Army Group North, but the divisions could not arrive before 23 July. When the garrison commander requested permission to evacuate Vilnius, Hitler rejected this request, promising that if something happened to supply the city by air. On 9 July Model and the commander of Army Group Centre, in a conference with Hitler, proposed pulling back Army Group Centre to the line Riga– Dvinsk–the Dvina River, but Hitler declared that this part of the Baltic coastline was needed by Grand Admiral Dönitz for training submarine crews. Also, Finland's position depended to a great degree on the Wehrmacht holding the Estonian coast.[111]

On 8 July Vilnius was encircled by the 5th Guards Tank Army, the 5th Army and also units of the 11th Guards Army and N.S. Oslikovskii's cavalry-mechanized group. On the previous evening, 7 July, the garrison had been reinforced by the 16th Parachute Regiment's 2nd Battalion. Major General Reiner Stachel, who had been appointed commandant of Vilnius, which Hitler had ordered to be defended as a 'fortress', arrived with it. With the arrival of reinforcements, the strength of the garrison rose to 4,000 men. Yet another combat group, under the command of Lieutenant Colonel Theodore Tolsford, which had been dispatched to reinforce the garrison of Vilnius, had been encircled in the Lentvaris area, 10km from Vilnius. In a conversation with Model on 9 July, Reinhardt, the commander of the Third Panzer Army, called the order to defend Vilnius 'madness'. Model agreed with him and promised to pass this up the chain of command. But on this day he was unable to convince Hitler to authorize a breakout by the garrison of Vilnius.

It was only on 11 July that Hitler decided to heed Heusinger's arguments and authorized a breakout. On 12 July the German 6th Panzer Division, which had 61 tanks and 31 tank destroyers, was dispatched to Kaunas. It was able to relieve the garrison of Vilnius and bring 5,000 men out of the encirclement.[112] The 6th Panzer Division had been reinforced with a battalion of Panthers from the *Grossdeutschland* Division's panzer regiment, which doubled the number of tanks to 136. The breakout and the relief attack were carried out on the night of 12/13 July under Reinhardt's personal leadership. Tolsdorf's group, which had linked up with the garrison breaking out of Vilnius, was also saved.[113]

As early as the end of June the Chief of the General Staff, K. Zeitzler, proposed withdrawing Army Group North behind the Western Dvina and thus not only avoid the risk of being cut off from Germany by Soviet forces operating along the 'Bagration' front breaking through to the Baltic coast, but also to free up half of Army Group Centre's forces for launching a counterblow to the south. But Hitler rejected this plan. Meanwhile, due to the Third Panzer Army's withdrawal, the southern flank of Army Group North was now threatened. The First Baltic Front's divisions poured into the 40km breach between the two Army Groups in the direction of Riga. Zeitzler attempted to convince Hitler: 'My *Führer*, you have twice forced me to operate against my convictions, the first time at Stalingrad, and then in the Crimea. I will not allow you to do this a third time'. Having declared that 'the war is lost in the military sense', and should be ended, he asked Hitler to relieve him from his position. Zeitzler fell seriously ill after this and did not return to military service.

Meanwhile, in the beginning of July the ill Zeitzler was temporarily replaced by the chief of the General Staff's operational section, Lieutenant General Adolf Heusinger, who continued to insist on the withdrawal of Army Group North to the Western Dvina. Both Army Group commanders – Colonel General Georg Lindemann and Field Marshal Walter Model – agreed with this plan. Lindemann officially requested the withdrawal of his Army Group to the line Riga–Daugavpils and, in the event of a refusal, promised to request to be relieved. On 4 July he was replaced by Colonel General Johannes Friesner. However, the latter also supported the idea of a withdrawal. On 9 July Friesner and Model once again unsuccessfully attempted to convince Hitler of the necessity of a retreat.[114]

On 20 July an unsuccessful attempt was made on Hitler's life. Heusinger was severely wounded in it. Hitler considered Zeitzler indirectly responsible for the attempt, the main role in which was played by army generals and officers, and relieved him as Chief of the General Staff. Heinz Guderian replaced him, while keeping the post of Inspector of Armoured Forces. After 16 July the Soviet offensive along the front of Army Group Centre slowed down due to logistical problems. Now the main role was played by the infantry, and not the seriously worn-out tank troops. Model planned to stabilize the front with the aid of reserves along the line Brest-Litovsk–Kaunas, in front of which his forces were waging holding actions. The German Third Panzer Army was successfully repelling attacks by formations of the Third Belorussian Front, attacking from Vilnius, in the Kaunas area. But the gap with Army Group North had widened, thanks to the First Baltic Front's advance. Model had to extend the northern flank of his Army Group, which made the retention of Kaunas impossible. The Second Belorussian Front forced the Neman in the Grodno area, but was halted by a counterblow by units of the newly-recreated German Fourth Army. Insofar as the headquarters of the Ninth Army had been temporarily moved from the front, the Second Army made up the southern flank of Army Group Centre. The First Belorussian Front's right wing was slowly pressing it from Pinsk toward Brest-Litovsk. In Model's estimation, even in the event of the arrival of all requested reinforcements by 21 July, Army Group Centre's 16 formations would have to battle against 160 Soviet formations. It seemed as though it would finally be possible to reestablish a continuous front. But at this time the retreat of Army Group North Ukraine began.[115]

It would seem that given such an overwhelming, tenfold superiority in the number of formations and, accordingly, in everything else – men, tanks, planes and artillery – that the Soviet forces should have completely destroyed Army Group Centre. However, this did not occur. It's possible that one of the reasons that they were unable to fully take advantage of their overwhelming superiority was that that a significant part of the rank and file of the four Soviet Fronts taking part in Operation 'Bagration' consisted of recruits from among the local inhabitants and partisans called up directly into the units during the course of the operation itself and who had almost no combat training. By the way, the quality of German reinforcements in 1944 had also fallen significantly. The former Wehrmacht major Helmut Ritgen, who served in the 6th Panzer Division, noted 'the low quality and low level of the reinforcements' training'.[116] It's likely that the inability of the Red Army's ground force commanders to coordinate with aviation also played a role. After all, under conditions of the Soviet Air Force's overwhelming superiority and Army Group Centre's weak anti-aircraft defences, Soviet reconnaissance aircraft should have been able to detect the arrival of German mobile formations at the front without too much difficulty. Then these formations should have been subjected to mass attacks from the air, while superior Soviet tank and mechanized units and formations should have moved up to meet them. The experience of Operation 'Bagration' shows that a German panzer division usually defeated in battle a Soviet tank or mechanized corps, which had 2–3 times more tanks. This is probably why in order to neutralize a German panzer division the Soviet command found it necessary to simultaneously dispatch against it no less than two tank or mechanized corps. In this case, even if both Soviet corps had suffered heavy losses, the losses by the German division would have made it incapable of launching new counterblows without significant armoured reinforcements. However, Soviet combined-arms and tank commanders failed to demonstrate the art of manoeuvre and the ability to quickly concentrate the necessary forces at the decisive point.

Chapter 6

The Voyage of the *'Wiking'*

On 13 July the offensive by the First Ukrainian Front began, which threw back Army Group North Ukraine's main forces to the Carpathians. Simultaneously, units of the German Second Army came under attack. On 12 July the commander of the same army's I Cavalry Corps, Cavalry General Gustav Harteneck, reported to the headquarters of the Second Army: 'The 129th Infantry Division is too tired. People no longer even hear the artillery cannonade. The weapons are not in order, because there are no cleaning tools at hand. They are no longer holding their positions; instead of this, they run away.' It was on the following day that a powerful Soviet attack was launched against precisely this division. 'The 129th Infantry Division simply does not want to fight any longer.'[1]

On 12 July Model announced to the commander of the Second Army, Colonel General Weiss: 'The position of your army – to wage battle as an act to slow down the Russians' advance – is completely absurd. We are presently in a crisis situation, which it is necessary to overcome by all possible means. The conduct of combat operations must be directed toward inflicting as much loss as possible on the Russians.'

On that same day the Second Army chief of staff, Major General von Tresckow, reported to the Army Group chief of staff Lieutenant General Krebs: 'The Russians cannot be held with these forces. Orders must be issued for operations directed at slowing their advance.' Krebs replied: 'When the order to defend was issued, 30km were covered. What will happen when we order them to carry out holding actions? ... You must issue your orders in accordance with the field marshal's orders!'[2] Model was demanding that the troops fight according to the cry of 'Not a step back!' but at the same time inflicting maximum losses on the enemy. However, these two principles often don't go together.

Five days later, on 18 July, the First Belorussian Front's left wing struck two of the Fourth Panzer Army's corps. As K.H. Frieser notes:

> It's paradoxical, but following the retreat by Army Group Centre the operational configuration of the German forces was now more favourable than before 22 June. Then the Belorussian balcony, as seen from Kovel', stretched more than 500km to the east, so that after a successful breakthrough the First Belorussian Front's left wing could advance unhindered into the rear of Army Group Centre. Meanwhile, however, the German front in this sector was pushed so far back to the west that Army Groups Centre and North Ukraine were almost side by side. Aside from this, Field Marshal Model had as a precautionary measure evacuated the Kovel' salient, which was difficult to defend,

during 4–8 July, in order to avoid a pre-planned encirclement similar to the one which took place around Vitebsk and to garner reserves by shortening the front.[3]

The defence of Kovel' no longer made any sense, because the Soviet forces in Belorussia must soon reach Brest.

On 16 July 1944 *Stavka* issued a threatening order, entitled 'On the Shortcomings of Committing the 11th Tank Corps into Battle', signed by Stalin and A.I. Antonov. It stated the following:

> ... on the First Belorussian Front, during the enemy's withdrawal from Kovel', the 11th Tank Corps received the assignment to pursue the retreating enemy. Neither the commander of the 47th Army, Lieutenant General Gusev, who was entrusted with the 11th Tank Corps, nor the commander of the 11th Tank Corps, Major General of Tank Troops Rudkin, being unaware of the actual situation, organized a reconnaissance of the area. The enemy pulled back his forces to a previously prepared line and organized a powerful anti-tank defence there. The 11th Tank Corps went into battle without artillery support and did not even deploy its self-propelled artillery regiments. The tank corps' infantry and the rifle divisions' infantry did not attack behind the tanks.
>
> Marshal of the Soviet Union Rokossovskii, the commander of the First Belorussian Front, who was personally overseeing the troops' operations along the Kovel' axis, did not inspect the 11th Tank Corps' organization for the battle. As a result of this extremely poor organization of the tank corps' commitment into the fighting, two tank brigades, which were thrown into the attack, irreparably lost 75 tanks.
>
> The *Stavka* of the Supreme High Command warns Marshal of the Soviet Union Rokossovskii as to the necessity going forward of attentively and scrupulously preparing the commitment of tank formations into battle and orders:
> 1. To issue a reprimand to the commander of the 47th Army, Lieutenant General Gusev, for carelessness displayed by him in organizing the 11th Tank Corps' commitment into battle.
> 2. That Major General of Tank Troops F.I. Rudkin be removed from the post of commander of the 11th Tank Corps and be placed at the disposal of the commander of the Red Army's armoured and mechanized troops.[4]

However, as the Russian historians Vladimir Pinaev and Aleksandr Tomzov write:

> It's thought that the 11th Corps' heavy losses in the Maciejowa area were the result of mistakes by the corps command. However, this opinion looks more like an attempt to shift the blame from the guilty to the innocent party. The capability of Rudkin's corps to carry out reconnaissance was quite limited. Either the First Belorussian Front's intelligence organs should have carried out reconnaissance, or the 47th

Army's, to which the 11th Corps was attached, to check on the strength of the German forces along the path of the offensive. But this was not done.

The Soviet forces were sure than that they were attacking the infantry's defensive positions. However, at Maciejowa, besides infantry, there were lying in ambush 40 German Tiger tanks, from the 5th SS Panzer Division *Wiking*, 14 Nashorn assault guns (8.8 cm guns that were significantly more dangerous than the Panthers' 7.5 cm guns), about ten StuG IIIs, as well as towed anti-tank guns. The bitter result of the offensive was the irreparable loss of 79 T-34s and four SU-76 self-propelled guns.[5]

The report by the 36th Tank Brigade describes the battle on 8 July as follows:

Having overcome the barbed wire obstacles and a number of trenches, we unexpectedly met up with the enemy's powerful anti-tank defence, with a well-organized fire system from self-propelled guns and Tiger tanks. The enemy, having created an anti-tank sack, allowed the tanks to approach to close range and then fell upon the attacking tanks with all sorts of weapons, employing *panzerfausts*, bottles with flammable liquid, and anti-tank rifles, while they fired from tanks and self-propelled guns from the depth of the defence. Possessing a more favourable line, the enemy set fire to up to 30 tanks in the course of an hour.

The tank battalions were engaged in heavy fighting with a numerically superior enemy, and were completely unsupported by artillery from the 118th and 18th Howitzer Regiments. In response to the tank troops' request to open fire on the enemy and his weapons impeding the tanks' advance, the artillery commanders replied that the firing positions were too far away and the range of fire did not allow them to fire to accompany the tanks . . .

As a result of bitter fighting, the brigade lost 42 tanks burned and was forced to fall back to the eastern slopes of height 220 and go over to the defensive. During the course of the fighting it was established that the enemy had transferred to this sector the 5th Panzer Division *Wiking* from the Chelm area, which had up to 70 tanks and 40 self-propelled guns . . . According to our information on the group of the enemy's tank units, there were up to ten tanks of various types along this sector. The brigade headquarters and the unit commanders were completely unaware of the presence of the SS Panzer Division *Wiking*, which had been transferred to this sector of the front.

Matters were no better in the 65th Brigade, according to its report:

During the period of combat on 08.07.44 the brigade suffered losses in personnel, weapons and combat equipment: 17 T-34 tanks with 76mm guns, of which one burned and 16 (the number of knocked-out and burned tanks has not been established) remained in the depth of the enemy defence. Twenty-three tanks with 85mm guns, of which eight burned and 15 (the number of knocked-out and burned tanks has not been established) remained in the depth of the enemy defence. Among the personnel ten officers, 26 sergeants and four enlisted men were killed; 12 officers, 28 sergeants and 14 enlisted men were wounded; 25 officers, 81 sergeants and two enlisted men remained in the depth of the enemy's defence, along with their equipment. In all, 108 men. The fate of the latter is unknown.

On the evening of 7 July the 47th Army's intelligence report stated:

Radio intelligence: the Second Army is in Terespol', the LVI Panzer Corps in Podgorodno, the SS Panzer Division *Wiking* is in Labunya, with subordinate units in Vlodava and Lyuboml', the 16th Panzer Division is in Sokal', and the headquarters of the artillery units is in Podgorodno. According to data from our neighbour on the right, the enemy was continuing to defend along his previous positions.

Conclusion: The enemy, while covering himself with powerful rearguards, continues to slowly fall back to the second defensive line of Smidyn'–Maciejowa. By shortening his front, the enemy has pulled out the 342nd Infantry Division and has evidently transferred it to the Kukuriki–Podgorodno–Khvorostuv area in order to prepare a defensive line.

The 47th Army's intelligence report for 9 July noted:

Prisoner testimony: prisoners taken on 08.07.44 in the area north-east of Smidyn' and in the area of Height 200.0 (south-east of Smityn') belong to the second company of the *Germania* Panzergrenadier Regiment. At the preliminary interrogation in the unit they testified that the *Germania* Panzergrenadier Regiment and the SS Panzer Division *Wiking* arrived at the given sector from Chelm on 02.07.44. There are 110 men in the 10th Company and up to 30 tanks in the tank battalion (the SS *Wiking*'s tank battalion), which is operation with them.

Conclusions . . . The enemy is consolidating along the occupied line, having reinforced his combat units with elements of the SS Panzer Division *Wiking*.[6]

Marshal Vasilii Ivanovich Chuikov, who commanded the 8th Guards Army, recalled:

I had occasion to encounter an 'elastic defence' as early as here, around Kovel', along the 47th Army's sector.

On 6 July the enemy abandoned the Kovel' salient and fell back 20km. In the 47th Army's headquarters they believed that the Hitlerites had begun a general withdrawal, without checking this through additional reconnaissance.

There was a basis for such an evaluation of the enemy's actions. North of *Poles'ye* our troops by this time had won a major victory.

THE VOYAGE OF THE 'WIKING'

On 3 July Minsk was liberated. Due to its defeat around Minsk it was possible that the German command had made the decision to withdraw along the Kovel' axis for the purpose of strengthening his defence. What could our command undertake in such a case? To prevent the Hitlerites from breaking contact, to pursue the retreating enemy, to break into his combat formations, to split up his retreating units, and to even attempt to encircle part of his forces. Insofar as the enemy was abandoning fortified positions, it would seem that the opportunity was being created to commit mobile formations with the task of gaining operational freedom. The 11th Tank Corps was thrown into the pursuit of the retreating enemy on 8 July. Of course, a scrupulous reconnaissance should have been carried out and the enemy's movements followed from the air. But this would have required time. And time is precious in such situations. The enemy, while falling back, might have had time to occupy the next defensive line, while the entire idea of a tank attack was that it reach these fortifications before the enemy, cutting off his retreating units. The corps was alerted and thrown forward.

The corps' forward units moved at top speed. They overtook the retreating German infantry and ran into a defensive position, which had previously been prepared for such a case. The German command, before removing its units for the retreat, moved anti-tank artillery formations to the second position, placing it for flanking and cross fire. Our tanks loitered under destructive aimed fire along previously registered areas . . . The corps suffered heavy losses. To make a long story short, the tank troops fell into an ambush. A planned and thought-out ambush.[7]

Actually, the matter transpired quite differently from the way Chuikov imagined it. Vasilii Ivanovich probably heard that Kovel' was being defended by the SS *Wiking* Division and that this division had launched an attack against the 11th Tank Corps. And so he decided that the *Wiking* Division had lured Rudkin's corps into an ambush and had launched a counterblow. But the fact of the matter is that *Wiking* was defending Kovel' only until the beginning of May 1944 and on 8 May, after the fighting for Kovel' had ended, the division was pulled back for reforming and was at the SS proving ground in Haidelager, in the Dembitsa area not far from Cracow. By the end of May the 1st Battalion of the division's tank regiment had 27 Panzer IVs. On 1 June *Wiking*'s 5th Battalion of assault guns was broken up and 22 Stug IVs were transferred to the 1st Panzer Battalion, which did not take part in the subsequent fighting around Maciejowa (now Lukow). On 25 June *Standartenführer* Johannes Muhlenkamp's combat group, which included the 2nd Panzer Battalion (the 1st Panzer Battalion had not yet completed its training and outfitting) on Panthers and the 3rd Panzergrenadier Battalion, left the proving ground and by 3 July had concentrated in Maciejowa, 80km from Kovel', which it had already been decided to abandon by this time, and nearly due south of Chelm. On the night of 5 July the main forces of the German 342nd Infantry Division were pulled out of the Kovel' salient and by the evening of 5 July its rearguards had abandoned the city. During the following several days Muhlenkamp's panzer troops had several small firefights with the enemy to the north of the Kovel'–Chelm railway. As of 1 July they had 23 operating Panzer IVs and another four undergoing repair,

OPERATION BAGRATION: AN INCOMPLETE TRUTH

69 operating Panthers and another two undergoing repairs in the 2nd Battalion and 17 operating Stug IVs and another four undergoing repairs. There were also five Panther command vehicles. On 8 July 21 Jagdpanzer IV tank destroyers were transferred to the panzer regiment, but they were too late to take part in the fighting around Maciejowa and, it would seem, took no part at all in *Wiking*'s fighting, because they were later transferred to some other division.

During the day of 5 July Soviet aviation bombed the German positions between Krugel' and Smidyn', thanks to which Muhlenkamp became convinced that the main Soviet attack would soon be directed against this area in order to seize Chelm and the crossings over the Bug River. He shared his fears with Lieutenant General Johannes Block, the commander of the LVI Panzer Corps, who agreed that Muhlenkamp's group should be pulled back to the Maciejowa area, where a switch position should be created for opposing the Russian breakthrough. On 8 July a large number of Soviet bombers attacked the German positions and then there were committed into the fighting, according to German estimates, approximately 400 tanks and self-propelled guns, which overestimated the actual amount of Soviet armoured equipment by 1.5 times (another German source speaks of approximately 295 Soviet tanks and self-propelled guns, which is closer to reality).[8] The corps should have had an authorized strength of 208 tanks in its three tank and one motorized rifle brigades. Another 21 tanks were in the heavy tank regiment and 42 SUs in the two self-propelled artillery regiments, which yields an overall armoured strength of 271 vehicles. The 7th Company's platoon, which was commanded by a Finnish SS *Obersturmführer*, Ulf-Ola Olin, was stationed in front of the main forces. Muhlenkamp ordered him to allow ten Russian tanks to pass and to then open fire. In this way the attention of the Russian tank troops were distracted to Olin's platoon, and at this moment all of the 2nd Battalion's tanks opened fire. The fighting lasted 30 minutes. One hundred and three Soviet tanks were destroyed, while there were no irreparable Panther losses in Muhlenkamp's group. Several Panthers were damaged.[9]

Since Soviet aviation had bombed the positions near Maciejowa, this meant that they knew there were German forces there. And in the intelligence report, which was received by the 47th Army's headquarters on the evening of 7 July, the Smidyn'–Mateyuv defensive line was mentioned, but not the location of units there from the *Wiking* Division, which was still listed as being in the Labunya–Vlodava–Lyuboml' area. Rudkin expected to encounter there ten, but not 76 German tanks (Muhlenkamp could only have that many tanks if the two Panthers undergoing repairs on 1 July, if all five commanders' Panthers and if one 'Panther' had not been put out of action during 1–8 July). What is important here is not some sort of specially-prepared ambush (this was a classic switch position), but poor intelligence work, both in the 47th Army and in the 11th Tank Corps, which failed to spot the presence of a major enemy group of tanks along the 11th Tank Corps' route. Its defeat enabled the Germans to hold an important crossing over the Bug and to block the approaches to Brest from the south.

The two Soviet tank brigades' – 36th and 65th – irreparable losses amounted to, according to their reports, 82 tanks. However, the German data, based on a calculation of Soviet vehicles left on the battlefield, speaks of 103 armoured vehicles. The 50th Independent Guards Heavy Tank Breakthrough Regiment (IS-2s) also took part in the fighting as part of the 11th Tank Corps. The 20th Tank Brigade and the 1461st and 1493rd Self-Propelled Artillery Regiments did not take part in the fighting. The heavy tank regiment had an authorized strength of 21 tanks, but it's doubtful that all were destroyed around Maciejowa. It's most likely that the 21 lost tanks not shown in the reports, aside from the losses of the 50th Guards Heavy Tank Regiment, also include tanks from the 36th Brigade remaining on the battlefield but not shown in the report. Aside from this, although it was maintained in the *Stavka* order that the corps did not have time to deploy its self-propelled artillery regiments, according to data supplied by Vladimir Pinaev and Aleksandr Tomzov, four SU-76s were destroyed in the fighting near Maciejowa. Then the losses of the 50th Regiment and the undercounted losses of the 36th Brigade must account for an overall 17 vehicles. The German side determined the number of destroyed Soviet T-34 tanks and T-34-85s and, possibly, IS-2s at 99,[10] which together with the four SU-76s makes for 103 destroyed armoured vehicles.

In an account by the First Belorussian Front's commander of the armoured and mechanized troop directorate on the results of 'Bagration', it was pointed out that

> the armour protection of the T-34-85 against the anti-tank weapons employed by the enemy is unsatisfactory – more than 90 per cent of the shell hits against the tanks caused holes or breaks in the armour. 50 per cent of the hits against T-34-85s were on the turret, because the turrets of the T-34-85 and particularly the turrets of the KV-122 are very big in comparison with the body of the tank. On the forward side the surface of a T-34-85 destroyed is almost equal to that on the body surface.[11]

In a Wehrmacht report of 11 July the fighting on 6–10 July in the area between Kovel' and Maciejowa is described in the following manner:

> In the Kovel' area the forces of the army and SS troops repelled an offensive by ten rifle divisions, a tank corps and two tank brigades in four days of stubborn defensive fighting. During the fighting they inflicted significant losses on the enemy in men and materiel. During the course of combat 295 enemy armoured vehicles were destroyed by all kinds of weapons at the front and in the rear. The 342nd Infantry Division, from the area of the Rhine and the Moselle, under the command of Major General Nickel, and the 26th Infantry Division, from the area of the Rhine and Westphalia, under the command of Lieutenant General de Boer, and a combat group from the 5th SS Panzer Division *Wiking*, under the command of SS *Standartenführer* Muhlenkamp, demonstrated outstanding valour.[12]

The number of Soviet tanks and self-propelled guns destroyed in the fighting is probably greatly exaggerated, although Muhlenkamp's tank troops destroyed some number of Soviet tanks and self-propelled guns on other days besides 8 July, while the two infantry divisions and the Luftwaffe inflicted some losses on the Soviet armour. The Soviet attack on 8 July proved to be unexpected for Muhlenkamp's group (the first ones to notice the Soviet tanks were two officers who were shaving at that moment in their bathing suits), but following bombing by Soviet aviation and the appearance of the T-34s, they were able to rapidly recover from the surprise and open fire.[13]

OPERATION BAGRATION: AN INCOMPLETE TRUTH

But, as early as 11 July the *Wiking* Division's units abandoned their positions near Maciejowa and began to move to the Bialystok area. This happened before the time, when on the night of 11/12 July the 2nd Panzer Battalion destroyed another 18 tanks during counter-attacks in the Skaino–Krugel'–Krasnoduby (Krasnodub'ye) triangle. On 12 July in the headquarters of the Second Army in Bielsk, the commander of the *Wiking* Division, *Gruppenführer* Herbert Gille, declared to Henning von Tresckow: 'If you think that we can hold the enemy's pressure here with our forces, then you are mistaken. There can be no thought of an offensive without the risk that our forces will be destroyed.' On the evening of 12 July the headquarters of the 5th Panzer Regiment and the 2nd Panzer Battalion began to fall back to the west and on the morning of 14 July they arrived in Brest-Litovsk.[14]

On 14 July the headquarters of the Second Army informed the headquarters of the *Wiking* Division: 'The route for the units moving by motor transport is Brest, Kamenets-Litovskii, Belovezha, Khainovka, Narew. The division should be ready for operations in the east, north-east and south-east; carry out reconnaissance of the route and increase the capacity of the bridges for tanks.'

The division's other units moved in 33 trains along the railway and were supposed to concentrate in the Chelm–Lublin–Siedlce area. The division's units moved by motor transport began to arrive in Brest-Litovsk as early as the evening of 14 July, thanks to their high march discipline. Gille's adjutant, *Untersturmführer* Lange, reported:

> On approximately 14 July 1944 the SS 5th Panzer Division *Wiking*, which had arrived from various billeting areas, was subordinated to the Second Army (approximately the Brest-Litovsk–Bialystok sector). Division commander Gille delivered a report at the Second Army's command post to the west of Bialystok. I accompanied him.
>
> We found the Second Army's chief of staff, Major General Henning von Tresckow, in his office. He was carrying on a telephone conversation with Army Group Centre headquarters and reported on the enemy's capture of several inhabited locales and signs of a breakdown and the chaotic situation among the allied forces [the Hungarians, B.S.]. While the telephone conversation continued, Gille put in his personal commentary on this matter: 'But, Herr General, this is incorrect. There's no enemy there. My *Wikings* are headed there. We just flew over this area . . .'
>
> This embarrassed Tresckow and he quickly ended the telephone conversation.
>
> Following an approximately five-minute briefing, the chief of staff accompanied my division commander to the commander of the Second Army, Lieutenant General Walter Weiss [he had actually been a colonel general since 30 January 1944, B.S.].

On the evening of 14 July Krebs informed Tresckow how he should employ the SS *Wiking* Division: '*Wiking* cannot be employed in detail. *Wiking* must be in the reserve in the event of a breakthrough. The field marshal's order is as follows: to hold the Russian, and no matter where a penetration occurs, to hold the line approximately 10km behind it. It is intended to carry out counter-attacks with *Totenkopf* and *Wiking*; *Totenkopf* will be employed in the Fourth Army's sector.' Model advised Weiss: 'Employ the *Wiking* Panzer Division wisely; not in the forests. It would be best in the area around Harteneck's corps.'

At 1130 on 15 July *Wiking* received information from the Second Army headquarters: 'It is more likely that the division's first task will be the destruction of the enemy on the southern wing of Harteneck's group. Establish contact with it immediately, in order to effectively carry out the necessary preparations.'

By midday on 15 July those units of the division which were being transferred by motor transport had arrived in the Bialystok area. In all, 558 vehicles passed through the control post in Bielsk. The panzer regiment's command post was located in Bialystok, along with three companies. At 1400 the division received an order by telephone: 'The panzer division is to move immediately in the direction of Khainovka. The division commander is to immediately arrive at army headquarters in a *Storch*; trains are to be dispatched in the appropriate manner.' But in a telegraphic order, received at 2050, a different mission was assigned:

> The SS 5th Panzer Division *Wiking* is gathering on both sides of Khainovka in such a way as to prevent any advance by the enemy from the Belovezh Forest to the west, north or south by through offensive blows in an eastern, south-eastern or north-eastern direction. Insofar as it is possible, the division's task is to halt the offensive by the enemy already in the woods, by sending part of its forces forward.

Early on the morning of 16 July two-thirds of those units which were being moved by motor transport, as well as seven trains, arrived in Khainovka, having covered 50km. New instructions arrived at 1155: 'Reconnoitre a movement to Kamenets-Litovskii, in order to attack the enemy who is advancing on Brest . . . You should attack over the Lesna to the east as quickly as soon as possible.'

The division chief of staff, *Obersturmbannführer* Schonfelder, informed Tresckow that the division's artillery had not yet arrived, to which the latter replied: 'If the enemy moves on Brest this will create an extreme threat to the XX and XXII Army Corps. You must attack.' Specific instructions for the direction of movement followed four hours later: 'Move without delay, with a large as possible combat group, to the Kamenets-Litovskii bridgehead. Pull back as strong forces as possible to the eastern bank, so as to be able to attack and in order to establish contact with the XXIII Army Corps' north-western wing.'

At 1715 Gille rejected the demand by the army headquarters to abandon his forward posts in the Khainovka area, in order to oppose a potential threat from the enemy forces attacking from the Belovezha area, thus dividing his forces: 'We are not a division, we are a combat group. Only one-third of the division is available. The attack which I plan to launch must affect the situation. For this, I need everything that I have . . . At present, the tanks and motorized infantry are moving along two roads.'

Six hours later the *Wiking*'s forward units arrived at Kamenets-Litovskii along the eastern bank of the Lesna River. This was already the third concentration area for the division, more than 100km from the first, over the course of a little more than 30 hours. Muhlenkamp's group, which consisted of a panzer regiment and the *Germania* Panzergrenadier Regiment's 3rd Battalion on armoured personnel carriers, established its command post on the morning of 17 July at the fork in the road on the south-eastern edge of Kamenets-Litovskii, where one road led to Pelishche, and the other to Vidomlya. Muhlenkamp disposed of 20 combat-ready Panthers. Another 17 Panthers arrived on that day. Two companies from the 1st Panzer Battalion also arrived.

The Soviet forces were attacking from Pruzany against the north-western wing of the XXIII Army Corps. According to German estimates, the Soviet forces included a mechanized corps, a cavalry corps and three rifle divisions from I.A. Pliev's cavalry-mechanized group, which were moving into the gap between the flanks of the XXIII Army Corps and Harteneck's group in a south-western direction on Brest. Thus by the evening of 16 July Model had decided that 'proceeding from the threatening development of the situation, the SS Panzer Division *Wiking* had to be transferred to the area east of Kamenets-Litovskii, even despite the fact that it had not been fully concentrated in the Biala-Podlaska–Khainovka area, in order to attack eastward at midday on 17 July and enable the left wing of the XXIII Army Corps to punch through back to the defensive line'.

At 1100 on 17 July Muhlenkamp attacked with his available forces and reached the crossroads to the north of Pelishche. Hohnle's combat group from the 7th Infantry Division launched an attack toward his combat group. By midday both groups had linked up. The forward Soviet units that had already reached the Vidomlya area were cut off from their communications. Meanwhile, two companies from the 1st Panzer Battalion, which had just arrived in Kamenets-Litovskii, attacked Soviet forces in the Vidomlya area. Two kilometres north of Vidomlya they encountered a powerful Soviet defence with tanks and anti-tank guns. The 3rd Company destroyed three anti-tank guns and one Sherman, but itself lost three Panzer IVs irreparably, with another tank damaged. The battalion commander, the battalion adjutant, the commander of the 4th Company and several NCOs were wounded by a direct shell hit on the bridge over the Lesna, where they were holding a conference. The 1st Battalion was inferior to the *Wiking*'s 2nd Battalion, both in terms of the training of the rank and file, which did not have time to complete its training in Heidelager, and in the quality of its armoured equipment, because the Panzer IVs, even when modernized, were highly inferior to the Panthers. The 1st Battalion's report on the fighting on 17 July states the following: 'The entire operation demonstrated that a reconnaissance in force with tanks does not always bring the kind of success to which we have become used in other reconnaissance subunits, mainly due to the unique quality of the combat equipment and its poor suitability for such tasks, which inevitably results in heavy losses.' Things went far more successfully with *Wiking*'s 2nd Panzer Battalion. Its 2nd Company captured Szczerbowo and Podbzany 7km to the south-east of Kamenets-Litovskii. This is how the headquarters of the German Second Army evaluated the results of the fighting of 17 July: 'As a result, the enemy was deprived of a good opportunity to break through to Brest to the south-east of the Belovezh Forest . . . During the day the Second Army achieved a significant defensive success. The forward units of the attacking wedge, which was directed against Brest, were cut off and are in danger of being destroyed.'

By the morning of 18 July the 2nd Battalion's companies linked up with the 1st Battalion's companies in the western part of the bridgehead. *Wiking* was assigned a task for 18 July to eliminate the enemy's forces that had broken through and been cut off from their rear, and to then throw the Soviet troops beyond the Lesna. Gille was preparing to conduct reconnaissance only until the arrival of the division's artillery regiment, but at 0900 Weiss issued the order: 'The division must attack today and destroy the enemy.'

That same morning the 1st Panzer Battalion's technical service platoon reported the destruction of an enemy truck, an armoured personnel carrier and an anti-tank gun in Rudavich, near the crossing over the Lesna, 11km from Vidomlya. Early in the morning the enemy, in battalion strength and supported by 13 76.2mm anti-tank guns, attacked from the woods 2km to the east of Pruska Wilowiska. In reply, the 4th Company of the 5th SS Panzer Regiment's 1st Battalion counter-attacked in the Topole area along with the *Germania* Regiment's 1st Battalion, which had just arrived along with the headquarters company and the 5th Panzer Regiment's technical service platoon. One anti-tank gun was destroyed and another captured. The 2nd Battalion's 7th and 8th companies attacked height 178 and the villages of Czemery and Rani, which were respectively 7.5km to the east and 5km to the south of Kamenets-Litovskii. Following the capture of Czemery the 2nd Battalion reached the banks of the Lesna Leva River.

In the German Second Army's war diary the results of the fighting on 18 July were summed up in the following manner:

> Although the forward units of the Soviet 4th Guards Cavalry Corps were temporarily cut off from their rear lines of communications, today they continued to advance further toward the Bug north-west of Brest. The recently established contact between the 7th Infantry Division and the 5th SS Panzer Division *Wiking* is interfering with the supply of these forces and is thus creating the prerequisites for their elimination.
>
> The 7th Infantry Division and the 5th SS Panzer Division *Wiking* managed to close the breach to the south-east of Kamenets-Litovskii by attacks from the north and south, thus cutting off the enemy's powerful infantry, armour and cavalry forces, which have already advanced to the west across the Bielsk–Brest railway to the Bug to the north of Janow-Podlaski from their rear communications lines. At present both divisions are attacking to the north-east, in order to occupy the line of the Lesna Leva River and to establish contact with the 102nd Infantry Division.

The Soviet forces, in order to ease the cavalry-mechanized group's situation, began an enveloping movement further to the north. In the XXIII Army Corps' war diary for 19 July, it was noted:

> The 65th Army, which has concentrated in the wooded area of the Belovezh Forest, today began operations to envelop Brest from the west. There are at present almost no German or allied forces along its route of advance through Kleszczele to the south-west toward the Bug. The XXIII Army Corps was ordered to rapidly pull the 5th SS Panzer Division *Wiking* and all available forces from the front line and to dispatch them deep into the 65th Army's flank.

But on 19 July *Wiking* had to stabilize the front of the XXIII Corps near the Lesna. The 1st Panzer Battalion was moved on the night of 19 July to the centre of Kamenets-Litovskii. At 0915 it established contact with the *Westland* Regiment's 1st Battalion in

Klepacze, 7km north of Kamenets-Litovskii, as well as with the 35th Infantry Division's blocking forces in Dimitrovicha. About 500 Red Army soldiers, who were attempting to advance to the west and south-west, had infiltrated to the area Sziszowo–Czernaki–Podbiala. In the morning the 35th Infantry Division was able to retake Podbiala.

At 1600 the 5th Panzer Regiment's 4th Company attacked in the direction of Sziszowo, having halted in Khulewicz, while advancing along Height 156. It cleared with fire a path to the village for *Westland*'s 1st Battalion. The panzer company itself bypassed the village and approached it from the north, which enabled the infantry to take the village following the elimination of the stubbornly defending Soviet forces in its northern part. From the height of the rise to the north of the village the Germans controlled the Lesna Prava Creek, which flowed into the Lesna Leva not far away. In the evening the company, which was armed with assault guns, successfully repelled an attack by a Soviet battalion, undertaken with powerful artillery support.

At the same time the 8th Company on 19 July was helping units which had been encircled in Vidomlya, an attack to the east from its positions on Height 182.5 on the outskirts of Rani, which was supported by the regiment's 2nd Battalion, against the last enemy bridgehead beyond the Lesna near Podzeczan, was unable to reduce it in size. Enemy counter-attacks on Czemery were beaten back. Topole was once again occupied by the Germans. According to the Second Army's war diary, the XXIII Army Corps, 'finally established a continuous front running from north to south'.[15]

Now *Wiking* was heading against the 65th Army, the rapid movement of which to the south-west toward Bielsk demanded that Gille's division be immediately thrown against it. The commander of the cavalry-mechanized group, General Issa Aleksandrovich Pliev, recalled this fighting:

> The Hitlerites threw their operational reserves against the cavalry-mechanized group from various directions. Bitter fighting broke out. The enemy managed to encircle our troop formation and the encirclement ring began to grow smaller. Because the Front's main forces were far behind us we could not count on their assistance.
>
> The very first thing we did was to take up an all-round defence, which was supported by an old border fortified area. We created a fire group from elements of rocket, field and anti-aircraft artillery, tanks, and self-propelled guns, which was thrown into the most threatened sectors of the encirclement ring. Thanks to front aviation – the pilots delivered shells, bullets and fuel and picked up the wounded at night. Where should we break out – to the east, the north, or to the south? But the Hitlerites were probably waiting for them here and had set up ambushes. And if we break out to the west? So we carried out a false breakout demonstration to the east. The enemy hurriedly began to remove his main forces from the western side of the encirclement ring and shift them to the area of the false activities. Having chosen a particularly dark night, Pliev led his group in the opposite direction.
>
> Without leaving a single wounded soldier behind, our forces successfully came out of the encirclement. While the fascists were trying to figure out, what, where and why, they had already gone deep into the woods. The cavalry-mechanized group subsequently routed the

enemy's rear areas and communications and, in conjunction with other arriving forces, took up defensive positions along the eastern bank of the Vistula . . .[16]

In the Kovel' area the First Belorussian Front had five combined-arms armies, one tank army, 416,000 men, 21 rifle divisions, 1,748 tanks and self-propelled guns, 8,335 guns and mortars and 1,465 planes, not counting Long-Range Aviation, against two German corps. There was one rifle division, 356 guns, and 83 tanks and self-propelled guns per kilometre of front. Within two days Soviet forces had forced the Western Bug. On 22 July the 2nd Tank Army entered the breakthrough. The German VIII Army Corps on the left flank was cut off from Army Group North Ukraine. Its divisions fell back to the north and were included in Army Group Centre in the Brest area. The German LVI Panzer Corps was forced to fall back to the south-west, to the Vistula. A 100km gap opened between the two Army Groups. On 24 July Rokossovskii's troops took Lublin. On 29 July the 69th Army captured the first bridgehead across the Vistula in the Pulawy area. The First Belorussian Front's right wing, in advancing to the west, attacked the German Second Army, as its left wing, while moving north, tried to get into its rear. The 70th Army attacked Brest-Litovsk. To the south-west, the 11th Tank Corps and the 2nd Guards Cavalry Corps, behind which the 47th Army was moving, were attacking toward Siedlce, cutting off the German Second Army's path of retreat. The Soviet 2nd Tank Army moved on Warsaw from the Pulawy bridgehead. The First Belorussian Front's tank units broke through near Kleszczele, between Brest and Bialystok. The German Second Army was threatened with a two-sided envelopment, because it was being enveloped from the north by units of the Second Belorussian Front.

In a 23 July directive on the conduct of operations on the Eastern Front, Hitler demanded that the existing front line be held, including Brest-Litovsk, as a 'fortress'. At the same time he demanded a mobile defence, while maintaining that 'the offensive is the best defence'. Nonetheless, Model was forced to pull back the Fourth Army from the salient around Grodno and then, due to the enemy breakthrough near Kleszczele, requested permission to abandon Brest-Litovsk. But even on 26 July, when Brest-Litovsk had already been encircled for an entire day, Hitler ordered it be defended 'to the complete destruction of the garrison'. However, Model explained to the *Führer* that such a decision would only result in the rapid elimination of two German divisions without any kind of significant damage to the enemy. That same evening Hitler authorized a breakout. During the course of heavy fighting on 27–29 July the Brest garrison was able to break out to the west, with the assistance of a relief attack from without.

The 4th, 5th and 7th Panzer Divisions and five infantry divisions were transferred from Army Group North Ukraine to Belorussia, and from the rear there were also transferred there the *Grossdeutschland* Division, which was being reformed, and the SS divisions *Wiking* and *Totenkopf*, as well as the *Hermann Göring* Parachute-Panzer Division from Italy. The 12th Panzer Division and three infantry divisions were dispatched from Army Group North to the 'Bagration' front. But on 20 July the 12th Panzer Division had only one combat-ready tank and 53 tank crews on hand.[17]

Model carried out two counterblows along the Second Army's front in order to prevent its being encircled. The SS *Wiking* Panzer Division and the 4th Panzer Division, one of the Wehrmacht's elite formations, attacked Soviet forces that had broken through

OPERATION BAGRATION: AN INCOMPLETE TRUTH

near Kleszczele, which enabled them to peacefully pull back the Second Army's divisions. The SS *Totenkopf* Panzer Division was also transferred from the Fourth Army and attacked Soviet forces near Siedlce and halted on 27 July the 11th Tank Corps, which had recovered from its rout near Maciejowa, the 2nd Guards Cavalry Corps and the 47th Army's divisions. The Soviet forces suffered heavy losses in tanks and were thrown back.[18]

In the beginning of June German intelligence had uncovered an increase in enemy activity in front of the 4th Panzer Division's positions around Kovel'. During the following two weeks reinforcements of men and materiel reached the division, including the 2nd Panzer Battalion, which had been mastering the Panthers in Germany as early as the autumn of 1943. The battalion had mainly received Ausf. A Panthers, as well as Panthers of the earlier Ausf. G type. A fresh infusion of Panzer IV tanks arrived for the 1st Battalion, thanks to which the overall number of tanks in the 4th Panzer Division rose to 130. The 49th Anti-Tank Battalion got several Marder IIs and Jagdpanzer IVs. The 4th Reconnaissance Battalion got several Luchs light reconnaissance tanks with 20mm guns, several light armoured Sd.Kfz.222 transports, eight Sd.Kfz.232 armoured cars, and the 12th and 33rd Panzergrenadier Regiments also got a small number of Sd.Kfz.250 and Sd.Kfz.251 armoured personnel carriers, although these were insufficient even to fully outfit a single battalion in each of the regiments. On 22 June, when the reconnaissance in force began before Operation 'Bagration', the 4th Panzer Division was alerted and dispatched to Army Group Centre, where it entered the fighting at the beginning of July. According to a division report, on 6 July it killed 227 Soviet soldiers and destroyed 11 tanks and self-propelled guns, although nothing was reported about prisoners. During the second half of July, while experiencing difficulties with the delivery of fuel and ammunition, the 4th Panzer Division was reinforced with 17 assault guns from the 904th Battalion and 12 Tigers from the 507th Battalion. This partially compensated for losses in armoured equipment suffered by the division in the preceding heavy fighting. For example, in the evening of 8 July there were only 13 combat-ready Panzer IVs and 25 Panthers. On 17 July all of the 4th Division's armoured equipment was thrown into the fighting along the Narew in order to support the 129th Infantry Division. The German units repelled with great decisiveness the Soviet attacks, which were poorly coordinated and launched with insufficient air support. During the 20–21 July fighting the 4th Panzer Division counted 405 Soviet soldiers killed and only 25 wounded, which speaks to the ferocity of the combat. The Germans did not take prisoners, understanding that it would be very difficult to evacuate them. Several guns were also captured. The 4th Panzer Division's personnel losses were comparatively small and it was reinforced by several armoured vehicles. By the evening of 21 July the division disposed of 13 combat-ready Panthers, 21 Panzer IVs, six Panzerjäger tank destroyers with 47mm guns, eight assault guns and 16 Tigers, as well as six command tanks. Twenty-seven Panthers, 40 Panzer IVs, nine Panzerjägers, four Jagdpanzer IVs, and 16 assault guns were undergoing minor repairs, with 27 Panthers, 23 Panzer IVs, one Panzerjäger, 16 Jagdpanzer IVs, and one assault gun undergoing major repairs for up to three weeks. In two weeks of heavy fighting eight assault guns, 12 Panthers, and three Jagdpanzer-IVs, were destroyed or damaged, as well as lighter armoured vehicles, including, evidently, a certain number of Panzer IVs. The remaining tanks and assault guns undergoing repairs were out of action for technical reasons. By the morning of 27 July there were 32 combat-ready Panthers,

29 Panzer IVs, nine Panzerjägers, five Jagdpanzer IVs and three Tigers, as well as six command tanks. By this time the 904th Assault Gun Battalion from the 4th Division had been removed. There were 27 Panthers, 40 Panzer IVs, nine Panzerjägers, one Jagdpanzer IV and seven Tigers undergoing minor repairs, with nine Panthers, six Panzer IVs, one Panzerjäger, 14 Jagdpanzer IVs and 12 Tigers undergoing major repairs. At the end of July the 4th Panzer Division began the march to Warsaw, where it fought against the Soviet 2nd Tank Army. The division was divided into two combat groups. Hans Kristern's combat group consisted of the 35th and 12th Panzergrenadier Regiments, the 4th Reconnaissance Battalion, the 103rd Artillery Regiment's 2nd Battalion, the 79th Engineer Battalion, the 79th Anti-Tank Battalion's 3rd and 4th Companies, the 290th Anti-Aircraft Battalion, and units from the 79th Signals Battalion. Lieutenant Colonel Gerlach von Gaudecher's combat group included the 33rd Panzergrenadier Regiment, the 1071st Infantry Regiment (an independent infantry regiment attached to the division), the 1st and 3rd Battalions of the 103rd Artillery Regiment, the 507th Panzer Battalion, the 1st Company of the 159th Construction Battalion, and the 1st and 2nd Companies and part of the 4th Company from the 49th Anti-Tank Battalion. On 1 August the 4th Panzer Division had 19 combat-ready Panthers, 28 Panzer IVs, 12 Panzerjägers, ten Jagdpanzer IVs and 29 Tigers, as well as four command tanks. There were 23 Panthers, 18 Panzer IVs, two Panzerjägers, two Jagdpanzer-IVs, and 15 Tigers undergoing minor repairs, and 25 Panthers, 17 Panzer IVs, two Panzerjägers and six Jagdpanzer-IVs undergoing major repairs. In all, there were 69 combat-ready tanks and tank destroyers in the 4th Panzer Division, with another 29 in the attached 507th Panzer Battalion.

On 2–3 August the 4th Panzer Division reported destroying 11 Soviet tanks. On 4 August this number rose to 53, and during eight days of exhausting fighting, from 2 through 9 August, the division destroyed 108 tanks, two self-propelled guns, 20 field guns and 45 anti-tank guns. Five hundred and forty-four Red Army soldiers were killed and 52 captured. The German losses were small, but the strength of the combat elements fell to 2,325 men. On 11 August the division was shifted to Courland. The first collisions with Soviet troops around Riga proved to be successful for the 4th Panzer Division. In several days, according to its report, about 1,000 Russians were killed and about 2,000 men captured. Also, up to 200 guns and 100 tanks and self-propelled guns were destroyed or captured.[19]

The *Wiking* Division and the 4th Panzer Division jointly attacked and halted the Soviet forces that had broken through near Kleszczele.[20] This is what the former commander of the 65th Army, General – then Colonel General – Pavel Ivanovich Batov, related about this battle:

> Night came on 23 July. The army observation post was in the woods near the lateral road, directly opposite the centre of the 80th and 105th Corps' operational formation. To the south, nearly 20km away, the 69th Sevsk Division was holding a bridgehead over the Western Bug, while the guards troops of the 37th Division and 15th Sivash Division covered the entire right flank.
>
> Radetskii, Lipis and Veskii were at the observation post. We discussed the possibility of reinforcing the attack along the left flank. Colonel Nikitin almost ran into the overhead cover. Light from the

OPERATION BAGRATION: AN INCOMPLETE TRUTH

kerosene lamp dimly illuminated his face, and this is perhaps why it seemed unusually pale.

'What's happened?'

'A radio conversation by the commander of the 5th SS Panzer Division *Wiking*, Galla [actually, this is SS *Gruppenführer* Herbert Gille, B.S.] with the commander of the 4th Panzer Division Petsel [actually, with Lieutenant General Clemens Betzel, B.S.] has been intercepted. Gall is in Wysokie-Litovsk and Betzel is in Bielsk. They are getting ready to launch meeting attacks against our forces to link up in the Kleszczele area.'

One could have expected anything, but not this. No one supposed that such a threat could emanate from the north, from Bielsk. This was a miscalculation by our intelligence. The Germans had correctly evaluated the weakness of our right flank. The enemy's counterblow pursued limited aims – to link up the Wysokie-Litovsk group of forces with the Bielsk group. In order to speed up the resolution of this task, General Galla had requested the commander of the German 4th Panzer Division to render him assistance in clear over the radio.

The army command post was in Kleszczele; that is, it could come under attack. I summon Bobkov to the telephone: 'Sound the alarm. Move the command post immediately to Gainovka.' I left with Radetskii to the edge of the woods, where telegraph apparatuses had been mounted on a car. We had to wait a long time until they called Rokossovskii. Finally the following words appeared on the ticker tape: 'The commander is on the line.'

I report: 'A radio conversation had been intercepted. The enemy is preparing meeting counterblows from the area of Bielsk and Wysokie-Litovsk toward Kleszczele. I'm preparing the troops to repel the enemy's tanks. There are insufficient forces. Our combat formations have been thinned out. I have no reserves.' Rokossovskii ordered: 'Take measures to hold your present position. Assistance will be rendered.'

This short conversation had just concluded, when from the north, south and west the roar of an artillery cannonade began to grow. The enemy's counterblow had begun. I remain in Kleszczele with Radetskii: communications cannot be lost with the corps for a minute.

I.I. Ivanov was the first to report:

'The enemy has attacked the 69th. He is attempting to throw our units off the bridgehead. The division is defending successfully.'

We had determined this direction of the counterblow as a secondary one.

The order is given to Ivanov: 'Prepare to repel the tanks from the north, from Bielsk. The main danger will be there . . .' I get in touch with D.F. Alekseev. I can tell that things are hot by the corps commander's voice.

'A division of infantry is attacking from the direction of Bol'shoe Turno. Thirty-five tanks, two armoured trains and self-propelled artillery are supporting it. The attack is being launched against the 354th. The division's units have fallen back 3km and have taken up an all-round defence in the area of the inhabited locale of Augustinka.

'The situation in the 80th Corps is even more intense. Having repelled five counter-attacks, the 356th Division and the 115th Brigade suffered losses. The divisional artillery lacks the strength to hold the attack by the enemy's armoured fist. Also, the corps' rifle units have a large number of soldiers that have never been under fire. I have thrown in two rocket launcher platforms to assist Baranov's retreating units.'

Alekseev reports again: 'The enemy is continuing to develop the offensive to the north-east and is trying to encircle the 44th Division. The guards troops have fallen back to the Zales'ye area. They have taken up defensive positions. One regiment has become separated and is fighting in encirclement.' I barely had time to draw conclusions and communicate my decision to the corps commander, when Ivanov came on the line: 'One hundred tanks are attacking the 15th and 37th Divisions from the direction of Bielsk. The enemy is splitting our combat formations. My command post has been cut off from the troops.'

A hundred tanks from the north and as many from the south. In this situation there remained nothing else to do but to squeeze the army's group of forces' main forces toward the centre, to abandon part of the occupied territory, to shorten the front line, and to take up an all-round defence. There is very little time in which to issue this order to the troops. We decide to transmit the order in the clear, over the radio, while masking the planned defensive lines with numbers from a coded map. In order not to lose a precious minute, I order that all the corps' radios be put on the same wavelength. The order is received by all the corps commanders simultaneously. Ivanov immediately reports that he has lost communications with the 69th Division. It was necessary to assign this division the following task: to abandon the bridgehead over the Western Bug and to come and assist the corps' headquarters. But how can I communicate this? Colonel Rondarev, a staff officer, was standing next to me. 'Allow me to break through on a motorcycle.' I shake Rondarev's hand firmly.

'Hurry, but be careful.'

He raced off on the motorcycle toward the Western Bug. He managed to pass through along the roads not occupied by the enemy to the 69th's command post and pass on the order. By midday it had become clear that the northern and southern German groups of forces would be able to link up. It was time for the army commander's operational group to fall back on Gainovka, in order to organize from there an attack along the enemy that had broken through. The noise of battle grew nearer. But it was still necessary to report on the situation to Rokossovskii. Nikolai Antonovich and I jumped into our cars and set off for the telegraph operators. Rokossovskii replied quickly.

I report: 'The enemy is launching a meeting counter-attack from two directions to Kleszczele. The army headquarters has been pulled back to Gainovka. I'm here with an operational group and we are directing the battle at . . .'

OPERATION BAGRATION: AN INCOMPLETE TRUTH

I wasn't able to finish the report. Nikolai Antonovich interrupted me: 'Germans!'

We could see through the bus's open door that in the high rye, about 300m distant, the turret of a German tank had appeared. The gun barrel turned in our direction and at that moment a loud explosion was heard. The enemy sent his first shell into a poorly-camouflaged truck on which the runner of a telegraph apparatus had been mounted.

'Everybody follow me!'

We run toward the field of rye, where our camouflaged *Willys* [jeeps] were by the road. From behind there's a second explosion. The telegraph apparatus had begun to burn. Fortunately, the telegraph operators were able to run away with us. The *Willys* sped along the field of rye to Gainovka, We literally passed by within tens of meters of a German tank unit's combat formations. The thick rye saved us.

They told us that the Front commander had been very worried by the sudden breaking off of the conversation and asked over the radio: 'Where's Batov?' Receiving no answer, he sent a squadron of fighters to reconnoitre. We saw the planes flying over the areas of Kleszczele and Czeremcha, but the pilots did not spot our vehicles. There was a joker among them: he reported from his aircraft by radio to his immediate superior that he saw along the road from Kleszczele to Gainovka . . . scattered military-issue plates.

We reached our command post in the evening. Before long G.K. Zhukov and K.K. Rokossovskii arrived.

'Report on your decision.'

'The plan for eliminating the German breakthrough has already been worked out. It's been decided to launch an attack on Kleszczele from the Gainovka area with the forces of two newly-arrived battalions from the army's reserve regiment and separate units of the 18th Corps, with fire support from Guards mortar battalions. Alekseev's corps is simultaneously attacking from the south.'

'The decision is the correct one, but with too few forces', admitted G.K. Zhukov. 'We must not only restore direct communications with the corps, but we must capture a bridgehead over the Bug. We'll give you a hand.'

It turns out that that Lieutenant General Ivan Alekseevich Gartsev's 53rd Rifle Corps, from Romanenko's army, and the Don Corps's 17th Tank Brigade, which was undergoing reformation, were heading our way. The arrival of these forces was expected during the night.

During the remaining hours we were in constant contact with the corps commanders. All the comrades reported calmly. Our nervousness, which had been caused by the tanks' stunning attack, had passed. The 37th's Guard troops saved Ivanov. They broke through to the corps' command post and helped them get out of the encirclement. Later, when the entire course of events for 23 July was noted on the corps' maps, it became clear that the 37th Guards' artillery troops had helped me and Radetskii as well.

Upon the appearance of tanks in the area of Krasnoe Selo, the division commander decided to immediately move an independent Guards anti-tank battalion from Czeremcha to the unnamed heights north of Kleszczele and to cover the roads with fire. The artillery troops moved at high speed. Guards Major Aleksei Sergeevich Kalmykov, a Hero of the Soviet Union and the battalion commander, was in the lead vehicle . . . At that time the enemy tanks had already broken through to the heights. Kalmykov's battalion blocked their path. The tanks fire. All of this took place right in front of the division's artillery commander, Guards Major Nikolai Nikitich Lukht, who led the artillery troops of the 86th Guards Rifle Regiment to new firing positions after the tank destroyers.

'Prepare for battle!' he commanded.

The artillery crews deployed their guns directly on the road. They fired point-blank on the enemy. Five enemy vehicles were burning. More tanks are crawling out on the crest of the height. Seeing the fate of the lead vehicles, the German tank crews turn back. The enemy put in groups of automatic riflemen to outflank the artillery troops. Only the gun layers remained at their guns, while the remaining troops went into battle against the German infantry. This attack was also repulsed. The tanks appeared again. It continued this way for nearly two hours, until the enemy gave up on his plan to reach Kleszczele by the shortest route. The Guards troops' brave resistance delayed by a good deal a breakthrough by the German tanks. The enemy was forced to attempt to bypass the artillery batteries along the forest roads. Thus at first only a few German vehicles appeared near Kleszczele. One of these had shot up our telegraph apparatus . . . On 24 July I.A. Gartsev's and D.F. Alekseev's rifle corps, in conjunction with the 17th Tank Brigade, routed the Germans around Kleszczele and in two days of fighting restored the army's previous position. The enemy lost more than 40 tanks, up to 50 guns and more than 5,000 officers and men, although he was nonetheless able to remove part of his combat equipment and formation headquarters from Bielsk. The remaining forces of the Wysokie-Litovsk group of forces fell back along the road to Drohiczyn.[21]

P.I. Batov sought to assure his readers that the main objective of the German counterblow was to get the SS *Wiking* Division out of encirclement, when the goal was actually to eliminate the Soviet bridgehead over the Bug and to halt the offensive by the 65th Army. To judge by everything, Pavel Ivanovich overstated the number of enemy tanks. On 2 August the *Wiking* Division and the 4th Panzer Division between them had 144 tanks and assault guns. Of course, there could have been a little more armoured equipment on 23 July, but to judge from the description cited in P.I. Batov's memoirs, the Germans did not suffer heavy irreparable losses in the 23 July fighting and the German losses of 40 tanks claimed by the commander of the 65th Army appear exaggerated. Moreover, by 2 August the number of tanks and assault guns could have increased due to repairs and the delivery of new vehicles. The 65th Army managed to restore its previous position comparatively easily only because immediately following the successful counterblow, the SS *Wiking* and 4th Panzer Divisions were transferred to the Warsaw area and arrived at their new concentration areas on 31 July and 2 August, respectively.

From the German side, *Wiking*'s fight with the 65th Army was viewed in the following manner. At 1800 on 19 July the XXIII Army Corps received an order from the Second Army headquarters:

> An enemy force of unknown strength has occupied Kleszczele following its exit from the Belovezh Forest.
>
> The XXIII Army Corps quickly pulled the 5th SS *Wiking* Division out of the front line, and it moved to the north-west together with other units, so as to be maximally strong to the east of the Brest-Litovsk railway and to rout the enemy to the north-east of Kleszczele and to establish contact with Mercker's group to the north-east of Orla. The enemy's forces to the north-west of Brest must be blocked by part of the [available] forces and eliminated, insofar as the fulfilment of the first assignment allows this.

Von Tresckow dispatched his orders to the division chief of staff and his assistant with the words: 'Delay the enemy! Nothing is holding in the West. The road to the Reich is open!'

On 21 July Henning von Tresckow, who had taken an active part in the anti-Hitler plot and who, upon learning of the failure of the attempt on Hitler and understanding that sooner or later the Gestapo would get to him, committed suicide. He went out into no-man's land in the area to the north-east of Novoselok and, while imitating a firefight, blew himself up with a hand grenade.

The *Wiking* Division slowly broke contact with the enemy, while inflicting losses on them. By this time the division already had its own artillery regiment, which had arrived with the latest trains. At 0900 on 21 July Gille's division left its concentration area near Kamenets-Litovskii and set out for the north-west. The panzer regiment, the headquarters of which was in Woisk, 12km from Kamenets, pulled its 1st Battalion at night from its positions to the north of Sziszowo. The battalion remained in the western part of Woisk until 1400. The headquarters company reached the woods to the west of Jasionowka at about 1530. At the same time the 3rd Company and the headquarters arrived at Maniewicze, 3km to the south. Closer to evening the 4th Company was pulled out of the Kamenets bridgehead. At first, the 2nd Battalion fought along a 40km sector. It counter-attacked in the direction of Height 178.4 and Czemery, along the eastern edge of the Kamenets bridgehead, to the south of the Lesna. The main forces of the 2nd and 3rd Battalions of the *Germania* Regiment attacked to the north-west and reached the Sipurka Creek. The 5th Company attacked the villages of Kalenkowicze and Padborcze, 25km to the north-west of Kamenets. The 7th Company ended up being drawn into fighting 10km to the west of Dolbizna and Klewicze.

The enemy had already crossed the Brest-Litovsk rail line north of Kleszczele and was moving to the south-west and forced the division to regroup and move to the north, in order to block the way of the 65th Army's forward units. On the morning of 21 July the division once again attacked from Wysokie-Litovsk. The panzer regiment, which had one Panzer IV (with a long barrel), 44 Panthers and 13 assault guns, crossed the Czeremcha–Brest rail line approximately 10km south of Czeremcha with its 1st Battalion. It had left Tumin, to the west of the railway line, and headed north in the direction of Bobrowka, parallel to the railway. Several Soviet cavalry patrols were quickly pushed out of Tumin. Powerful enemy columns continued to advance unhindered to the south of the Czeremcha–Nurzec railway. A destroyed bridge to the north-west of Tumin interfered with the immediate attack by the 1st Panzer Battalion, which had no engineers at all. They had to spend several hours looking for a crossing. At this time a large part of the 2nd Battalion was still fighting approximately 6km to the south-east of Czeremcha. The 7th Company pulled the enemy back near Dolbizna, while the 6th Company, which meanwhile had been moved up from the Kamenets bridgehead, attacked in the outskirts of Awlus, to the south-east of Czeremcha. The 8th Company and the company's engineers, in accordance with orders from the corps and division, deployed further to the west and attacked to the north the columns that were moving along the Wolka–Nurzec–Tymianka road.

Only at 2000 on 21 July did the 1st Panzer Battalion reach Bobrowka and establish contact with the 5th and 7th Companies of the *Westland* Regiment's 2nd Battalion. Meanwhile, Soviet forces were threatening to seize a bridge over the Bug to the south-east of Siemiatycze. On 22 July the *Wiking* Division was given a task from the Second Army headquarters: 'Enemy units, which are moving along the Brest–Bialystok railway to the west must be cut off from their rear supply lines, which must restore the continuity of the army's front.'

Meanwhile, the headquarters of the XXIII Army Corps was reporting to the Second Army's headquarters:

> The *Wiking* Division must first create the basis for the beginning of operations. It is planned to concentrate the division and shift it to the north. One regiment is to attack toward the north-east of Chola (to the east of the line Brest–Czermecha); one group one group is to attack from Bobrowka to the north; one group has been distracted toward Nurzec . . . The 292nd Infantry Division has been attached to the *Wiking* Division . . . The terrain is hard to traverse and the enemy is strong. The enemy is very strong in the woods. Aerial reconnaissance may not spot him there.

There were problems with supplying the division, because Pliev's encircled cavalry-mechanized group had not been destroyed and had cut the railway in the Wysokie area.

On 22 July the 3rd Panzer Company, along with *Westland*'s second battalion, threw Soviet forces out of Zubacze. The *Wiking* Division was opposed by divisions of the Soviet 65th Army's 105th Rifle Corps. It was noted in the corps' war diary for 21 July:

> Having created . . . three groups for operating from three directions for splitting up the corps' combat formations, the enemy began to carry out this operation from 2400 on 20.7.44. He launched the offensive to the north on Nurec and Rogacze, creating a direct threat to the corps' headquarters, and with part of his forces attacking to the west along the railway to Nurec station, splitting up the corps' forces into two groups, and cutting off the division's headquarters and that of the corps from the troops. By 1900, they had taken Rogacze and Medwezki, and Nurec station along the western axis.[22]

OPERATION BAGRATION: AN INCOMPLETE TRUTH

This is what the Soviet 65th Army's war diary said about the fighting on 22 July: 'The enemy counter-attacked at 1700 with up to two regiments of infantry, along with 70 tanks and self-propelled guns, against the 75th Guards Rifle Division's elements in the general direction of Nurec and Czeremcha (western). At the cost of heavy losses, the enemy managed to break through to the woods south of Medwezki and Nurec.' The number of German tanks has been inflated here by 1.8 times. On 23 July *Obersturmführer* Karl Nicolussi-Leck's 8th Panzer Company captured Czeremcha, destroying eight SU-76s from the 65th Army's 1899th Self-Propelled Artillery Regiment, losing two Panthers knocked out. The 8th Company then moved to height 181.2 to the north of Czeremcha, where in Kleszczele he established contact with forces from the German 4th Panzer Division, which were attacking from the north.[23]

Soviet forces attempted to recapture Czeremcha, which changed hands several times. Early on the morning of 24 July *Wiking*'s 4th Panzer Company destroyed two T-34s and one 76.2mm anti-tank gun by the railway embankment in Czeremcha. The overall situation demanded the withdrawal of *Wiking* to the western bank of the Bug. On 25 July, when the *Wiking* Division was already withdrawing to the Bug, the *Westland* combat group, consisting of the 1st Panzer Battalion from the *Westland* Regiment and the 1st Battalion of *Wiking*'s artillery regiment, were holding a new defensive line while the division's remaining units were withdrawing. At the same time, the 4th Panzer Company relieved the 8th Panzer Company near Kleszczele at 2300 on 25 July, in order to block the movement of enemy columns along the Kleszczele–Dasza road. The 3rd Panzer Company, which comprised the panzer regiment's mobile reserve, threw Soviet forces out of Keszczele on 25 July. According to German estimates, Soviet losses amounted to 30 killed, who remained on the battlefield, with one field gun and one anti-tank gun captured. At 1700 there followed a new Soviet attack, which by German estimates, included 200 men and 12 tanks, which broke into Czeremcha from the west. They were halted by fire from a composite anti-aircraft machine gun from a platoon out of the headquarters company of the 1st Panzer Battalion. *Westland*'s 1st Company destroyed two T-34s with anti-tank guns, and another five T-34s were destroyed by the 3rd Company's Panzer IVs. The remaining T-34s were destroyed by the 8th Company's Panthers, which were attacking from the south and striking the enemy tanks from the flank. The commander of the 1st Panzer Battalion's headquarters company, *Obersturmführer* Cenghas, described this episode in the following report:

> We were in position around Czeremcha and in the woods to the west of Czeremcha. At about 1000 the Russians broke through in the eastern part of Czeremcha. There were decisive defensive efforts on the part of two guns from the anti-aircraft platoon. The old defensive line was restored.
>
> Closer to 1700 I saw how our infantry had fallen back. The sounds of battle reached us from the woods. An NCO from the *Westland*'s command post reported that it was necessary to send forward a composite anti-aircraft machine gun. The Russians were getting ready to attack in significant strength.
>
> Anti-aircraft machine gun no. 2 was moved to the main defensive line and opened fire against the edge of the woods. Suddenly 12 T-34s emerged from the woods. At the same time we received orders from

the battalion to move both anti-aircraft machine guns back, insofar as they were helpless against tanks. However, according to the order by the commander of *Westland*'s 1st Battalion, the anti-aircraft machine guns remained at their positions, and while carrying out dodging manoeuvres with the help of their engines, attempted to get away from the tanks, several of which had passed by. Two T-34s were knocked out by *Westland*'s 14th Company. One of the 14th Company's anti-tank guns then got a direct hit and was put out of action.

Anti-aircraft machine gun no. 1 managed to destroy two 76.2mm anti-tank guns and cut the infantry off from its tanks, which is why they suffered heavy losses. As a result, the Russians were able to enter Czeremcha only on their tanks. Later on, they lost all their tanks, when they entered the fire zone of our tanks and the 8th Company, which moved up with its Panthers. Both anti-aircraft guns had been pulled back, because they had carried out their assignment. One man was wounded in the stomach, but remained at his gun. At night the previous positions were occupied once again.

On the morning of 26 July the Soviet attacks resumed, supported by field and anti-tank guns, mortars and 'Katyushas'. The Red Army troops once again were able to break into Czeremcha and were once again thrown out after Soviet tanks were unable to overcome the German defence. The 7th Panzer Company continued to fight 10km from Czeremcha and 10km from Bereziszcze, and the 5th Company was able to throw the Russians off Height 176, to the north of Werpol, 17km from Czeremcha, and the 6th Company counter-attacked along the Biala Podlaska–Terespol highway. Westfall's reinforced combat group, within the confines of the main withdrawal, fell back from its positions near Keszczele and in Czeremcha on the night of 27 July.

The 1st Panzer Battalion's main forces concentrated in the Tokary area 17km from Czeremcha. The 4th Company lost two assault guns while attempting to evacuate a damaged gun. Both were destroyed, the damaged gun and the towing gun. As a result of attempts to evacuate, time was lost and the company had to attempt to break through the Soviet forces' combat formations. The 3rd Company relieved the 8th Company in its positions 5km north-west of Wilanowo, and the latter crossed the Bug. On the night of 28 July the 1st Panzer Battalion reached the woods near Makowicze. Its companies were subjected to Soviet air attacks, particularly the 4th Company south of Tokary. Near Siemiatycze, on the bridgehead along the northern bank of the Bug, a platoon from the 3rd Panzer Company was covering the withdrawal of a battalion from the 292nd Infantry Division. All of the damaged tanks and assault guns were evacuated over the Bug even before evening, and the last units of the 1st Panzer Battalion crossed the river at 2100 on 27 July and headed for the Zakalinki area.

However, the changed situation on the night of 28 July forced us to deploy the 1st Panzer Battalion from east to west. Now it was directed against Kozuchowek, more than 90km from Brest-Litovsk. All of the wheeled vehicles safely overcame this 80km march on 28 July, but many tanks and assault guns broke down, and in each company there remained only from three to six armoured vehicles. On 29–30th the 1st Battalion's repair services were engaged in restoring the damaged tanks and assault guns. Rokossovskii decided to repel the counterblow of five, as he believed, German divisions (including two panzer divisions), north-west of Wysokie and south-east of Bielsk-Podlastki with the forces of the 48th and 65th Armies and one corps from the 28th Army. In reality, only two panzer divisions were to launch the counterblow, and these were forced to fall back on the night of 27 July in connection with their transfer to another area. Rokossovskii was preparing to encircle the Germans' Brest group of forces with an attack from the north-east by the main forces of the 28th Army, from the south-east with the 70th Army, and from the east with the 61st Army's 9th Guards Rifle Corps along converging axes. The 65th and 47th Armies' formations were also supposed to reach the Western Bug River and prevent the Brest group of forces from being relieved from without. However, the two armies were unable to reach the Western Bug.[24]

The Brest garrison, led by the commander of the 251st Infantry Division, Lieutenant General Maximillian Felzmann, was able to break out to the west. A curious entry regarding this breakout remained in the combat diary of the German Second Army. 'The encirclement ring closed on the evening of 27 July. On 27 July the order was issued for the breakout ... We were able to get 700 wounded out. The artillery guns that had to be left behind were blown up ... Nothing remained in Brest except for alcohol (to distract the Russians). All the rest – forts, bridges, bunkers and 70 rail cars, which had been moved to a bridge – was blown up. The *Hiwis* behaved magnificently!'

At 1300 on 31 July the 1st Panzer Battalion left for the north-west and, having covered about 60km, ended up 35km to the east of Warsaw, where the *Wiking* Division was gathering. As early as 24 July the First Ukrainian Front's right wing had taken Lublin and the First Belorussian Front forced the Bug at Wlodawa, 60km south of Brest-Litovsk, the defence of which made no sense. The Soviet 3rd Tank Corps broke through the German Second Army's western wing toward Warsaw.

On 31 July the 1st Panzer Battalion arrived in the area east of Stanislawow. Stanislawow itself had been retaken by units of *Wiking* as early as the evening of 30 July, while several tanks and trucks had been captured.

On the evening of 31 July the headquarters of Army Group Centre issued a directive on the continuation of the offensive on 1 August:

> The attack for the purpose of closing the breach to the east of the Warsaw bridgehead must be undertaken with the first rays of the sun on 1 August 1944, from Stanislawow to the west by the SS IV Panzer Corps. For this purpose, the headquarters of the Second Army is to transfer to the SS IV Panzer Corps a tank group and three battalions from the SS *Totenkopf* 3rd Panzer Division on the evening before.
>
> The Ninth Army is to clear the Warsaw–Radzymin road by attacking from the south-west on 1 August.

As the enemy had already penetrated to Siedlce, *Totenkopf* was authorized to abandon the city. On the morning of 1 August its right wing established contact with *Wiking*'s engineer battalion. By the evening of 1 August the main forces of the *Germania* Regiment and the tanks of the 2nd Panzer Battalion had established contact from the west with the 19th Panzer Division on Height 129, to the north of Okuniew. Throughout 1 August new Soviet forces attacked to the south of Stanislawow, in Mlenczien, and to the south-east of Grebkow.

The 3rd and 4th Companies, along with *Westland* and the engineer battalion, repeatedly carried out counter-attacks in the area of Ludmilow and Sokolja and were able to restore their previous defensive line. The rain has made the roads impassable for wheeled transport.

By the evening of 2 August a breakthrough toward Radzymin was carried out by the 19th Panzer Division from the south-west and by units of the 4th Panzer Division from the north-east. The breakthrough units of the Soviet 2nd Tank Army were blocked and unable to advance to the north.

On 3 August these units, which were suffering from a fuel shortage, were pushed back to Welomin and to the area to the east. They attempted to break through to the south and south-east along the north front of the *Wiking* Division. In order to prevent this, a battalion from the *Germania* Regiment was activated, reinforced by the 2nd Battalion's tanks. They operated against Soviet forces to the north of Michalow. Even tracked vehicles moved on the local roads with difficulty.

The final breakthrough to the west for the purpose of destroying the encircled troops on 4 August was contained in an order by the German Second Army: 'All available forces should be concentrated along the western wing in order to establish contact by means of an offensive and to maintain it with the Ninth Army, which has moved forward at 0800 on 4 August from the Michalow area through Dluga Koscielna.' Despite the enemy's growing pressure along the southern front, the German Second Army finally created a continuous front and also destroyed the encircled units of the Soviet 2nd Tank Army.

On 2 August the SS 5th Panzer Regiment had eight Panzer IVs with long-barrelled 75mm guns, 45 Panthers and 12 assault guns combat ready, which was less than the authorized strength of a single panzer battalion. As Ewald Klapdor notes, 'one should note the magnificent work of the technical services in maintaining many combat vehicles in working condition after two weeks of extreme wear and tear'.[25]

On 29 July *Wiking*'s strength was 2,200 men. This meant for 3 August 247 men per kilometre of front. The *Totenkopf* Division, which was mostly defending, could put up 78 combat troops per kilometre. On the average the German Second Army had 115 combat personnel per kilometre of front in its divisions and analogous formations. On 6 August Herbert Gille headed the SS IV Panzer Corps. *Standartenführer* Eduard Deisenhofer commanded the division for six days, and on 12 August he was relieved by *Standartenführer* Johannes Muhlenkamp. *Obersturmbannführer* Fritz Darges, Martin Bormann's and Hitler's former adjutant, became the commander of the SS 5th Panzer Regiment.

On 10 August a counter-attack by the 2nd Battalion threw out of Stanislawow Soviet forces which proceeded to break in once again. On the night of 12 August *Wiking* pulled out of the fighting and took up a prepared defensive zone: the railway 4km to the south of Tluszcz–the western extremity of the woods near Grabow–the woods to the south-east of Sulejow. Due to the worsening situation with its neighbour to the left, the 5th Jäger Division, the left-wing *Westland* Regiment retreated more than 10km to the north-north-east, at the same time as the right wing of the *Germania* Regiment, which served as a strongpoint, only shifted insignificantly. The division's entire front had earlier been oriented to the south-west; at that moment it shifted to the south-east.

On 14 August units of the *Wiking* Division repelled the final Soviet attacks in the Sulejow area, which changed hands several times. Nicolussi-Leck's 8th Company, which had thrown the Soviet forces out of the town, irreparably lost two Panthers. Then a quiet set in for a few days. Before this, at 2300 on 14 August, the *Wiking* Division evacuated Sulejow. A Soviet rifle battalion, with 20 T-34s and self-propelled guns, occupied a position in the woods to the south and south-west of Sulejow.

On 15 August Soviet troops attacked the *Germania* Regiment's 2nd Battalion and occupied Jasienica, which, however, was retaken with a counter-attack, along with Height 105. Soviet troops also penetrated to the northern bank of an arm of the Cinka stream. As a result of the counter-attack by the 3rd Panzer Company, they managed to recapture height 99 one kilometre to the south of Wilczanica.

At 0900 on 18 August a major Soviet offensive on Warsaw began. Along the *Wiking* Division's sector the Germans managed to prevent a Soviet breakthrough to the north-west. By 24 August the strength of the *Wiking* Division had fallen to 10,335 men. There was fighting near Wymyslow, to the north-west of Sulejow and in Wolka Sulejowska. *Wiking*'s 1st Panzer Battalion suffered heavy losses, but it also destroyed 17 Soviet tanks – six Shermans, six T-34s, four T-34-85s and one flamethrower tank, as well as ten anti-tank guns. And along the sector of the *Germania* Regiment's 2nd Battalion, Soviet troops took Tluszcz and Height 107. The 7th and 8th panzer companies counter-attacked and destroyed 12 Soviet tanks and inflicted heavy losses on the infantry, halting the Soviet advance in the area of Jasienica. But the German infantry was thrown back and the tanks from *Wiking*'s 2nd Panzer Battalion were left without infantry cover.

On *Wiking*'s right flank, near the boundary with the SS *Totenkopf* Division, on the night of 19 August the Germans fell back to their main defence line Klembow–Zonza River–south of Krusza–Wolka Kozlowska–Postoliska–Mokrowis. Soviet aviation was active, employing heavy bombs. Several of the 2nd Panzer Battalion's companies attempted to break out through the line of Soviet tanks under the cover of darkness. In breaking out, the Germans once again were helped by composite anti-aircraft machine guns. During 19 August *Wiking*'s 1st Panzer Battalion destroyed five Soviet tanks, and the 2nd Battalion 15.

On the night of 21 August *Westland*'s worn-out battalions were pulled back to Laskow, north of the Radzymin–Wyszkow road in order to put themselves in order. The 3rd and 4th Panzer Companies covered the withdrawal. The entry in the war diary of the 5th SS Panzer Regiment's 1st Battalion for 21 August reads: 'The 3rd and 4th Companies are covering the withdrawal and the panzergrenadiers' reconstitution, while occupying positions favourable for defence against the attacking enemy. The crews in the woods, encircled by the Russian infantry and without infantry support, are putting up resistance and giving the panzergrenadiers the necessary time in order to reform and occupy positions on heights 106 and 103 near Slopsk.'

Obersturmführer Cenghas reported on the activities of the 1st Panzer Battalion's anti-aircraft platoon:

The battalion headquarters was located in front of the infantry line. The anti-aircraft platoon had consolidated in the direction of Wolka-Slopsk, with weapon no. 2. There was no longer infantry in front. Weapon no. 2's forward post was observing how the Russian infantry went into the south-eastern part of Wolka-Slopsk, first with 20 soldiers, and then after 100m, another 25–30 soldiers. Well-placed continuous fire from all four barrels forced the Russians to fall back in panic. In any event, the Russians suffered losses as a result of being fired on in an ambush.

After approximately two hours the enemy once again moved forward in several detachments. He managed to position a mortar. After we once again opened fire the enemy covered our position with mortar fire. There were four wounded next to weapon no. 4 within one or two minutes. The weapon had to immediately change its position.

Only the commander and his tank remained at the battalion command post. Nothing more remained there. The command post had moved to Marianow.

On *Wiking*'s right flank, where the *Germania* Regiment was defending, the Soviet troops took Trojany along the Radzymin–Wyszkow railway. On 23–24 August the Germans managed to repel the majority of the Soviet attacks. But on the 25th the German defence crumbled.

On the evening of the 25th *Wiking*'s 6th and 8th Companies, along with the tanks from the *Totenkopf* Division, were located in the triangle Zawady–Los–Mokre. Further to the north the Soviet tanks had advanced as far as the southern bank of the Bug near Czarnow, bypassing Ludwinow. As a result, by evening they were between elements of *Wiking* and elements of the 1131st Infantry Brigade. The exhausted infantry was pulled back to a smaller bridgehead around Slenzany.

On the morning of 25 August Soviet artillery destroyed the 24-ton bridge to the Slenzany bridgehead. On this day Soviet troops repelled all German counter-attacks in this area. The *Wiking* Division irreparably lost eight Panzer IVs and four assault guns. Such heavy losses in armoured equipment were caused by the fact that the tanks and assault guns had shot off all their ammunition and had to be abandoned on the bridgehead and blown up because it was impossible to evacuate them. The Soviet losses, according to German estimates, were three Shermans and two T-34s, and two anti-tank and ten field guns. Aside from this, the attacking Soviet troops suffered heavy losses in killed and wounded.

Colonel Wilhelm Soet, the commander of the 1131st Infantry Brigade, which had been temporarily attached to the *Wiking* Division, upon the completion of the fighting on 27 August, reported:

The withdrawal was magnificently supported by *Hauptsturmführer* Saumenicht's panzer battalion [*Wiking*'s 1st Panzer Battalion, B.S.]; cooperation with the battalion may also be described as exemplary in the preceding days . . . In my opinion, the panzer crews did not want to abandon the hardened grenadiers until the last of them had crossed, and then, after the final shot had been fired, they blew up their vehicles so that their panzers would not fall into enemy hands. It's possible that a retreat together with the 1st Battalion [of infantry] would have preserved the panzers, but powerful pressure by a superior enemy would have resulted in heavy losses for the [infantry] battalion.

Thus I do not accuse of anything the tank crews whom I know as calm warriors.

This is typical, as the German commanders preferred to lose more tanks if it would help reduce losses among the infantry.

Although the *Wiking* Division lost the southern bank of the Bug, it was able to significantly slow down the pace of the Soviet offensive. Following the forcing of the Bug at Wlodawa, the First Belorussian Front covered more than 170km in ten days. But in order to cover the next 40km required more than 30 days. Following the end of the fighting the 1st Panzer Battalion, leaving only the 4th Company at the front, was pulled back to Lodz for reforming at the end of August.[26]

The example of the elite SS *Wiking* Division during Operation 'Bagration' shows how events might have developed had it not been for the Allies' landing in Normandy in June 1944, or had it not been as successful as actually transpired. Then Hitler might easily have been able to concentrate an additional 4–5 elite and fully-equipped panzer divisions on the Eastern Front. More than likely, they would have been concentrated somewhere in the Kovel' area, behind the boundary between Army Groups North Ukraine and Centre, in order, if necessary, to employ them where the Soviet offensive seemed most likely. And the example of the *Wiking* Division shows how these divisions might have changed 'Bagration's' course and outcome. In all, over a month of fighting, this division was able to rout one tank corps, create serious problems for two Soviet cavalry-mechanized groups and, in conjunction with another panzer division, one combined-arms army, as well as to rout a tank army on the approaches to Warsaw with another three panzer divisions. And if there had been five such divisions at the start of 'Bagration'? They would not have been able to defeat the entire mass of Soviet troops concentrated for 'Bagration', but an extra five panzer divisions might have been able to put all the armour gathered for 'Bagration' out of action in about three weeks and, together with other divisions, to inflict even greater personnel losses on the Soviet troops than was actually the case. The main thing is that additional panzer divisions would have covered the retreat of Army Group Centre's main forces to the Berezina and would have prevented the formation of large 'cauldrons'. In this case, 'Bagration' would likely not have lasted longer than two to three weeks. The front would have halted at the Berezina and the rout of Army Group Centre would not have occurred

Chapter 7

The Voyage of the 'Pseudo *Wiking*'

Peter Neumann's memoirs (or diary), *The Black March. The Personal Story of an SS Man*, became a worldwide bestseller in the 1950s and early 1960s. Actually, the bestsellers were the English-language translations of this book, the first of which appeared in 1959.[1] It was never published in German and all translation were either taken from the French text, which was published in 1956, or, as in the case of the Russian translation, were taken from one of the English-language translations. Moreover, there was never a Peter Neumann among the *Wiking* Division's officers. The suspicion immediately arises that the author of *The Black March* was not a German at all, but a Frenchman, and the French-language text of 1956 is not a translation but the original (by the way, the French name for the book is a lot simpler: *SS!*). This means that the author should most likely be looked for among those who wrote in French. The well-known Russian publicist Vol'fgang Akunov assumed that

> a significant part of the bloody history of Peter Neumann and his friends-comrades was simply rewritten by Ovidii Gorchakov from the adventure novel (that is, not even a 'novel-chronicle' in the manner of the unforgettable searcher for the Amber Room, Yulian Semenov, but a purely artistic work!) by the French author Georges Bernage (who disguised his real name under the pseudonym of 'Peter Neumann', probably because in case he were caught taking too many liberties with the facts, or even the outright falsification of history, and who gave his creation the form of a supposedly authentic diary of an officer from the SS *Wiking* Division), which came out in France (in French) after the end of the Second World War under the title of *The Black March*.[2]

The Soviet writer and former front-line intelligence officer, Ovidii Gorchakov, in his novella *Maksim is not in Contact* and several other works, actually liberally cited *The Black March*, taking it for the real diary of a *Wiking* Division officer. One could attempt to seriously test V. Akunov's hypothesis were it not for one curious circumstance: the historian and publisher, Georges Bernage was only born in 1949 and could in no way have written the memoirs of an SS officer, even fictitious ones. Meanwhile, another French writer, Pierre Daix[3] (1922–2014), is very good for the role of the author of *The Black March*. He was not only a writer, but a journalist as well and following the war was editor of the communist journal *Ce soir*, and also published biographies of Pablo Picasso and Aleksandr Solzhenitsyn. He joined the French Communist Party at the end of September 1939. He later broke with the communists in 1973 and left their ranks, which owed a great deal to his favourable realtions with Solzhenitsyn. Pierre Daix died in Paris on 2 November 2014, at the age of 92. His biography for the war years has still not been cleared up. He maintained that he was in Mathausen and other Nazi concentration camps. Daix related that while reading Aleksandr Solzhenitsyn's novella *A Day in the Life of Ivan Denisovich*, 'I came to understand that the nature of Stalin's and Hitler's camps was the same'.[4] Daix's enemies maintained that he had not been in Mathausen, but had only been dispatched as forced labour to Germany and Austria, or had simply served in the Todt organization.

Be that as it may, the fact that in 1954 he published a novel *Un tueur* (*The Murderer*), which was published in the Soviet Union under the title *A Murderer is Needed*, leads one to suspect him as the author of *The Black March*. The novel's main hero, the former French SS soldier Daniel Laverdon, has only just been released from prison (the action takes place in 1954). Thankfully, this inveterate rogue and scoundrel dies at the end of the book. It's quite possible that the experience of *The Murderer* gave Daix the idea for the hero of his next novel-pamphlet – the German SS officer Peter Neumann, Hitler's 'new man', called to rule in Germany and in Europe – and even gave him his own name, Pierre (Peter). This is the same repulsive type as Laverdon. An illustrative example is how he strangles his Jewish fiancée with his own hands (a Jewish fiancée for an SS officer is about as likely as a British lady as the fiancée of a Papuan cannibal). At the end of *The Black March* Neumann either perished on the streets of Soviet-occupied Vienna, or is captured (although the SS *Wiking* Division took no direct part in the defence of Vienna). However, nothing written in *The Black March* has much to do with the real *Wiking* Division. An example is how in an SS officers' school the students are forced to dig in during a tank attack and those who dig insufficiently-deep foxholes are doomed to die under the treads of the tanks. Here the author of *The Black March* is parodying in his own way the order by Marshal S.K. Timoshenko, who after taking up the post of defence commissar following the Finnish War, demanded the employment of live ammunition during exercises. The defence commissar actually sanctioned such a practice in his 16 May 1940 order 'On the Troops' Combat and Political Training during the Summer Period of the 1940 Training Year'. This order contains the demand that 'The infantry should be trained to follow behind a fire wall, adhering to it at a distance of 200m allowed by the explosions of shells'.[5] This meant, in practice, firing on troops with live rounds, which in the event of the rounds falling short, led to casualties among the participants in the exercises. As early as the April meeting of the higher command element on the results of the Finnish War, at which Stalin was present, to a statement by one of the commanders' 'After all, it is forbidden to fire live rounds during peacetime', the commander of the Archangel Military District, V.N. Kurdyumov, who was shortly afterwards appointed chief of the Red Army's combat training administration, replied:

> KURDYUMOV. Nevertheless, in the Leningrad Military District we trained the troops in cooperation by artillery firing at the firing ranges over the heads of our troops. We accompanied the infantry attack with artillery fire. Dmitriev and other comrades present here also fired.
>
> A VOICE. I also fired, although this is forbidden. This is what we're talking about.

KURDYUMOV. Do you want the order to read, fire away, and if you kill someone, no one will be held responsible?

A VOICE: A rolling barrage was forbidden, as this was viewed as an incorrect and harmful action.

KURDYUMOV. We are teaching the infantry cooperation with the other combat arms at all camp gatherings. But we can't do it like that. To say train, and if you have any casualties, then no one will be responsible. You can't write that.[6]

Actually, the initiator of the employment of live ammunition during exercises was not in fact Timoshenko, but Stalin himself. According to Marshal S.M. Budennyi's account, not long after the Finnish War, Stalin stated:

'I do not recognize those manoeuvres where the soldiers do everything in a conventional manner, in which they shoot, attack and even dig trenches in a conventional manner. People must train as if they were in a real battle. And for this reason we must not spare the ammunition. Only in a complex situation will the soldier learn to operate with confidence.'

'But there might be accidents', observed one of the commanders.

'Yes, there might be', Stalin replied. 'But in wartime we will suffer heavy losses if we do not teach the troops to handle their weapons, to know how to attack and to know how to defend.'[7]

It didn't make much sense to employ live ammunition during exercises. It was far more important to train the gunners to fire accurately, and the artillery, aviation and infantry commanders to closely cooperate with each other. This required a greater number of firing-range exercises and the ability to skilfully employ communications equipment. And the employment of live ammunition during manoeuvres had no effect on this.

We will not get into all of the nonsense found in *The Black March*. We will halt only on those which touch upon the period of Operation 'Bagration'. On 29 May 1944 Neumann was summoned to the unit's headquarters on the front line, where a certain Major Stressling informed him: 'The headquarters in Charlottenburg has entrusted you with an important mission. I need brave soldiers who have already proven themselves in action. Thus I have picked your people for a trip to Belorussia. I have summoned you to warn you that your people have to be ready by tomorrow morning.'

It's simply impossible to make sense of this mountain of nonsense. The headquarters of the *Wiking* Division was never in Charlottenburg, near Berlin. Daix, and Neumann after him, thought that the headquarters of the SS troops was located there, which also does not correspond to reality. There were a number of SS establishments, including the *Führer*'s plenipotentiary for the overall supervision of the NSDAP's spiritual and ideological education, in Charlottenburg, but not the SS troops' headquarters (the SS Main Operational Administration), which was located on the Prinz Albrecht-Strasse. And it defies understanding why the headquarters of the SS troops is transmitting instructions directly to the *Wiking* Division's battalion commander. It's unclear why the SS officer, Stressling, is called a major, when it would be correct to call him a

OPERATION BAGRATION: AN INCOMPLETE TRUTH

sturmbannführer. What is also completely senseless is that the unit in which Neumann served could, on 29 May be on the front line, if as early as 8 May, after the end of the fighting around Kovel', the *Wiking* Division had been pulled out of the line for reformation and was at the Haidelager SS firing range in the Debica area, not far from Cracow. At the same time, Neumann and his men make their way to Minsk, for some reason, through Brest-Litovsk. If Daix believed that the *Wiking* Division was still in the Kovel' area, then it would have been simpler to use the Kovel'–Minsk branch line. Neumann's subunit was supposed to clear out, together with the SS 16th Division ('*Reichsführer SS*') and the SS 9th Division (*Hohenstaufen*), about which the author of the diary learns only on 8 June. At this time the SS 16th Division was operating in Italy and the SS 9th Division had left the Kovel' area for Normandy. Thus they could not have taken part in any kind of anti-partisan operation in Belorussia. On 28 June Neumann wrote in his diary: 'We were ordered to detain deserters and to immediately execute them in the case of resistance. It's clear! SS headquarters has foreseen everything, even in a retreat. We have to carry out this terrible work. The Russians are breathing down our neck, and they are not sentimental.'

Insofar as not a single element of the *Wiking* Division was in Belorussia at this moment, the reader may view this entry as complete nonsense.

On 29 June Neumann describes an epic scene along the Mogilev–Minsk highway:

> The checking of all military trucks and cars moving west is being conducted along the Mogilev–Minsk road.
>
> Those officers and soldiers who cannot present furnish written orders confirming that they are carrying out their military duties are mercilessly shot.
>
> Stressling, who is commanding the operations, has evidently received this order within the last hour.
>
> A 'Mercedes', camouflaged with branches, halts at our blockhouse. In the car are a captain and two other officers. To judge by their pale faces, they have probably guessed what this means.
>
> About 40 SS soldiers in black greatcoats stand on both sides of the road with their automatic rifles at the ready. The Wehrmacht officers look at them as if they don't understand anything. Or, it's possible that they understand only too well.
>
> I approach them and salute.
>
> 'This is an SS checkpoint. Your travel orders, please'.
>
> The captain pulls out from the pocket of his pull-over blouse [there were no such things in the Wehrmacht, B.S.] a piece of paper and hands it over to me. I examine the paper and return it.
>
> 'I'm sorry, Captain. But this is a pass to the front zone. I need a permission document to pass. Is this all that you can show me?'
>
> There is stark animal fear on the faces of all three officers. These are clearly staff officers who, in the absence of strict supervision by the command, have decided to take off for Minsk at their own risk, at a time when the mobilization of all resources was necessary to hold the Bolsheviks.
>
> Running from the battlefield is nothing but treason.
>
> Stressling comes up:

THE VOYAGE OF THE 'PSEUDO *WIKING*'

'Get out of the car, and be quick about it!'

The three officers get out. An SS soldier immediately gets into the car and moves it off to the side of the road.

'Your documents, gentlemen' says a stone-faced Stressling.

He studies them carefully and then raises his eyes.

Ninth Army headquarters? What are you doing here on the road?

'We're traveling to Minsk, Major . . .'

'Oh, you're traveling to Minsk, are you?', says Stressling in a bass voice. 'It seems to me that you won't make it there!'

'But you have no right . . .'

'So, I don't have any right?'

He calls me forward:

'Neumann! Get rid of this band of traitors!'

Within a few minutes they are leading the three staff officers into the field, to the side of the road. I don't know if this is the proper thing to do, but I am obliged to obey Stressling's orders. After all, this is the first time I've commanded an execution squad. And those that are to be shot are Germans. I try to make sense of my feelings and nearly with horror I discover that everything that is taking place leaves me quite calm. It's as if this were happening to someone else.

'Are you really preparing to shoot us?' one of the officers gasps.

'It's useless, Guro', says another officer. 'These are SS men, a band of dirty murderers!'

I line up my four soldiers with their backs to the road. Three others guard the officers. I turn to the SS soldier who is holding his automatic rifle at his hip.

'Make ready!'

'Heil Hitler', the captain shouts.

'You dirty pig', the SS soldier replies.

'Fire!'

Four automatic rifles simultaneously pour fourth their death-dealing burst and the staff officers fall to the ground without a sound. I come up to them. There's no need to finish them off.

There were no SS subunits with Army Group Centre, just as there were no executions of retreating soldiers and officers, who were quickly included into composite units. Here Daix is more likely reproducing the practice of Soviet blocking detachments. Such blocking detachments appeared in the Wehrmacht only during the last months of the war. There were not yet any during 'Bagration'. The Ninth or Fourth Armies did not defend Mogilev, and the Ninth Army's staff officers, who were stationed in Bobruisk, could not have appeared on the Mogilev–Minsk highway.

On 1 July new wonders happen with Neumann: 'We were ordered to carry out a punitive operation in a small village near Minsk. One captain, whom I had seen earlier, commands the operation. He has a square jaw, a stern face, a scar on his left cheek, and the rank and insignia of the 1st Panzer Division "*Leibstandarte* Adolph Hitler".'

On 1 July, on the eve of the abandonment of Minsk, the Germans clearly had no time for punitive operations against a single village. The Germans might have tried to

OPERATION BAGRATION: AN INCOMPLETE TRUTH

destroy or drive those same partisans out of a village only if that village blocked their way to the west. But then they would have attacked with forces significantly greater than a platoon. To be sure, an 'automatic rifle company' joins the SS platoon (there were no such companies in the Wehrmacht, as opposed to the Red Army and the NKVD troops). There was no way any SS soldiers and officers from the *Leibstandarte* could have been around Minsk that day, insofar as they were fighting in Normandy.

The clearing of the village is described in a deeply mythic manner:

> It's as hot as a heated stove, and the soldiers take off their pull-over blouses [again, which they Wehrmacht did not have, B.S.] and tuck them into their belts.
>
> Naked to the waist, without their high-necked jackets, they approach the partisans meter by meter.
>
> Here and there lie the bodies of women.
>
> A group of half-naked (!) women were crowded around one of the 'Maksim' machine guns.
>
> The machine gun has evidently jammed. In a few seconds we reach them without any losses on our side.
>
> One of the women takes aim at us with a 'Degtyaryov' [a 'Degtyaryov' machine gun, with a fully-loaded magazine, weighed about 12kg – obviously not a weapon for women! B.S.]. She has no time to shoot. An SS soldier throws himself on her and knocks the weapon out of her hands. The woman throws herself on him with a savage howl, scratching him with her nails. The soldier pushed her away with one hand, points the barrel of his automatic rifle and forces her to be quiet.
>
> But there is too much shooting going on everywhere and too many bullets flying around us to busy ourselves with women.
>
> The SS soldier hits his captive with the butt of his carbine.
>
> It doesn't seem as though the woman presents any danger now, so I interfere: 'Drag her into the truck. And make sure she's well guarded!'
>
> The soldier is clearly relieved. He grabs the prisoner by the shoulder and roughly pushed her forward. I observe him for a few seconds. The SS soldier hold the partisan with one hand and with the other – takes a few liberties, which calls forth the woman's savage howls.
>
> She'll calm down. The soldier deserves the reward that came his way.
>
> The clearing of the village is carried out methodically. One after the other, the buildings are cleared of rebels [in general, the Germans called the partisans 'bandits', B.S.].
>
> Grenades and the automatic rifles' 9mm bullets are a sure guarantee of their future loyalty.
>
> Suddenly, there resounds a dull noise from the side of the road.
>
> A tank column passes by at full speed, heading for the west.
>
> To the west! I don't like the looks of this.

It sounds as if only on 1 July did Neumann discover that the Germans were hurriedly retreating! Immediately afterwards comes 16 August, when Neumann joins the *Wiking* Division on the Vistula.[8]

THE VOYAGE OF THE 'PSEUDO *WIKING*'

One is easily convinced that the real author of *The Black March* had little idea of the realities of fighting in Belorussia in June and July of 1944 and brings all of the *Wiking* Division's operations down to punitive actions, but says nothing about the *Wiking* Division's successful battles against Soviet forces in July and August 1944.

In all likelihood, Daix wrote his diary-pamphlet as a counter-propagandistic work against a book by one of the creators of the SS troops, SS *Oberstgruppenführer* Paul Hausser, *SS Troops in Action* (*Waffen-SS im Einsatz*), which came out in 1953 (Gottingen: Plesse Verlag) and the memoirs of other former SS men who tried to write only good things about the SS and who sought to prove they had been undeservedly designated as a criminal organization at the Nuremburg war crimes trials. Daix, on the other hand, concentrates not on the *Wiking* Division's combat successes, but on the crimes committed by the SS, but lacking information about *Wiking*'s real crimes, he mostly made up the crimes of his fictitious personage, Peter Neumann.

It's quite likely that the idea of coming up with the diary of Peter Neumann was suggested to Pierre Daix and the Parisian publishing house Editions France-Empire by the history of the memoirs of Colonel Kirill Dmitrievich Kalinov, *The Soviet Marshals have the Floor*.[9] The Russian émigré, poet and journalist Kirill Dmitrievich Pomerantsev first told in his memoirs about this book that came out in 1950 and made a great sensation, in a sketch about to his acquaintance with the famous Soviet diplomat-defector G.Z. Besedovskii, who lived in France:

> I became acquainted with Grigorii Zinov'evich Besedovskii during the second half of the '50s, although I don't remember exactly when. [Here K.D. Pomerantsev's memory has led him astray. To judge from later events, his acquaintance with Besedovskii took place in the second half of the '40s, because K.D. Kalinov's memoirs, written by them, had already been published in French as early as 1950, B.S.] . . .
>
> When I became acquainted with him, he was already a completely different person. He was around 60 years of age. A brilliant raconteur and fabricator who knew several foreign languages (prior to Paris, he had been first secretary at the Soviet embassy in Rome, and before that in Tokyo), he had already put out several 'sensational' false works. I will relate one of them.
>
> Once, while at the house of my acquaintance, the writer V.P. Krymov (who had published in Russia the famous journal *The Capital and Country Home*), I was acquainted with B., a colonel with the French General Staff. Upon learning that I was a Russian journalist, B. asked me whether I had read *The Memoirs of Colonel Kalinov*. He explained to me that they contain Marshal Bulganin's military doctrine, which is now being studied in the General Staff. I was forced to disappoint the colonel: The *Memoirs* had been written by me in my apartment, supported by a 'Gloria' cocktail of cognac and milk (an excellent drink!) and Kalinov was even 'christened' Kirill in my honour. I will not describe the colonel's embarrassment: it's not hard to imagine . . .
>
> *Kalinov* was followed by the *Notebooks* of Stalin's nephew (killed during the Second World War), which were also fabricated by Besedovskii . . .[10]

OPERATION BAGRATION: AN INCOMPLETE TRUTH

I saw Besedovskii for the last time in October 1962, during the Khrushchev–Kennedy 'missile crisis', when several institutions were preparing to evacuate from Paris, and the always-careful *Le Monde* published a front-page article under the title 'On the Eve of War?' (or something like that). He arrived after lunch, while continuing to walk with a noticeable limp, and my first question was – 'Will there be a war?' Besedovskii burst out laughing: 'What war? There won't be any war. Our boys can't fight and Khrushchev knows that well. The "sovietologists" are sounding the alarm because they understand about as much about Soviet politics as certain kinds of animals understand oranges. Khrushchev will surrender while saving face, which is what negotiations are being conducted about.'

As we know, this is what happened. But this episode opened my eyes to Besedovskii and explained his 'bold' behaviour. The absence of fear of being kidnapped or killed by the Chekists. In actuality, his false works in no way interfered with Moscow and only succeeded in confusing the Western capitals and in some sense was even beneficial to the Kremlin. Thus I do not exclude the possibility that some kind of 'gentlemen's agreement' may have been concluded between him and the Soviet embassy. And I found out how he wrote his books during our last meeting. He had something like a card catalogue with the names of all the Soviet and foreign rulers. Say, for example, it was written there that Stalin was in some such city on some such date, where he made a speech, while Molotov met with a British or French minister in another city. And this was actually the case, although Besedovskii himself invented what they said. For example, he once suggested to me that we open a news agency together. I was amazed: 'And where will we get our news?' 'No need to worry about the news: we'll have more than we need!' I, of course, refused, but he did not insist.[11]

But Besedovskii (1896–after 1962) actually had his own agency, moreover even before the war, but he did not cooperate with newspapers, but with the intelligence of the Allied nations (Besedovskii never cooperated with German intelligence). The former Polish intelligence official, the émigré Jerzy Niebrzycki (1902–68), who wrote under the pseudonym of Ryszard Wraga for the Paris *Rebirth* and a number of other publications, related in 1950 how in 1948 he met in Paris his former 'informer-correspondent from Vienna', a Russian who

> . . . was not badly informed in his time regarding various kinds of 'fabricators' of information, the most dangerous parasites for any intelligence service. Ten years had changed him little. He remained the same restless and sharp man and would also squeal the first word of each phrase and also spoke immediately about everything without finishing a single thought. I nevertheless noticed that he seemed to have become more respectable, but, looking closely, I decided that the only reason for this was his irreproachably fashionable coat, his no less irreproachable and fashionable tie, and his even more irreproachable and fashionable

hat. Following all sorts of mutual greetings I decided to learn the secret of the origin of all this irreproachability.

'But, dear Ivan Petrovich, I don't ask about you. I see that you are looking good and are a dandy. Who are you working with?'

Ivan Petrovich was in no way insulted He had always been an intelligent man and knew that if an émigré looks like a fop, then everybody has the right to wonder: where does he get his money.

'I won't hide it. Now I'm in the pink. Knock on wood'. (Ivan Petrovich loved it when people considered him a linguist and from time to time would toss off such phrases that everyone was truly puzzled: 'What language is this?' But, 'Knock on wood', I understood). During the war and immediately after it was every which way. But now I can live. And I can tell you: the Arctic pulled me out!'

'What Arctic?'

What do you mean? Don't you know the Arctic? Papanov, Vodop'yanov and such folk. The Soviet Arctic! Of course! A very profitable country, I can tell you that! A Colorado and the Klondike . . ., or whatever. It's a veritable golden duck. I can tell you that now. Now I'm such a specialist that Schmidt himself couldn't catch up with me'.

'So, tell me!'

'Understand that the matter was such. I went very hungry in '46. And then there descended on Paris all sorts of intelligence services from all kinds of countries. In this sense Paris has always enjoyed a good reputation: you can always find some kind of information here. I, as you know, was never involved with forgeries. And, as you know, I always had some kind of information. If only about these fabricators of all sorts of mobilization plans and military establishments, or protocols of the "last meeting of the Politburo". A worthy piece of information and a real "service" will pay any amount of money for such information'.

'I began to take a close look and finally came up with one young man, a representative of a major power with hard currency [undoubtedly the US, B.S.]. *Nomina*, as they say, *sunt odiosa*. The gentleman did not name the hotel, but you can guess for yourself. I see that he's not a bad kid. He spends the entire day running like a madman around cafes where "informers" and "sources" gather. It's clear that "headquarters" has supplied him with a lengthy list. He would bustle around; smoke a pipe and read *Pravda*, *Soviet Patriot* and *The Socialist Herald*. In a word, it was immediately clear that he was a "specialist". I became acquainted and got into a conversation with him. At our third meeting I got down to business: this is the way it is . . . Would you be interested? And here I am with my last ten francs in my pocket and with only the gloomiest prospects. But the young man proved to be amazingly firm. "No", he would say, "all of that is nonsense. Now", he says, "drop all your syntheses and opinions (that's what he said: opinions). What are needed now are elements for an exact analysis. Facts are necessary! Facts, facts, facts . . . For example, if you could get me something concrete about the

Kuzbass or the Arctic. Figures, diagrams of various kinds, photocopies of orders, stenographic records of meetings, schedules ..."'

'I was completely stunned. How is this, I think to myself, to get information on the Arctic from Paris? This is the new atomic school come into its own. Where did the principle go that you always repeated: *Quand et comment.* But you must understand: ten francs and no hope of getting the next ten. "Eh", I think to myself, "to hell with your new school! I didn't invent it and I won't be to blame". So, I made a triumphant face and cry out: "My dear fellow, why didn't you ask me immediately about these Arctic facts. Facts are the least part of it. I still have the most serious notes along those lines . . ."'

'In a word, as you know, what won't an enterprising man with ten francs in his pocket come up with? The young man proved to be very bright and quick-witted. After a two-hour conversation I left with 200, what do you call them? In hard currency, that is, in my pocket. The first thing I did was to run off to a foreign book store. I bought up a bunch of books about the Arctic. I acquired a wonderful map. And then I made a down payment on an enormous radio receiver. Not just a radio, but a real 20-cylinder Lincoln. I ran into the National Library. Well, in a word, within two weeks I appear before my *Lavrans* and present my first report. I drew up all sorts of maps and laid down red dots. New names and surnames – as many as you like. My calculations were right on target. I see that the young man is hard-headed. "Facts, facts", he keeps repeating, although he doesn't have a clue as to what these facts are. And you know better than I that the harder the currency the more cumbersome the bureaucracy in the given country. This was my calculation: while my report is making its way to "headquarters", while they admire it, while it lands in the *des Etudes*, while the specialists read, and until they evaluate it, three or four months go by and I'm set up for half a year. So, we'll see. You see, there are different kinds of specialists. Some specialists are easier to fool than a yellow-billed sparrow. Well, in a word, it's been half a year since I've been a *sures bien sur* on Arctic affairs. I've become extremely adept in this matter. The Soviet government could invite me as an advisor. I've "built" so many ports, wharfs and ships during this time. And they are doing something in the Arctic, and if they are doing something, then why should others think up something else rather than I? The theory of probability, you understand. And I'm happy, and the 'specialists' are happy. Now I have a large library and, what is most interesting, from time to time I read in various magazines my own inventions as scientific "facts". In the final analysis, I don't know what is the truth as what is the fruit of my imagination.'

Wraga assumed, not without reason, that the *Memoirs of Colonel Kalinov* were a production of the same kind as 'Ivan Petrovich's' works about the Arctic, but at the same time the main idea of the book *The Soviet Marshals Have the Floor* is that if you closely examine it, the book coincides amazingly with the general line of Soviet propaganda. Disinformation plus inspiration, as they say in specialist slang. What could be better?[12] Western readers learned from Kalinov's book about the Red Army's decisive contribution to the defeat of the German army in the Second World War. Here the Red Army's losses during the Second World War at 14.6 million killed, and perished. In reality, the army's losses were almost twice as large. But, in any event, this figure seemed more believable than the one mentioned by Stalin in 1946, which put Soviet losses during the war at seven million military and civilian dead, a figure which was never believed in the West. At the same time, the Russian originals of 'Kalinov's' memoirs and those of other Soviet defectors, as well as those of several other people, which were actually written by Besedovskii and his numerous co-authors, never came out in Russian. Thus Russian émigrés in the West could not read them. Among them were a lot of participants in the war who were able to unmask the false works without any problem, finding in the works of Besedovskii and company a mass of nonsense and factual mistakes. On the other hand, the absence of Russian-language editions guaranteed that no one would attempt to bring the books into the USSR. That picture of the war, which in Moscow they considered acceptable for Western readers, was considered harmful for Soviet citizens, because it so differed from the official propaganda. For the same reason, Daix did not publish his *The Black March* in German, although if one wanted to one could translate it or find a reliable translator. Publishing *The Black March* in German would have been extremely dangerous. After all, it would have been read by actual veterans of the *Wiking* Division and they would have quickly unmasked the fake. There would have been a scandal in Germany which would have undermined faith in the French- and English-language editions. Besedovskii put out yet another two false memoir books about the Second World War. These are the memoirs of General Andrei Andreevich Vlasov, who headed the ROA [Russian Liberation Army], under the eloquent title of *I Chose the Scaffold. The Secret Memoirs of General Vlasov, the Soviet Traitor*[13] and the memoirs of the supposed former assistant military attaché in France, Ivan Nikitich Krylov – *My Work in the Soviet General Staff*.[14] Vlasov's memoirs were supposedly written down by the same Kirill Dmitrievich Kalinov, so one may assume that Besedovskii wrote them along with K.D. Pomerantsev. Grigorii Zinov'evich also produced two works by Stalin's 'nephew', Budu Svanidze, *My Uncle Stalin*[15] and *Georgii Malenkov*, as well as *Notes for a Journal*, by the former People's Commissar of Foreign Affairs Maksim Litvinov.[16]

Most likely, 'Ivan Petrovich' lied to Wraga about his visits to libraries and his independent search for information about the Arctic, which was presented to the gullible Americans as having been received from Soviet displaced persons and, it was even possible, from some kind of mythical agents who had supposedly remained in the USSR. In all likelihood, Wraga's interlocutor worked in Besedovskii's agency and accumulated a card catalog on the Arctic within the confines of his work there. It's clear that this agency did not only publish false memoirs, put also delivered information for the western special services, which, naturally, were not openly published. In all likelihood, Besedovskii began his activities even before the war. At least one time, in 1932, Besedovskii sold to Polish intelligence through go-betweens the 'Plan for Mobilizing the USSR Red Banner Baltic Fleet' for 1932, supposedly 'on the basis of data from the RKKA Naval Administration, compiled by a Red naval officers and former worker in the same administration's operational section'. In reality, this 'Plan', by all accounts, was compiled by Aleksandr Aleksandrovich Sobolev (1890–after 1945), the former Soviet naval attaché in Sweden and Finland, who defected in 1930 and who had no part in compiling the mobilization plan for the Baltic Fleet in 1932.[17] It was not the authenticity of the document that was important to Besedovskii and his collaborators, which is why they included information from open sources and testimony by defectors. They did not have any spies in the USSR.

As the American historian Paul Blackstock noted, 'since 1955 Besedovskii's pen and imagination have not been active. But his place was taken by a gifted student from the same school – Viktor Aleksandrov'. (one of the translators of 'Kalinov's' memoirs into French). In a letter to Wraga Besedovskii openly maintained:

> As for me, I write books for idiots. Can you imagine that anyone in the West would read my books, which you call apocryphal, if I, in citing Kaganovich, Zhukov and Mikoyan, or Bulganin, were to try and get across the manner, sense and form of their speech? . . . But when I depict Stalin or Molotov in their pajamas, when I related the most awful possible stories about them, without thinking about what is the truth and what is invention, be sure that not only the intellectuals will read me, but also the most important government figure of capitalism, in heading out for a peace conference, will take up my book before he lies down to sleep in his Pullman car . . . Allah gave money to the stupid, so that the smart ones could live.[18]

In the same way, Pierre Daix, in creating his *The Black March*, was not counting on expert historians, but on the wider public that had only a very approximate and inexact idea of the realities of the Second World War.

It's possible that after 1955 Besedovskii simply stopped fabricating false Soviet memoirs, insofar as that had become more difficult to do, because there was already a lot more open information about the USSR and the Soviet army in the west and to concentrate on passing information on the Western special services, which he, to all appearances, did during the Cuban Missile Crisis. But, besides this, he could have taken part in the creation of false memoirs about the SS, such as *The Black March*, at least as far as financing their publication and then receiving a commensurate income.

Chapter 8

The Salvation of Army Group Centre

On 28 July the First Baltic Front received a directive aiming it at East Prussia:

> The main task of the Front's troops is to cut off the enemy group of forces operating in the Baltic States from its communications in East Prussia, for which purpose the *Stavka* of the Supreme High Command orders the following: Following the capture of the Siauliai area, to develop the main attack in the general direction of Riga, while part of the Front's left wing will attack toward Memel, for the purpose of cutting off the maritime railway that connects the Baltic States with East Prussia.[1]

On that same day an analogous directive was received by the Third Belorussian Front:

> 1. To develop the offensive with the forces of the 39th and 3rd Armies with the task of capturing Kaunas no later than 1–2 August 1944 by an attack from the north and south. Subsequently, all of the Front's forces are to attack to the borders of East Prussia and no later than 10 August capture the line Raseiniai–Jurburg–Eydtkuhnen, where they are to securely consolidate in preparation for an invasion of East Prussia, in the general direction of Gumbinnen, Insterburg and Preussisch-Eylau.
> 2. Keep the boundary line with the First Baltic Front as before, and from 2400 on 29.07 with the Second Belorussian Front as far as Augustow, as before, and then Stradaunen, Rhein and Heilsberg (all locales for the Third Belorussian Front inclusively).[2]

Also on the 28th the Second Belorussian Front was directed to seize a bridgehead over the Narew:

> 1. To develop the offensive, while launching the main attack in the general direction of Lomza and Ostroleka, with the task of no later than 8–10 August to capture the line Augustow–Graewo–Stawiski and to seize a bridgehead on the western bank of the Narew River in the Ostroleka area.
> 2. Upon carrying out the above-indicated task, the troops are to securely consolidate and prepare for an invasion of East Prussia in the general direction of Mlawa and Marienburg. Keep in mind that part of the forces in the Mlawa area are to attack toward Allenstein.

3. To establish as of 2400 on 29.07 the following boundary lines: with the Third Belorussian Front as far as Augustow, as before, and then Stradaunen, Rhein and Heilsberg (all locales for the Third Belorussian Front inclusively); with the First Belorussian Front as far as Rozan, as before, and then Ciechanow–Strasburg–Graudenz (all locales for the Second Belorussian Front inclusively).[3]

The main role in the offensive on Polish territory was to be played by the First Belorussian Front. On 28 July it was given the following directive:

1. Following the capture of the Brest–Siedlce area, the Front's right wing is to develop the offensive in the general direction of Warsaw with the task of capturing Praga no later than 5–8 August and to seize a bridgehead on the western bank of the Narew in the Pultusk–Serock area. The Front's left wing is to seize a bridgehead on the western bank of the Vistula River in the Deblin–Zwolen–Solec area. The captured bridgeheads are to be employed for attacking to the north-west in order to roll up the enemy's defence along the Narew and Vistula rivers and thus secure the forcing of the Narew River by the Second Belorussian Front's left wing and the Vistula River by its own forces. The Front is to subsequently attack in the general direction of Torun and Lodz.
2. The following boundary line is to be established from 2400 on 29.07: For the Second Belorussian Front as far as Rozan, as before, and then Ciechanow, Strasburg and Graudenz (all locales are for the Second Belorussian Front inclusively); with the First Ukrainian Front as far as Konskie and then to Piotrkow and Ostrow (20km south-west of Kalisz). Both locales are for the First Belorussian Front inclusively.[4]

On 29 July Vasilevskii and Zhukov were tasked not only with coordinating, but with controlling the operations of the Third Belorussian and First and Second Baltic Fronts and the First Ukrainian and First and Second Belorussian Fronts, respectively.[5] On that same day a special directive to the First Ukrainian and First Belorussian Fronts was issued on how to force the Vistula:

> The order by the *Stavka* on forcing the Vistula River and seizing the bridgeheads named in the order to the armies should not be understood as meaning that the other armies should sit on their hands and not attempt to force the Vistula. The Front command is obliged to maximally support with crossing equipment those armies in the zone of which the Vistula is to be forced according to the order by the *Stavka*. However, the other armies, given the opportunity, must also force the Vistula River. The *Stavka*, in attaching great significance to the matter of forcing the Vistula, obliges you to inform all army commanders within your Front that the soldiers and commanders who have distinguished themselves in forcing the Vistula will receive special decorations and orders all the way to being awarded the title of Hero of the Soviet Union.[6]

THE SALVATION OF ARMY GROUP CENTRE

On 31 July Hitler declared to Jodl at a meeting at the *Wolfschanze*, his headquarters at Rastenburg in East Prussia:

> Jodl, when I look at the major problems today, the first of them is the problem of stabilizing the Eastern Front – we cannot overlook that right now – and I ask myself regarding the situation, whether it's really so bad that our forces are concentrated relatively close to each other. Because there are not only shortcomings, but advantages as well. If the area which we are now in can be held, then this is an area in which we can still live and we have no enormous communications zones. Assuming, of course, that we will actually supply the combat group with what we have created in previous communications zones. Then this will be a real force. If we don't do this, then the communications zone will shift to Germany, and if we create a deeper army service zone in the rear, where there is no necessity of an army zone.

Hitler also pointed out that it was necessary to hold France, because the submarine war was being waged from its shores. He recognized that the forces available in the West

> . . . are not likely sufficient to defend that narrow front. If we can say that about 75 per cent of our mobile forces and a certain amount of our non-mobile forces are located here, and I shift them to such a line, then we can see the complete hopelessness of holding such a line with the forces available to us, regardless of where we built it. We must understand that changes in France may take place only in that case where we are able – if only for a certain time – to establish air superiority. This is why I believe that we must do everything possible, no matter how difficult this may be now, to prepare the Luftwaffe elements that are now being created in the Reich, for employment as the last reserves in the worse possible circumstances. In order to employ them, I can't say right now how things will play out, but they must be employed where we will possibly be able to once again make changes. Unfortunately, this will take many weeks and we won't be able to cope with this any faster. Thus I have no doubts: if we could have thrown in another 800 fighters in order to immediately bring their numbers up to 2,000 simultaneously, like we probably could do now, then this entire crisis could be immediately overcome: there would be no more crisis. We will even be able to wage war here, only if we are able to restore the Luftwaffe to some degree. Thus I've thought about the question: what are the most dangerous moments that could take place during the war? This first, of course, would be a breakthrough in the East, with the real threat to the German fatherland – be that in the Upper Silesian industrial zone or in East Prussia, with the accompanying difficult psychological consequences. But I believe that with those forces which we now dispose of, we will overcome this human crisis, this crisis of morale. This cannot be separated from the event which took place here.

Hitler also stressed the decisive role of the Western Front, which demanded his constant attention: 'I can't leave the western campaign to Kluge. This is absolutely impossible, because everything depends on this. The troops won't understand it if we sit just sit in East Prussia while decisive actions are taking place here. No one can know if we're here or further behind. The most valuable parts are here, while the Ruhr area is behind us!'[7]

In the *Führer*'s monologue the Eastern and Western Fronts already figure, at a minimum, as equal entities, and Hitler even gives priority to stabilizing the Eastern Front, but, most likely, because he thought they had managed to stabilize the Western Front. But as early as 1 August, with the capture of Avranches by the Americans, there arose the threat of the collapse of the German front in Normandy. As early as 7 August the Allies began their offensive and on 19 August the main German forces defending in Normandy had ended up in a 'cauldron' in the Falaise area, from which only a small number managed to extricate themselves. At that critical moment Hitler was forced to throw all his mobile reserves to the Eastern Front in order to prevent the loss of the line of the Vistula and Narew and the rout of Army Group North, which had been cut off from Germany. This, however, did not prevent disaster from striking Army Group South Ukraine in Romania. Thus, when examining Operations 'Overlord' and 'Bagration', one should speak of their mutual dependence. All the way up to the end of July 1944, the concentration of the German panzer troops' and the Luftwaffe's efforts in the West aided to a great degree the success of 'Bagration'. But it was precisely in August that 'Bagration' forced the Germans to shift all their mobile forces to the Eastern Front, which meant they could not prevent the disaster at Falaise. After this the surviving divisions had to fall back to the Siegfried Line along the German border, because there was no possibility of defending along the line of the Seine – the river was too lengthy for the few German troops and there were no fortifications along it. Kurt von Tippelskirch admitted: 'Since the Russians launched a new offensive on 22 June in the East against Army Group Centre, which led to a complete rout of the front within a few days and for the halting of which it was necessary to gather all possible forces, one could count even less than ever on the movement of sufficient reinforcements to Normandy.'[8]

One should not doubt that up until the beginning of August Stalin attached great significance to the rapid forcing of the Vistula and the capture of Warsaw. On 31 July there appeared a directive to the three Belorussian Fronts and the First Ukrainian Front, as well as to the command of the pro-Soviet Polish 1st Army regarding relations with the Home Army:

1. In light of the fact that Polish territory to the east of the Vistula has for the most part been freed from the German aggressors and that there is no necessity of continuing the combat work of the Polish partisans in this part of Polish territory, the *Stavka* of the Supreme High Command orders the armed detachments of the Home Army subordinated to the Polish Committee of National Liberation and wishing to continue fighting the German aggressors to be placed at the disposal of the commander of the Polish 1st Army (Berling), in order to feed them into the regular Polish army. These partisans are to turn in their old weapons, so as to get new and better weapons.
2. In light of the fact that enemy agents are striving to penetrate into the Red Army's areas of combat operations and establish themselves on

liberated Polish territory under the guise of Polish detachments of the Home Army, the *Stavka* of the Supreme High Command orders that armed detachments constituting part of the Home Army or other similar organizations, undoubtedly having within them German agents, are to be immediately disarmed upon being discovered. The officers of these detachments are to be interned and the enlisted and NCO personnel are to be dispatched to separate reserve battalions of Berling's Polish 1st Army. Weapons taken from these detachments are to be turned over to the army artillery depots. For this purpose, the commander of the Polish 1st Army is to form by 7 August of this year separate reserve battalions: for the Third Belorussian Front in the Vilnius area, for the Second Belorussian Front in the Bialystok area, for the First Belorussian Front in the Lublin area, and for the First Ukrainian Front in the Jaroslaw area. Enlisted men and NCOs sent to the separate reserve battalions are to be carefully checked by the Polish 1st Army's information section. Those who pass the check are to be dispatched to the Polish 1st Army's reserve regiment in the city of Lublin.

3. Progress on the disarmament of and the number of enlisted and NCO personnel dispatched to the Polish 1st Army, as well as the number of interned officers, is to be reported to the General Staff every five days, beginning on 1 August of this year.[9]

In practice, there were no Home Army detachments which would have agreed to recognize the authority of the Polish Committee of National Liberation. Thus only the directive's articles dealing with the disarmament of the Home Army's detachments and the internment of its command (officer) element in special camps had real significance. Simultaneously, there was issued a directive for mobilizing into the Polish Army on liberated Polish territory only through the Polish Committee of National Liberation, but actually by the Red Army command with the formal permission of the Polish Committee. At the same time, mobilization by representatives of the London government was forbidden: 'Mobilization carried out on Polish territory by various Polish organizations having no relationship to the Polish Committee of National Liberation is illegal and those persons carrying out such a mobilization are subject to immediate arrest as German agents causing confusion among the Polish population.'[10] The Soviet leadership, for the purpose of discrediting members of the Home Army and other Polish governmental structures in exile, declared them 'German agents', which they most certainly were not.

At the beginning of August there remained in the 5th Guards Tank Army only 28 combat-ready tanks, which were combined into a single brigade.[11] On 8 August P.A. Rotmistrov was hurriedly removed from the post of commander of the 5th Guards Tank Army for such heavy losses and received no more appointments to the army at the front. His successor, V.T. Vol'skii, took command of the army only on 19 August, which shows the unplanned character of Rotmistrov's relief from the post of army commander. On 30 July the First Baltic Front, while attacking in the gap between Army Groups Centre and North, reached the shore of the Baltic Sea in the Tukums area, thus cutting land communications between them. Army Group North Ukraine had been thrown back 200km to the Carpathians and beyond the Vistula. And what was even worse for the Germans, following the capture of Avranches on 1 August by the Americans, the entire

OPERATION BAGRATION: AN INCOMPLETE TRUTH

German front in Normandy was in danger. The Wehrmacht had no reserves. To the south of Kaunas, Soviet troops broke through in the gap between the Third Panzer and Fourth Armies and had nearly reached the border of East Prussia. On 2 August Wehrmacht units, for the first time since the start of the war, were fighting on German territory in the area of the East Prussian town of Schirwindt, which was bombarded by the 33rd Army's 142nd Artillery Brigade. But the most serious was the situation of the German Second Army. There were no German troops in the 60km area between its right flank in Siedlce and Warsaw. On 25 July Model decided to create a new front along the Vistula from Pulawy to Warsaw and to link up his flank with that of Army Group North Ukraine. This task was to have been resolved by the Ninth Army's headquarters, which had been pulled out of Bobruisk. For the time being it was staffed by highly exotic auxiliary and security formations such as the 1st Company of the 818th Azerbaijani Battalion or the 2nd Company of the 791st Turkestan Battalion, the combat value of which was close to zero. The sole combat-capable formation was the newly-arrived 73rd Infantry Division, which was completing its reformation and the training of its personnel following heavy losses in the Crimea, where it had been nearly completely destroyed. This division was stationed south-east of Warsaw for defending the suburb of Praga.[12]

On 23 July 'Foreign Armies East', in its latest appreciation of the situation, came to the conclusion that 'The Soviet command views the ongoing operations as decisive for the outcome of the war'. At the same time, Gehlen's service concluded with relief that Soviet troops were attacking from Kovel' to the west, and not to the north-west, on Warsaw and the border of East Prussia. But German intelligence still feared that Soviet troops might turn from Kovel' to East Prussia. On that day the headquarters of Army Group Centre was already busy with 'the placement of forces for the battle for Warsaw'.[13]

In K.H. Frieser's opinion:

> Only on 27 July 1944 was Rokossovskii ordered to turn part of his forces along the left front to the north 'in the general direction of Warsaw'. But now this attack was being launched too late. Moreover, the attack was launched by only a small part of those troops which the Red Army might have concentrated in this area if the decisive point of the main efforts had been moved there as early as the beginning of the summer of 1944. Then, instead of Radzievskii's 800 combat vehicles, 8,000 tanks or even more might have attacked Warsaw. Instead of this, the Red Army scattered its enormous forces along the entire Eastern Front, concentrating its main efforts in the marshy and primeval forests of Belorussia. The ease which an operational breakthrough was achieved in Kovel' from the very outset shows just how much more disastrous it would have been for the German eastern army if the decision had been carried out in this strategically more effective place in June 1944. But even Radzievskii's attack, although it was not now launched in full strength, was extremely dangerous from the German point of view, insofar as it was aimed at the rear of the German front along a completely undefended sector to the east of Warsaw. Army Group Centre was ultimately saved by Stalin's decision that the First Belorussian Front's left wing attack first to the west, in the direction of Lublin and Pulawy, and not immediately to the

north-west in the direction of Warsaw. This afforded Model sufficient time to halt at the last moment the exhausted Soviet armoured elements. And thus a second 'miracle on the Vistula' took place, analogous to the one in 1920, in which through Stalin's fault a decisive defeat of the Red Army took place in the same place as the result of a counterblow by the Polish marshal Jozef Pilsudski.[14]

Here one might object that Tukhachevskii, and not Stalin, was responsible for the Red Army's defeat in the Battle of Warsaw in 1920. The idea that an initial attack in the Kovel' area to the north toward Warsaw and the East Prussian border would have led to a more impressive result, seems accurate.

On 27 July the Soviet 2nd Tank Army, having reached the Vistula in the Pulawy area, turned toward Warsaw. It disposed of 800 out of approximately 1,800 tanks and self-propelled guns from the First Belorussian Front's left wing. At the moment of the 2nd Tank Army's commitment into the breakthrough, it numbered: 473 T-34s, 140 M4A2 Shermans, 42 IS-2s, ten MK-9s, 65 SU-85s, 63 SU-76s and 19 SU-57s. In all, there were 812 tanks and self-propelled guns. The Germans hoped to delay the tanks in the Lublin area. But there were only trenches with hastily constructed wood and earth machine-gun nests. To be sure, the Germans widely employed Lublin's stone buildings for defence. However, the defenders' forces were very weak – two security battalions, an SS police regiment and 12 assault guns. But the first attempt to take Lublin by the forces of the 8th Guards Tank Corps was unsuccessful. As the corps headquarters reported, 'In attempting to take the city on the march with tanks alone, the corps encountered the enemy's powerful fire resistance and was unsuccessful'. Without infantry cover the tanks proved to be too vulnerable to anti-tank weapons on the streets of the city. On 23 July, in the Lublin area, a shot from a rifle (possibly by a sniper), seriously wounded the commander of the 2nd Tank Army, Lieutenant General of Tank Troops S.I. Bogdanov, in the shoulder. Major General A.I. Radzievskii, the army's chief of staff, took command of the army. On 24 July the 8th Guards Tank Corps' 28th Guards Motorized Rifle Brigade and the forward units of the 8th Guards Army and the 7th Guards Cavalry Corps reached the city. According to a report by the 8th Guards Tank Corps, 'In order to cause panic among the enemy, the Sherman tanks entered the fighting with their sirens on'. But this did not make much of an impression on the enemy and the fighting for Lublin continued until midday on 25 July. In this fighting the 8th Guards Tank Corps lost 15 T-34s, ten Shermans and five SU-85s, for a total of 30 tanks and self-propelled guns, as well as three armoured cars and seven motorcycles. Personnel losses amounted to 119 killed and 339 wounded. Among those killed was the commander of the 301st Guards Self-Propelled Artillery Regiment, Lieutenant Colonel M.S. Ionis. Losses among the 3rd Tank Corps, the 8th Guards Army and the 7th Guards Cavalry Corps during the fighting for Lublin are unknown. Before the start of the fighting for Lublin the 2nd Tank Army had lost 272 tanks and self-propelled guns due to technical and combat reasons (including 132 as the result of enemy action), of which 159 vehicles had been repaired by the start of the fighting for Lublin. During the fighting for Lublin the army lost 96 tanks and self-propelled guns: 41 T-34s, 26 M4A2 Shermans, one IS-2, ten SU-85s and 18 SU-76s. Of this number, irreparable losses were eight T-34s, four Shermans, four SU-85s and three SU-76s, for a total of 19 vehicles. It's most likely that the 30 tanks and self-propelled guns are the 8th Guards Tank Corps' overall losses in the fighting for Lublin, which accounted for 31.25 per cent of the 2nd Tank Army's losses for this period. One may assume that in the fighting for Lublin this corps irreparably lost about six tanks and self-propelled guns. It's likely that the 3rd Tank Corps suffered the same number of irreparable losses. From the start of the Lublin–Brest operation until 26 July the 2nd Tank Army's irreparable losses totalled 36 T-34s, ten Shermans, four SU-85s and seven SU-76s.[15]

In August 1945 the Commander-in-Chief of Allied Forces in Europe, Dwight Eisenhower, made a visit to the USSR. Marshal G.K. Zhukov accompanied him in the journey around the country. During his stay in Moscow and on the flight to Leningrad they spoke a lot about the recent war, and clearly not without drink. Eisenhower was interested in how the Red Army overcame German minefields. In his *Crusade in Europe*, he cites his conversation with Zhukov on this matter:

> Highly illuminating to me was his description of the Russian method of attacking through mine fields. The German mine fields, covered by defensive fire, were tactical obstacles that caused us many casualties and delays. It was always a laborious business to break through them, even though our technicians invented every conceivable kind of mechanical appliances to destroy mines safely. Marshal Zhukov gave me a matter-of-fact statement of his practice, which was, roughly '. . . When we come to a mine field our infantry attacks exactly as if it were not there. The losses we get from personnel mines we consider only equal to those we would have gotten from machine guns and artillery if the Germans had chosen to defend that particular area with strong bodies of troops instead of mines. The attacking infantry does not set off the vehicular mines, so after they have penetrated to the far side of the field they form a bridgehead, after which the engineers come up and dig out channels through which our vehicles can go.'
>
> I had a vivid picture of what would happen to any American or British commander if he pursued such tactics, and I had an even more vivid picture of what the men of any one of our divisions would have had to say about the matter had we attempted to make such a practice a part of our tactical doctrine. Americans assess the cost of war in terms of human lives, the Russians in the over-all drain on the war on the nation. The Russians clearly understood the value of morale, but for its development and maintenance they apparently depended upon over-all success and upon patriotism, possibly fanaticism.
>
> As far as I could see, Zhukov had given little concern to methods that we considered vitally important to the maintenance of morale among American troops: systematic rotation of units, facilities for recreation, short leaves and furloughs, and, above all, the development of techniques to avoid exposure of men to unnecessary battle-field risks, all of which, although common practice in our Army, seemed to be largely unknown in his.[16]

At least one episode of overcoming German minefields was documented for Operation 'Bagration' and it happened on 26 July 1944, not far from the Polish border. A war veteran, the Leningrader Boris Mikhailovich Mikhailov, was sure over the course of several decades that his friend, who was in the same year as he in the Tashkent Infantry-Mortar School, Zhorka (Georgiii Porfir'evich) Pavlikov, had perished in 1944, because one of his friends wrote that he had been killed: 'But in 1987 my school friend, and now the main designer in one of the Petersburg military-industrial complex institutes, Len'ka Vol'fson, said that he knew a veteran by the name of Pavlikov who works as the section chief at a 'closed' military factory in Petropavlovsk. One thing led to another and . . . It's him! Zhorka!' In 1989 B.M. Mikhailov came to see G.P. Pavlikov in Petropavlovsk, in Kazakhstan, and the latter told him his story:

> They sent us from Termez to the front on 2 May. In the beginning of June we arrived near Roslavl', in the Smolensk Oblast'. From there they sent us in groups to the divisions of the Second Belorussian Front. I ended up in the 110th Rifle Division's 1289th Rifle Regiment. The division was attacking and was reinforced on the march with captured service workers from the German army, healthy men . . . [the author means *Hiwis*, B.S.]. They gave me a platoon of such men and took us to the bank of a creek near the town of Zambrow, which was already in Poland, and ordered me to take the soldiers forward after the artillery preparation and to keep an eye on them, so that they wouldn't hide and run off. I got the soldiers up. We ran across the creek. Further on were bushes. There's shooting all around. Shells are exploding on all sides. I run and see how the soldiers, here and there, jump up and then fall. I can't understand what the matter is. But suddenly I went up in the air and ended up on the ground.
>
> There's a terrible pain in my legs. I look and one foot is lying off to the side. Long, white tendons trail from it to my leg. The other foot is turned at a right angle in the shin. My hands are in one piece, as is my head. I stretch out and my hands are in front of me. I grab the grass and move forward. I thus made it to the creek. There a medic and a soldier came up to me. I tell them: 'Bandage me up'. They looked and see that the foot is dangling, but they put it back together and began to bandage me. Suddenly one of them began to shout: 'I'm hit, I'm hit!' and he grabbed his stomach and ran off. Then there was another explosion. The shell landed on the creek bank. The medic who was bandaging me fell on me. I look at him: he's missing half of his skull and the sticky brains are scattered everywhere. I got out from under the medic and crawled to a hill. There someone else came up. I don't remember anything else. They amputated one leg below the knee and I lay in the hospital for a whole ten months with the other. At first it began to knit and then knitted improperly. A large bone blister formed.

B.M. Mikhailov commented on this episode in the following manner: 'I look and touch the deformed shin with a big protrusion on the old man's angular leg. How much you had to put up with, you poor guy! What bastard sent you to lead a bunch of doomed men over a minefield? What for? So that today, while still alive and covered with orders down to your navel, to flaunt yourself on the television screens, telling everyone about your combat feats and not feeling any pangs of conscience for the senseless deaths of soldiers? "War writes everything off".'[17]

One should add that in all likelihood B.M. Mikhailov incorrectly listed the patronymic of his friend. According to the 'Feat of the People' database, the name and patronymic of Junior Lieutenant G.P. Pavlikov was Georgii Prokop'evich (or Prokof'evich). The mistake is quite understandable, if you take into account that Mikhailov probably never called his friend by his patronymic. In 1968 G.P. Pavlikov was awarded the Order of the Red Star, probably due to his serious wounding that made him an invalid, in 1945 the medal 'For the Victory over Germany in the Great Patriotic War of 1941-1945', and in 1985 the Order of the Patriotic War, 1st Class. Pavlikov was born in Petropavlovsk, in the North Kazakhstan Oblast', where he also lived and worked after the war.[18] According to information contained in the 'Immortal Regiment' database, Georgii Prokop'evich Pavlikov was born on 16 January 1925 and died on 8 May 2007, on the eve of Victory Day, in Petropavlovsk.[19] B.M. Mikhailov (1925–2005), who died two years before his friend, fought in Romania and Hungary to the end of the war, fortunately without once being wounded, and was awarded during the war with two orders of the Red Star and the Order of the Patriotic War, 2nd Class, and in 1985 with the Order of the Patriotic War, 1st Class.

This example shows that as opposed to the widely-held opinion, in 1944 and 1945, when the Red Army's victory was no longer in doubt, the command did not spare people, just as it had done in the beginning of the war. If the former *Hiwis* were at least guilty before the Soviet regime due to their previous service for the Germans (and this did not justify sending them through a minefield to certain death or mutilation), then Georgii Prokop'evich Pavlikov, who had just graduated from a military school, was not guilty of anything and landed in a minefield only because he commanded a platoon consisting of former *Hiwis*.

On 25 July, the day the fighting for Lublin came to an end, the 16th Tank Corps, upon arriving at the Vistula, because of poor anti-aircraft defence 'suffered significant and unjustified losses in personnel and equipment' from enemy aviation, as the headquarters of the 2nd Tank Army noted. At the same time,

> the commander of the 16th Tank Corps, Major General of Tank Troops Dubovoi, did not plan or organize the battle and poorly commanded the course of the fighting. The brigade commanders, not feeling firm leadership, in turn, did nothing, fobbing off the control of the battle to the battalion commanders. Thus the corps reached the Deblin area and fought in separated groups from the front, without bypassing Deblin from the north and south ... A large part of the indicated shortcomings were also noted in the 3rd Tank Corps while taking the Pulawy area. The commander of the 3rd Tank Corps, Major General of Tank Troops Vedeneev and his staff, also did not plan and control the dynamics of the battle. The 3rd Tank Corps' battle for Deblin developed haphazardly.[20]

In the fighting for Deblin the 16th Tank Corps lost eight tanks burned, 12 tanks knocked out, 69 men killed and 274 wounded. The army headquarters accused the corps commander of 'throwing all of the corps' forces into the fighting along the road in a single direction, and the enemy's presence led to its standing in place and to excessive losses'.[21]

THE SALVATION OF ARMY GROUP CENTRE

The 8th Guards and 1st Polish Armies followed behind the 2nd Tank Army, while ahead and to the right the 11th Tank and 2nd Guards Cavalry Corps and the 47th Army had already begun their attack against the left flank of the German Second Army near Siedlce, in order to cut off Army Group Centre's path of retreat to the west. Rokossovskii's directive of 27 July ordered them to seize crossings over the Narew at Zegrze and Serock, and then the bridges over the Vistula near Modlin, cutting off the German group of forces in the Vistula–Narew–Bug triangle from Warsaw. The offensive by the Soviet 2nd Tank Army on Warsaw, which began on 27 July, at first hit only air. On the following day the army disrupted communications between the German Second Army and the new Ninth Army that was still undergoing formation. The Soviet tank troops were opposed only by the Luftwaffe's attack aircraft. On 29 July the Soviet 2nd Tank Army cut the Warsaw–Siedlce highway with three tank corps. On the left flank the 16th Tank Corps was moving on Praga, but was halted by the 73rd Infantry Division. The 8th Guards Tank Corps moved on Okuniew, encountering only minor resistance. On the right flank the 3rd Tank Corps, while encountering no resistance, reached Radzymin on 30 July, 15km north-east of Warsaw. The Soviet tank formations were in the deep rear of the German forces and only 3km from the strategic bridge over the Narew at Zegrze. On 31 July Soviet forces took Siedlce.

On 1 August the 8th Guards Army forced the Vistula at Magnuszew and created a bridgehead. On that same day the Warsaw uprising began. The main supply routes of the German Second, Fourth and Ninth Armies ran through Warsaw. In K.H. Frieser's opinion, '1 August was a fateful day, because the Eastern Front threatened to collapse like a house of cards'.[22]

On 2 August a directive was issued to the Second and Third Ukrainian Fronts for the conduct of the Iasi–Kishinev operation. At that moment they still did not know in the *Stavka* that in Warsaw an uprising by the Home Army had broken out, just as they had not assumed that in the coming days the 2nd Tank Army would be defeated on the approaches to Warsaw. The time for beginning the operation was not indicated in the directive.[23]

On 15 July (11 July, according to other data), the *Hermann Göring* Division, which was occupying positions to the south of Florence, began to move to the Eastern Front on 72 trains. The division arrived in its full complement there on 27 July and was dispatched to the area north-east of Warsaw, where together with the SS *Wiking* Division it encircled a Soviet tank corps in the Wolomin–Radzymin area. Model reported that thanks to the valiant struggle of the *Hermann Göring* Division they had managed to hold Warsaw. On 8 August the division carried out a counter-attack against the Soviet bridgehead between Magnuszew and Warka. The division even contained a certain number of outdated tanks.[24] On 5 August a company of assault guns under the command of Captain Hans-Joachim Bellinger, from the *Hermann Göring* Division, supposedly destroyed 36 T-34s.[25]

Four German panzer divisions launched a surprise counter-attack east of Warsaw, and the Soviet tank formations, which were prepared for an offensive, fell into a trap. Model made a risky move, concentrating here three panzer divisions from Army Group Centre. Aside from this, the *Hermann Göring* Parachute-Panzer Division, which had earlier halted the offensive by the Allies, which continued following the capture of Rome, arrived in Warsaw from Italy. Taken together, the four divisions had 223 tanks and 54 assault guns and tank destroyers. It was believed that this should suffice to defeat the Soviet 2nd Tank Army's three tank corps, which numbered about 800 tanks and self-propelled guns. On 2 August the German divisions disposed of the following armoured equipment:

- The 19th Panzer Division, which had been transferred from Army Group North Ukraine: 26 Panzer IVs, 26 Panthers and 18 Marder III light tank destroyers;
- The *Hermann Göring* Parachute-Panzer Division: 35 Panzer IVs, five Panthers and 23 Jagdpanzer IV tank destroyers;
- The SS *Wiking* Panzer Division: eight Panzer IVs, 45 Panthers and 13 assault guns;
- The 4th Panzer Division: 40 Panzer IVs and 38 Panthers.

In accordance with Model's plan, an enveloping attack on Okunew would be undertaken during the first phase of the operation, in order to cut off the rear of the Soviet 3rd Tank Corps, which had advanced far to the north. During the second phase the four divisions were supposed to undertake a concentric attack against the encircled Soviet 3rd Tank Corps. Then they would attack the 8th Guards Tank Corps and, finally, the 16th Tank Corps. But the attacking divisions still had to be gathered from different sectors of the front to the area east of Warsaw and have their simultaneous attack from four different directions organized. As K.H. Frieser notes, 'Taking into account the enemy's numerical superiority, they needed to concentrate the necessary troops in the right place at the right time'.[26]

Before the arrival of the *Hermann Göring* Division from Italy, the 73th Infantry Division was supposed to repel the pressure by the Soviet 2nd Tank Army, but on 27 July its defence in the Garwolin area, which had been established in just one day, was penetrated by the 8th Guards Tank Corps. As noted in a report by the 60th Guards Tank Brigade, 'The enemy's units were encircled and defeated by a turning movement from the north and north-west. Many enemy soldiers and officers were taken prisoner and headquarters documents were seized from units of the 73rd Infantry Division.' On 29 July the commander of the 73rd Infantry Division, Lieutenant General Friedrich von Franek, was captured. The Soviet tank troops operated successfully against German infantry, when the latter lacked armour support and a sufficient number of anti-tank guns. Franek testified during his interrogation:

> In view of the shortage of time, cooperation between the *Hermann Göring* Panzer Division and the 73rd Infantry Division was not organized. On the morning of 27.7.1944 the combat group defending GARWOLIN was attacked by Russian tanks. The fighting continued until midday. Having suffered heavy losses, the group fell back to the line STAROGRUDSKA–STAROGRUD. On the evening of 27.7.1944 I received orders to hold the defensive line at all costs. The 186th Infantry Regiment fell back in disorder and there were no communications. All measures were taken by me. However, the regiments, having lost communications with me, began to fall back in disorder in the direction of WARSAW. I was captured by Russian tank troops. The division's units suffered enormous losses, particularly the 186th Infantry Regiment.[27]

THE SALVATION OF ARMY GROUP CENTRE

On 25 July units of Major General Wilhelm Schmalz's *Hermann Göring* Division began to arrive in the Warsaw area. The first to arrive was the reconnaissance battalion's 2nd Company, which on the morning of 26 July had two collisions with Soviet reconnaissance detachments and supposedly even knocked out one T-34. It transpired that Soviet troops were astride the road 3km from Siedlce. By 27 July the division's entire reconnaissance battalion, the artillery, an anti-tank battalion and a parachute-assault battalion had already arrived. The *Hermann Göring* Division also received the 27th Panzer Regiment's/19th Panzer Division 1st Battalion, with 72 Panthers. By the evening of 27 July the first 28 Panthers had arrived with the *Hermann Göring* Division. They were supposed to attack to the west of Parysow.

The 944th Security Battalion held the German front in the Warsaw area near Karczew, adjacent to the Vistula. Further on was the 70th Infantry Regiment; the 170th Infantry Regiment was defending near Kolbiel, and the 186th Infantry Regiment's positions were located on the division's far left flank, with its centre in Sienice as far as Ceglow (all from the 73rd Infantry Division). The *Hermann Göring* Division's reconnaissance battalion, which was defending from Ceglow to Mrozow, was adjacent to the 73rd Division's left flank, while the parachute-assault battalion was in the reserve.

As of 27 July the following was considered combat-ready in the Soviet 2nd Tank Army: 3rd Tank Corps – 125 T-34s, seven SU-85s, 16 SU-76s and four SU-57s (altogether 154 tanks and self-propelled guns); 8th Guards Tank Corps – 50 T-34s, 93 Shermans, 14 IS-2s, 18 SU-85s, 15 SU-76s and four SU-57s (altogether 193 tanks and self-propelled guns); 16th Tank Corps – 151 T-34s, ten IS-2s, 13 SU-85s, 15 SU-76s and four SU-57s (altogether 193 tanks and self-propelled guns). Another 30 tanks and self-propelled guns were in individual units not forming part of the corps. Thus the 2nd Tank Army had 570 combat-ready tanks and self-propelled guns. In five days the army lost due to various reasons 244 vehicles. On 26 July the following was reported in a message to the army headquarters:

> The army continued to operate without air cover, despite the army commander's insistent requests to the Front commander. During the day the army's troops lost up to 40 motor vehicles burnt and knocked out due to bombing and machine gun-cannon fire by enemy aviation . . . Enemy aviation launched bombing raids and continuously strafed the corps' combat formations and roads, which was a palpable brake on the army's vigorous actions.

In the morning the *Hermann Göring* Division's anti-tank battalion, with 11 Jagdpanzer IVs and two Panzer IVs, arrived at Otwock. From this they formed a combat group under the command of Captain Hans-Joachim Bellinger and dispatched it to the area to the north-west of Sienice. There it collided with seven Soviet tanks and knocked out one of them. At midday combat group 'Bellinger' encountered head-on the main forces of the 8th Guards Tank Corps, the 58th and 59th Guards Tank Brigades, in the Sienice–Pogorzela area. At 1600 the Germans were thrown out of Sienice and Pogorzela, having irreparably lost one assault gun. By the close of 28 July the last Panthers from the 27th Regiment's 1st Battalion had arrived. Meanwhile, tanks from Major I.N. Fundovannyi's 50th Tank Brigade, supported by Major D.G. Gurenko's 1107th Self-Propelled Artillery Regiment, arrived 4km east of Minsk-Mazowiecki. Other tank units from the 3rd Tank

OPERATION BAGRATION: AN INCOMPLETE TRUTH

Corps moved out from Ceglow in the direction of Lekawica. Near Ceglow they were counter-attacked by a battalion of Panthers from Kaluszyn and from Minsk-Mazowiecki. The 8th Guards Tank Corps' forward units were also counter-attacked around Sienice. The commander of the XXXIX Panzer Corps, Dietrich von Saucken, who on 1 August was promoted to general of panzer troops for his success in the fighting around Warsaw, observed the counter-attack. According to German data, on 28 July 12 Soviet tanks and 16 trucks were destroyed. The data were seriously understated. The 8th Guards Tank Corps alone reported the loss of five burnt Shermans and eight T-34s burnt, while one SU-85's barrel had been shot through. Twenty-six vehicles, 12 motorcycles and two armoured personnel carriers were set on fire by enemy air raids. Eleven men died and 26 were wounded, with the notation that 'losses are still being checked', which testifies to the fact that actual personnel losses were far higher. The 3rd Tank Corps reported having irreparably lost four T-34s, with another seven T-34s knocked out. Sixty-six men were killed or wounded. One hundred and thirty-four tanks and self-propelled guns – 108 T-34s, six SU-85s, 16 SU-76s and four SU-57s – remained combat ready.

The headquarters of the 2nd Tank Army did not attach any significance to these counter-attacks, possibly because the corps' headquarters were reporting highly-inflated data on the enemy's losses. The 8th Guards Tank Corps reported the destruction of five German tanks, two anti-tank guns and up to two battalions of infantry. The 3rd Tank Corps reported destroying six German tanks and seven assault guns, as well as 14 field guns. In reality, the Germans suffered nothing like these losses. The following was written the 2nd Tank Army's combat journal: 'Up to two companies of tanks and infantry from the Minsk-Mazowiecki area in the direction of Menja station; up to a company of infantry, supported by 10–15 tanks, from the Kaluszyn area in the direction of the town of Ceglow. The counter-attacks were repelled.'

On the morning of 29 July the *Hermann Göring* Division received another 15 Jagdpanzer IVs and two Panzer IVs. The 8th Guards Tank Corps then seized Sienice and approached Pogorzele. Its units destroyed three Jagdpanzer IVs and one Panzer IV from combat group 'Bellinger'. Here a company of IS-2s under Senior Lieutenant N.A. Kamyshev, from the 62ns Independent Guards Heavy Tank Regiment, distinguished itself. By evening units of the 173rd Infantry Division had fallen back to the line Swider–Duchnow–Okuniew. Captain A.V. Leferov's 87th Independent Motorcycle Battalion, with seven T-34s, routed the 944th Security Battalion in the Karczew area and then occupied Otwock. On the evening of 29 July units of the 2nd Panzergrenadier Regiment's 2nd Battalion and the 1st Panzergrenadier Regiment's 3rd Battalion arrived. On 29 July the *Hermann Göring* Division's irreparable losses were one Panzer IV and six Jagdpanzer IVs. The 8th Guards Tank Corps irreparably lost eight T-34s, seven Shermans, two IS-2s and two SU-85s. Four T-34s, three Shermans and one IS-2 were knocked out. Thirty-three men were killed and 41 wounded. On the morning of 30 July there remained 29 T-34s, 59 Shermans, 13 IS-2s, 14 SU-85s and 12 SU-76s combat ready, for a total of 127 tanks and self-propelled guns. Seventeen T-34s, 42 Shermans, two IS-2s, four SU-85s, and four SU-76s were undergoing repairs. Four IS-2s were en route.

On 30 July the 16th Tank Corps occupied Wiazowna, Miedzylesie and Zakret, having pushed back units of the 73rd Division's 70th and 170th Infantry Regiments. But as early as 1130 there followed a counter-attack by Colonel Karl-Richard Kossman's combat group, which included the 74th Panzergrenadier Regiment's headquarters and 2nd Battalion, and the 27th Panzer Regiment's/19th Panzer Division 1st Battalion.

THE SALVATION OF ARMY GROUP CENTRE

The group recaptured Wiazowna, but was then itself cut off by the 16th Tank Corps' 6th Independent Guards Heavy Tank Regiment and was forced to attempt to break out of the encirclement with the aid of the parachute-assault battalion. The attempt by the 1st Parachute Panzergrenadier Regiment's combat group supported by the 1st Battalion's/27th Panzer Regiment 3rd Company to attack on Wolomin ended in failure. The *Hermann Göring* Division, which included the 27th Panzer Regiment, reported destroying 11 T-34s, mainly from the 16th Tank Corps. The 8th Guards Tank Corps lost irreparably one T-34 and one Sherman, with another Sherman damaged.

According to the plan by the 2nd Tank Army's command, the army was to launch its main attack east of the Warsaw highway, in order to bypass the Warsaw fortified area. In the 2nd Tank Army's report, it was stated that:

> The enemy, upon discovering the threat from the south-east by the 2nd Tank Army's group of forces in the PRAGA–WARSAW area, by 31 July 1944 had halted the ARMY'S offensive. The German command is undertaking emergency measures to organize and strengthen the defence of the Warsaw and Praga fortified areas. The enemy has been strengthening the Praga sector from the east and north-east, partly with new and partly with tank units transferred from the BREST area. As a result of the battles conducted and wide-ranging reconnaissance before the 2nd Tank Army's front, by the close of 31.7.1944 the following enemy group of forces has been determined: the SS 5th *Wiking* Panzer Division has been concentrating in the area of the STANISLAWOW woods. The SS 3rd *Totenkopf* Panzer Division has been concentrating in the area GUZOWATKA–ZAWADY–MOKROE. The *Hermann Göring* Panzer Division along the sector CZARNA–STRUGA–MARKI. The 19th Panzer Division's 27th Panzer Regiment has been operating along the sector ZIELONKA–MILOSNA STARA–ZBYTKI, as well as the remnants of the 73rd Infantry Division and the 6th Warsaw Security Regiment. The 4th Panzer Division was moving from the north-east to the LASKOW–TROJANY–KOZLY area.
>
> Having evaluated the situation, the 2nd Tank Army's military council has made the following decision: The Warsaw fortified area is not to be attacked with tanks. Detailed reconnaissance of the enemy's weak spots is to be carried out with motorized rifle units, with the subsequent commitment of tanks for the purpose of capturing PRAGA.
> 1. The army is to be gathered into a fist and concentrated in the following areas: 3rd Tank Corps: the main forces in WOLOMIN, leaving powerful detachments for cutting the RADZYMIN–WARSAW highway; 8th Guards Tank Corps: OKUNIEW–SULEJOWEK–GALINOW; 16th Tank Corps: to hold the line MILOSNA STARA–MIEDZYLESIE–ZBYTKI. 2. The defence's forward line is to be KOBELJAW–OSSOW–SULEJOWEK–MILOSNA STARA–ZBYTKI. The army is to be covered from the east and partially from the north-east against units of the enemy's Brest–Bialystok group of forces arriving in the PRAGA area. The defence is to be ready by 1200 on 1 August 1944. In adopting the decision, the army

commander had in mind the arrival of one rifle division from the 125th Rifle Corps to STANISLAWOW for securing the 2nd Tank Army's communications. The division, as later proved to be the case, did not reach the STANISLAWOW area.[28]

By the morning of 31 July units of the 2nd Tank Army had driven units of the *Hermann Göring* Division out of Minsk-Mazowiecki. But on that day the *Hermann Göring* Division committed 18 combat-ready Panzer IVs, which had arrived the previous evening, into the fighting. By the close of 31 July the division had 12 Panzer IVs and 18 Jagdpanzer IVs combat ready. The division destroyed two T-34s and lost irreparably two Panzer IVs, while another 7–8 Panzer IVs were damaged.

The 8th Guards Tank Corps did not advance on 31 July. From 21 through 31 July the corps lost 33 T-34s, 37 Shermans, four IS-2s, three SU-85s and five SU-57s, for a total of 82 tanks and self-propelled guns. Two hundred and fifty-three men were killed, 735 wounded, 39 burned, 18 concussed and 20 were missing in action. Overall losses were 1,065 men. Twenty-nine T-34s, 55 Shermans, ten IS-2s, and 12 SU-76s remained in line, for a total of 120 tanks and self-propelled guns, while the neighbouring 3rd Tank Corps lost 83 T-34s, seven SU-85s, 12 SU-76s and four SU-57s, for a total of 106 tanks and self-propelled guns.

On 31 July the *Hermann Göring* Division lost one Panzer IV. By the evening of 31 July the division had 32 Panzer IVs (20 of which took part in suppressing the Warsaw uprising during 2–4 August), 18 Jagdpanzer IVs and three Marders. The *Hermann Göring* Division's irreparable and medical losses in July were 1,181 men (these also include losses on the Italian front). From 28 through 31 July four Panzer IVs and eight Jagdpanzer IVs were lost.[29]

Model took personal charge of the offensive. At first he disposed of only the *Hermann Göring* Division. By no means had all of its armoured equipment arrived from Italy, but as early as 28–29 July a few of the *Hermann Göring* Division's tanks that had already arrived, along with units of the 73rd Infantry Division, and were able to prevent the seizure of Praga by formations of the Soviet 2nd Tank Army. Meanwhile, the 19th Panzer Division had been pulled from its sector of the front in the Bialystok area, and on 29 July its units were able to hold an important bridge over the Narew at Zegrze.[30]

On 30 July the commander of the 2nd Tank Army reported to the First Belorussian Front command:

> The presence of the fortified line of the Warsaw fortified area is confirmed by the commander of the 73rd Infantry Division, Lieutenant General Franek (taken prisoner by us). There are pillboxes that have been occupied by artillery units. Minsk-Mazowiecki is occupied by the *Hermann Göring* Panzer Division. The 3rd Tank Corps' main forces captured Kobylka, 8km north-east of Warsaw. The 16th Tank Corps has captured Poguljanka and has come up against a heavily-fortified sector along the line of the woods to the west of Milosna Stara. The 8th Guards Tank Corps is engaged in a stubborn fight along the line Minsk-Mazowiecki–Glianka (8km from Minsk-Mazowiecki) against the *Hermann Göring* Panzer Division. I have decided the following: To

THE SALVATION OF ARMY GROUP CENTRE

move the 3rd and 16th Tank Corps more quickly to the outskirts of Praga and to link up their flanks. To cut off Warsaw from the east, north-east and south-east. The 8th Guards Tank Corps is to cover itself against Minsk-Mazowiecki from the south. Its main forces are to bypass the *Göring* Panzer Division's defence. The 8th Guards Tank Corps is to be pulled back to the Okuniew–Izabela–Podjuzefina, while supporting the activities of the 3rd and 16th Tank Corps from the east. I am moving the reserve 109th Tank Brigade to the woods to the north-east of Minsk-Mazowiecki and, with an attack by the 3rd and 16th Tank Corps from the east, to destroy the *Göring* Panzer Division in the Minsk-Mazowiecki area, while preventing its withdrawal and linkup with the main forces along the north-eastern axis. The enemy's aviation is bombing the corps' combat formations without respite. I urgently request: to wipe from the face of the earth Minsk-Mazowiecki, where the concentration of about 100 tanks and self-propelled guns has been established. To cover the army's area with fighter aviation. Our aviation does absolutely nothing. Speed up the delivery of fuel and oil. I am beginning to wear myself out.[31]

On 29 July Radio Moscow transmitted an appeal to the Polish communists and residents of Warsaw, which spoke of the approach of Soviet troops to Warsaw and the arrival of the moment when the defenders of Warsaw would come to grips with the enemy in battle. 'The sons of Warsaw will join the Allied forces, so as to with active struggle with the occupiers on the streets of Warsaw, in its buildings, factories and depots, not only to hasten the moment of final victory, but also to save national treasure and the lives of your brothers . . . Repeated broadcasts with an appeal for an armed uprising in Warsaw and about the nearness of assistance for the rebellious residents of Warsaw were broadcast over the Kosciuszko radio station.'[32]

Winston Churchill recalled how on 2 August in London news of the Warsaw uprising became known:

> . . . we anxiously waited for more. The Soviet radio was silent and Russian air activity ceased. On August 4 the Germans started to attack from strong-points which they held throughout the city and suburbs. The Polish Government in London told us of the agonizing urgency of sending in supplies by air. The insurgents were now opposed by five hastily concentrated German divisions. The Hermann Goering Division had also been brought from Italy, and two more S.S. divisions arrived soon afterwards. I according telegraphed to Stalin.
>
> 'Prime Minister to Marshal Stalin, 4 Aug. 1944
>
> At urgent request of the Polish Underground Army we are dropping, subject to weather, about sixty tons of equipment and ammunition into the south-west quarter of Warsaw, where it is said a Polish revolt against the Germans is in fierce struggle. They also say that they appeal for Russian aid, which seems to be very near. They are being attacked by one and a half German divisions. This may be of help to your operation'.

OPERATION BAGRATION: AN INCOMPLETE TRUTH

The reply was prompt and grim.

> 'Marshal Stalin to Prime Minister, 5 August 1944
> I have received your message about Warsaw.
>
> I think that the information which has been communicated to you by the Poles is greatly exaggerated and does not inspire confidence. One could reach that conclusion even from the fact that that the Polish emigrants have already claimed for themselves that they all but captured Vilna with a few stray units of the Home Army, and even announced that on the radio. But that of course does not in any way correspond to with the facts. The Home Army of the Poles consists of a few detachments which they incorrectly call divisions. They have neither artillery nor aircraft nor tanks. I cannot imagine how such detachments can capture Warsaw, for the defence of which the Germans have produced four tank divisions, among them the Hermann Goering Division'.[33]

On 1 August the attack began by the 19th Panzer Division on Okuniew from the west and the SS *Wiking* Division from the east. At 1915 they met north of Okuniew, having cut off the Soviet 3rd Tank Corps located north of Radzymin. Model personally led the attack by the 4th Panzer Division and units of the 19th Panzer Division. On 3 August the Soviet 3rd Tank Corps had concentrated in the Wolomin area. The 4th Panzer Division attacked from the north-east, the *Wiking* Division from the south-east, the *Hermann Göring* Division from the south-west, and the 19th Panzer Division from the north-west. The majority of the Soviet formations in the Wolomin area were destroyed. On 4 August other formations of the Soviet 2nd Tank Army were attacked, and those of the 47th Army, which had rushed to its aid. The fighting was concentrated around Okuniew, where the Soviet 8th Guards Tank Corps occupied positions. The Germans wanted to destroy it, but here the situation was complicated for them in other sectors of the front. On 4 August they had to pull the 19th Panzer Division back, and the *Hermann Göring* Division on 5 August. They moved to the Magnuszew bridgehead and the 8th Guards and Polish 1st Armies, which with the support of powerful tank formations, were attempting to expand the bridgehead. On the evening of 4 August the German troops in Okuniew went over to the defensive, insofar as the task of defeating the Soviet forces to the east of Warsaw and preventing their immediate offensive on the city had been carried out.

On 5 August the headquarters of the 2nd Tank Army reported to the headquarters of the First Belorussian Front:

> The enemy forces, including the SS *Totenkopf* Panzer Division, the *Hermann Göring* Panzer Division, the SS *Wiking* Panzer Division, the 19th Panzer Division, the 73rd Infantry Division, an assault battalion, the 24th Construction Battalion, and artillery units, attacked units of the 3rd Tank Corps and the 8th Guards Tank Corps at 1100 on 3.8.1944 from the following directions: Radzymin – 40 tanks, Klembow – 40 tanks and armoured personnel carriers. Struga – 20 tanks and infantry, Turow – 18 tanks and infantry, the woods 2.5km south-west of Okuniew – 16 tanks and a battalion of infantry, Poswietne – 14 tanks and infantry, and Kraze Stara – 20 tanks and an armoured train operating from the Zelenka area.

THE SALVATION OF ARMY GROUP CENTRE

On 3.8.1944 the 2nd Tank Army, with the 3rd Tank Corps and part of the 8th Guards Tank Corps's forces, was fighting to destroy the enemy's tanks and infantry. The 3rd Tank Corps' 50th and 51st Tank Brigades were fighting against superior enemy forces along the line Duczki–the railway running through Wolomin–Nadarzyn, and suffered heavy losses and did not leave the area of combat operations, with the exception of individual tanks and 46 men from the 50th Tank Brigade's motorized battalion. The army's losses: 58 tanks and self-propelled guns burned or knocked out, of which 42 remained on territory occupied by the enemy. Sixteen guns of various calibres and 17 vehicles were crushed. The commanders of the 50th and 51st Tank Brigades, including Hero of the Soviet Union Colonel Mirvoda and Major Fundovnyi, with their staffs, were wounded and remained in the territory occupied by the enemy.

According to information from the headquarters of the 2nd Tank Army, during the period from 20 July through 8 August 1944, the army irreparably lost 210 tanks and 34 self-propelled guns.[34]

On 4 August the Soviet 3rd Tank Corps irreparably lost 47 tanks, six 76mm guns, two 57mm guns, one 120mm mortar, and 160 men killed or wounded, while up to 500 did not emerge from the encirclement. On that day there remained in the army 394 combat-ready tanks and self-propelled guns. Another six tanks were being transported.

On 6 August the commander of the First Belorussian Front ordered: 'The 2nd Tank Army is to turn over its combat sector to the troops of the 47th Army and the 2nd Guards Cavalry Corps and is then to concentrate in the area to the east, west and south of Minsk-Mazowiecki.' At the moment of its movement from the front on 8 August, the 2nd Tank Army had 373 combat-ready tanks and self-propelled guns. In the fighting from 1 through 8 August the 2nd Tank Army, minus the 3rd Tank Corps, irreparably lost 94 T-34s, one IS-2, six Shermans, eight SU-85s and seven SU-76s, for a total of 116 vehicles, including two armoured personnel carriers, seven 76mm guns, ten 57mm guns, 11 45mm guns, one 120mm mortar and eight 82mm mortars, for a total of 37 guns. Personnel losses were 409 men killed, 1,271 wounded and 589 missing in action, for a total of 2,269 men. The 3rd Tank Corps's losses during the period from 30 July through 6 August were 91 T-34s and SU-85s and seven SU-76s, for a total of 98 vehicles, as well as two armoured personnel carriers, seven 76mm guns, ten 57mm guns and three 45mm guns, and one 120mm mortar and eight 82mm mortars, for a total of 29 guns. Personnel losses were 1,265 men, including 236 killed, 636 wounded, 373 missing in action and ten sick.[35] Thus, the Soviet 2nd Tank Army's losses in the first ten days of August 1944 were, at a minimum, 645 killed, 1,055 missing in action and 1,907 wounded, for a total of 3,607 men. According to a report by the headquarters of the 2nd Tank Army, its losses during the period of combat from 20 through 31 July 1944 were as follows: 582 killed, 1,581 wounded and 52 missing in action, and during the period from 20 July through 8 August it lost 991 men killed, 2,852 wounded and 442 missing in action.[36] The irreparable losses in the report by the headquarters of the 2nd Tank Army seem low by several orders. The summary of irreplaceable losses by the 2nd Tank Army, minus the 3rd Tank Corps, for 1–8 August and those of the 3rd Tank Corps for the period from 30 July through 6 August are 1,607 men, when according to the army report the irreparable losses for the period from 20 July through 8 August are only 1,433 men. Losses for the German Ninth Army during the first ten days of August 1944 were 758 men killed, 1,397 missing in action and 3,163 wounded, for a total of 5,318 men.[37]

During the tank battle around Warsaw, Soviet forces suffered heavy losses. On 4 August there remained only 263 tanks and self-propelled guns in the Soviet 2nd Tank Army, as opposed to 22 July, at the start of the offensive, when it had 812 tanks and self-propelled guns. On 5 August the 2nd Tank Army had to be pulled out of the front line for reforming. From 21 through 31 July 1944 Army Group Centre captured 1,442 prisoners, and from 1 through 10 August 2,525 prisoners.[38] Probably nearly all of them were taken during the fighting with the Soviet 2nd Tank Army. Most likely, the data on this army's irreparable losses has been understated by a factor of several times, because in its reports only 1,055 men are shown. Even employing obviously understated Soviet data on losses, the 2nd Tank Army lost only 1.27 times less than the German Ninth Army, and as for overall losses – 1.47 times less. But during this period the Ninth Army was also fighting against the 8th Guards Army, the Polish 1st Army and part of the 47th Army's forces.

The *Hermann Göring* Division lost 15 tanks and assault guns (six Panzer IVs, eight Jagdpanzer IVs and one Marder) irreparably during the period from 25 July through 5 August. The SS *Totenkopf* Division lost three Panzer IVs, 26 Panthers, two Tigers and one assault gun irreparably from 23 July through 10 August, for a total of 32 vehicles. The SS *Wiking* Division in the fighting from 2 through 5 August lost irreparably six Panzer IVs and two StuG-III assault guns, for a total of eight tanks and assault guns. From 3 through 6 August the 4th Panzer Division lost irreparably five Panthers, seven Panzer IVs and two Marders, for a total of 14 armoured vehicles. From 1 through 5 August the 19th Panzer Division irreparably lost 13 Panthers, one Bergpanther recovery vehicle, and five Panzer IVs and Jagdpanzer IVs, for a total of 19 tanks and assault guns.[39] Overall irreparable losses for the five German panzer divisions in the battle near Warsaw were 88 tanks and assault guns. The Soviet 2nd Tank Army, according to the 'Information of Losses Suffered by the 2nd Tank Army's Forces from 20 July through 8 August 1944' (actually, from 22 July through 6 August) which was prepared by the army's staff, the army lost irreparably 244 tanks and self-propelled guns, including 155 T-34s, 48 Shermans, four IS-2s, three MK-3 Valentines, 18 SU-85s, 15 SU-76s and one SU-57. The army also lost 36 guns, 11 mortars, 11 armoured cars and 82 motor vehicles. The army staff estimated the personnel losses for this period at 991 men killed, 2,852 wounded and 422 missing in action, or 4,265 men.[40] The data on personnel losses is extremely understated, because during the period under observation Army Group Centre captured 3,967 prisoners, mainly from the 2nd Tank Army. It's most likely that the losses in armoured equipment are understated, but even according to available data they are 2.8 times the German ones.

As Frieser believes, Stalin wanted to quickly seize Warsaw during the first stage of the operation, as testified to by the vigorous lunge toward the Polish capitol by the 2nd Tank Army. Stalin

> clearly wanted to pre-empt the Polish resistance movement. It was assumed that the Red Army would quickly take Warsaw or, at least the suburb of Praga on the right bank of the Vistula. Moreover, Soviet units had already crossed over the Vistula at Magnuszew and seized a bridgehead, which had evidently created the prerequisites for encircling

THE SALVATION OF ARMY GROUP CENTRE

Warsaw from the south, also with aid from the second half of the pincers from the north. Under these circumstances Model's counterblow was a complete surprise.

But following the defeat that the 2nd Tank Army suffered at the gates of Warsaw and the start of the Warsaw uprising, Stalin's intentions changed:

> After several Soviet armies had arrived as reinforcements there took place what the insurgents had least expected: units of the Red Army waited – as the Poles could see – at the gates of Warsaw, undertaking nothing until the Germans crushed the uprising. The situation may be described as follows: at first the Soviets wanted to take Warsaw, but were unable; later they could have taken Warsaw, but didn't want to any more. There are no available dossiers in the Soviet archives that could offer a clear answer to this question, and thus the polemic between historians on the subject of Stalin's 'restraining' order continues to this day.[41]

Difficulties also arose in the other Soviet armies forcing the Vistula. Lieutenant Colonel V.K. Svekrovin, the General Staff representative with the headquarters of the 69th Army, reported on 6 August:

> The enemy, while holding the heights along the western bank of the Vistula between the bridgeheads of the 91st and 61st Rifle Corps, has the opportunity of observing the troops' combat formations and all the crossings over the Vistula in the army's zone. As a result, during daylight the crossings are under enemy fire, which extremely limits the transfer of troops, equipment and supplies over the river. It is necessary for the army's forces to take immediate measures to capture the heights occupied by the enemy between the bridgeheads of the 91st and 61st Rifle Corps. This will enable the army to speed up the forcing of the Vistula River and at the same time to significantly reduce personnel and equipment losses.
>
> 5. It is necessary to note the poor work of the anti-aircraft artillery covering the bridgeheads and the absence of bridgehead cover by our fighter aviation, which allows the enemy's aviation to operate unhindered against the crossings and the troops' combat formations.[42]

Colonel Drabkin, the General Staff's representative with the 8th Guards Army, reported on 3 August on the difficulties of forcing the Vistula:

> The 8th Guards Army's troops, during the course of 2 August 1944, conducted unsuccessful fighting on the western bank of the Vistula and continued to cross over infantry, artillery, ammunition, and horses. I consider the reason for the unsuccessful offensive battle for broadening the bridgehead on the western bank of the Vistula River to be the following:
> a) The infantry's indecisive actions without a corresponding amount of reinforcement equipment, namely: the absence of tanks and an insufficient amount of artillery on the western bank of the Vistula River, particularly during the first half of the day.

OPERATION BAGRATION: AN INCOMPLETE TRUTH

b) The enemy's resistance has increased, because the latter plans, according to prisoner testimony, to throw our units off the bridgehead, employing for this his aviation. During the course of 2.8.1944 the enemy's aviation put out of action a large amount of crossing equipment, which slowed down the crossing of troops and equipment during 2.8.1944.

The absence of a bridge and an insufficient amount of floating crossing equipment prevents us from throwing the mechanically-towed division artillery, tanks and other equipment across to the western bank in a timely manner . . .

An attempt to cross tanks over to the western bank of the Vistula underwater did not yield results, as the first two KV tanks remained under water and on this note the tank crossing was ended. It is necessary to speed up the construction of a heavy pontoon bridge for the crossing of heavy equipment (tanks and wheeled artillery).[43]

As K.H. Frieser notes:

The 'Foreign Armies East' section, under the leadership of Major General Gehlen, had long ago determined the point of Archimedes in which the German front might be operationally dislodged. This was the Kovel' salient, from which the Red Army's armoured units could rapidly advance to the Baltic through Warsaw and encircle two German Army Groups. Then the entire Eastern Front would have collapsed and the road to Berlin opened. Looking back, it seems quite probable that just such an offensive for the purpose of encirclement would have been crowned with success. Today, as opposed to the Soviet leadership at the beginning of the summer of 1944, we possess exact information about the real correlation of forces on both sides and the subsequent course of events. In any event, during the summer of 1944 the Red Army quickly achieved an operational breakthrough in any direction. On 18 July the First Belorussian Front began a supporting offensive on Kovel' [Kovel', which was abandoned by the Germans without a fight, because after the abandonment of Minsk its defence no longer made any sense, was liberated by Soviet troops as early as 6 July, so it would be more correct to say 'from Kovel'", B.S.], and although only its left wing took part in the offensive, the defenders were simply swept aside. In all, within a few days a nearly 100km breach was formed in the German front. Thus it is easy to imagine the landslide that would have been put in motion if Operation 'Bagration' had been conducted from Kovel' in the direction of Warsaw, and not from the Belorussian balcony in the direction of Minsk. Finally, this was the largest mass of forces which had ever been deployed for an offensive. Nonetheless, the Red Army command committed a mistake by dispersing its strategic potential at the operation level. Laudatory Soviet historiography repeatedly cited Stalin's 'ten blows' (offensives) in 1944, but a closer look shows that there were several blows more. The fact is that in the summer of 1944 the Soviet command did not risk gathering its forces for a decisive and fatal blow, but limited itself to inflicting a number of wounds on the enemy. Instead of a decisive strategic offensive along a single sector, it carried out a series of operational blows along the entire front. Operation 'Bagration' against Army Group Centre was only the main attack among the other attacks in the summer of 1944. After it there followed other major offensive operations, which from the very beginning were designed to shock the enemy, as a result of which all four German Army Groups on the Eastern Front were attacked simultaneously.[44]

As Frieser believes, the Soviet command preferred to disperse its forces, because in the past the concentration of forces along the axis of a single main attack led to very great losses and quite limited results. As an example, he points to the Soviet counteroffensive around Moscow in 1941–2 and their offensive in the south in February–March 1943, which ran into Manstein's counterblow.[45] However, in 1942 the Red Army was attacking not only in the Moscow area, but practically along the entire front. And this continued all the way up to the start of the German summer offensive in accordance with Plan 'Blue'. And simultaneously with the Stalingrad counteroffensive the Red Army began its equally powerful offensive against the Rzhev–Vyaz'ma salient. In the beginning of 1943, aside from the offensive in the south, the *Stavka* began a simultaneous offensive along the central sector of the front on Kursk and Sevsk and a similar dispersal of Soviet forces contributed to the success of the German counteroffensive around Khar'kov. And during and after the Battle of Kursk almost all of the Soviet Fronts attacked, and not just the Voronezh and Central Fronts. I think that a similar dispersal of forces may be explained by the Soviet *Stavka*'s (specifically, Stalin, Zhukov, Shaposhnikov and Vasilevskii) desire, in violation of the canons of military art, to attempt to be strong everywhere. In reality, they managed to achieve this only by the summer of 1944, when the Eastern Front had been weakened by the transfer of the majority of the Wehrmacht and SS's panzer and panzergrenadier divisions to the West to repel the Allied landing in France. If one looks at the plan for Operation 'Bagration', knowing its course and result, then with the aid of hindsight, the optimal means for the Red Army's operations during the summer of 1944 appears as follows: on 22 June the First Ukrainian Front is the first to begin an offensive in the same strength as it actually had in the middle of July, when it began its offensive on L'vov and Sandomierz. After Army Group North Ukraine had committed all of its mobile reserves into the fighting, some time at the end of June, the First Belorussian Front's left wing, reinforced in comparison with the actual course of events both at the expense of the same Front's right wing and at the expense of the Second and Third Belorussian Fronts, should have begun its offensive. But the offensive should have developed not in the direction of L'vov and Lublin, as was actually the case, but along the axis Kovel', Warsaw, East Prussia and the Baltic shore. Having only the 20th Panzer Division as a mobile reserve, Army Group Centre could not have repelled such an offensive. In this case the routes of retreat for all three armies in the 'Belorussian balcony' would have been cut off, and besides them the German Second Army, which actually suffered little as a result of Operation 'Bagration', would also have been routed. Soviet losses would have been significantly smaller than during the actual course of events, because the Soviet troops would not have had to break through the defence of the German Third Panzer and Fourth and Ninth Armies, but mainly destroy the enemy's encircled groups of forces which had almost no ammunition. But one must keep in mind that earlier Soviet forces had unsuccessfully tried to storm Kovel' for a long time and

OPERATION BAGRATION: AN INCOMPLETE TRUTH

that Soviet intelligence knew that it was precisely here that the Germans were expecting the main attack during the summer campaign of 1944. Thus it seemed logical to launch the main attack where the enemy did not expect it. Besides this, the course of Operation 'Bagration' leads one to think that the Soviet command, as usual, overestimated the Germans' forces and believed that they had transferred far fewer divisions and aircraft to the West than was actually the case. The *Stavka* did not expect such rapid and complete success for Operation 'Bagration' and was not ready to immediately concentrate forces along a single direction (the most promising was the Warsaw direction).

As concerns the situation that developed following the defeat of the Soviet 2nd Tank Army on the approaches to Warsaw, Stalin had a choice. He could have temporarily postponed the conduct of the Iasi–Kishinev operation against Army Group South Ukraine in Romania and transferred the 6th Tank Army, which was designated for this operation, to the Warsaw area, reinforcing it with the 2nd Tank Army's remaining armoured equipment and carried out an offensive to encircle the Warsaw group of forces from the Pulawy and Magnuszew bridgeheads. If this offensive had coincided with the offensive by German divisions in the north to restore the land communications between Army Groups Centre and North, then the few German panzer formations remaining in the Warsaw area would not have been able to repel the Soviet offensive. The Germans would have been forced to fall back to the Oder and the war would probably have been shortened by at least several months. In this case it is unlikely that German forces would have remained in Romania, the government of which would most likely have preferred to join the anti-Hitler coalition, even without the defeat of Army Group South Ukraine during the course of the Iasi–Kishinev operation. However, it seems that Stalin was not at that moment interested in a rapid end to the war. This is not only because of the Warsaw uprising, which was organized and headed by the Home Army which was subordinated to the Polish government in exile based in London. Finally, following the capture of Warsaw, they could have disarmed the insurgents and sent them to reinforce the Polish 1st and 2nd Armies, which were formally subordinated to the puppet National Liberation Committee in Lublin, but actually to the Red Army command. However, of course, to dissolve several tens of thousands of Warsaw insurgents in these armies was much more difficult than a few insurgents in Vilnius. They could have arrested the leaders of the uprising and then condemned them on trumped-up charges, having recognized them as responsible for attacks by the Home Army's fighters on the Red Army's soldiers. This is how they treated the Home Army's detachments that sought to liberate Vilnius, and they later condemned the Home Army's leaders, headed by General Leopold Okulicki, whom they lured into negotiations and arrested. Of course, it would have been better to avoid a scandal with the Western Allies due to the disarmament and arrest of the Warsaw insurgents, so Stalin had nothing against the Germans suppressing the uprising before the Red Army took Warsaw, and therefore did not hurry to liberate the Polish capital. But no less a role was played by the fact that the leader did not need the too-rapid capitulation of Germany. Stalin wanted to have time to seize all his designated spoils before the capitulation, fearing that the Western Allies might trick him and, for example, not turn over the Balkans, by committing their troops there immediately following the capitulation. And the Iasi–Kishinev operation was supposed to open the road to the Balkans for the Red Army.

Thus on 16 August Stalin issued directives to the Second and Third Ukrainian Fronts to begin the Iasi–Kishinev operation on 20 August. And on that same day he ordered the First Belorussian Front to transfer the 4th Guards Cavalry Corps to the Second Ukrainian

THE SALVATION OF ARMY GROUP CENTRE

Front, and the 2nd Guards Cavalry Corps to the Third Ukrainian Front. In the same way, on the same day the First Ukrainian Front received orders to transfer the 6th Guards Corps to the Second Ukrainian Front.[46] Thus not only were Soviet troops not transferred from Romania to Poland, which might have realistically hastened the end of the war but, quite the opposite, the group of Soviet forces in Poland was weakened by three Guards corps, which were dispatched to Romania for developing the success. On 31 July the 3rd Guards Mechanized Corps seized Tukums on the shore of the Gulf of Riga. Between Raseiniai and the Gulf of Riga all the German forces consisted of several dispersed combat groups, which would create the threat of the fall of Riga and the breakthrough of Soviet troops into Courland. Thirty of Army Group North's divisions were cut off in Estonia and Latvia. The Germans immediately attempted to eliminate this dangerous wedge. On 5 August the offensive was resumed by the Second and Third Baltic Fronts, which by this time had already suffered heavy losses, having lost 1,325 tanks after 22 June 1944.[47]

On 8 August Guderian presented the plan for Operation '*Doppelkopf*' (literally the 'double head', the name of a card game popular in the German army), which was supposed to close the 'Baltic hole' and restore land communications between Army Groups North and Centre. Two of the five panzer divisions which were supposed to take part in the counteroffensive were still being transferred from Romania.[48] The fact is that the arrival of Soviet forces at the shores of the Baltic threatened an attack on Riga from the west and the subsequent destruction of all of Army Group North, the main forces of which were still defending near Narva and in eastern Latvia, and whose sole mobile reserve, the 12th Panzer Division, had long since been transferred to Army Group Centre.

A.M. Vasilevskii, quite reasonably fearing German counterblows in the area of Tukums, Dobele and Siauliai, in his words, on the evening of 2 August,

> ... reported to the Supreme Commander-in-Chief that in order to further carry out its assigned tasks, the First Baltic Front needs additional and immediate reinforcement and once again reminded him of the 5th Guards Tank Army. Besides this, I requested that he transfer here at least one corps from the Second Baltic Front's 4th Shock Army, compensating the latter with two rifle corps from the *Stavka* reserve. I.V. Stalin promised to carry out these requests and on the following day A.I. Antonov reported that the corresponding decision had been made. At the same time, it was planned to move the tank army to Raseiniai and, with an attack to the north-west, toward Kelme, defeat the German group of forces concentrated west of Siauliai. Also, within two days the *Stavka* authorized the return of the 4th Shock Army, consisting of two corps, from the Second Baltic Front to the First Baltic Front. The third corps was dispatched to reinforce the Second Baltic Front's 22nd Army.[49]

On 3 August the corresponding *Stavka* directive followed:

1. Rotmistrov's army is to be immediately employed for attacking from the Ariogala area to the north-west in the general direction of Kelme, for the purpose of defeating the enemy group of forces concentrating against Siauliai. Rotmistrov's army is to be subordinated to Bagramyan.
2. To immediately transfer one rifle corps from the Second Baltic Front's 4th Shock Army to the First Baltic Front.[50]

On that day the Germans were able to take back Birzai and the 357th Rifle Division ended up being surrounded.[51] At 1430 on 5 August, units of the 60th and 22nd Guards Rifle Corps of the First Baltic Front's 43rd Army went over to the offensive to relieve the 357th Division. However, because of a shortage of ammunition they were unable to suppress the enemy's artillery. The 19th Tank Corps, which was committed into the fighting in the evening, suffered heavy losses from the Tigers of the 510th Heavy Panzer Battalion. During 6 August the 43rd Army's attacking troops were able to advance only 8km along a narrow sector, but they drove the Germans out of Birzai. On the night of 7 August the 19th Tank Corps was able to reduce the distance to the encircled troops to 5km. By midday on 7 August the division was relieved.[52]

On 5–6 August the *Grossdeutschland* Division repelled attacks by units of the 33rd and 39th Armies on the East Prussian border town of Schirwindt. On 14 August units of the German 252nd and 212th Infantry Divisions, which had been reinforced with two companies from the 510th Heavy Panzer Battalion, the SS 500th Parachute Battalion and by units of the 7th Panzer Division, which had begun Operation *'Grif'*, while preparing for Operation *'Doppelkopf'*, retook Raseiniai, which had earlier been occupied units of the 5th Guards Tank and 39th Armies. The 29th Tank Corps' 25th Tank Brigade here lost all of its 30 tanks. The 29th Corps' 31st and 32nd Tank and 53rd Motorized Rifle Brigades attempted to break through to the units encircled in Raseiniai, but were beaten off by the 510th Battalion's Tigers. In the fighting of 14–15 August the 29th Tank Corps lost 185 men killed (of these, 130 were from the 25th Tank Brigade) and 570 men wounded. Forty-nine T-34-85s were lost irreparably and six T-34-85s were knocked out. The Germans took more than 300 prisoners and 37 Soviet tanks, while losing two Tigers knocked out. Meanwhile, Baron Tilo von Werthern's panzergrenadier brigade from the *Grossdeutschland* Division, which had three Panzer IVs and eight assault guns, retook Kalnujai, where the 18th Guards Tank Brigade was located, but on 15 August the 2nd Guards Motorized Rifle Brigade and the 3rd Guards Tank Corps' 3rd and 19th Guards Tank Brigades counter-attacked and recaptured it. The corps lost 42 men killed and 285 wounded. Nineteen T-34s were irreparably lost and seven T-34s and two IS-2s were knocked out from the newly-arrived 14th Guards Heavy Tank Regiment. Wertern's brigade lost two tanks and four assault guns damaged.[53]

On 9 August the *Grossdeutschland* Division took back Vilkaviskis in a surprise attack by surrounding and destroying the garrison.[54] It was here that Guderian made a fatal error. At this moment he should not have transferred panzer divisions from Romania to the northern flank of Army Group Centre, but quite the opposite – one or two panzer divisions from Army Group Centre should have been transferred to Army Group South Ukraine. Then Romania, to all appearances, following the beginning of the Soviet offensive in Moldavia, would still have gone over to the other side, but it's possible that German Army Group South Ukraine could have avoided encirclement and fallen back to Transylvania and Hungary without great losses. However, of course, at that moment Guderian could not predict where exactly the next Soviet attack would land.

The following units were to take part in the counteroffensive:

- General of Panzer Troops Dietrich von Saucken's XXXIX Panzer Corps, which consisted of the 4th, 5th and 12th Panzer Divisions, was to be deployed between Memel and Liepaja and from there cover the 80km to Army Group North's positions in Jelgava. The tanks for reinforcing the corps were to be transported by sea. The corps also contained Major General Count Hyacinth von Strachwitz's combat group. It consisted of two panzer brigades – the 101st, which included the remnants of the 18th Panzergrenadier Division, and SS *Sturmbannführer* Martin Gross's brigade, which had been created around an SS reserve-training regiment in Dundaga and which numbered up to 2,500 men.

- General of Panzer Troops Otto von Knobelsdorf's XL Panzer Corps was to attack from the Tauroggen area toward Siauliai, first with the 14th Panzer Division and the *Grossdeutschland* Panzergrenadier Division, to which the 7th Panzer and 1st Infantry Divisions were to later attach themselves.

There were 141 tanks and 54 assault guns in both corps. By the end of the operation on 26 August, the number of tanks and assault guns had grown to 299, due to the arrival of new units. The First Baltic Front, which began the offensive on 22 June with three armies, supported by 687 tanks and self-propelled guns, during the course of the operation all the way to the middle of August, was reinforced by the 51st and 2nd Guards Armies, the 5th Guards Tank Army, and the 3rd Guards Mechanized and 19th Tank Corps. To be sure, during this time they took from it the 4th Shock Army and transferred it to the Second Baltic Front. The First Baltic Front had the 1492nd Self-Propelled Artillery Regiment, with 21 SU-76s, the 3rd Guards Heavy Tank Regiment, with 15 KVs, the 3rd Guards Mechanized Corps, with 11 T-34s, 20 M4A2 Shermans, 18 Mk IX Valentines, 19 SU-122s, 11 SU-85s and 13 SU-76s, for a total of 92 armoured vehicles; the 1st Tank Corps' 89th (25 T-34s) and 159th (24 T-34s) Tank Brigades, and the 5th Guards Tank Army, with two KVs, 77 T-34s, two SU-85s and 33 SU-57s, for a total of 115 tanks and self-propelled guns, and some other formations for repelling the German counterblow in the area of Siauliai and Tukums.[55] It's interesting that the Germans somewhat underestimated the Soviet tank forces. For example, according to the testimony of Soviet prisoners, there remained only 40 combat-ready tanks in the 5th Guards Tank Army out of an original 500. And the German command believed this information, although, as we have become convinced, the 5th Guards Tank Army at that time had twice as many combat-ready tanks.[56] Aside from this, Bagramyan disposed of the 1st Tank Corps' 117th Tank Brigade, as well as the 1437th, 1514th, 1402nd, 1490th and 1491st Self-Propelled Artillery Regiments, the 346th Guards Heavy Self-Propelled Artillery Regiment, and the 2nd Guards Army's 32nd Guards Heavy Tank Regiment, the 6th Guards Army's 34th Guards Tank Brigade, 43rd Army's 10th Guards Tank Brigade, the 377th Guards Heavy Self-Propelled Artillery Regiment, and the 1203rd Self-Propelled Artillery Regiment, and the 51st Army's 15th Guards Independent Tank Regiment, the 336th Guards Heavy Self-Propelled Artillery Regiment, and the 1022nd, 1102nd and 1489th Self-Propelled Artillery Regiments. Aside from this, the Front reserve contained the 79th, 101st and 102nd Tank Brigades, the 8th Guards Tank Regiment, the 19th Tank Corps' 867th and 1452nd self-propelled artillery regiments, the 39th Guards and 143rd Tank Brigades, the 2nd and 64th Guards and 105th Independent Tank Regiments, the 10th Assault-Engineer Brigade's 47th and 119th Tank Regiments, and the 333rd and 335th Guards Heavy Self-Propelled Artillery Regiments.[57] Even if one assumes that all of these units and formations had only one-third of their tanks and self-propelled guns out of their authorized strength combat-ready and not take into account the First Baltic Front's motorized rifle and mechanized brigades, which also disposed of their own armoured equipment, Bagramyan should have disposed of, at a minimum, approximately 300 tanks and self-propelled guns, and thus had no less than a twofold superiority over the attacking German Third Panzer Army. By taking into account arriving reinforcements, this superiority was more likely threefold.

Hitler demanded an attempt to encircle the Soviet forces in Lithuania. Thus following the establishment of land communications between Army Groups Centre and North, the German troops were 'to turn to the south in the direction of Kaunas . . . and strike in the rear the enemy forces facing the Third Panzer Army's eastern front'. It was planned that by means of this grandiose castling move that two German panzer corps, with the assistance of Army Group North's infantry divisions, would encircle several armies from the Soviet First Baltic and Third Belorussian Fronts simultaneously. Hitler even believed that they could manage to encircle '50 or 60 whole divisions', which was clearly a fantasy, as was, by the way, the idea of encircling several Soviet armies.[58]

On 16 August, the day of the start of the counterblow, Model was appointed commander-in-chief of the Western Front; Reinhardt replaced him as the head of Army Group Centre, and Colonel General Erhard Raus headed the Third Panzer Army, arriving there on 17 August. The German offensive proved unexpected for the Soviet command. It widely employed anti-tank brigades and regiments for defence. According to German estimates, in 12 days of fighting 595 Soviet tanks and self-propelled guns were destroyed. Significant tank forces – the 5th Guards Tank Army and the 1st Tank and 3rd Guards Mechanized Corps – were employed for counterblows. On 17 August the Luftwaffe supported the offensive with 114 attack aircraft and dive bombers, 116 fighters, and 30 reconnaissance aircraft, but air superiority passed to the Soviet air force very quickly. Here not only the Soviet aviation's numerical superiority, but also the Luftwaffe's extreme shortage of fuel, played a role. During the conduct of Operation '*Doppelkopf*' the Sixth Air Fleet followed these instructions from 13 August: 'A scrupulous calculation of the distribution of fuel is a necessary operational measure, having priority over all other considerations'. And in the 'Operational Considerations Regarding Operation "*Doppelkopf*"', which were issued by the Sixth Air Fleet command on that same day, it was noted that: 'the IV Air Corps' combat units stand ready, but will probably not be deployed because of the fuel situation'.

This is the way Alfred Iedtke, the commander of a panzergrenadier battalion in the 5th Panzer Division, described the first day of the offensive in the Papiile area:

> The panzer group overcame the advanced Russian units only through fighting and had still not penetrated sufficiently deeply into the enemy's defence; thus the shift to the south meant that, while bypassing a town, it came under heavy anti-tank fire, both from there and from the left flank. This was the result of the excellently directed fire from the Russian artillery . . .
>
> There were still more unpleasantness from the Russian anti-tank guns, which were well placed in the woods approximately 6km to the north-east of Papile. But resistance was soon overcome. In the neighbouring woods (at a depth of about 8km) we caught a battalion of Russian artillery by surprise, which was quickly captured by our tanks.

> The enemy's weak resistance in Mazunai was quickly suppressed. We moved in the direction of Kruopiai. The area was crawling with Russians, but there was no organized resistance. It appeared that they were from scattered or rear units. The morale of our people was outstanding. After numerous fighting retreats, we were, at last, once again attacking, just like in the old days.[59]

The *Grossdeutschland* Division captured the railway bridge over the Venta River at Kursenai. Another bridge was captured by the 14th Panzer Division near Saukenai, but it had been damaged by artillery fire. The 7th Panzer Division encountered fierce resistance north-east of Kelme and was unable to advance. The 4th Panzer Division captured the village of Vegeriai, but was only able to advance 5km on 17 August. The 12th Panzer Division operated a little more successfully. The 5th Panzer Division's southern combat group reached Gaudikiai, where it encountered a powerful anti-tank defence. It advanced approximately 15km in two days.[60]

The Soviet 51st Army's staff believed that the German 4th and 5th Panzer Divisions attacking it had 200 tanks, which exaggerated their actual strength by more than two times.[61] In all, for Operation '*Doppelkopf*' the German troops had 281 tanks and assault guns.[62]

On 18 August, according to Iedtke's testimony, units of the 5th Panzer Division ran into a large group of Soviet anti-tank artillery 3km to the north-east of Gaudikiai, which opened a heavy fire, while

> individual anti-tank guns were well masked on the edge of the woods along both sides of the road, which we were supposed to seize, having covered approximately 6km by way of the woods. Our artillery opened a heavy fire against the edge of the woods. At our request, the final salvo included several smoke shells. We then attacked and broke into the woods under the cover of a smoke screen. The Russians ran away, leaving 10–12 anti-tank guns.
>
> Advancing further, we discovered that the forest road was little more than a cutting, about 60–80m wide, with several young saplings. The Russians had stationed even more anti-tank guns along key positions, which were difficult to discover and which were defended by infantry. Thus we had no other choice but to attack with dismounted panzergrenadiers along both sides of the road and attempt to clear our path against the anti-tank guns, while at the same time our tanks had barrelled forward. This was a labour-intensive undertaking and we advanced slowly, because the woods on both sides of the road was full of Russian infantrymen, against which we had to guard our tanks and half-track all-terrain vehicles, which were among the tanks and which were driven only by the driver and navigator. Yet another unpleasantness was that the road had been mined. The mines had been laid quite recently, thus Captain Pilke's engineers were able to locate them relatively easily and disarm them. Within two or three hours we had reached the end of the woods. The first tanks and all-terrain vehicles moved forward into Versiai, which was located a kilometre ahead, and reported that it was free of the enemy. We lined up along the edge of the woods and

the company commanders gathered their subunits that had gotten mixed up in the woods. We were able to see Zagare, some 5km to the north. Lieutenant Colonel Herzog appeared and ordered us to continue reconnoitring to the north and to guard both main roads in the north and south until the arrival of the 14th Panzergrenadier Regiment's 2nd Battalion. At that moment there sounded the devilish explosion of a 'fire wizard' – undoubtedly from numerous 'Katyushas' – simultaneously along the edge of the woods and in the gap behind it. When we were already passing by, heading to our designated blocking positions, there arrived a radio message from the regimental headquarters: 'Immediately fall back to Gaudiakai'. This could not be the truth. I got in touch by walkie-talkie with the regiment's signals section. 'The radiogram is correct. There is an unpleasantness on the right flank. Hurry!'

So we head back along this ridiculous forest road. Moving ahead of us were the panzergrenadier company, then three platoons of panzers, then the main part of the battalion, and in the rear a panzer platoon with panzergrenadiers. This panzer platoon with the panzergrenadiers was supposed to hold the edge of the woods near Verniai until we were convinced that we had once again reached the western part of the edge of the woods. Even when we were moving back, I heard the sounds of fighting in the direction of Gaudiakai. Captain Elmers, the commander of the 2nd Panzergrenadier Company, which was moving forward, reported over the radio: 'Enemy tanks are fighting our artillery'. A battalion of our artillery was stationed on a rise to the north of Gaukiakai and was now waging a close-quarters battle with 15–20 Shermans. Several guns were firing over open sights. The Shermans were located very conveniently for my two panzer platoons along the edge of the woods, because the majority of them had their rear facing us. Before long Captain Eisser, who had proven himself in many battles and had been awarded the Knight's Cross, had shot up almost all of the enemy tanks with his panzers. Two or three enemy tanks made their way to the woods, but were later found abandoned by their crews and blown up.[63]

Captain Nockel, from the 5th Panzer Division, also recalled:

Throughout the night of 17/18 August the enemy passed by the right flank of the attacking division in three tank groups, each of which contained 25–30 tanks, mainly Shermans and 'Iosif Stalins', and in the morning attacked our right flank between Gaudiakai and Kruopiak behind powerful artillery support. Their aim was to destroy our wedges and halt our attack. This attack was beaten off with heavy losses for the enemy. The rearguard tanks of the 31st Panzer Regiment's 2nd Battalion knocked out nine enemy tanks to the east of Gaudiakai. In the Gaudiakai area the artillery was firing over open sights and Eisser's panzer company (3rd Company) together knocked out 25 enemy tanks. Around Krupoiai the division's anti-tank battalion under the command of von Ramin knocked out 25 enemy tanks moving in march column. The division was mentioned in a Wehrmacht order for the destruction of 56 tanks. The fact that the tanks had attacked Gaudiakai without infantry support surprised us very much. Firing from all their guns, they captured my headquarters and Lieutenant Colonel Herzog's headquarters along the edge of the woods to the east of Gaudiakai. They were moving directly against a battery of the 116th Panzer Artillery Regiment's 2nd Battalion, which had been deployed in an open valley. Here they came to their destruction under artillery crossfire. The battery suffered heavy losses.[64]

The German tank attacks were quite successful, but they lacked motorized infantry for defending the flanks and combating Soviet anti-tank guns. The offensive by the German XXXIX Panzer Corps in the direction of Jelgava was halted at the halfway point in Zagare. The XL Panzer Corps, which was attacking along the right flank, was also unable to recapture the area around Siauliai from superior Soviet forces. But the situation was saved by Strachwitz's group, which was originally only carrying out flank protection duties. The group was given the additional task of attacking along the northern wing along the shore, but Strachwitz was able to set about carrying out both missions only on 19 August, because only by that time were his group's tanks delivered by sea. Having only 60 tanks and assault guns and taking advantage of the distraction of the main Soviet forces to the fighting in the Zagare and Siauliai areas, he carried out a breakthrough and on 20 August linked up the Sixteenth Army's vanguard, thus reestablishing land communications between the two Army Groups. Strachwitz's group received artillery support from German warships. On 20 August a squadron under the command of Vice-Admiral August Tile entered the Gulf of Riga. The heavy cruiser *Prinz Eugen*, fired 284 203mm shells against the Soviet positions near Tukums, clearing the path for Strachwitz's group. And the destroyers *Z-25* and *Z-28* fired 168 150mm shells in support of Army Group North's vanguard, which was attacking from the east. This led not only to losses, but to a powerful psychological shock among the defending Soviet troops. An entire Soviet tank brigade, consisting of 48 tanks, was supposedly destroyed by fire from the *Prinz Eugen*. Among the Soviet troops there spread rumours about the employment by the Germans of V-1 and V-2 misisles. Later the fighting shifted to the northern wing, where it continued until 27 August. Overall, during the course of Operation '*Doppelkopf*', the Germans advanced 50km in depth along a 180km front. Thanks to the success of this operation, Operation 'Bagration' was brought to an end.[65]

The 7th Panzer Division captured Kelme in heavy fighting. Lieutenant General Hasso von Manteuffel's *Grossdeutschland* Division advanced as far as Siauliai, where its tanks got stuck in the swampy soil. Lieutenant General Martin Unrhein's 14th Panzer Division got into fierce combat in the woods. Knobelsdorf's XL Panzer Corps advanced only 40km. Lieutenant General Karl Decker's 5th Panzer Division advanced 20km and got bogged down in the woods, where its vanguard was encircled and broke out to the division's main forces only with great difficulty. A Soviet counter-attack drove the 5th Panzer Division back to its original positions. The XXXIX Panzer Corps' 4th and 12th Panzer Divisions encountered heavy resistance and advanced only 10km.

The 101st Brigade from Strachwitz's group, reinforced with an SS panzergrenadier battalion from Gross's brigade, was supposed to have captured the Berzupe railway station and then attack along the group's right flank in the direction of Berze and Bikste, having established a guard in Dzukste, was supposed to have attacked the western part of

Tukums, moving from the south. Two brigades were supposed to have attacked through Kummern or along the shore to link up with General of Cavalry Philipp Kleffel's group from the Sixteenth Army, which was defending the Riga sector.[66] The German 5th Panzer Division destroyed more than 50 Soviet tanks in the fighting for Kruopiai.[67]

Colonel General Erhard Raus, the commander of the Third Panzer Army, who was commanding the operation, recalled:

> The route of the planned attack (130km in depth) led first through swampy and wooded terrain, then through a slightly hilly and open valley, which was cut by several rivers and, finally, once again rested against swampy and wooded terrain. Only in the area immediately to the north, surrounding Dobele and Tukums, was the terrain more convenient for a panzer attack. Here was the best and shorter route to Army Group North (approximately 40km). Nonetheless, the arriving panzer divisions were gathered to the south of it for the offensive. The reasons for the unconditional choice of the southern axis of attack were the developing situation and the goal of the offensive. There were reasons to fear that the forces along the northern flank, which consisted of covering divisions (the Army Group's training division) and the Baltic security formations (*Schutzmannschaftt*), would not be able to repel a new offensive by the Russians to the west. On the other hand, in the southern area were located the newly-arrived *Volksgrenadier* divisions (548th, 549th and 551st), which probably possessed great defensive power. Beside this, there were rail lines and the Riga–Königsberg highway in this area, which guaranteed the attacking formations more rapid movement. Finally, the OKH hoped to quickly break the Red Army's front along its western face and thus deployed forces for attacking in detail, as soon as they were freed from the front.[68]

As Raus concluded:

> ... the overall operation, following insignificant initial successes, was unsuccessful due to the great length of the line to such a degree that partial successes could not influence the other actions, not to mention uniting for achieving a complete victory. However, the operation distracted to itself such powerful Russian formations that Strachwitz's group, which had arrived late, managed, with the assistance of the cruiser *Prinz Eugen*, to capture Tukums and break through the Soviet corridor to Riga, which was held by small forces. These actions, of course, in no way guaranteed the liberation of Army Group North.[69]

Strachwitz's group defeated the 346th Rifle Division, which was defending the shore. According to a report by the division headquarters, its losses for 20 August and during the withdrawal during the night of 21 August were 250 men killed and 1,986 who did not make it out of the encirclement (it's likely that the majority of them became prisoners). The division lost almost all of its artillery, transport and medical battalion.

In order to secure reliable communications between the two Army Groups, Raus captured the commanding heights in the Dobele area. In order to guarantee surprise, the area occupied by the *Grossdeutschland* Division was at first abandoned, and then once again attacked by five panzer divisions. The Soviet side did not expect that the attack would be made through an area just abandoned by the Germans, and the German tanks were able to rapidly cross it and seize the heights near Dobele.[70]

On 26 August Saucken reported to Raus: 'Up until now we have destroyed more than 800 enemy anti-tank guns and thus have forced the enemy to bare almost completely the other sectors of the front . . . there are few artillery munitions. We had to pull back our heavy field howitzers from the line of fire, because they only had a few shells left for self-defence.'

On 27 August the German 4th Panzer Division unsuccessfully attempted to capture Bene. In the evening the division commander, Karl Betzel, reported to Saucken: 'Bitter and continuous fighting, with extremely heavy losses, over the last several days against a determined opponent, who enjoys a quite significant superiority in men and weapons, has so exhausted the troops that a pause of one or two days is desperately needed before resuming the attacks.'[71] However, the Army Group Centre command and that of the Third Panzer Army decided to end '*Doppelkopf*', because the chances of taking Jelgava and establishing a wider corridor between the two Army Groups were considered illusory. In 12 days the Germans had advanced approximately 50km and halted approximately 30km from Jelgava. The XXXIX and XL Panzer Corps' divisions had tied down the main Soviet forces, which permitted Strachwitz's group to capture Tukums. The former chief of staff of the 12th Panzer Division, Gerd Niepold, considered that one of the reasons for not being able to take Jelgava and completely destroying the Soviet armoured group was the lowering of the quality of the panzergrenadiers during the fourth year of the war against the USSR. The reinforcements during the past months were significantly less well trained than those soldiers who entered Soviet territory on 22 June 1941.[72]

Here one must note that by the autumn of 1944 the quality of the Soviet infantry, compared with June 1941, had worsened to an even greater degree than the quality of the Wehrmacht's infantry, insofar as very often Soviet commanders were throwing into battle practically untrained reinforcements, which were making up for the enormous losses that were an order of magnitude higher than those of the Germans. But the Red Army's artillery and tank troops had not suffered such large irreparable losses as the infantrymen and in 1944 there were already no small number of experienced soldiers in their ranks, and they had begun to train the tank troops better than during 1941–3, which reduced the gap in the level of combat training with the Germans, who in 1943–4 were devoting less time to training tank troops and artillerymen than before. As before, a large percentage of experienced tank troops remained in the Wehrmacht's tank and artillery units. The Germans' task was eased by the fact that the Soviet 51st Army reported on the attack on Tukums from the north and south as being with 300 tanks, which exaggerated the enemy's strength by a large factor. During the second half of the day on 20 August a report arrived, which also did not correspond to reality, that the enemy had carried out a landing with 35 landing ships, after which both divisions of the 1st Guards Rifle Corps were pulled out of the Tukums area to the line Mitava–north-west of Dobele–Auce. As the Russian historians Aleksandr Polishchuk and Andrei Ulanov believe,

> The breakthrough by von Strachwitz's group is an example of what kind of operational success may be achieved by even a small formation which is in the right place at the right time. The subsequent course of combat

OPERATION BAGRATION: AN INCOMPLETE TRUTH

events showed in the example of the Soviet command's actions to what kinds of consequences in making operational decisions an inaccurate evaluation of the enemy's forces and mistaken reports may lead.[73]

I.Kh. Bagramyan maintained: 'I had no doubt that that without immediate assistance these divisions would be threatened with destruction. But we could not help them with anything. Thus I granted permission for the withdrawal of units of the 346th and 417th Rifle Divisions. Kreizer issued them an order to try and break out to the line Jelgava–north-west of Dobele–Auce.'[74] Strachwitz's group and the 14th Panzer Division were transferred to Army Group North, which in this manner received mobile reserves.

During the period from 11 through 31 August 1944 the German Third Panzer Army lost 4,395 men killed, 16,157 wounded and 3,352 missing in action.[75] It's likely that the majority of these losses was suffered during the course of the fighting in the Siauliai and Tukums area. In the period from 11 through 31 August Army Group Centre took 4,246 prisoners.[76] Evidently nearly all of them were captured during the course of the battles described. Another 2,525 prisoners were taken in the first ten days of August.

According to the First Baltic Front's operational reports for the period from 1 through 28 August inclusively, German losses were 43,840 men killed, 1,879 captured and 1,135 tanks and assault guns destroyed, captured or knocked out.[77] Actually, during 1–31 August the Third Panzer Army lost only 5,839 men killed, 21,806 wounded and 5,308 missing in action.[78] Taking into account the number of missing in action, the 1,879 men captured by the First Baltic Front appears to be quite truthful. Then the overall losses of the German Third Panzer Army in August 1944 may be estimated at 9,268 men killed, which is 4.7 times less than the estimate of the Wehrmacht's losses in killed by the headquarters of the First Baltic Front.

The Germans won a tactical victory and roughly handled the First Baltic Front's mobile formations and also removed the threat of an attack against Riga from the south, which could have led to the encirclement and defeat of Army Group North. The weakened Soviet troops could not immediately resume the offensive against the Army Group. But, as it soon transpired, in and of itself the prolonged absence of land communications between Army Groups Centre and North could not lead to the defeat of Army Group North, insofar as the supply of the latter could was still carried out predominantly by sea, even when there existed a land corridor. When in October 1944 land communications between the two Army Groups were finally lost, Army Group North was able to safely fall back to Courland, where until the end of the war it attracted to itself far more Soviet troops than there were Germans remaining on the Courland peninsula. Thus one may conclude after the event that it would have been better for the German command to have employed part of the panzer formations slated for carrying out Operation '*Doppelkopf*' in Romania for the subsequent salvation of Army Group South Ukraine.

On 29 August Vasilevskii was relieved of managing the operations of the Third Belorussian Front, but continued to guide the operations of the three Baltic Fronts within the confines of conducting the Riga offensive operation.[79] In Soviet and Russian historiography this day is considered the final day of Operation 'Bagration'. On 29 August all the Fronts taking part in Operation 'Bagration' received orders to fully or partially go over to the defensive. The First Baltic Front, having gone over to the defensive with its left wing, was supposed to go over to the offensive with its right wing during 5–7 September within the confines of the Riga operation (the offensive was later moved to 15 September). The Third Belorussian Front went over to the defensive completely. The Second Belorussian Front's right wing was to go over to a static defence and the forces of the 49th and 3rd Armies were to reach the Narew River by 4–5 September and seize a bridgehead along the western bank of the river in the Ostroleka area, after which it was also to go over to a static defence. The troops of the First Belorussian Front's right wing were supposed to continue the offensive, in order to reach the Narew River as far as its mouth by 4–5 September and to seize bridgeheads along the river's western bank in the Pultusk–Serock area after which they were to go over to a static defence.[80]

Thus the Soviet command renounced liberating Warsaw in the immediate future. At the same time, the opportunities for doing this were in August and they had not disappeared in September. As of 1 August 1944 the *Stavka* VGK reserve numbered two rifle corps with six rifle divisions, three mechanized corps, one tank corps, two tank brigades, three independent tank regiments and seven self-propelled artillery regiments. If only half of the enumerated forces had been thrown against the Vistula, if necessary, by subordinating them to one of the three army headquarters in the *Stavka* reserve,[81] then the German front near Warsaw would not have held out, all the more as the Germans had to transfer part of their panzer divisions to the north for carrying out operation '*Doppelkopf*'. Even half of the tank and mechanized formations in the *Stavka* reserve was numerically superior to the number of tanks and self-propelled guns in the German group of forces around Warsaw. If they had thrown there all of the tank and mechanized formations in the Soviet *Stavka*'s reserve the First Belorussian Front's superiority in armoured equipment would have become overwhelming. As of 6 August the German panzer divisions around Warsaw had approximately 252 armoured vehicles combat ready.[82] At the same time, a Soviet tank corps in 1944 had an authorized strength of 258 tanks and self-propelled guns and a mechanized corps 246 tanks and self-propelled guns.

The situation had not fundamentally changed by 1 September. There were already five rifle and airborne corps, with 14 rifle and airborne divisions, two mechanized corps, one tank corps, one independent tank brigade, one independent tank regiment and four self-propelled artillery regiments.[83] And these forces would have been sufficient to change the course of the battle around Warsaw, all the more so because the 2nd Tank Army was also taking part in the September fighting in the Warsaw area. Its 8th Guards Tank Corps, having taken on the 3rd Tank Corps' surviving tanks, took part together with the 47th Army in the September offensive on Praga. And the 8th Guards Army's 16th Tank Corps and 11th Independent Guards Tank Brigade was fighting on the Magnuszew bridgehead. At the moment when the 2nd Tank Army was pulled out of the fighting on 5 August, it had 400 armoured vehicles in line and another 102 vehicles in ongoing and intermediate repair. It's most likely that the corps that took part in the September fighting had been reinforced with both repaired and armoured equipment and that sent from the factories.[84] Given the desire, they would not have pulled the 2nd Tank Army into the *Stavka* reserve on 6 September, and, having restored the 3rd Tank Corps, once again thrown it into the fighting for Warsaw together with the arriving reserves. Only Stalin had no desire to do so.

Hitler, on 31 August 1944, at a meeting in the *Wolfschanze* with Keitel, the chief of staff of the Western Front (the commander-in-chief in the West), Lieutenant General Siegfried Westphal, and the chief of staff of Army Group Centre, Lieutenant General

OPERATION BAGRATION: AN INCOMPLETE TRUTH

Hans Krebs, declared: 'You know that Field Marshal Kluge has committed suicide. There is a very strong suspicion that had he not committed suicide then he would have inevitably been immediately arrested.' The *Führer* accused Kluge and other plotters of intending to capitulate to the Western Allies in order to fight against the Russians together with them. Hitler called this idea a 'completely idiotic concept' and accused the plot participants of the 'criminal surrender of German territory in the East', at a minimum to the Vistula and, possibly, as far as the Oder and Elbe. Hitler also suspected the former ambassador in Moscow, von der Schulenburg, of intending to act together with the Russians against the Western Allies, and yet another part of the plotters – of an attempt to get the Russians and Western Allies to quarrel and called these attempts 'completely naïve'.[85] Actually, Kluge and the other participants of the '20 July plot' were preparing, in the event of their seizure of power, to halt combat activities on all fronts and only attempt to defend Germany's 1937 boundaries.

According to Soviet data, during the first 12 days of Operation 'Bagration' Soviet aviation carried out about 55,000 sorties, for a total of 153,000 sorties for the entire operation, which was a record for the entire war.[86] However, it is quite characteristic that despite having air superiority during the course of Operation 'Bagration', Soviet forces lost the tank battles, which did not tell against the overall victorious outcome of the operation for the Soviet side, but prevented them from fully reaping the fruits of victory.

According to Soviet estimates, the German command had concentrated against the First Baltic and the three Belorussian Fronts almost 2.3 times more men, 1.4 times more guns and mortars and 8.4 times the number of combat aircraft, but 2.2 times fewer tanks and self-propelled guns than against the Anglo-American troops in Normandy. As V.O. Daines believes, the Germans had 1,980 tanks and assault guns and 161 aircraft against the Allies in Normandy.[87] I should note that the comparison with 161 aircraft that took an immediate part in repelling the landing in Normandy is incorrect, insofar as the 'Reich' Air Fleet, the largest in the Luftwaffe, and which was responsible for the air defence of Germany, was operating only against Anglo-American air power at this time. Following the beginning of the landing in Normandy the Fleet's main forces, or approximately 515 combat-ready day fighters, 421 combat-ready night fighters and 302 combat-ready bombers were thrown against the Western Front. Along with several other types of aircraft, the 'Reich' Air Fleet had 1,348 combat-ready aircraft. The X Air Corps, which was tasked with directly opposing the landing, had 93 combat-ready anti-ship aircraft at the end of May 1944. Besides this, the Third Air Fleet, which was based in France, western Germany, Belgium, and the Netherlands, also had the IX Air Corps with 137 regular bombers. Besides this, the Third Air Fleet had six groups (squadrons) with 115 day fighters. Taking into account reconnaissance aircraft, night fighters and some other types of aircraft, the Third Air Fleet had 539 combat-ready aircraft before the Normandy landing.[88] Along with the 'Reich' Air Fleet, there were about 1,887 combat-ready aircraft at the invasion front in Normandy, which is 3.1 times more than the number at the disposal of the Luftwaffe along the 'Bagration' front. Moreover, German data speak to the fact that in Normandy the Germans employed about 2,500 tanks and assault guns, including those that had been transferred from the Eastern Front (particularly the 9th and 10th SS Divisions from the SS Panzer Corps) after the Normandy landing, but still before the beginning of Operation 'Bagration'.[89] And by the start of the Soviet offensive, Army Group Centre did not have the 900 tanks and assault guns that V.O. Daines allots to it. According to data from the official

THE SALVATION OF ARMY GROUP CENTRE

German history, *The German Reich and the Second World War*, on 22 June 1944 Army Group Centre disposed of 118 tanks and 377 assault guns, for a total of 495 armoured vehicles.[90] Thus the amount of German armoured equipment in Normandy was 5.05 times more than in Army Group Centre.

The distribution of armoured equipment and aviation clearly shows that in June 1944 Hitler and the Wehrmacht command attached far more importance to repelling the landing in Normandy, and not to holding Army Group Centre's front. And the Sixth Air Fleet, which was supporting Army Group Centre, had on 20 June only 920 aircraft, of which only 602 were combat-ready (and not 1,352, as V.O. Daines believes), including only 61 day and 31 night fighters.[91] And this was against 5,200 tanks and self-propelled guns and 6,800 combat-ready aircraft in the four Fronts taking part in Operation 'Bagration'. This yielded the Soviets a superiority of 10.5 times in armoured equipment and 11.3 times in aircraft. The number of combat-ready Luftwaffe aircraft that took part in the beginning of the battle in Normandy was one aircraft more than the amount of German aircraft along the entire Eastern Front. The First, Fourth, Fifth and Sixth Air Fleets, which on 31 May 1944 had 1,886 combat-ready aircraft, were fighting there,[92] while by 22 June the number had decreased even further (from 688 aircraft in the Sixth Air Fleet to 602). If one excludes from the calculation transport aircraft, of which there were only nine in the 'Reich' Air Fleet and none in the Third Air Fleet at all, then the advantage in favour of Normandy is even more obvious – 1,878 to 1,729.

On 31 May 1944 Army Group South Ukraine's tank and motorized divisions had 29 assault guns (26 combat-ready), 185 Panzer IV tanks (120 combat-ready), 107 Panthers (56 combat-ready), and 28 Tigers (14 combat-ready), for a total of 349 armoured vehicles (216 combat-ready). Here and further on we are not taking into account armoured equipment in the assault gun brigades. Army Group North Ukraine numbered 84 assault guns (75 combat-ready), 296 Panzer IVs (272 combat-ready), 194 Panthers (177 combat-ready), and 176 Tigers (157 combat-ready), for a total of 750 armoured vehicles (681 combat-ready). Army Group Centre numbered 63 assault guns (47 combat-ready), 73 Panzer IVs (57 combat-ready) and 37 Tigers (29 combat-ready), for a total of 173 armoured vehicles (133 combat-ready). Army Group North numbered 49 Panzer IVs (35 combat-ready), 12 Panthers (five combat-ready) and 57 Tigers (37 combat-ready), for a total of 118 armoured vehicles (77 combat-ready). In all, on the Eastern Front there were 176 assault guns (140 combat-ready), 603 Panzer IVs (484 combat-ready), 313 Panthers (238 combat-ready), and 298 Tigers (233 combat-ready), for a total of 1,390 armoured vehicles (1,095 combat-ready). Here we are not counting the SS 9th and 10th divisions from the SS II Panzer Corps, which although they were located in Army Group North Ukraine's area, were listed as being in the OKH reserve and were dispatched to Normandy immediately after the landing. Actually, these data overstate the actual number of armoured vehicles by including divisions, which while they were counted as being part of the corresponding Army Groups, were actually undergoing reforming in the deep rear, or were not combat capable and could not be immediately dispatched to the front. We are speaking here about the following divisions – *Grossdeutschland*, with 89 armoured vehicles (50 combat-ready), *Wiking*, with 126 armoured vehicles (124 combat-ready), *Totenkopf*, with 36 armoured vehicles (25 combat-ready), and the 4th Panzer Division, with 70 armoured vehicles (68 combat-ready). By excluding these units the actual number of armoured vehicles should be reduced to 1,069 armoured vehicles (828 combat ready).[93]

OPERATION BAGRATION: AN INCOMPLETE TRUTH

By 1 June 1944 there were 30 assault gun and assault artillery brigades overall on the Eastern Front (the 177th, 184th, 185th, 189th, 190th, 210th, 226th, 228th, 237th, 243rd, 244th, 245th, 259th, 270th, 278th, 281st, 286th, 300th, 301st, 303rd, 311th, 322nd, 325th, 600th, 904th, 905th, 909th, 911th, and 912th Assault Gun Brigades and the 667th Army Assault Artillery Brigade), which numbered 615 combat-ready StuG IIIs, 40 StuGs, 95 StuG IVs, and 42 StuH howitzers. One hundred and fifty-eight assault guns and 25 assault howitzers were undergoing repairs. In all, there were 798 armoured vehicles in the assault artillery and assault gun brigades.[94]

Thus the overall strength of armoured vehicles on the Eastern Front will increase to 798 vehicles (615 combat-ready) and reach 1,867 (1,443 combat-ready). By adding in the assault artillery brigades the strength of the armoured vehicles in Army Group Centre increases approximately to 314 assault guns (about 242 combat-ready). We get such a result if of the 377 assault guns included in Army Group Centre as of 22 June 1944, we subtract 63 assault guns as part of the divisions. Then the number of armoured vehicles in Army Group Centre will increase to 487 vehicles (375 combat-ready). Thus an additional 484 assault guns (373 combat-ready) should be added for the remaining Army Groups on the Eastern Front, which will increase the number of armoured vehicles in them to 1,380 (1,068 combat-ready). On the eve of the beginning of Operation 'Bagration' Army Group Centre accounted for about 26.1 per cent of all armoured vehicles on the Eastern Front (26 per cent of all combat-ready armoured equipment). The combat-ready armoured strength of the group of German forces in Normandy exceeded the strength of all combat-ready armoured vehicles on the Eastern Front by approximately 1.7 times, and the strength of combat-ready armoured vehicles in Army Group Centre by 6.7 times. Until the end of June, but chiefly after the start of Operation 'Bagration', the Eastern Front's panzer and panzergrenadier divisions and independent panzer battalions received 512 armoured vehicles as reinforcements, including Army Group South Ukraine – 79 vehicles, including 59 in a division being reformed; in Army Group North Ukraine – 303 vehicles, including 89 in a division being reformed; in Army Group Centre – 66 vehicles; and in Army Group North – 23 vehicles. The greatest number of armoured reinforcements was received by Army Group North Ukraine, but this was due to the fact that more panzer and panzergrenadier divisions were located here, many of which were already preparing to transfer or were being transferred to Army Group Centre's front. We should note that in May 1944, for the first time the number of German tanks in the West exceeded the number of tanks in the East. Then there were 1,654 armoured vehicles in the West and 1,044 in the East, with another 1,157 vehicles in Germany, for a total of 3,855. After 6 June the 9th Panzer Division and a panzer training division, which were being dispatched to the Eastern Front, were deployed to Normandy, so the gap increased even more. In August, at the end of Operation 'Bagration', the indices were nearly equal: there were 1,723 armoured vehicles in the West and 1,691 in the East. In September, following 'Bagration', 1,534 armoured vehicles remained in the West and 1,485 in the East.

Chapter 9

The Sides' Losses

Army Group Centre suffered its greatest losses during the period from 22 June through 10 July. According to final data from the OKW loss service (*Wehrmacht-Verlustwesen*), German losses for this period were 264,444 men, including 6,622 killed, 22,165 wounded and 235,657 missing in action. The greatest losses were in the Fourth Army, which amounted to 130,670 men (5,315 killed, 16,879 wounded and 108,485 missing in action). Of the number of missing in action, about 15,000 men returned to the ranks, so that overall losses may be estimated at approximately 250,000 men.[1]

There remained in the German Fourth Army only a few independent units smaller than a division, while the Ninth and Third Panzer Armies retained a reinforced corps each. Twenty-eight Wehrmacht divisions were routed and were no longer able to operate as combat-capable formations.

However, Soviet losses were extremely high. From 23 June to the end of July 1944 the forces of the four Soviet Fronts taking part in Operation 'Bagration' lost 440,879 men, including 97,232 killed.[2] Insofar as Soviet data on the number of killed has been understated, on average, by approximately a factor of three, one may assume that the actual number of killed was about 282,000 men, with overall losses of about 625,700 men. In order to compare these losses with the German ones, one must add to the losses shown of the Fourth, Ninth and Third Panzer Armies the losses of the German Second Army during the period from the last ten days of June to the end of July. They were 1,674 killed, 7,157 wounded and 1,687 missing in action, for a total of 10,518 men. This army became the only army in Army Group Centre which almost completely retained its combat capability during the course of Operation 'Bagration' and by the beginning of August had not lost its combat capability, although it suffered quite heavy losses during the month of August. One must also take into account the losses by the Fourth, Ninth and Third Panzer Armies during the last 20 days of July. There are no data for the Ninth Army and one may assume that it actually is part of those 250,000 men who were lost in the cauldrons in Belorussia. For the Fourth Army and Third Panzer Army losses were: 1,390 men killed, 7,154 wounded and 2,462 missing in action for the Fourth Army, and 1,860 men killed, 8,751 wounded and 1,734 missing in action for the Third Panzer Army. This makes for a total figure of 23,351 men, including 3,250 killed, 15,905 wounded and 4,196 missing in action.[3] Army Group Centre's overall losses for the period from 22 June to 31 July 1944 may be estimated at 283,869 men. Soviet losses were 2.2 times those of the Germans.

On 17 July 1944 57,600 German officers and soldiers taken prisoner in Belorussia marched in columns along the Garden Ring and other streets of Moscow, headed by 19 generals. Street-cleaning vehicles followed behind the prisoners, cleaning Moscow's streets of the traces of those who in 1941 had dreamed of a parade in Moscow and who

OPERATION BAGRATION: AN INCOMPLETE TRUTH

in 1944 became participants in a shameful march. Thus, Stalin wanted to demonstrate to the entire world the results of Operation 'Bagration'.

According to OKW statistics (*Wehrmacht-Verlustwesen*), in the period from 21 June through 31 August 1944 Army Group Centre's losses were 26,397 killed, 262,929 missing in action and 109,776 wounded, for a total of 399,102 overall losses. Taking into account those surrounded men who reached the German positions but who did not become an OKW statistic, K.H. Frieser estimates Army Group Centre's overall losses during 'Bagration' at 390,000 men.[4]

During the period from 21 through 30 June 1944 Army Group Centre took 406 prisoners, 2,582 in July and 6,771 in August, for a total of 9,759 prisoners.[5]

In accordance with the data of the staff entrusted with winding up Army Group Centre's affairs, which had been gathered by 1 March 1945, Army Group Centre's losses during Operation 'Bagration' were as follows.[6]

Losses By Army Group Centre's Divisions Destroyed in June–August 1944

Division	Strength	Remaining Alive	Died	Missing in Action	Fate Unknown
31st Infantry	14,000	4,032	85	2,992	6,891
78th Assault	16,599	4,049	142	2,647	9,761
36th Infantry	10,549	2,076	93	1,738	6,642
196th Infantry	13,000	4,824	83	253	7,840
57th Infantry	14,224	2,348	59	3,961	6,888
267th Infantry	12,654	1,277	57	5,081	6,239
18th Panzer Grenadier	13,987	3,064	155	4,404	6,364
110th Infantry	12,844	1,463	137	4,356	6,888
337th Infantry	13,581	6,097	218	2,000	5,266
25th Panzer Grenadier	13,323	4,086	205	4,357	4,675
Feldherrnhalle Panzergrenadier	14,433	3,418	204	3,160	7,651
4th Luftwaffe Field	11,800	1,195	45	5,670	4,890
6th Luftwaffe Field	9,831	1,374	35	5,038	3,384
9th Luftwaffe Field	9,100	4,446	235	446	3,973
95th Infantry	10,000	2,762	107	2,521	4,610
197th Infantry	12,000	4,905	81	2,766	4,248
45th Infantry	12,870	2,769	232	5,150	4,719
206th Infantry	12,200	1,301	33	5,530	5,336
246th Infantry	11,653	1,210	11	5,045	5,387
256th Infantry	10,700	4,249	141	4,673	1,637
299th Infantry	11,000	4,654	154	2,710	3,482
6th Infantry	13,681	1,407	73	6,155	6,046
383rd Infantry	12,929	2,150	119	4,175	6,485

THE SIDES' LOSSES

Division	Strength	Remaining Alive	Died	Missing in Action	Fate Unknown
134th Infantry	13,870	5,243	277	3,615	4,735
296th Infantry	11,045	2,256	210	4,421	4,158
260th Infantry	11,350	2,538	149	2,847	5,816
Units subordinated to corps and army	23,600	6,899	43	4,493	12,165
Security Troops (probably including the 286th Security and 707th Infantry (Security) Divisions, but without collaborationist formations)	47,000	16,720	286	8,015	21,979
TOTAL	393,823	102,812	3,669	108,219	179,123

The appearance of the 9th Luftwaffe Field Division, which in January–February 1944 suffered heavy losses in the fighting around Leningrad, remains a mystery. One may assume that this division was being reconstituted in Belorussia or Poland and was thrown into the fighting after the start of 'Bagration' and got into an encirclement.

Army Group Centre's losses in the period from 21 June through 31 August 1944, according to far from complete data, were 20,780 killed, 28,254 missing in action and 92,324 wounded.[7] But this is without taking into account the data from the staff for the winding up of Army Group Centre's affairs, which takes into account losses from units and formations that ended up being encircled. It determines that of the 393,823 men who were encircled, 102,812 remained alive and 3,669 surely perished, and 108,219 were missing in action, and the fate of 179,123 men remained unknown as of 1 March 1945.[8] Practically all of them, just like those missing in action, should be regarded either as killed or taken prisoner. So Army Group Centre's overall irreparable losses for the indicated period may be determined as 340,045 men. For the period from 1 March through 1 October 1944 the three Belorussian Fronts and the First Baltic Front took 153,770 prisoners.[9] Practically all of them were captured during 'Bagration'. Then the number of killed in Army Group Centre during the period from 21 June through 31 August 1944 may be estimated at 186,275 men. Army Group Centre captured 9,756 prisoners.[10] Then the number of Soviet troops killed may be estimated at 515,700 men. The correlation of men killed during the course of 'Bagration' may be estimated at 2.8:1, irreparable losses at 1.5:1, and overall losses at 2.6:1, in all cases in favour of the Germans. In terms of losses, Operation 'Bagration' became the Wehrmacht's greatest defeat on the Eastern Front after Stalingrad.

According to official data, Soviet troops during the Belorussian offensive operation (Operation 'Bagration'), from 22 June through 29 August 1944, lost 178,507 men irreparably and another 587,308 wounded and sick. Besides this, the Polish 1st Army lost 1,533 men killed and missing in action, and 3,540 wounded and sick.[11] In our estimation, the data by the collective responsible for *The Stamp of Secrecy has been Removed* underestimates Soviet irreparable losses by approximately three times. Thus actual Soviet irreparable losses may amount to about 525,500 men. At the same time, independent Soviet divisions suffered heavy losses during 'Bagration'. For example, during the Bobruisk garrison's breakout to the west on 29–30 June, the 356th Rifle Division lost 1,785 men killed, wounded and missing in action.[12] During the fighting on 30 June–1 July in the area of the village of Oktyabr', the fresh 82nd Rifle Division suffered such heavy losses that it was pulled back into the rear. At the end of July, having been reinforced, the division ran into the SS *Wiking* Division in the Czeremcha area and suffered such heavy losses that it took two months to restore it.[13]

In 1944 the Red Army suffered its greatest losses in July and August, when Operation 'Bagration' was being conducted in Belorussia and Poland, along with the offensive by Soviet forces in Galicia and the Iasi–Kishinev operation. As of 1 July 1944 the number of wounded and sick in hospitals amounted to 915,244 men and as of 1 August 1,025,190 men.[14] Taking into account the wounded and sick who returned to their units, those discharged as invalids and for an extended leave, as well as those dying in hospitals, the overall number of new wounded and sick that entered the hospitals in July 1944 may be determined at 641,500 men.

The enemy's losses in Soviet reports are exaggerated by several times, while their own irreparable losses are undercounted by several times. Let's take the 31st Army's (Third Belorussian Front) war diary for May 1944 – the last month before 'Bagration'. During this period, according to entries in the journal, which were based on combat reports, the army's troops inflicted a loss of 2,226 men killed on the enemy. Part of the German Fourth Army – approximately an army corps – fought against the 31st Army. According to German data, the losses for the entire Fourth Army for May 1944 were 526 men killed, 78 missing in action and 2,238 wounded.[15] Taking into account the fact that no more than a third of the German Fourth Army's forces (the 31st Army's headquarters estimated this at two infantry divisions, one panzergrenadier division and part of the forces of yet another division) were operating against the 31st Army, it is unlikely that its actual irreparable losses in the fighting against the 31st Army exceeded 200 men. Thus data on the enemy's irreparable losses in May 1944 in the reports by the Soviet 31st Army are exaggerated by approximately 11 times.

And how many men, according to army reports, did the 31st Army lose in May 1944? According to incomplete data (there is no information on losses for 6 May), the army's losses were 360 killed and 1,100 wounded. According to the army headquarters' information, the losses were fewer – 279 killed, and 883 wounded, with another 25 men non-combat irreparable losses.[16] The 31st Army's irreparable losses are approximately 1.8 times more than the irreparable losses of the German Fourth Army's units facing it for May. At the same time, the 31st Army supposedly suffered no missing-in-action losses, which is hard to believe. For example, on 1 May the Germans retook in a counter-attack the stronghold of Protasovo, which had been occupied in the morning by elements of the 10th Independent Punishment Battalion. According to official data, the battalion's losses were 65 killed and 79 wounded. At the same time, it states that only the battalion's remnants survived. One may assume that a significant part of the punishment troops, who ended up being encircled, were taken prisoner or went missing in action. In army reports irreparable losses were usually understated by approximately three times, so the 31st Army's losses in killed and missing in action in May 1944 may be estimated at approximately 1,080 men, which is 5.4 times the loss suffered by the German divisions opposing it. In May 1944 the 31st Army received 12,145 reinforcements, of which only 417 men were sent to combat support and rear units. In April there were only 2,706 reinforcements with stated losses of 413 killed, one missing in action, three non-combat irreparable losses, and 981 wounded. At the same time the numerical strength of the army's divisions on 1 April 1944 was: 220nd Rifle Division – 3,490 men; 192nd Rifle Division – 3,340 men; 331st Rifle Division – 3,602 men; 88th Rifle Division – 3,546 men, and; the 152nd Fortified Area – 4,126 men, for a total of 17,524 men. By 31 May the strength of the 31st Army's divisions had changed in the following manner: 192nd Rifle Division – 4,467 men; 88th Rifle Division – 4,833 men; 331st Rifle Division – 5,968 men; 220th Rifle Division – 7,009 men; the 152nd Fortified Area – 4,458 men; the 174th Rifle Division – 4,293 men; the 62nd Rifle Division – 4,867 men; the 352nd Rifle Division – 6,087 men, and; the 173rd Rifle Division – 5,986 men. Thus the strength of those four divisions and fortified area in the 31st Army on 1 April, by the end of May amounted to 26,735 men; that is, they had increased by 9,211 men. In April these divisions and fortified area lost 241 men killed, one missing in action and two non-combat irreparable losses, as well as 538 wounded, for a total of 782 men, and received reinforcements of 2,396 men. In May these divisions and fortified area lost 160 men killed (while at the same time the fortified area supposedly lost only 22 killed, which is clearly understated, because the 10th Independent Punishment Battalion, which was part of the unit, lost no less than 65 men killed in the fighting for Protasovo on 1 May), 547 wounded and also non-combat irreparable losses of eight men, for a total loss of 715 men. In May these divisions and fortified area received 8,974 reinforcements. Correspondingly, by the end of May they should have numbered 27,397 men, but only numbered 26,735 men. It's most likely that the difference in 662 men is unaccounted-for combat irreparable losses. According to reports by the 31st Army's headquarters, these formations' irreparable losses in April and May 1944 numbered 1,074 men; that is, 2.6 times more. We should note that during these two months the 31st Army's front line did not change, there could not have been an unaccounted-for call-up directly into the units, and losses were an order less than during major operations, so that they understated them to a lesser degree than during 'Bagration'.

Soviet troop strength from 1 July through 1 August 1944 fell from 11,047,090 to 10,865,345 men. Taking into account the fact that German troops in the East only captured 6,143 prisoners in July 1944, the Red Army's losses in men killed in this month may be estimated at 471,300.[17] In July 1944 the Red Army's losses in wounded, according to Ye.I. Smirnov's table, were 132 per cent of the average monthly level for the war. Then the overall number of killed, according to our methodology, may be estimated at 660,000 men. The difference with the estimate on the basis of the monthly dynamic of troop strength and the number of wounded and sick in hospitals is about 189,000 men. The difference arose, most likely, because in July the strength of the reinforcements that reached the troops significantly exceeded the monthly level for 1944 and was 150,000–200,000 men more than that figure adopted by us of 937,100 men. After all, it was necessary not only to make good the heavy losses suffered in the last ten days of June, when 'Bagration' began, and in July, but to also increase the numbers to augment the Soviet offensive. Also, in July the direct call-up into units in connection with the liberation of large territories with rather numerous populations was practised. By 1 September 1944 the number of wounded and sick in hospitals rose to 1,098,548 men. The number of wounded and sick that entered the hospitals in August 1944 may be estimated at 604,800 men. Taking into account the fact that, according to Ye.I. Smirnov's table, the fall in the numbers of wounded in August by 36,700 in comparison with September, appears unlikely. One may assume that actually in August, for some kinds of reasons, several tens of thousands fewer servicemen were returned to their units than in July (as a variant: there were fewer demobilized invalids, perhaps due to their being enrolled). We conditionally accept that in August there were approximately the same number of wounded and sick as in July; that is, approximately 641,500 men.

From 1 August through 1 September 1944 Soviet troop strength fell from 10,865,345 men to 10,674,798. In August 1944 German troops on the Eastern Front took 14,393 prisoners.[18] The number of killed in the Red Army's ranks in August 1944 may be estimated at 471,700 men. If one employs the number of wounded and sick of 641,500 in calculations, then the number of killed may be estimated at 508,400 men.

According to Ye.I. Smirnov's table, in August 1944 the number of wounded was 140 per cent of the average monthly level for the war. Correspondingly, the overall number of killed in this month may be estimated at 700,000 men. This is 228,000 men higher than the result of the estimate on the basis of data on the monthly dynamic of the Red Army's strength and the number of wounded and sick in hospitals. One can assume that for these same reasons that we enumerated applicable to July 1944, the strength of the reinforcements that entered the Red Army in August 1944 was 200,000–250,000 men higher than the average monthly level for 1942–5 adopted by us.

If we compare the Soviet losses in wounded for June, July and August 1943 and 1944, they, and the losses in killed in proportion to them, were almost unchanged. In 1943 the number of wounded was 365 per cent of the average monthly rate for the war, and during that same period in 1944, which saw the highly successful Belorussian and Iasi–Kishinev operations, 360 per cent.[19] It was not that the Soviet troops had learned how to fight, but that there were significantly fewer German troops on the Eastern Front due to the Normandy landing. The Soviet personnel superiority had become overwhelming, there remained almost no German fighter aircraft in the East, and the best German panzer divisions were unsuccessfully attempting to repel the Allied landing in Normandy. As a result, German losses rose, but Soviet losses practically did not decline. Quite the opposite, the Germans, having significantly fewer men and materiel, inflicted on the Red Army in 1944 the same kinds of losses as in 1943. This is hardly surprising. By the end of the war the Red Army consisted chiefly of those liberated from captivity, practically untrained recruits from the occupied territories and mobilized *Ostarbeiters*, when at the beginning of the war a significant part of the Red Army's personnel had served a year in the army and more and had the experience of the 'liberation campaigns', Khalkhin-Gol and the Finnish War.

Due to the fact that the Soviet superiority in men, tanks, artillery and aircraft had become overwhelming, and due to the dispatch of a significant part of the German divisions and the overwhelming majority of the Luftwaffe's aircraft to the West, German losses on the Eastern Front, beginning from June 1944, rose sharply, and not only in prisoners, but in those killed. It was not that the Red Army had learned to fight, but the Wehrmacht was deprived of the opportunity to maintain sufficient forces in the East for any kind of successful defence.

In 1944 German aviation carried out 182,000 sorties on those fronts where the Western Allies were operating, and on the Eastern Front 342,500 sorties. But the correlation of losses was almost directly the opposite. In the West the Luftwaffe, according to calculations by the American researcher Don Cauldwell, lost 9,768 combat aircraft in 1944, and in the East only 2,406. The probability for Luftwaffe pilots to be shot down in the West was eight times higher than in the East.

Soviet Long-Range Aviation (ADD) was used to its full extent in Operation 'Bagration'. At the beginning of June 1944 it numbered 1,266 (1,134 combat-ready) night bombers, predominantly Il-4s, Il-2s and B-25s, and its total bomb load was 1,253 tons, which approximately corresponded to the total bomb load of all the Air Armies taking part in Operation 'Bagration'. The ADD's aircraft could drop bombs weighing 500kg and more, which enabled them to destroy concrete fortifications of which, to be sure, there were almost none in Belorussia. The *Stavka* ordered only 11 air corps from its reserve, reinforced to full strength, to Belorussia, as well as several air divisions. One thousand five hundred and six aircraft were dispatched to the 1st Air Army (Third Belorussian Front) and 1,047 to the 16th Air Army (First Belorussian Front). Both of these Fronts played the principal role in Operation 'Bagration'.[20]

On 23 June, the first day of the offensive, despite the poor weather, the Germans recorded more than 4,500 overflight sorties by Soviet aviation. The Luftwaffe's anti-aircraft artillery reported shooting down 23 aircraft and the German fighter pilots 43. But the Luftwaffe was only able to make 180 sorties. On the following day, due to the improved weather, the Soviet Air Force carried out 5,305 sorties.[21]

From 13 through 18 June the ADD's formations, working only at night, carried out a special operation to destroy the enemy's aviation on its airfields. One thousand four hundred and seventy-two sorties were carried out and 1,459kg of bombs dropped. Following the start of the offensive, the ADD's goal was the railway junctions. But its losses were heavy. Sixty-one ADD aircraft had been shot down by the end of June alone, the Germans' employment of radar contributing to this.

On the evening of 27 June the 16th Air Army launched a crushing attack against the group of German forces encircled south-east of Bobruisk. In 90 minutes 1,127 demolition bombs, weighing 50kg and 100kg, 4,897 small shrapnel bombs weighing 8kg, 10kg and 25kg, and 5,326 anti-tank bombs were dropped, and 572 rockets launched. The 526 aircraft that took part in the raid suffered no losses. According to Soviet accounts, possibly exaggerated, up to 150 tanks and assault guns were destroyed and damaged (Kessel's divisions simply did not have that many armoured vehicles), about 1,000 guns of various calibres, up to 6,000 motor vehicles, up to 300 truck tractors and 3,000 transport vehicles; more than 1,000 soldiers and officers were killed, as were up to 1,500 horses, and about 5,500 soldiers and officers were scattered.

By the beginning of July the Sixth Air Fleet numbered 1,135 combat aircraft and, moreover, in the Baltic States up to half of the First Air Fleet's force was employed (approximately 180 aircraft). Five Soviet Air Armies (1st, 3rd, 4th, 6th, and 16th) had 7,368 aircraft (6,665 combat-ready). About 1,000 ADD aircraft and 600 aircraft from air-defence units were also operating along the 'Bagration' front. However, the 6th Air Army (1,061 aircraft) was still in reserve and was committed into the fighting only on 18 July. But even without it, the Soviet Air Force had a numerical superiority of 6.1 times, and with it 6.9 times. Only the Luftwaffe's higher level of pilot training, rear support and command, which knew how to rapidly concentrate forces along those sectors where a Soviet breakthrough was planned, whether a counterblow was being conducted, or it was necessary to destroy a strategically-important bridge, levelled the playing field. In the log of the Luftwaffe's 55th Bomber Squadron, *Grif*, it was maintained that the poor tactical and gunnery training of the Soviet fighter pilots

> ... was particularly clearly manifested in the Luftwaffe's daytime
> raid on the crossings over the Vistula. Although the enemy attacked
> the 'Heinkels' in strength of two–three squadrons simultaneously

from two sides, from the rear and the sides, carrying out so-called oblique attacks, the fighters interfered with each other and they were unable to shoot down a single bomber. During their attacks the Soviet fighters completely failed to interfere with the Bf 109s from the cover group carrying out their task. Last year's results were repeated: the Soviet fighters proved to be helpless against a well-organized defence, based on the echeloning of groups of bombers according to height.

The Soviet 2nd Tank Army's forward units suffered heavily from enemy low-level air attacks on the approaches to Praga. In crossing the Berezina units of the 3rd Guards Mechanized Corps suffered from German attack aircraft. At the same time, the necessity of rapidly abandoning airfields, which were under threat of being captured by the advancing Soviet troops, while abandoning damaged aircraft, as well as supplies of fuel, munitions, which they were unable to take away, told most negatively on the Luftwaffe's activities.[22]

The Red Army Air Force's irreparable loss of aircraft during Operation 'Bagration' was on the average one per 80–90 sorties. The high losses were a consequence of the insufficient training given to young pilots. Of 4,709 pilots dispatched to fill out the air corps from the High Command Reserve, 4,075, or 87 per cent, were recognized as being in need of further instruction in a combat situation. There had never been such a high proportion before.[23]

From 23 June through 29 August 1944 the Red Army Air Force carried out 153,545 combat sorties, including the following: launching raids against enemy troops and equipment (35 per cent of the overall number); accompanying assault aviation (22 per cent); covering the ground forces (17 per cent); reconnaissance (13 per cent); and strikes against the enemy's rail shipments (8 per cent). Only about 5 per cent of all sorties were for attacking airfields, 'free hunting' and carrying out special assignments, etc.

Long-Range Aviation carried out 43 mass raids against the enemy's troops, rear areas and airfields (13,431 sorties), dropping 14,174 tons of bombs. Losses amounted to 124 aircraft, predominantly from German fighters. In July 1944, for the first time in the air war on the Soviet-German front, the number of sorties by German night fighters in the Sixth Air Fleet's area exceeded the number of sorties by day fighters.

During the rapid offensive the Air Force's rear services failed to move forward to new airfields in time and to supply them with everything necessary. Thus as early as the end of June the number of combat sorties in the 1st Air Army fell 3–5 times relative to the offensive's first days, while during the operation's second period, from 5 July through 29 August, an average of 2.5 fewer sorties were carried out per day than during the first period. The Luftwaffe had no such problems, because when moving a new German unit to a new airfield everything necessary for waging combat operations for a period sufficient for the organization of ground transport was moved with it by transport aircraft or bombers. While concentrating significant aviation forces along the axes of the counterblows and operating at high intensity, the Germans would create a numerical superiority along individual sectors of the front and would inflict serious losses, both on the ground forces and the Red Army Air Force. In a report by the 1st Air Army in the middle of August, it was stated: 'Flying personnel, not encountering organized enemy

THE SIDES' LOSSES

resistance until reaching the line of the Neman River, let its guard down in the air, while with the approach to the border of East Prussia the enemy's resistance increased significantly.'[24]

As the Russian military historian Andrei Smirnov explained: having generalized data on several dozen dogfights, according to which it was possible to verify by enemy documents the reports by the sides on the number of shot-down aircraft, on the average the Soviet side exaggerated the number of victories by 5.3 times and the German side an average of only 2.4 times.[25]

A table published in Khazanov's book will help us to evaluate the Soviet Air Force's actual losses during 'Bagration'.[26]

Changes in the 3rd Air Army's Numerical Strength in August 1944.

Formation/Unit	Aircraft Model	14 August	19 August	24 August	29 August
211th Assault Air Division	Il-2	99/-	72/15	43/23	40/19
332nd Assault Air Division	Il-2	72/15	48/19	38/26	42/11
335th Assault Air Division	Il-2	102/1	84/8	65/16	66/10
1st Guards Bomber Corps	Pe-2	166/-	171/1	212/1	269/12
334th Bomber Division	Tu-2	75/2	62/12	66/13	52/23
314th Night Bomber Division	Po-2	47/2	60/2	60/4	57/4
1st Guards Fighter Corps	La-5, Yak-9, Yak-3	181/19	200/37	151/48	130/40
11th Fighter Corps	P-39 Aerocobra	151/38	167/36	165/47	174/21
259th Fighter Division	Yak-7b, Yak-9, La-5	86/24	73/27	69/25	65/28
11th Independent Reconnaissance Air Regiment	Pe-2	21/2	17/4	19/2	17/4
105th Guards Independent Air Regiment	Po-2, R-5, C-47	38/2	38/2	39/2	44/3
399th Signals Air Regiment	Po-2	28/4	26/5	29/2	29/2

Changes in the 3rd Air Army's Numerical Strength in August 1944. (*Continued*)

Formation/Unit	Aircraft Model	14 August	19 August	24 August	29 August
206th Independent Aerial Spotter-Reconnaissance Air Regiment	Various models	33/3	28/6	28/6	28/6
TOTAL		**1,099/112**	**1,046/174**	**984/215**	**913/183**
Total Aircraft		1,211	1,220	1,199	1,096
Percentage of Aircraft out of Commission		9.2	14.2	17.9	16.7

Notes:
1. The numerator indicates the combat-ready aircraft and the denominator those not ready for combat.
2. Data were compiled at 1900 every day.

It's easy to count that during the period from 14 through 29 August the 211th Assault Air Division irreparably lost no less than 40 aircraft, the 332nd Assault Air Division no less than 34, and the 335th Assault Air Division no less than 27 aircraft. The losses by the 1st Bomber Corps are simply impossible to count, because the number of bombers in it grew continuously. This does mean there were no irreparable losses suffered by the air corps, but only testifies to its constant reinforcement with new equipment, while the number of arriving aircraft constantly exceeded the irreparable losses. The 334th Bomber Division lost no fewer than seven aircraft, while at the same time it is impossible to establish the division's losses for the period from 19 through 24 August, during which the number of aircraft rose. The 314th Night Bomber Division lost irreparably no less than three aircraft. However, it is impossible to determine the losses for the period from 14 through 29 August, when the number of aircraft in the corps constantly grew. The 1st Guards Fighter Corps lost no less than 67 aircraft, but it is impossible to establish its losses for the period from 14 through 19 August, during which the number of aircraft in the corps grew. The 11th Fighter Corps lost irreparably no less than 17 aircraft during the period from 24 through 29 August, and before 24 August its losses are impossible to determine, insofar as during that period the number of aircraft in the corps grew. The 259th Fighter Division lost irreparably no less than 17 aircraft. Before 19 August the 11th Air Reconnaissance Regiment irreparably lost no less than two aircraft, while its losses after 19 August are impossible to establish, because from 19 through 29 August the number of aircraft in the regiment did not change. The losses by the 105th Guards Independent Air Regiment are impossible to establish, because during the period from 14 through 29 August the number of aircraft in the regiment either remained the same or increased. The 399th Signals Air Regiment lost no less than one aircraft before 19 August, while subsequently the number of aircraft in the regiment did not change. The 206th Independent Aerial Spotter-Reconnaissance Air Regiment lost no fewer than two aircraft before 19 August, while subsequently the number of aircraft in the regiment remained unchanged.

THE SIDES' LOSSES

It works out that a calculation on the basis of the dynamics of the 3rd Air Army's formations' and units' strengths alone yields irreparable losses of 217 aircraft for the period from 14 through 29 August. At the same time, according to official data, based on reports by the air headquarters, in all of August 1944 the 3rd Air Army supposedly irreparably lost, due to combat and non-combat reasons, only 220 aircraft.[27] However, our calculations show that in only 15 days in August, even according to minimal estimates, the 3rd Air Army lost irreparably only three aircraft less than for all of August, if one is to believe the reports by the army's headquarters. Clearly, these reports should not be believed. Undoubtedly, the 3rd Air Army's actual losses in August 1944 were much higher than 217 aircraft. According to data cited in Khazanov's book, the 3rd Air Army numbered 1,089 combat-ready aircraft in the beginning of August.[28] To be sure, we don't know if they are speaking about all aircraft, or only combat-ready planes, without taking into account those undergoing repairs. In the first days of August the 3rd Air Army suffered only slight losses, but they began to increase, beginning on 7 August, when in connection with the beginning of German counter-attacks in the Jekabpils area, the Luftwaffe's effectiveness increased.[29] By 14 August the number of aircraft in the 3rd Air Army had increased to 1,211, including 1,099 combat-ready. However, one must take into account not only the losses suffered during 1–14 and 30–31 August, but also those losses during the 15–29 August time period, which are out of our realm of study. Let's begin with the fact that it was precisely the fighters and attack aircraft that suffered the greatest losses and thus new aircraft were constantly being fed into the corresponding formations and units to make good their losses. The number of aircraft in those units and formations of fighter and bomber aviation, where an increase in the air park of 192 aircraft was noted (we exclude the independent regiments that suffered comparatively small losses from our calculations). The number of aircraft in the enumerated divisions and corps for 14 August was 681. It works out that by 29 August the number of aircraft had increased by 1.282 times. If we assume that replacement aircraft arrived in the same proportion in those same corps and divisions where the number of aircraft did not grow (there were 399 such aircraft on 14 August), it means that no less than 113 additional aircraft were lost there, including no less than 82 aircraft in the three Il-2 'Sturmovik' divisions. Then the losses by the 1st Guards Bomber Corps, the 334th Bomber Division and the 314th Night Bomber Division may be estimated as 31.65 per cent of their strength on 14 August; that is, 92 aircraft (this number includes the seven aircraft previously counted in the 334th Bomber Division and three aircraft in the 314th Night Bomber Division). One may assume that the level of fighter losses was between the level of 'Sturmovik' losses and those for the bombers. Then the irreparable losses for the 1st Guards Bomber Corps, the 334th Bomber Division and the 314th Night Bomber Division may be estimated at 47.5 per cent of 499 aircraft – the number on 14 August – that is, 237 aircraft, including 17 aircraft counted earlier in the losses of the 11th Fighter Corps, 67 in the 1st Guards Fighter Corps, and 17 in the 259th Fighter Division. In this case the irreparable losses of all the formations and units of the 3rd Air Army during the period from 14 through 29 August may be estimated at 517 aircraft. Even if we assume that the intensity of the fighting during the remaining 16 days of August was lower and the 3rd Air Army's irreparable losses for these days were two times less, then they would amount to approximately 258 aircraft. In conclusion, this yields no fewer than 775 irreparably lost aircraft for August. This is 3.5 times more than the official data for the 3rd Air Army's losses in August 1944.

OPERATION BAGRATION: AN INCOMPLETE TRUTH

Khazanov cites official data, according to which the 3rd, 1st, 4th, 16th, and 5th Air Armies in July 1944 lost irreparably, due to combat and non-combat reasons, 694 aircraft and 785 in August.[30] If all of the Air Armies' losses were undercounted in the same proportion as the losses of the 3rd Air Army, then in July the losses of the Soviet Armies for July may be estimated at 2,430 aircraft, and 2,750 in August. It's more than likely that they did not report a certain part of their losses higher up. According to Khazanov, until the end of July, 'from the beginning of the offensive in Belorussia we lost about 400 combat aircraft (in the reports presented to I.V. Stalin combat losses of 306 aircraft were shown)'.[31] If we apply the coefficient of 306 to 3.5 times, then actual irreparable losses for Soviet aviation taking part in 'Bagration', during the period from 22 through 30 June may be estimated at approximately 1,070 aircraft. But a large part of the losses in aircraft, most likely, was due to those aircraft which had not earlier been included in the number of lost or damaged machines, because their pilots were not killed and were not missing in action, but which were written off upon the arrival of new equipment due to actual combat damage or wear and tear. In Khazanov's estimate, during the course of 'Bagration' the Luftwaffe lost irreparably, due to all reasons, a total of 1,200–1,500 aircraft.[32]

It's interesting that the overall correlation of irreparable losses of fighters on the Eastern Front for all of 1944 is 6.0:1 in favour of the Luftwaffe, which is close to our estimate of the overall correlation of losses of combat aircraft in Operation 'Bagration'.[33]

In this a major role was played by the fact that the Soviet Air Force carried out a far greater number of combat sorties than did the Luftwaffe and, accordingly, offered a far larger number of targets for German fighters and anti-aircraft guns. The gap in the level of pilot training remained, although it gradually decreased as the Luftwaffe's most experienced pilots had to be dispatched to air defence over Germany and to the Western Front to combat Allied aviation. Along the 'Bagration' front the Soviet Air Force carried out 39,365 sorties in July, and 52,017 in August, for a total of 91,382.[34] In Belorussia the Soviet Air Force was opposed by the Luftwaffe's Sixth and First Air Fleets. At the same time, part of the First Air Fleet was also operating along the Karelian Isthmus, in Army Group North's sector. These Air Fleets carried out 235,269 sorties for all of 1944.[35] Of this number, about 39,211 may be allotted to July and August, taking into account the dispersal of the First Air Fleet to other theatres, and thus is unlikely to be more than 30,000 sorties, which is three times fewer than the Soviet Air Force. A role was also played by the fact that, as in the case with armoured equipment, the Soviet aircraft repair service was significantly inferior to the German one and so restored a much lower number of damaged aircraft.

Khazanov notes that

> The chief result of the Luftwaffe's summer battles was the worsening of the situation in a number of areas. For example, the quality of personnel training fell due to the shortage of experienced instructors, while there was observed the loss of equipment superiority, which was present earlier, and there were significant difficulties in making losses good ... But the Anglo-American air raids on factories for producing synthetic fuel in Germany, as well as the occupation by Soviet troops of the large oil-producing areas in Romanian Ploesti, had catastrophic consequences. This told immediately on the air fuel situation for the German Air Force.[36]

THE SIDES' LOSSES

During June–August 1944, Army Group Centre suffered heavy losses among its higher command echelon. In all, 15 senior officers perished, including those who were promoted to general's rank posthumously. Of these, one general was killed by the Germans themselves, while another committed suicide so as not to be subjected to repressions as an active member of the 20 July plot. The remainder perished due to the action of Soviet troops and partisans, including those who committed suicide so as not to be captured.

Major General Otto Drescher, the commander of the 267th Infantry Division, was killed in a wood 3km south of the village of Merkine, in the Varena District of Lithuania, on 13 August 1944. Werner Froemert, who commanded the *Feldherrnhalle's* reserve brigade, was seriously wounded and died in hospital in Danzig on 28 July 1944. On 20 September 1944 he was posthumously promoted to major general, dating to 1 July 1944. Hans Hahne, who temporarily commanded the 197th Infantry Division, went missing in action near Vitebsk on 24 June 1944. In this case, he may be confidently numbered among the dead, because Hahne was not found in Soviet captivity.

SS *Brigadeführer* Bronislaw Kaminskii, the commander of the 29th (1st Russian) Grenadier Division in the Russian National Liberation Army's SS troops, units of which took part in repelling the Soviet forces' offensive during the course of Operation 'Bagration' and in suppressing the Warsaw uprising, was killed on orders of *Reichsführer SS* Heinrich Himmler on 28 August 1944 in the Beskids by an SD *sonderkommando*. The likely reasons for the killing were pillaging by units of the Russian National Liberation Army in Warsaw, and particularly the desire to remove the main competitor to General A.A. Vlasov among Russian collaborationists.

General of Artillery Robert Martinek, the commander of the XXXIX Panzer Corps, was killed near the town of Berezino, Minsk Oblast', on 28 June 1944.

Lieutenant General Rudolf Peschel, the commander of the 6th Luftwaffe Field Division, was killed by partisans near the settlement of Begoml' (Minsk Oblast') on 29 June 1944.

General of Artillery Doctor Georg Pfeiffer, the commander of the VI Army Corps, blew himself up along with his vehicle, having fallen into a partisan ambush on the road between the villages of Stekhovo and Mokrovichi (Belynichi District, Vitebsk Oblast') on 27 June 1944.

Lieutenant General Ernst Phillip, the commander of the 134th Infantry Division, committed suicide east of Bobruisk on 29 June 1944.

Luftwaffe Lieutenant General Robert Pistorius, the commander of the 4th Luftwaffe Field Division, was killed near the village of Svitino (Beshenkovichi District, Vitebsk Oblast') on 27 June 1944.

Lieutenant General Walter Scheller, the commandant of the Brest-Litovsk fortress, was killed near Brest-Litovsk on 22 July 1944.

Lieutenant General Otto Schunemann, the temporary commander of the XXXIX Panzer Corps, was killed during an air raid near the village of Pogost (Berezino District, Minsk Oblast') on 29 June 1944.

Helmut Werner Strempel, the commander of the 252nd Infantry Division's 461st Grenadier Regiment, and simultaneously commander of the 'Strempel' divisional group, was mortally wounded near the town of Madona (Latvia) and on that same day died at the 'Dambri' medical evacuation post, Medical Company No. 2/23. He was posthumously promoted to major general, effective 1 August 1944. Major General

OPERATION BAGRATION: AN INCOMPLETE TRUTH

Henning Hermann Karl Robert von Tresckow, the chief of staff of the Second Army, being an active participant in the plot against Hitler, following the failure of which he committed suicide, simulating his death in battle by blowing himself up with a hand grenade near the town of Ostrow Mazowiecka (Poland) on 21 July 1944.

Major General Albrecht Wustenhagen, the commander of the 256th Infantry Division, was killed near the village of Kokhanovka (Tolochin District, Vitebsk Oblast') on 28 June 1944. He was posthumously promoted to lieutenant general, effective 1 April 1944.

Lieutenant General Karl Ludwig Zutavern, the commander of the 18th Panzergrenadier Division, committed suicide near Bobruisk on 6 July 1944.[37]

As a result of Operation 'Bagration', 23 German generals were captured. Of these, two were executed (hanged) for war crimes, one committed suicide in captivity, three died in captivity from disease, and two of them while serving a 25-year sentence for war crimes. The remaining 18 generals survived Soviet captivity, of which 13 were condemned to 25 years for war crimes. In all, the losses amongst the Wehrmacht's generals killed and captured were 37 men, including one SS general. However, the death of one SS general (Kaminskii) and one Wehrmacht general (von Tresckow, who committed suicide) had no direct connection with combat operations and were entirely political. With the exception of these two cases, the number of killed and captured Wehrmacht generals during Operation 'Bagration' comes to 35.

Lieutenant General Rudolf Bamier, the commander of the 12th Infantry Division, was taken prisoner in the Mogilev area on 28 June 1944 by a capture group led by a battalion commander of the 609th Rifle Regiment/139th Rifle Division/50th Army/Second Belorussian Front, Captain V.V. Fatin. He was one of the 19 generals who took part in the parade of the captured Germans around Moscow on 17 July 1944. He was one of 50 German generals who in Soviet captivity, on 8 December 1944 signed the appeal 'To the People and the Wehrmacht', calling on the German population and army to rise up against the Nazi leadership and to put an end to the war. On 21 April 1950 he was repatriated to the GDR; he headed a police school in Glowen, and was then appointed to the post of chief of the commandant of Erfurt's military-technical school. He was transferred to the GDR Ministry of State Security in 1959 and on 31 December 1963 he retired. Rudolf Bamier died on 13 March 1972, at the age of 75, in the Gross Glienicke suburb of East Berlin.

Major General Heinrich Otto Gotftried Erdmansdorff, the commandant of the Mogilev fortified area, was taken prisoner in the Mogilev area on 28 June 1944 by a capture group led by a battalion commander of the 609th Rifle Regiment/139th Rifle Division/50th Army/Second Belorussian Front, Captain V.V. Fatin. He was took part in the parade of the captured Germans around Moscow and the appeal of the National Committee for a Free Germany, 'To the People and the Wehrmacht'. On 15 January 1946 he was indicted for war crimes in a trial conducted in the District Officers' House in Minsk. He was sentenced to death. On 30 January 1946 he was publicly hanged at the Minsk racetrack. Heinrich Otto Gottfried Erdmansdorff was 52.

Major General Herbert Michaelis, the commander of the 95th Infantry Division, was captured around Borisov on 28 June 1944. He was took part in the parade of captured Germans around Moscow on 17 July 1944 and signed the appeal 'To the People and the Wehrmacht. He was sentenced to 25 years in corrective-labor camps on 8 October 1948 by a military tribunal of the MVD troops of the Vitebsk Oblast' for war crimes. On 8 October 1955, as non-amnestied war criminal, we was turned over to the FRG authorities and freed. Herbert Michaelis died on 20 August 1969, at the age of 72, in Bonn.

THE SIDES' LOSSES

Lieutenant General Alfons Hitter, the commander of the 206th Infantry Division and commandant of the Vitebsk fortress, was captured around Vitebsk on 28 June 1944. He took part in the parade of the captured Germans around Moscow on 17 July 1944. On 3 December 1947 he was sentenced to 25 years of corrective-labour camps by a military tribunal of the Baltic Military District, sitting in the Vitebsk city theatre, for war crimes. On 8 October 1955, as a non-amnestied military criminal, he was handed over to the FRG authorizes and freed. Alfons Hitter died on 11 March 1968, at the age of 75, in Thomasberg, Lower Austria (Austria).

General of Infantry Friedrich Gollwitzer, the commander of the LIII Army Corps, was taken prisoner on 26 June 1944, not far from Vitebsk, by a scout, Junior Lieutenant Nikolai Yakimov, from the 464th Artillery Regiment/164th Rifle Division/39th Army. Gollwitzer took part in the parade of captured Germans around Moscow on 17 July 1944 and signed the appeal 'To the People and the Wehrmacht'. On 31 December 1947 he was sentenced to 25 years of corrective-labor camps by a military tribunal of the Belorussian Military District, sitting in the Vitebsk dramatic theatre, for war crimes. He was held in Lezhnev camp no. 48 for captured generals (in the Ivanovo Oblast'). On 6 October 1955, as a non-amnestied war criminal, he was handed over to the FRG authorities and freed. In 1964 the Amberg district attorney began an investigation into Gollwitzer on the matter of his assumed complicity in war crimes during the invasion of Poland in 1939. However, the investigation was halted due to a lack of evidence. Friedrich Gollwitzer died on 25 March 1977 in Amberg (Bavaria) at the age of 87.

Major General Adolph Gamann, the commandant of Bobruisk, surrendered in the Bobruisk area on 29 June 1944. On 17 July he took part in the parade of captured Germans around Moscow. On 30 December 1945 Gamann was sentenced to death by a military tribunal of the Bryansk garrison for the deaths of 96,000 Soviet prisoners and 130,000 civilians, as well as for impressing 218,000 Soviet citizens for work in Germany as commandant of Orel, Bryansk and Bobruisk. Gamann was also accused of murdering Soviet citizens, such as tens of thousands of Jews in Bobruisk in 1941, which took place when he was not the commandant of the city. Gamann was the commandant of Orel in during June 1942–July 1943, commandant of Bryansk in August 1943, and commandant of Bobruisk during September 1943–June 1944. On 30 December 1945 Adolph Gamann was hanged on Theatre Square in Bryansk. He was 60 years old.

Lieutenant General Hans-Walter Heyne, the commander of the 6th Infantry Division, was captured on 30 June 1944, in the Bobruisk area. In 1950 he was convicted of war crimes and sentenced to 25 years of corrective-labour camps. On 6 October 1955, as a non-amnestied war criminal, he was handed over to the FRG authorities and freed. Hans-Walter Heyne died on 29 August 1967 at the age of 73.

Major General Alexander Conrady, the commander of the 36th Infantry Division, was taken prisoner on 1 July 1944 in the Bobruisk area. On 8 December 1944 he signed the appeal of the National Committee for a Free Germany, 'To the People and the Wehrmacht'. On 4 November 1947 he was sentenced by a military tribunal of the Belorussian Military District, sitting in the Garrison Officers' House in Bobruisk, to 25 years for war crimes in corrective-labour camps. On 6 October 1955, as a non-amnestied war criminal, he was turned over to the FRG authorities and freed. Alexander Conrady died on 21 December 1983 at the age of 80.

OPERATION BAGRATION: AN INCOMPLETE TRUTH

Lieutenant General Baron Kurt-Jugen Henning von Lützow, the commander of the XXXV Army Corps, was captured on 3 July 1944 in the Bobruisk area in a woods east of the Svisloch' River. He was took part in the parade of German prisoners around Moscow on 17 July 1944 and on 8 December 1944 signed the appeal 'To the People and the Wehrmacht'. On 20 June 1950 he was sentenced by a military tribunal of the Moscow Military District MVD to 25 years of corrective-labour camps for war crimes. On 16 January 1956, as a non-amnestied war criminal, he was turned over to the FRG authorities and freed. Baron Kurt-Jugen Henning von Lützow died in Hannover on 20 July 1961 at the age of 68.

Major General Klaus Müller-Bulow, the commander of the 246th Infantry Division, was taken prisoner south-east of Polotsk, Vitebsk Oblast', on 27 June 1944. On 8 December 1944 he signed the appeal by the National Committee for a Free Germany, 'To the People and the Wehrmacht'. On 3 December 1947 he was sentenced for war crimes to 25 years in corrective-labour camps by the military tribunal of the Baltic Military District, sitting the Vitebsk city theatre. On 5 February 1954 Klaus Müller-Bulow died of heart failure and neurosclerosis in the USSR MVD's Sverdlovsk Camp No. 476 for prisoners of war, at the age of 61.

Major General Aurel Johann Schmidt von Nagyatad, the chief of the Ninth Army's 10th Main Engineer Command, was captured on 9 July 1944 in the village of Kabaki, Berezovka District, Brest Oblast'. On 17 July 1944 he took part in the parade of German prisoners around Moscow and on 8 December 1944 signed the appeal by the National Committee for a Free Germany, 'To the People and the Wehrmacht'. On 11 July 1948 he was freed and repatriated to Austria. He died on 23 May 1965 at the age of 73.

Lieutenant General Edmund Hoffmeister, the commander of the XLI Panzer Corps, was captured on 1 July 1944 in the Bobruisk area. On 17 July 1944 he took part in the parade of German prisoners around Moscow and on 8 December 1944 signed the appeal 'To the People and the Wehrmacht'. At the end of July 1944, shortly after the attempt on Hitler's life, he made a radio broadcast from Moscow in the name of the National Committee for a Free Germany, criticizing the Nazi regime. On 24 December 1944 the military tribunal of the MVD troops of the Gomel' Oblast' sentenced Hoffmeister to 25 years of corrective-labour camps for war crimes. On 20 February 1955 Edmund Hoffmeister died of heart failure in Camp No. 476, in Asbet, Sverdlovsk Oblast'. He was 57 years old.

Major General Gustav Gihr, the commander of the 707th Infantry Division, was captured on 27 June 1944 in the Bobruisk area. He took part in the parade of captured Germans around Moscow on 17 July 1944. On 8 December 1944 he signed 'To the People and the Wehrmacht'. In 1950 Gihr was sentenced to 25 years of corrective-labour camps for war crimes. On 11 October 1955, as a non-amnestied war criminal, he was handed over to the FRG authorities and freed. Gustav Gihr died on 31 October 1959 in Freiburg at the age of 65.

Lieutenant General Hans von Traut, the commander of the 78th Assault Division, was captured on 6 July 1944 in the area of the village of Smelovichi, Minsk Oblast'. In the 144th Artillery Brigade's combat journal there remains the following entry on the capture of Traut:

> 6 July. At 0600 in the woods 1.5km west of Karpilovka (the Mogilev–Minsk road), 30 soldiers and six officers, headed by Lieutenant General Traut, crossed the Mogilev–Minsk road, as a result of which the movement of our troops was halted. A group of sergeants and enlisted

men from the 3rd Battalion, consisting of eight men, led by First Sergeant F.P. Lekontsev, which was moving along this road, got into a fight with the Germans. As a result of a ten-minute battle, two officers and five soldiers were killed and the rest scattered. Lieutenant General Traut was captured and turned over to the headquarters of the 69th Rifle Corps.

On 17 July 1944 he was one of the 19 Wehrmacht generals who took part in the parade of captured Germans around Moscow and signed the appeal of the National Committee for a Free Germany, 'To the People and the Wehrmacht'. On 4 November 1947 he was sentenced to 25 years in corrective-labor camps by the military tribunal of the Belorussian Military District, sitting in the garrison officers' home in Bobruisk, for war crimes. On 6 October 1955, as a non-amnestied war criminal, he was turned over to the FRG authorities and freed. Hans von Traut died on 9 December 1974 in Darmstadt (Hesse) at the age of 79.

Major General Friedrich-Carl von Steinkeller, the commander of the *Feldherrnhalle* Panzergrenadier Division, was captured east of the village of Krupitsa, Minsk Oblast', on 7 July 1944. On 17 July 1944 he took part in the parade of captured Germans around Moscow. Steinkeller was one of the 50 German generals in captivity, who on 8 December 1944 signed the appeal of the National Committee for a Free Germany, 'To the People and the Wehrmacht'. On 19 November 1948 the military tribunal of the MVD troops of the Kiev District sentenced him to 25 years of corrective-labour camps for war crimes. On 9 October 1955, as a non-amnestied war criminal, he was turned over to the FRG authorities and freed. Friedrich-Carl von Steinkeller died on 19 October 1981 in Hanover (Lower Saxony) at the age of 85 years.

General of Infantry Paul-Gustav Volckers, the commander of the XXVII Army Corps, was captured on 9 July 1944, together with the corps headquarters, by soldiers from the 385th Rifle Division in the Mogilev area, west of Smilovichi, Cherven District, Minsk Oblast'. On 17 July 1944 he was paraded through the streets of Moscow at the head of a column of several thousand captured Germans and on 8 December 1944 signed the appeal 'To the People and the Wehrmacht'. On 23 January 1945 he died of bleeding on the brain in the Lezhnev prisoner of war camp No. 48 (NKVD USSR) at the age of 54 years.

Lieutenant General Vincenz Müller, the commander of the II Army Corps and temporary commander of the Fourth Army, surrendered on 8 July 1944 near Samokhvalovichi, Minsk District, Minsk Oblast', and issued orders for his corps to cease resistance. On 17 July 1944 he took part in the paarde of captured Germans around Moscow. On 3 August 1944 Müller became a member of the National Committee for a Free Germany and the Union of German Officers. He often broadcast commentaries through the 'Free Germany' radio station and simultaneously wrote articles in the *Freies Deutschland* newspaper. At the end of 1944 he, together with General Rudolf Bamler, attended special anti-fascist courses. On 8 December 1944 Müller signed the appeal by the National Committee for a Free Germany, and 'The Appeal by the 50 Generals'. He was held in special prison No. 20/V, at Planernaya Station, Moscow Oblast'. On 16 September 1948 he was transferred to repatriation camp No. 69, in Frankfurt-on-Oder, and released. While in the Soviet occupation zone he joined the German National Democratic Party. In September 1952 Müller became the chief of staff of the GDR People's Police and on 1 October 1952 was promoted to lieutenant general. From

OPERATION BAGRATION: AN INCOMPLETE TRUTH

1 March 1956 he was chief of the main staff and deputy minister of defence of the GDR. On 1 March 1958 he was retired in connection with a growing mental disorder. On 12 May 1961 Vincenz Müller committed suicide at the age of 66, jumping from the balcony of his building in East Berlin. Müller's memoirs, *I Found the True Fatherland*, were published posthumously in 1963.

Major General Gunther Klammt, the commander of the 260th Infantry Division, was captured on 9 July 1944 in the village of Uzlyany, Pukhovichi District, Minsk Oblast'. He was a member of the National Committee for a Free Germany and the Union of German Officers. Klammt was one of 50 German generals who, while in Soviet captivity, on 8 December 1944 signed the appeal by the National Committee for a Free Germany, 'To the People and the Wehrmacht'. On 20 December 1947 Klammt was sentenced to 25 years in corrective-labor camps for war crimes by the military tribunal of the Belorussian Military District, sitting in the Railway Workers' Club in Gomel'. On 6 October, as a non-amnestied war criminal, he was turned over to the FRG authorities and released. Gunther Klammt died on 16 May 1971, in Lubeck, Schleswig-Holstein, at the age of 73.

Lieutenant General Wilhelm Francis Ochsner, the commander of the 31st Infantry Division, was captured on 12 July 1944 in the Minsk area. He was held under guard in prison No. 1 in Minsk. On 4 November 1947 he was sentenced to 25 years for war crimes in corrective-labour camps by the military tribunal of the Belorussian Military District, sitting in the Garrison Officers' House in Bobruisk. On 10 October 1955, as a non-amnestied war criminal, he was turned over to the FRG authorities and released. Ochsner died on 5 December 1990, at the age of 91, in Marquartstein (Bavaria).

Lieutenant General Eberhard von Kurowski, the commander of the 110th Infantry Division, was captured on 21 July 1944 in the Grodno area. Kurowski,signed the appeal by the National Committee for a Free Germany, 'To the People and Wehrmacht'. On 20 December 1947 he was sentenced for war crimes by a military tribunal of MVD troops of the Belorussian Military District to 25 years in prison. On 6 October 1955, as a non-amnestied war criminal, he was turned over to the FRG authorities and freed. Von Kurowski died on 11 September 1957 in Stanzach (the Tyrol, Austria), at the age of 62.

Major General Joachim Engel, the commander of the 45th Infantry Division, was captured on 9 July 1944 by Soviet partisans in the Trostenets (Sloboda) area, near Minsk. On 17 July 1944 he became one of 19 Wehrmacht generals who took part in the paarde of captured Germans around Moscow. On 3 June 1948 Joachim Engel committed suicide in Gomel' prison No. 1, MVD, USSR, at the age of 51.

Major General Adolf Trowitz, the commander of the 57th Infantry Division, was captured on 7 July in the Minsk area. He joined the National Committee for a Free Germany and signed the appeal 'To the People and the Wehrmacht'. On 3 October 1949 Trowitz was sentenced by the military tribunal of MVD troops of the Kiev Oblast' to 25 years of corrective-labour camps for war crimes. On 8 October 1955, as a non-amnestied war criminal, he was turned over to the FRG authorities and freed. Adolf Trowitz died on 3 January 1978 in Hamburg.[38]

Lieutenant General Friedrich von Franek, the commander of the 73rd Infantry Division, was taken prisoner on 29 July 1944 in the area of the village of Wolka Mleka-Rudka, south-east of Warsaw, in a motor vehicle along with some of his staff, by a group of scouts from the 164th Tank Brigade/16th Tank Corps/2nd Tank Army, commanded by Senior Sergeant Mikhail Ivanovich Suchkov, who was awarded the Order of the Red

Banner for this feat. Franek was released from captivity on 22 July 1948 and repatriated to Austria. Friedrich von Franek died on 8 April 1976 in Vienna at the age of 83. He was the last German general captured during the course of Operation 'Bagration'.

Not a single Soviet general was captured during Operation 'Bagration'. However, there were those who died from wounds. In all, 13 Red Army major generals perished. The reasons for the deaths are from being blown up by mines and an artillery bombardment and, in at least one case, an air attack, while another died when his tank was hit by a shell. Thus the irreparable losses among the Soviet generals were 2.9 times fewer than among the German generals. This advantage was achieved exclusively at the expense of the captured generals, while the losses for generals who perished were different.

The commander of the First Belorussian Front's 9th Tank Corps, Major General of Tank Troops Boris Sergeevich Bakharov, died on 16 July 1944 near the village of Shakuny, Pruzany District, Brest Oblast', when his tank was destroyed by a direct hit by an anti-tank weapon.[39]

The commander of the M.V. Frunze 332nd Ivanovo Rifle Division/43rd Army/First Baltic Front, Major General Tikhon Fedorovich Yegoshin, was seriously wounded on 31 July 1944 during an enemy artillery bombardment along the road to his observation post on the bridgehead near the Dubna River, in the Daugavpils (Latvia) area and died the following day from his wounds.[40] The commander of the 35th Rifle Corps/3rd Army/First Belorussian Front, Major General Viktor Grigor'evich Zholudev, on 21 July 1944, while leading a group of officers, left for the front line in the Volkovysk area and perished in the fighting. On 11 November 1944 he was posthumously awarded the title of Hero of the Soviet Union.[41]

This is how the commander of the 3rd Army, Colonel General Aleksandr Vasil'evich Gorbatov, described Zholudev's death:

> When I arrived at corps headquarters they reported to me that General Zholudev had left for the 323rd Division. Upon checking the route, I set out after him, first to the division's command post, and then to the observation post, which was a kilometre from there. There they were making hasty arrangements to move, and not without reason: visibility from this observation post was very restricted. The corps commander and division commander were standing by their vehicles, ready for departure. I did not bother detaining them, but only asked if they knew the road to the newly-selected observation post and if there were communications there. They answered in the affirmative. The corps commander, upon leaving his vehicle, rode on ahead with the division commander, and I after them. There were no clearly defined roads, and the terrain was cut; at first we rode along a road in the field, and then by a forest road to the west. Then the vehicle ahead of us turned and then moved somewhat to the south-west along a slightly better road and turned to the north. It became clear to me that the division commander did not know the road to the new command post. At a stop I heard how the corps commander reproached him for this. I followed behind them, however, not getting involved in their argument, fearing to embarrass them and thus getting them completely confused.

OPERATION BAGRATION: AN INCOMPLETE TRUTH

When we had come out on a good field road – there was a field to our right and a woods to our left; three individual houses stood by the road; and a kilometre and a half in front of them was a small and gently sloping height, for which we were headed. It seemed suspicious to me that along the slope of the height facing us, no people, transport or firing positions could be discerned. I ordered my driver to catch up to the lead vehicle and to quietly signal for the people sitting in it to look back. When we approached more closely I said in a loud voice, so that they could hear me:

'Don't stop and go on ahead, only quietly. Listen to me carefully. You don't know where you're going. I'm going to count to three. When I say "three", everybody jump out of the vehicle and run behind the house.'

I told my driver:

'As soon as we jump out, turn around quickly and go back, behind the hillock.'

Near the third (last house), Zholudev, Maslov, myself, and my adjutants jumped out of the vehicles on my command and hid behind the house. At that moment they opened fire on us from three machine guns and ten rifles. The division commander's vehicle, which had been left on the road, was riddled with bullets. My vehicle was leaving at high speed, covered by clouds of dust, just like a smokescreen. Bullets were flying along the road, clattered against the smashed vehicle and got stuck in the house's walls.

The enemy was within 200m of us in a well-camouflaged trench. It was clear that the three machine guns were no longer being aimed at our vehicles in case they halted, but they would undoubtedly shoot us if we attempted to turn back, and if we had travelled forward for another half-minute, then we would have been captured by the enemy.

All seven of us stood behind the house. The shooting did not let up. The house was empty.

'Where did you take us?' I asked the deadly pale General Maslov.

He did not reply, only the pallor on his face changed to the colour of shame.

Zholudev answered for him.

'I said we were going the wrong way.'

Everything was clear. Our divisions were attacking along separate axes, not having a continuous front; we had gotten into the space between divisions.

We could not see our troops and the enemy could have made a sortie from his trench in order to capture us, so we could not delay and remain behind this house. But what could we do? How do we get out from behind this cover without getting immediately killed?

We decided to crawl along the rye field to the house that was 200m from us, and then to the next on, which was about a kilometre and a half behind it. We had to crawl through the short rye, keeping close to the ground.

It was hot. Soaked with sweat and spurred on by fear, we crawled, forgetting our exhaustion, and all the time we hear shots, although no longer aimed ones. We were about 25m from the second house, but we were separated from it by a stretch of ploughed field, along which it was useless to crawl. We took a break and prepared to sprint and simultaneously ended up behind the house; the enemy had noticed us too late. In this way we crossed behind the next house. We were already a half-kilometre from the enemy and the fear of being captured subsided, but the danger of being killed had not passed. We had to overcome another 500m in order to reach the woods or to hide behind the hillock. This was also not an easy task: we had to climb up the hill in view of the enemy. We decided to go, but quickly, while zigzagging, with a large interval between us. We left after a short breathing spell. They shot at us with machine guns and then from guns and mortars; the Germans probably understood what a great catch was getting away; perhaps they had noticed the red piping on three of us.

Generals Zholudev and Maslov were drawn to the corner of the woods closest to us, although I tried to stop them, telling them that the edge of the woods had probably been registered by the enemy. My adjutant and I continued to move along the field, in order to hide behind the crest of the height. As soon as our comrades began to approach the woods, an artillery salvo could be heard, and then we saw ten to twelve explosions near the edge of the woods. The strapping General Zholudev was thrown in the air by an explosion. I understood that an irreparable accident had occurred.

When we were out of the enemy's sight and the firing ceased, I sent my adjutant, I.A. Galushko, to the edge of the forest to find out what had happened. My vehicle had been shot up in several places, but the driver was unharmed. I followed my adjutant with my eyes. Seeing that he had halted near the edge of the woods and was waving his hands, I got into my vehicle and rode out to him. My foreboding did not let me down – we found the dead Zholudev and the concussed Maslov. Their adjutants and driver helped us to put Zholudev's body in the vehicle, and they set Maslov down, and we drove off slowly to the headquarters of the 323rd Rifle Division.

We buried Zholudev, and the deputy commander of the 348th Rifle Division, Colonel Praslov, the commander of the 40th Rifle Corps' artillery, Colonel Medvedev, and the assistant to the chief of the corps' intelligence section, Major Sheimovich, who were blown up by mines, in Volkovysk.[42]

On 13 July 1944 the deputy commander of the 13th Guards Rifle Corps/ 2nd Guards Army/First Baltic Front, Major General Ignatii Vikent'evich Klyaro, perished after stepping on an anti-tank mine in the town of Postavy, Vitebsk Oblast'.[43]

The commander of the 200th Rifle Division/4th Shock Army/First Baltic Front, Major General Ignatii Aleksandrovich Krasnov, died in battle on 6 July 1944 in the area of the village of Zvanitsa, Polotsk District, Vitebsk Oblast'.[44]

The deputy signals chief for the First Baltic Front, Major General of Signals Troops Yakov Osipovich Lagodyuk, perished on 27 July 1944 during an artillery bombardment on the outskirts of Daugavpils.[45]

OPERATION BAGRATION: AN INCOMPLETE TRUTH

The commander of the 369th Rifle Division/62nd Rifle Corps/49th Army/Second Belorussian Front, Major General Ivan Sidorovich Lazarenko, perished on 26 June 1944 4km from the village of Kholmy, in the Chausy area, as the result of a direct hit by a shell on his vehicle. On 21 July 1944 he was posthumously awarded the title of Hero of the Soviet Union.[46]

The commander of the 134th Rifle Division/61st Rifle Corps/69th Army/First Belorussian Front, Major General Vladimir Nikolaevich Martsinkevich, was mortally wounded on 30 July 1944 in the fighting for the Pulawy bridgehead and on that same day passed away. On 6 April 1945 he was posthumously awarded the title of Hero of the Soviet Union.[47]

The commander of the 80th Rifle Corps/65th Army/First Belorussian Front, Major General Ivan Leont'evich Ragulya, was mortally wounded during a Luftwaffe raid in the Baranovichi area and on 22 July died in hospital in Baranovichi.[48]

The commander of the 71st Guards Rifle Division/23rd Guards Rifle Corps/6thGuards Army/First Baltic Front, Guards Major General Ivan Prokof'evich Sivakov, was killed on 27 July 1944 during an artillery bombardment of his observation post near the Antalepte farmstead, in the Zarasai District of Lithuania. On 22 July, five days before his death, he was awarded the title of Hero of the Soviet Union.[49]

The commander of the 120th Red Banner Guards Rifle Division/41st Rifle Corps/3rd Army/First Belorussian Front, Guards Major General Yan Yanovich Fogel', was mortally wounded west of the town of Volkovysk, near the town of Novogrudok, on 8 July 1944 and died on 9 July in a hospital in the village of Dyatlovo, Baranovich Oblast'. On 10 April 1945 he was posthumously awarded the title of Hero of the Soviet Union.[50]

The commander of the 13th Guards Rifle Corps/2nd Guards Army/First Baltic Front, Guards Major General Kantemir Aleksandrovich Tsalikov, died on 21 July 1944, when his car blew up on an anti-tank mine near the village of Dudi, to the north of Kurkliai, in the Utena District of Lithuania.

The commander of the 343rd Rifle Division/49th Army/Second Belorussian Front, Anton Ivanovich Yakimovich, died on 25 August 1944, when his car blew up on an anti-tank mine in the area of the village of Pesy-Lipno (Zambrow County, Podlaskie Voevodship).[51]

***

Operation 'Bagration', as did Operation 'Overlord', – the Allied landing in Normandy which was developing parallel to it – showed that the inevitable defeat of Germany was not far off. The Wehrmacht no longer had the capability of concentrating a sufficient number of troops on either front in order to hold the enemy. The attempt to carry out a counteroffensive along one of two main fronts, the Western or the Eastern, would inevitably lead to a serious defeat on the other front. Following the completion of 'Bagration', the war in Europe continued for only a little more than eight months. For the Red Army, the victory in the battle in Belorussia during the summer of 1944 was particularly valuable, in that in this battle the German side, against commonly-accepted opinion, did not commit any major mistakes. The Soviet victory was the consequence of the forces and equipment that had come to be on the Eastern Front, as well as the skill of the Soviet generals, and was not due to any fatal mistakes by the enemy.

Notes

Chapter 1: Why Was the Western Front Command Removed in April 1944?

1. 'Beseda c byvshim nachal'nikom shtaba Zapadnogo and Tret'ego Belorusskogo frontov general-polkovnikom Pokrovskim Aleksandrom Petrovichem'. As recorded by Konstantin Simonov. Foreword and publication by L. Lazarev. *Oktyabr'*, 1990, no. 5, p. 121.
2. A.V. Isaev, *Operatsiya 'Bagration': 'Stalinskii Blitskrig' v Belorussii* (Moscow: Yauza: Eksmo, 2014), pp. 432–41.
3. *Russkii Arkhiv. Velikaya Otechestvennaya Voina*, vol. 13 (2-2). (Moscow: TERRA, 1997), Document no. 264, pp. 323–6.
4. N.M. Khlebnikov, *Pod Grokhot Soten Baterei* (Moscow: Voennoe Izdatel'stvo, 1974), p. 273.
5. I.Kh. Bagramyan, *Tak shli my k Pobede* (Moscow: Voennoe izdatel'stvo, 1977), p. 305.
6. P.A. Zhilin (ed.), *Boevoi Sostav Sovetskoi Armii. Chast' 4 (Yanvar'-Dekabr' 1944 g.)* (Moscow: Voennoe Izdatel'stvo, 1988), p. 189.
7. https:walter-weiss.livejournal.com/2633.html.
8. Simonov, 'Beseda', p. 129.
9. V.V. Abaturov, A.M. Litvin, and N.F. Azyasskii, *Osvobozhdenie Belarusi. 1943-1944 gg* (Minsk: Belorusskaya Nauka, 2014), p. 56.
10. Ibid., p. 57.
11. Ibid., p. 58.
12. Human Losses in World War II. Heeresarzt 10-Day Casualty Reports per Army/Army Group, 1943 [BA/MA RW 6/556, 6/558] (https://web.archive.org/web/20121029022426/http://ww2stats.com/cas_ger_okh_dec43.html)
13. Abaturov, *et al*, *Osvobozhdenie*, p. 58.
14. RGASPI, fond 83, opis' 1, delo 21, ll. 1-125.
15. Yu.V. Rubtsov, *Mekhlis. Ten' vozhdya* (Moscow: Veche, 2011), pp. 296–7.
16. A.M. Samsonov (ed.), *Osvobozhdenie Belorussii, 1944*, 2nd expanded ed. (Moscow: Nauka, 1974), p. 17.
17. L.N. Rabichev, *Voina vsyo Spishet. Vospominaniya ofitsera-svyazista 31-i armii. 1941-1945* (Moscow: Tsentropoligraf, 2010), pp. 135–6.

Chapter 2: The Poles'ye Tragedy

1. RGASPI, fond 625, opis' 1, delo 7, ll. 306-10.

Chapter 3: The Belorussian Partisan Movement through the Eyes of a Cadre Chekist

1. RGASPI, fond 625, opis' 1, delo 22, ll. 1184, 1186-88.

Chapter 4: The Prelude to 'Bagration'

1. K.H., Frieser (ed.), *Germany and the Second World War*. Edited for the Militargeschichtliches Forschungsamt (Research Institute for Military History), Potsdam, Germany. Translated from the German by Barry Smerin, Barbara Wilson. Edited by Barry Smerin. Vol. VIII (Oxford: Clarendon Press, 2017), p. 493; N. Belov, *Ya byl Ad'yutantom Gitlera* (Smolensk: Rusich, 2003), p. 432.
2. V.I. Dashichev, *Strategiya Gitlera – Put' k Katastrofe, 1933-1945: Istoricheskie Ocherk, Dokumenty i Materialy*. In four volumes (Moscow: Nauka, 2005), vol. IV, pp. 142–3.
3. Frieser, *Germany*, vol. VIII, p. 494.
4. I. Khyurter (ed.), *Zametki o Voine na Unichtozhenie. Vostochnyi Front, 1941-1942 gg. v Zapisyakh Generala Kheinritsi*. Translated from the German, with an introduction to the Russian edition by O.I. Beyda and I.R. Petrov (St. Petersburg: Izdatel'stvo Yevropeiskogo Universiteta v Sankt-Peterburge, 2018), p. 311.
5. H. Ritgen, *The 6th Panzer Division, 1937-45* (Oxford: Osprey Publishing, Ltd., 1982), p. 252.
6. Frieser, *Germany*, vol. VIII, p. 494.
7. Ibid., pp. 493–4.
8. Ibid., p. 495.
9. Ibid., p. 496.
10. S.J. Zaloga, *Bagration, 1944. The Destruction of Army Group Center* (London; Auckland; Melbourne; Singapore; Toronto: Osprey, 1997), p. 13.
11. J. Erickson, *The Road to Berlin: Stalin's War with Germany* (London: Orion, 2015 [e-book]), pp. 252, 263.
12. Ibid., p. 264.
13. V.O. Daines, *Vperyod, na Zapad! Operatsiya* 'Bagration' (Moscow: Veche, 2019), pp. 26–8.
14. Ibid., pp. 264–5.
15. A.I. Yeremenko, *Dnevniki. Zapiski. Vospominaniya. 1939-1946* (Moscow: Rossiiskaya Politicheskaya Entsiklopediya, 2013), p. 300.
16. RGASPI, fond 83, opis' 1,delo 29, ll. 99-107.
17. A.N. Mertsalov and L.A. Mertsalova, *Inoi Zhukov. Neyubileinye Stranitsy Biografii Stalinskogo Marshala* (Moscow: Terra, 1996), p. 68
18. Frieser, *Germany*, vol. VIII, pp. 497–8.

19. Ibid., p. 499.
20. Ibid., pp. 499–500.
21. P. Adair, *Hitler's Greatest Defeat. The Collapse of Army Group Center, June 1944* (London: Arms and Armour Press, 1996), p. 62.
22. Ibid., p. 64.
23. R. Vrublevskii, *Bobruiskii 'Kotel' 1944 goda* (Moscow: Yauza-Katalog, 2016), pp. 13–15.
24. Frieser, *Germany*, vol. VIII, pp. 503–06.
25. Ibid., p. 507.
26. R. Irinarkhov, *Triumf operatsii 'Bagration'. Glavnyi Stalinskii Udar* (Moscow: Yauza, 2014 [e-book]), p. 39.
27. Frieser, *Germany*, vol. VIII, p. 507.
28. Daines, *Vperyod*, p. 46.
29. Frieser, *Germany*, vol. VIII, pp. 507–08.
30. Ibid., p. 508.
31. Ibid., pp. 508–09.
32. Zaloga, *Bagration*, p. 40.
33. Frieser, *Germany*, vol. VIII, pp. 509–10.
34. Ibid., p. 512.
35. C.W. Wilbeck, *Sledgehammers: Strengths and Flaws of Tiger Tank Battalions in World War II* (Bedford, PA: The Aberjona Press, 2004), pp. 102–03.
36. K.M. Simonov, *Glazami Cheloveka Moego Pokoleniya. Razmyshleniya o I.V. Staline* (Moscow: Kniga, 1990), pp. 296–7.
37. Frieser, *Germany*, vol. VIII, pp. 514–15.
38. I.V. Timokhovich, 'Operatsiya "Bagration"', *Velikaya Otechestvennaya Voina. 1941-1945. Voenno-Istoricheskie Ocherki* ed. B.N. Petrov, Book 3, *Osvobozhdenie* (Moscow: Nauka, 1999), pp. 67–8.
39. G.F, Krivosheev (ed.), *Rossiya i SSSR v Voinakh XX Veka.kKniga Poter'* (Moscow: Veche, 2010), p. 322.
40. Frieser, *Germany*, vol. VIII, pp. 515–17.
41. Zhilin, *Boevoi Sostav*, ch. 4, pp. 160–1, 189–90.
42. *Russkii Arkhiv*, vol. 16 (5-4), p. 68.
43. Ibid., pp. 68–9
44. Ibid., p. 70.
45. Ibid., pp. 78–9.
46. Ibid., pp. 61–2.
47. Ibid., p. 80.
48. Ibid., p. 88.
49. Ibid., p. 82.
50. Ibid., p. 84.
51. Ibid., p. 85.
52. Ibid., p. 92.
53. Ibid., p. 85.
54. Daines, *Vperyod*, pp. 35–6.
55. *Russkii Arkhiv*, vol. 23 (12-4), pp. 205–06.
56. Ibid., vol. 16 (5-4), p. 92.
57. Ibid., vol. 13 (2-3), pp. 281–2.

58. Ibid., vol. 16 (5-4), pp. 93–5.
59. Ibid., p. 96.
60. K. Tippelskirch, *Istoriya Vtoroi Mirovoi Voiiny* (St. Petersburg: Poligon; Moscow: AST, 1999), pp. 596–7.

Chapter 5: The Rout

1. Frieser, *Germany*, vol. VIII, pp. 524–5.
2. Zaloga, *Bagration*, p. 26.
3. Ibid., p. 29.
4. Frieser, *Germany*, vol. VIII, pp. 526–8.
5. Ibid., p. 528, table V.II.6.
6. Ibid., p. 593.
7. Ibid., pp. 528–9, table V.II.7.
8. Zaloga, *Bagration*, p. 27.
9. Ibid., p. 36.
10. Frieser, *Germany*, vol. VIII, p. 535.
11. E. Klapdor, *Viking Panzers: The German 5th SS Tank Regiment in the East in World War II*. Translated from the German (Mechanicsburg, PA: Stackpole Books, 2011), p. 301.
12. Frieser, *Germany*, p. 527, table V.II.5.
13. Ibid., pp. 529–30.
14. Daines, *Vperyod*, p. 10; Zhilin, *Boevoi Sostav*, ch. 4, pp. 171–9.
15. Daines, *Vperyod*, p. 48.
16. Ibid., p. 49.
17. Timokhovich, 'Operatsiya', p. 58.
18. Zaloga, *Bagration*, p. 43.
19. Frieser, *Germany*, vol. VIII, p. 535.
20. Ibid., pp. 536–7.
21. Ibid., pp. 537–8.
22. Zaloga, *Bagration*, p. 53.
23. Frieser, *Germany*, vol. VIII, pp. 538–9.
24. *Russkii Arkhiv*, vol. 23 (12-4), pp. 264–7.
25. Bagramyan, *Tak shli*, pp. 333–4.
26. Daines, *Vperyod*, pp. 166–7.
27. Isaev, *Operatsiya*, p. 343.
28. Adair, *Hitler's Greatest Defeat*, p. 102.
29. Zaloga, *Bagration*, pp. 48–9.
30. Isaev, *Operatsiya*, p. 344.
31. V. Haupt, *Srazhenie Gruppy Armii 'Tsentr'* (Moscow: Yauza: Eksmo, 2006), pp. 346–7.
32. Frieser, *Germany*, vol. VIII, pp. 539–41.
33. Isaev, *Operatsiya*, pp. 350–1.
34. Ibid., pp. 328–34.
35. Ibid., p. 135.
36. Vrublevskii, *Bobruiskii*, pp. 19–78.
37. Adair, *Hitler's Greatest Defeat*, p. 117.

NOTES

38. Frieser, *Germany*, vol. VIII, p. 542.
39. Isaev, *Operatsiya*, pp. 386–8.
40. Tippelskirch, *Istoriya*, p. 599.
41. Frieser, Germany, vol. VIII, pp. 543–4.
42. S. Chernikov, *Proba Pera Komfronta Chernyakhovskogo*//Warspot, 2019, 27 Iyunya, https://warspot.ru/15004-proba-pera-komfronta-chernyahovskogo; Frieser, *Germany*, vol. VIII, pp. 547.
43. Wilbeck, *Sledgehammers*, p. 103.
44. S. Chernikov, *Proba Pera Komfronta Kommentarii*.
45. Frieser, *Germany*, vol. VIII, p. 557.
46. *Russkii Arkhiv*, vol. 16 (5-4), pp. 100–01.
47. Isaev, *Operatsiya*, p. 418.
48. Haupt, *Srazhenie*, pp. 332–3.
49. V. Myuller, *Ya Nashel Podlinnuyu Rodinu. Zapiski Nemetskogo Generala* (Moscow: Progress, 1974), p. 297.
50. Ibid., p. 298.
51. Tippelskirch, *Istoriya*, pp. 602–03.
52. Isaev, *Operatsiya*, p. 418.
53. Ibid., pp. 423–4.
54. Frieser, *Germany*, vol. VIII, p. 544.
55. Ibid., pp. 544–5.
56. Tippelskirch, *Istoriya*, pp. 602–03.
57. Adair, *Hitler's Greatest Defeat*, p. 118.
58. Vrublevskii, *Bobruiskii*, pp. 107, note 1.
59. Isaev, *Operatsiya*, pp. 404–05.
60. Ibid., pp. 405–06.
61. Ibid., pp. 408–09.
62. Ibid., p. 391.
63. Vrublevskii, *Bobruiskii*, pp. 283–5.
64. Ibid., pp. 290–2.
65. M. Sinitsyn, *Dnevnik Polkovnika 383-i Pekhotnoi Divizii Vermakhta Artura Yuttnera o Boyakh v Raione Bobruiska v Iyune-Avgusta 1944 g. Chast' 3*//belhistory.by.2021, 14 iyulya, https://zen.yandex.ru/media/belhistory_by/dnevnik-polkovnika-383-i-pehotnoi-divizii-vermahta-artura-iuttnera-o-boiah-v-raione-bobruiska-v-iiuneavguste-1944-g-chast-3-60eee4dc5f08a3516320b388
66. Vrublevskii, *Bobruiskii*, pp. 80–123.
67. Ibid., pp. 124, 133.
68. Ibid., p. 271.
69. Ibid., p. 276.
70. Ibid., p. 275.
71. Ibid., pp. 124–228.
72. Ibid., pp. 134–40.
73. Isaev, *Operatsiya*, p. 424.
74. Frieser, *Germany*, vol. VIII, p. 546.
75. Adair, *Hitler's Greatest Defeat*, pp. 141–5.
76. Ibid., pp. 122–4.
77. Frieser, *Germany*, vol. VIII, pp. 546; Adair, *Hitler's Greatest Defeat*, pp. 126–30.

78. Adair, *Hitler's Greatest Defeat*, p. 131.
79. Frieser, *Germany*, vol. VIII, pp. 547–8.
80. *Russkii Arkhiv*, vol. 16 (5-4), p. 101.
81. Frieser, *Germany*, vol. VIII, p. 549.
82. Daines, *Vperyod*, pp. 185–6.
83. Adair, *Hitler's Greatest Defeat*, pp. 153–5; 'Gen. Lt. Otto Drescher, how was he killed?//https://forum.axishistory.com/viewtopic.php?t=85168.
84. Adair, *Hitler's Greatest Defeat*, p. 155; Generalleutnant Paul Schurmann (1895-1978)//https:forum.axishistory.com/viewtopic.php?t=200108.
85. Timokhovich, 'Operatsiya', p. 68.
86. Frieser, *Germany*, vol. VIII, p. 551.
87. Tippelskirch, *Istoriya*, p. 603.
88. *Russkii Arkhiv*, vol. 16 (5-4), pp. 101–04.
89. Ibid., pp. 102, 104.
90. Ibid., pp. 104, 107.
91. Ibid., pp. 110–11.
92. Ibid., p. 107.
93. Ibid., p. 110.
94. Ibid., pp. 110–11.
95. Ibid., p. 111.
96. Ibid., p. 112.
97. Ibid., p. 113.
98. Klapdor, *Viking*, p. 301.
99. *Russkii Arkhiv*, vol. 16 (5-4), p. 113.
100. Frieser, *Germany*, vol. VIII, p. 554.
101. Ibid., p. 554; R. Hinze, *Der Zusammenbruch der Heeresgruppe Mitte im Osten 1944* (Stuttgart: Motorbuch Verlag, 1980), p. 261.
102. Adair, *Hitler's Greatest Defeat*, p. 154.
103. Frieser, *Germany*, vol. VIII, pp. 555–6.
104. Zhilin, *Boevoi Sostav*, ch. 4, pp. 189–94.
105. Frieser, *Germany*, vol. VIII, p. 556.
106. G.K. Zhukov, *Vospominaniya i Razmyshleniya*. In two vols. (Moscow: Olma-Press, 2002), vol. 2, p. 230.
107. Ibid., p. 239.
108. Frieser, *Germany*, vol. VIII, pp. 556–7.
109. Tippelskirch, *Istoriya*, p. 601; *Mirovaya Voina, 1939-1945* (Moscow: AST; St. Petersburg: Poligon, 2000), p. 426.
110. Frieser, *Germany*, vol. VIII, p. 557; Adair, *Hitler's Greatest Defeat*, p. 132.
111. Adair, *Hitler's Greatest Defeat*, pp. 164–5.
112. Ritgen, *The 6th Panzer Division*, p. 38. In August the 6th Panzer Division had to repel a new Soviet offensive along the East Prussian border. On 26 August the 6th Panzer Division was transferred to the Narew in the capacity of an army mobile reserve. Here it sought to repel Soviet attempts to invade East Prussia from the south.
113. Frieser, *Germany*, vol. VIII, p. 561. Frieser believes that 3,000 men of the Vilnius garrison's 4,000 men were saved. It is not excluded that about 2,000 men made up Tolsdorf's group.

NOTES

114. Frieser, *Germany*, vol. VIII, pp. 559–60.
115. Ibid., pp. 562–3.
116. Ritgen, *The 6th Panzer Division*, p. 37.

Chapter 6: The Voyage of the '*Wiking*'

1. Klapdor, *Viking*, p. 298.
2. Ibid., p. 299.
3. Frieser, *Germany*, vol. VIII, pp. 563–4.
4. *Russkii Arkhiv*, vol. 16 (5-4), pp. 47–8.
5. V. Pinaev and A. Tomzov, *Boevoi Put' Tankista: Viktor Romanov i ego IS-2*. Warspot, 2015, 13 sentyabrya, https://warspot.ru/3904-boevoy-put-tankista-viktor-romanov-i-ego-is-2
6. A. Ulanov, 'Zvezda', kotoroi ne bylo//Warspot, 2017, 30 iyunya, https://warspot.ru/9394-zvezda-kotoroy-ne-bylo.
7. V.I. Chuikov, *Konets Tret'ego Reikha* (Moscow: Sovetskaya Rossiya, 1973), pp. 22–3.
8. J. Trigg, *Hitler's Vikings. The History of the Scandinavian Waffen-SS: The Legions, the SS-Wiking and the SS-Nordland* (Stround, Gloucestershire, UK: The History Press, 2012), p. 245.
9. D. Oliver, *Viking Summer. 5 SS-Panzer Division in Poland, 1944* (Tatternhoe, Bedfordshire, UK: ADH Publishing, 2012), p. 4; Pinaev and Tomzov, *Boevoi Put' Tankista: Viktor Romanov I ego IS-2*. Warspot, 2015, 13 sentyabrya, https://warspot.ru/3904-boevoy-put-tankista-viktor-romanov-i-ego-is-2
10. Klapdor, *Viking*, p. 279.
11. Isaev, *Operatsiya*, pp. 413–14.
12. Klapdor, *Viking*, p. 279.
13. Ibid., pp. 278–9.
14. Ibid., pp. 300, 280.
15. Ibid., pp. 301–11.
16. Kochukov, A. 'KMG i ego Mechty'. *Krasnaya Zvezda*, 2003, 29 Noyabrya, http://old.redstar.ru/2003/11/29_11/5_01.html.
17. Klapdor, *Viking*, p. 297.
18. Frieser, *Germany*, vol. VIII, pp. 565–6.
19. R. Michulec, *4 Panzer Division on the Eastern Front (2): 1944* (Madrid: Concord Publications Company, 1999), pp. 3–4.
20. Frieser, *Germany*, vol. VIII, pp. 579–80.
21. P.I. Batov, *V Pokhodakh i Boyakh* (Moscow: Voennoe Izdatel'stvo, 1974), pp. 421–7.
22. P. Ponomarenko, 'Chitaem' staruyu fotografiyu: boevaya gruppa 'Mulenkamp' v Pol'she//Warspot, 2019, 16 fevralya, https://warspot.ru/14080-chitaem-stariyu-fotografiyu-boevaya-gruppa-myulenkamp-v-polshe
23. Ibid.
24. Daines, *Vperyod*, p. 277.
25. Klapdor, *Viking*, p. 323.
26. Ibid., pp. 324–55.

Chapter 7: The Voyage of the 'Pseudo *Wiking*'

1. P. Neumann, *The Black March. The Personal Story of an SS Man* (New York: Bantam, 1958). But this and other translations were not done from the German, but from the French edition: P Neumann, *SS!* (Paris: Editions France-Empire), 1956. The stereotype French edition appeared in 1958. Unsurprisingly, the translator from the German was not indicated, and there was no reason for the readers to suspect that Neumann kept his diary in French. The author of the diary nowhere indicates any kinship relations with the French or even his knowledge of the French language. Quite the opposite: the text of the diary is shot through with hatred for France and the French.
2. V. Akunov, *Chernyi Marsh i Legenda*//Mezhdunarodnaya voenno-istoricheskaya assotsiatsiya, 21 iyunya 2012, http://www.imha.ru/2012/06/21/chernyy-marsh-i-chernaya-legenda.html#.YSfSvM92Uk
3. In the USSR and in Russia he was often called 'P'er Deks, although in French this is pronounced 'P'er De'.
4. *Kontinent*, no. 9, 1976, p. 436.
5. *Russkii Arkhiv*, vol. 13 (2-1), p. 139. This order stated the following: 'Carry out one demonstration exercise in each unit with combat SOV (highly-poisonous substances) while overcoming a fortified zone' (p. 144), which also inevitably led to losses among the participants of the exercise. The defense commissar's order no. 30, of 21 January 1941, 'On the Troops' Combat and Political Training for 1941': demanded: 'Carry out inspection on overcoming sectors infected with combat highly-poisonous substances', and 'To work out in combined-arms exercises', among other things, 'an infantry attack with the employment of artillery chemical rounds and chemical mines' (p. 219).
6. *Zimnyaya Voina 1939-1940. Kn. 2. I.V. Stalin i Finskaya Kampaniya. (Stenogramma Soveshchaniya pri TsK VKP(b)* (Moscow: 'Nauka', 1999), p. 128.
7. S.M. Budennyi, *Proidennyi Put'*. Chapters from the fourth book. *Don* (1975), no. 3, pp. 26–8.
8. P. Noiman, *Chernyi Marsh. Vospominaniya Ofitsera SS. 1938-1945*. Translated from the English by L.A. Igorevskii (Moscow: Tsentrpoligraf, 2012), pp. 262–71.
9. C. Kalinov, *Les Marechaux Sovietiques Vous Parlent* (Paris: Stock, Delamain et Boutelleau, 1950).
10. V.M. Molotov's (Skryabin's) presumed nephew was Vasilii Vasil'evich Kokorin (1923–52) (Skryabin on his mother's side), was captured in April 1942 and was used by the Germans for propaganda purposes. Following the war he was repatriated to the USSR, imprisoned under guard and shot on 26 March 1952 for betraying the Motherland. (I.A. Reshin and A. Pochtarev, 'Plemyannik' Molotova pod sledstviem i sudom//*Nezavisimoe Voennoe Obozrenie*, 2000, 9 iyunya, https://nvo.ng.ru/history/2000-06-09/5_nephew.html). However, I was unable to locate such a work published in France. It's possible that K.D. Pomerantsev's memory betrayed him and he actually had in mind the memoirs of Stalin's 'nephew', which was the work of Besedovskii's pen and that of his collaborators.
11. K.D. Pomerantsev, *Skvoz' Smert'. Vospominaniya* (London: Overseas Publishing Interchange, Ltd., 1986), pp. 134, 138–9.

12. R. Wraga, *O Sovetskikh Marshalakh, Arkticheskom Metode i Vtorosteppykh Detalyakh. Vozrozhdenie (La Renaissance)* 1950, no. 10, pp. 189–93.
13. *J'ai Choisi La Potence; Les Confidences Du General Vlassov, Felon Sovietique* (Paris, 1947).
14. I.N. Krylov, *Ma Carrier a L'Etat-Major Sovietique.* Traduction de Stephan Makhloff et Serge Maffert (Paris, 1949).
15. B. Svanidze, *Mon Oncle Joseph* (Paris, 1952); B. Svanidze, *Georgiy Malenkov* (London, 1954).
16. M. Litvinov, *Notes for a Journal.* Introduction by E.H. Carr and a prefatory note by Walter Bedell Smith (New York, 1955).
17. B.V. Sokolov, *Operatsiya 'Trest' i Pol'skaya Razvedka* (Moscow: Veche, 2018), pp. 350–82.
18. P.W. Blackstock, 'Books for Idiots: False Soviet Memoirs', *Russian Review*, 1966, vol. 25, no. 3 (July 1966), pp. 290, 185–286.

Chapter 8: The Salvation of Army Group Centre

1. *Russkii Arkhiv*, vol. 16 (5-4), p. 117.
2. Ibid.
3. Ibid., p. 118.
4. Ibid., pp. 118–19.
5. Ibid., p. 120.
6. Ibid., pp. 120–1.
7. D. Glantz (ed.), *Hitler and his Generals: Military Conferences, 1942-1945.* English edition introduction by Gerhard L. Weinberg; original edition introduction and notes by Helmut Heiber; translated by Roland Winter and Krista Smith (New York: Enigma Books), 2002, pp. 444–6, 457.
8. Tippelskirch, *Istoriya*, p. 555.
9. *Russkii Arkhiv*, vol. 16 (5-4), pp. 122–3.
10. Ibid., p. 123.
11. Daines, *Vperyod*, p. 317.
12. Frieser, *Germany*, vol. VIII, pp. 567–8.
13. Ibid., p. 568.
14. Ibid., p. 584.
15. I.V. Nebol'sin, *Lyubimaya Stalinym. 2-ya Gvardeiskaya Tankovaya Armiya v Boyu* (Moscow: Eksmo; Yauza, 2016), pp. 502–03, 508–09.
16. D. Eisenhower, *Crusade in Europe* (New York: Da Capo Press, 1977), pp. 465–8.
17. B.M. Mikhailov, *Na Dne Blokady i Voiny* (St. Petersburg: Izdatel'stvo VSEGEI, 2000), pp. 187–9. B.M. Mikhailov also notes: 'In the offensive battles of the war's last year our infantry suffered enormous losses. There was no one to replace the infantry units that had been bled white . . . So, all of the "healthy men" who were captured by us were not shot, but put in uniform and now, as Soviet soldiers under the eye of Russian officers and holding detachments, were driven forward, as if forcing them to wipe off the shame of treason with blood'. Ibid., pp. 188–9.

18. http://podvignaroda.ru/?#id=1100469489&tab=navDetailManCard; http://podvignaroda.ru/?#id-1514186495&tab-navDetailManUbil
19. http://www.moypolk.ru/soldier/pavlikov-georgiy-prokopevich; see also https://1418museum.ru/heroes/25580582/
20. A. Polishchuk and A. Ulanov, *2-ya Tankovaya Protiv Krestnikov 'Tolstogo German'*//Warspot.ru, 2018, 31 oktyabrya, https://warspot.ru/132750-2ya-tankovaya-protiv-krestnikov-tolstogo germana
21. Nebol'sin, *Lyubimaya*, p. 510.
22. Frieser, *Germany*, vol. VIII, p. 569.
23. *Russkii Arkhiv*, vol. 16 (5-4), p. 124.
24. G. Williamson, *The Hermann Göring Division* (Oxford: Osprey Publishing, 2003), pp. 12–13.
25. B. Quarrie, *Fallschirmpanzerdivision Hermann Göring* (Oxford: Osprey, 1978), p. 21.
26. Frieser, *Germany*, vol. VIII, p. 579.
27. Nebol'sin, *Lyubimaya*, pp. 515–16.
28. Ibid., pp. 522–3.
29. Polishchuk, Ulanov, *2-ya Tankovaya protiv krestnikov 'Tolstogo German'*// Warspot.ru, 2018, 31 oktyabrya, https://warspot.ru/132750-2-ya-tankovaya-protiv-krestnikov-tolstogo germana
30. Frieser, *Germany*, vol. VIII, pp. 579–80.
31. Nebol'sin, *Lyubimaya*, p. 520.
32. *Russkii Arkhiv*, vol. 14-3(2), pp. 434–5.
33. W.S. Churchill, *The Second World War*. Vol. VI *Triumph and Tragedy* (Boston: Houghton Mifflin Co., 1985), pp. 115–16.
34. *Russkii Arkhiv*, vol. 14 (3-1), pp. 232–3, document no. 24, p. 234, document 26.
35. Nebol'sin, *Lyubimiya*, pp. 534, 540–1, 545–6.
36. *Russkii Arkhiv*, vol. 14(3-1), pp. 233–4.
37. Human Losses in World War II. Heeresarzt 10-Day Casualty Reports per Army/Army Group, 1944 (BA/MA RW 6/559) (https://web.archive.org/web/20121029022744/http://ww2stats.com/cas_ger_okh_dec44.html)
38. Human Losses in World War II. AOK/Ic POW Summary Reports [BA/MA RH 2/2807, 2/2621, 2/2622K, w/2633K, 2/2635K, 2/2636-2642, 2/707, 2/2773, IfZ ED 48] (https://web.archive.org/web/20130423093335/http://ww2stats.com/pow_ger_okh_aok.html)
39. Nebol'sin, *Lyubimaya*, pp. 547–8.
40. Ibid., p. 548.
41. Frieser, *Germany*, vol. VIII, pp. 582–3.
42. *Russkii Arkhiv*, vol. 14 (3-1), p. 234, document 27.
43. Ibid., p. 228, document no. 19.
44. Frieser, *Germany*, vol. VIII, pp. 599–600.
45. Ibid., p. 600.
46. *Russkii Arkhiv*, vol. 16 (5-4), pp. 127–8.
47. R. Bagdonas, *The Devil's General. The Life of Hyacinth Graf Strachwitz, The Panzer Graf* (Philadelphia, PA; Oxford: Casemate Publishers, 2013 [electronic copy]), p. 342.
48. Frieser, *Germany*, vol. VIII, p. 585.
49. A.M. Vasilevskii, *Delo Vsei Zhizni* (Moscow: Politizdat, 1978), p. 436.

NOTES

50. *Russkii Arkhiv*, vol. 23 (12-4), p. 336.
51. Daines, *Vperyod*, pp. 295–6.
52. Ibid., pp. 297–9.
53. Srazhenie za Raseiniai 14-16 avgusta 1944 goda//30 sentyabrya 2012, https://altyn73.livejournal.com/199379.html. The Germans estimated the irreparable losses for Soviet armoured equipment during Operation '*Grif*' at more than 60 tanks, which corresponds with the actual losses. (P. Buttar, *Between the Giants. The Battle for the Baltics in World War II* [Oxford: Osprey Publishing, 2013], pp. 215–16.)
54. Buttar, *Between the Giants*, p. 213.
55. A. Polishchuk and A. Ulanov, *Tupik 'Dvuglavoi'*//Warspot.ru,2019, 20 noyabrya, https://warspot.ru/9089-tupik-dvuglavoy
56. Buttar, *Between the Giants*, p. 214.
57. Zhilin, *Boevoi Sostav*, ch. 4, pp. 218–19.
58. Frieser, *Germany*, vol. VIII, pp. 586–7.
59. Buttar, *Between the Giants*, p. 217.
60. Ibid., pp. 218–19.
61. Ibid., pp. 219–20.
62. Ibid., p. 231.
63. Ibid., pp. 220–2.
64. Ibid., p. 222.
65. Frieser, *Germany*, vol. VIII, pp. 587–9.
66. Bagdonas, *The Devil's General* [electronic copy], pp. 345–7.
67. Buttar, *Between the Giants*, p. 228.
68. E. Raus, *Panzer Operations. The Eastern Front Memoir of General Raus, 1941-1945*. Compiled and translated by Steven H. Newton (Cambridge, MA: The Perseus Books Group; Da Capo Press, 2005), p. 295.
69. Ibid., p. 296.
70. Ibid., pp. 296–7.
71. Buttar, *Between the Giants*, p. 229.
72. Ibid., p. 230.
73. A. Polishchuk and A. Ulanov, *Solyonaya Voda dlya Tovarishcha Stalina*//Warspot.ru, 2018, 20 oktyabrya, https://warspot.ru/13178-solyonaya-voda-dlya-tovarishcha-stalina
74. Bagramyan, *Tak shli*, p. 414.
75. Human Losses in World War II. Heeresarzt 10-Day Casualty Reports per Army/Army Group, 1944 (BA/MA RW 6/559) (https://web.archive.org/web/20121029022744/https://ww2stats.com/cas_ger_okh_dec44.html)
76. Human Losses in World War II. AOK/Ic POW Summary Reports [BA/MA RH 2/2087, 2/2621, 2/2622K, 2/2633K, 2/2635K, 2/2636-2642, 2/2707, 2/2773, IfZ ED 48] (https://web.archive.org/web/20130423093335/http://ww2stats.com/pow_ger-okh_aok.html)
77. Daines, *Vperyod*, p. 308.
78. Human Losses in World War II. Heeresarzt 10-Day Casualty Reports per Army/Army Group, 1944 (BA/MA RW 6/559) (https://web.archive.org/web20121029022744/http://ww2stats.com/cas_ger-okh_dec44.html)
79. *Russkii Arkhiv*, vol. 16 (5-4), p. 132.
80. Ibid., pp. 133, 16, 137.

81. Zhilin, *Boevoi Sostav*, ch. 4, p. 238.
82. Nebol'sin, *Lyubimaya*, pp. 547–8.
83. Zhilin, *Boevoi Sostav*, pt. 4, p. 270.
84. Nebol'sin, *Lyubimaya*, pp. 563, 551–2.
85. Glantz, *Hitler and his Generals*, pp. 465–7.
86. Frieser, *Germany*, vol. VIII, p. 592.
87. Daines, *Vperyod*, p. 357.
88. A. Price, *The Last Year of the Luftwaffe: May 1944 to May 1945* (London: Greenhill Books, 2001), pp. 10–12, 14.
89. J. Buckley, *British Armour in the Normandy Campaign* (London: Frank Cass & Routledge, 2004), p. 120.
90. Frieser, *Germany*, vol. VIII, p. 528, table V.II.6.
91. Ibid., p. 529, table V.II.7.
92. Price, *The Last Year of the Luftwaffe*, p. 14.
93. T.L. Jentz (ed.), *Panzertruppen. The Complete Guide to the Creation & Combat Employment of Germany's Tank Force*, vol. 2: *1943-1945* (Atglen, PA: Schiffer Publishing, Ltd., 1996), p. 205. Here, as was the case with German armoured equipment in Normandy, Marders, Wespes and Hummels are not counted, but this is not of significance for comparison. Besides this, in our opinion, the Wespes and Hummels should probably be included among the artillery, and not with armoured vehicles. These self-propelled guns, having light armour (15–30mm), while at the same time possessing quite heavy-calibre guns of 105mm and 150mm respectively, were not designated for engaging Soviet tanks and self-propelled guns, but chiefly to be used against the enemy's infantry and artillery. The analogous Soviet self-propelled guns (the SU-122, ISU-122, SU-152 and SU-152) had much thicker armour and were built for engaging the enemy's tanks and self-propelled guns.
94. http://tankfront.ru/deutschland/StuG.html

Chapter 9: The Sides' Losses

1. Frieser, *Germany*, vol. VIII, pp. 552–3.
2. I.V. Timokhovich, 'Operatsiya', p. 77.
3. Human Losses in World War II. Heeresarzt 10-Day Casualty Reports per Army/Army Group, 1944 (BA/MA RW 6/559) (https://web.archive.org/web/20121029022744/http://stats.com/cas_ger_okh_dec44.html)
4. Frieser, *Germany*, vol. VIII, p. 591.
5. Human Losses in World War II. AOK/Ic POW Summary Reports [BA/MA RH 2/2087, 2/2621, 2/2622K, 2/2633K, 2.2635K, 2/2636-2642, 2/2707, 2/2773, IfZ ED 48] (https://web.archive.org/web20130423093335/http://ww2stats.com/pow_ger_okh_aok.html)
6. Human Losses in World War II. Abwicklungsstab, Group C (A.Gr.Center) {BA/MA RH 15/290] (https://web.archive.org/web/20130208211950/http://ww2stats.com/cas_ger-var-abwc.html)
7. Human Losses in World War II. Heeresarzt 10-Day Casualty Reports per Army/Army Group, 1944, [BA/MA RW 6/559] (http://web.archive.org/web/20160304175048/http://ww2stats.com/cas_ger_okh_dec44.html)

NOTES

8. Human Losses in World War II. Abwicklunghsstab, Group C (A.Gr.Center) [BA/MA RH 15/290] (http://web.archive.org/web/20160411222116/http://ww2stats.com/cas_ger_var_abwc.html)
9. V.P. Galitskii, 'Vrazheskie voennoplennye v SSSR (1941-1945 gg.)', *Voenno-Istoricheskii Zhurnal*, no. 9 (1990), table 2, p. 41.
10. Human Losses in World War II. AOK/Ic POW Summary Reports [BA/MA RH 2/2087, 2/2621, 2/2622K, 2/2633K, 2/2635K, 2/2636-2642, 2/2707m 2/2773, IfZ ED 48] (http://web.archive.org/web/20160304195737/http://ww2stats.com/pow_ger_okh_aok.html)
11. Krivosheev, *Rossiya*, p. 322.
12. Vrublevskii, *Bobruiskii*, p. 196, note 2.
13. Ibid., p. 275, note 1.
14. Here and afterwards calculations are according to: G.F. Krivosheev and A.V. Kirilline (eds), *Velikaya Otechestvennaya bez Grifa Sekretnosti. Kniga Poter'/* (Moscow: Veche), 2010, pp. 39–40, table 6.
15. Human Losses in World War II. Heeresartz 10-Day Casualty Reports per Army/Army Group, 1944, [BA/MA RW 6/559] (http://web.archive.org/web/20160304175048/http://ww2stats.com/cas_ger_okh_dec44.html)
16. Calculation according to: TsAMO, fond 386, opis' 8583, delo 368 (https://pamyat-naroda.ru/documents/view/?id=440105071&static_hash=a7348db7a2fee7ba047db914f499a 1av1); TsAMO, fond 241, opis' 2593, delo 352 (https://pamyat-naroda.ru/documentsview/?id-113985184&static_hash=a73484db7a2fee7ba047db914f499a 1av1); TsAMO, fond 386, opis' 8583, delo 367 (https://pamyat-naroda.ru/documents/view/?id=440105069&static_hash=a73484db7a2fee7ba047db914f499a 1 av1)
17. Human Losses in World War II. Abwicklungsstab, Group C (A.Gr.Center) [BA MA RH 15/290] (https://web.archive.org/web/20130208211950/http://ww2stats.com/cas_ger_var_abwc.html)
18. Ibid.
19. Ye.I. Smirnov, *Voina i Voennaya Meditsina* (Moscow: Meditsina, 1979), p. 188.
20. D. Khazanov, 'Aviatsiya v operatsii "Bagration"', *Aviatsiya i Vremya*, 2014, no. 5, pp. 36–8.
21. D. Khazanov, 'Aviatsiya v operatsii "Bagration"', *Aviatsiya i Vremya*, 2014, no. 6, p. 41.
22. Ibid., pp. 41–4.
23. D. Khazanov, 'Aviatsiya v operatsii "Bagration"', *Aviatsiya i Vremya*, 2015, no. 1, p. 34.
24. Ibid., pp. 34–5.
25. A.A. Smirnov, *'Sokoly', Umytye Krov'yu. Pochemu Sovetskie VVS Voevali Khuzhe Luftwaffe?* (Moscow: Yauza: Eksmo, 2010), pp. 38–66.
26. D.B. Khazanov, *Aviatsiya v Operatsii 'Bagration'* (Moscow: Fond 'Russkie Vityazi', 2019), p. 509.
27. Ibid., p. 444, table 3-2.
28. Ibid., p. 385.
29. Ibid., pp. 385–7.
30. Ibid., p. 444, tables 3-1 and 3-2.
31. Ibid., p. 204.

32. Ibid., p. 446.
33. Aviamaster (Kondrat'ev V. Bukhgalteriya Vozdushnoi Voiny, 2016, 12 iyunya), https://vikond65.livejournal.com/493077.html
34. Khazanov, *Aviatsiya*, p. 444, tables 3-1 and 3-2.
35. A. Zabolotskii and R. Larintsev, Poteri Lyuftwaffe na Vostochnom Fronte/Ugolok Neba. Aviatsionnaya Entsiklopediya, tabl 4, http://www.airwar.ru/history/av2ww/axis/germloss/germloss.html
36. Khazanov, *Aviatsiya*, p. 448.
37. D.N. Minaev, Admiraly i Generaly Vermakhta, SS i Politsii, Pogibshie i Propavshie bez Vesti na Vostochnom Fronte//Zhurnal 'Samizdat', http://samlib.ru/m/mminaew_d_n/generals_z_2_shtml
38. A. Sharkov and Yu. Bestvitskii, 'Rasplata. Generaly Vermakhta: Prestuplenie, Plenenie i Trava Zabvenie'. *Belarus' segodnya*, 2005, 29 marta, http://www.sb.by/articles/rasplata-generaly-vermakhta-prestuplenie-plenenie-i-trava-zabveniya.html;Nemetskia generaly v sovetskom plenu. Ch. 1-16, https://ronin-077.livejournal.com/
39. M.G. Vozhakin (ed.), *Velikaya Otechestvennaya: Komkory. Voennyi Biograficheskii Slovar'*, vol. 2, pp. 106–07
40. N.B. Akberdin, I.I. Basik, S.A. Botsvin, N.I. Nikiforov, I.A. Permyakov and M.V. Smyslov (eds), *Velikaya Otechestvennaya. Voennyi Biograficheskii Slovar'* (Moscow: Kuchkovo Pole, 2014, vol. 3. *Komandiry Strelkovykh, Gornostrelkovykh Divizii, Krymskikh, Polyarnykh, Petrozavodskikh Divizii, Divizii Rebol'skogo Napravleniya, Istrebitel'nykh Divizii*, pp. 914–15.
41. Vozhakin, *Velikaya*, vol. I, pp. 18–19.
42. A.V. Gorbatov, *Gody i Voiny* (Moscow: Voennoe Izdatel'stvo, 1989), pp. 285–7.
43. Vozhakin, *Velikaya*, vol. I, pp. 266–7.
44. Ibid., pp. 297–8.
45. Geroi Vtoroi Mirovoi: general-maior Yakov Osipovich Lagodyuk//Grani.lv, 8 maya 2012, https://www.grani.lv/daugavpils/25545-geroi-vtoroy-mirovoy-general-mayor-yakov-osipovich-lagodyuk.html
46. Akberdin, *et al*, *Velikaya Otechestvennaya*, vol. 4, pp. 560–2.
47. Ibid., pp. 738–40.
48. Ibid., vol. 5, pp. 150–2.
49. Ibid., pp. 390–2.
50. Ibid., pp. 786–8.
51. Ibid., pp. 1103–05.

Index

Soviet Fronts and German Army Groups are spelled out in full. Soviet armies are designated by numbers, while all others are spelled out in full. Soviet corps are designated by numbers, while German corps are designated by Roman numerals. Divisions and smaller units on both sides are designated by numbers. Soviet infantry units are referred to as rifle, while similar units of the other combatants are referred to as infantry. Soviet armoured units are referred to as tank or mechanized, while similar German units are referred to by the term panzer, or panzergrenadier. For purposes of brevity, no units smaller than a division are listed. In those cases in which confusion might occur, the nationality of the unit is indicated.

Abakumov, V.S., 29
Adair, P., 70
Afonin, I.M., 61–3
Alekseev, D.F., 178, 180–1
Allenstein, 73, 203
Antonov, A.I., 53, 83, 93, 164
Archangel Military District, 192
Ardennes, 65, 153
Ardennes Offensive, 150,
Army Group A, 18, 66
Army Group B, 67, 69
Army Group Centre, vi, 8, 18, 31, 40, 52, 54, 64, 65–6, 69–80, 86–91, 93–7, 103, 108, 110–11, 114–15, 121, 126, 128, 144, 149, 151, 153, 156–63, 170, 175–6, 186, 190, 195, 206–07, 213, 215, 222, 225, 227–8, 230, 235–43, 253
Army Group North, 18, 31, 50, 54, 65–6, 69, 73, 77, 95–6, 115, 153–4, 160–1, 175, 206–7, 226–8, 230, 233–4, 236, 239–40, 252
Army Group North Ukraine, 8, 18, 31, 50, 52, 54, 69–74, 76–7, 93, 108, 110, 115, 159, 162–3, 175, 190, 207–8, 214, 225, 239–40
Army Group South, 18, 31, 41, 66
Army Group South Ukraine, vi, 8, 18, 54, 69, 76, 206, 225–6, 228, 236, 239–40
Army Group Vistula, vi, 64, 66
Augustow, 155, 203–4
Augustow Canal, 155
Austria, 192, 255–6, 258–9

Bf 109 (fighter), 247
BT-7 (tank), 13
Bagramyan, I.Kh., 10, 30, 63–4, 95–6, 227, 229–30, 235–6
B-25 (bomber), 247
Bakharov, B.S., 259
Baku, 68
Balck, H., 145
Balkans, 17, 31, 71, 226
Baltic Front, 20
Baltic Military District, 255–6
Baltic Sea, 53, 69, 153–4, 160–1, 207, 224–5, 227
Baltic States, 69, 74, 154, 203, 248
Bamier, R., 254
Baranovichi, 48, 54, 104, 110–12, 114–15, 142, 146, 148, 152, 157, 262
Barbarossa, Plan 64
  Operation, 65, 66, 69, 76
Batov, P.I., 128, 177, 180–1
Bavaria, 65–6, 68, 150, 255
Belgium, 51, 66, 238
Belorussia, vi, 8, 18, 39, 41, 46, 50, 55, 65–6, 68, 71–2, 75–8, 80, 127, 164, 175, 193–4, 197, 208, 241–2, 244, 248, 252, 262
Belorussian Front, 15, 20
Belorussian Military District, 255, 257, 258
Belovezh Forest, 171–3, 182
Berchtesgarden, 94, 97

Berezina River, 66, 71, 73–9, 83–5, 87, 97, 102, 104, 107–16, 119–23, 126–8, 130–1, 133–4, 136–7, 139, 143–4, 146–7, 190, 247
Berezino, 83, 85, 113–15, 147, 253
Bergpanther (recovery vehicle), 222
Berlin, vi, 1, 150, 153–4, 193, 224
   Operation, 38
Berling, Z.H., 82, 206–7
Betzel, C., 178, 235
Bialystok, 73, 139–40, 152, 170–1, 183, 207
Bielsk, 170, 171, 173–4, 178–9, 181
Blancbois, G.A., 141–2
Blomberg, W. von, 70
Bobruisk, 54–5, 70–1, 73, 75, 78, 80, 84, 87, 93–4, 99, 101–07, 112, 114–16, 119–22, 126–33, 135, 137–42, 150, 156, 195, 208, 244, 247, 253–8
Bogdanov, S.I., 209
Bogushevsk, 18, 27
   Operation, 13–14, 16–17
Borisov, 83, 85, 87, 107–09, 111–13, 143–6, 254
Bormann, M., 187
Brandenburg, 66
Brendal, E., 103
Brest (Brest-Litovsk), 54, 69, 70, 73, 79, 140, 142, 152, 156, 161, 164, 168, 170–3, 175, 182–3, 185–6, 194, 204, 217, 253
Brody, 111, 159
Bryansk, 65, 68, 255
Budennyi, S.M., 19
Bulganin, N.A., 24–6, 38, 57, 197, 202
Burdeinyi, A.S., 98, 144
Burroughs, M.B., 53
Busch, E., 64–5, 69–70, 72, 75, 77–80, 87–8, 93–5, 97, 113–14, 116, 127–8, 159
Butlar, E. von, 159

Carpathian Mountains, 55, 69, 76, 163, 207
Caucasus, Battle of, 55
Caucasus Mountains, 68
Cauldwell, D., 246
Cavalry-Mechanized Group, 96, 99, 110, 142–3, 146, 172, 174, 183
Central Front, 55, 225
Chelm, 165, 166–8, 170
Chernyakhovskii, I.D., 11, 40, 55, 61, 63–4, 110–11
China, 46
Chuikov, V.I., 166–7
Churchill, W.S., 219

Ciechanow, 204
Civil War, Russian, 10
Conrady, A., 106, 117, 123, 131–4, 138, 255
Courland, 116, 177, 236
Cracow, 64, 167, 194
Crimea, 50, 55, 69, 78, 161, 208

Daines, V.O., 93, 238, 239
Danzig, 69, 253
Daugavpils, 73, 161, 259, 261
   see also Dvinsk
Deane, J.R., 53
Deblin, 204, 212
Debrecen, 146
Decker, K., 78, 143–4, 146, 233
Demme, R., 101, 128–9, 131–2, 136, 138–9
Demyansk, 64
Denmark, 49
Dietrich, S., 146
Dnepr Military Flotilla, 119
Dnepr River, 63, 66, 71, 78, 83, 85, 87, 96, 97
Dnestr River, 50, 78
Dollman, F., 68
Don Corps, 180
Don Front, 55
Don River, 65
Donitz, K., 64, 160
'Doppelkopf', Operation, 227–8, 230–1, 233, 235–6
Drescher, O., 253
Drohiczyn, 181
Drut' River, 71, 101, 108, 114, 126, 128
Dubovoi, I.V., 212
Dvina River, 160
Dvinsk, 160
   see also Daugavpils

VIII Army Corps, 89, 175
8th Guards Army, 50, 213, 215, 220, 222–3, 237
8th Guards Tank Corps (Polish), 83, 209, 213–21, 237
11th Army, 109
11th Fighter Corps, 249, 250–1
11th Guards Army, 40, 64, 80, 85, 98–9, 151, 160
11th Panzer Division, 50
11th Tank Corps, 155, 164–5, 167–8, 175–6, 213, 215
18th Guards Rifle Corps, 62
18th Panzergrenadier Division, 88–9, 229, 242, 253

INDEX

80th Rifle Corps, 177, 179, 262
81st Infantry Division, 96
82nd Rifle Division, 136–7, 244
83rd Guards Rifle Division, 109
84th Guards Rifle Division, 98
88th Rifle Division, 245
89th Rifle Corps, 81
East Berlin, 254, 258
East Germany, 112
   see also GDR
East Prussia, vi, 50, 53, 66, 69, 91, 147, 151, 153–4, 203, 205–6, 208–9, 225, 228, 249
East Prussian Operation, 65
Eighth Army, 41
Eighth Army (Italian), 65
Eisenhower, D.D., 210
Elbe River, 238
Eleventh Army, 69
Engel, J.C., 117–19, 121, 123–4, 133, 138, 258
England, 49, 50
Erdmansdorff, H.O.G., 254
Estonia, 74, 78–9, 154, 160, 227
Europe, 192, 210, 262

FRG (Federal Republic of Germany), 254, 255–8
I Cavalry Corps, 156, 163
IV Air Corps, 230
IV SS Panzer Corps, 186–7
XL Panzer Corps, 68, 107, 229, 233, 235
XLI Panzer Corps, 65, 70, 89, 99, 102, 116, 119–21, 126–8, 133–4, 137–8, 141, 256
LIII Army Corps, 89, 94–5, 255
LV Army Corps, 89, 107, 125, 140
LVI Panzer Corps, 166, 168, 175
1st Air Army, 247–8, 252
1st Cavalry Division (Hungarian), 90
1st Guards Bomber Corps, 249, 251
1st Guards Cavalry Corps, 142
1st Guards Fighter Corps, 249–50, 215
1st Guards Rifle Corps, 235
1st Guards Tank Corps, 99, 119, 123, 126, 128, 132–3, 142, 146, 152
1st Tank Corps, 229–30
1st Infantry Division (German), 229
1st Infantry Division (Polish), 12–3
1st Mechanized Corps, 152
1st SS Panzer Division (Leibstandarte Adolf Hitler), 31, 195
   see also Leibstandarte

1st Tank Corps, 104
4th Air Army, 247, 252
4th Air Corps, 89
4th Guards Cavalry Corps, 152, 173, 226
4th Luftwaffe Field Division, 89, 242, 253
4th Panzer Division, 51, 65, 72–3, 97, 142–3, 175–8, 182, 184, 187, 214, 217, 220, 222, 228, 231, 233, 235, 239
4th Rifle Division, 59
4th Shock Army, 95, 96, 153, 227, 229, 261
5th Air Army, 252
5th Army, 19, 26, 40, 80, 85, 99, 111, 151, 160
5th Guards Rifle Division, 109
5th Guards Tank Army, 11, 70, 76, 78, 82, 96, 99, 107, 109–10, 113, 143–6, 151, 153, 160, 207, 227–30
5th Jaeger Division, 188
5th Light Infantry Division, 89
5th Panzer Division, 72–3, 78, 97, 109–13, 115, 140, 143–7, 157, 159–60, 175, 228, 230–1, 234
5th SS Panzer Division (Wiking), 137, 165–6, 169–71, 173, 178, 182, 217
   see also Wiking SS Panzer Division
5th Rifle Division, 99
5th Shock Army, 50
14th Infantry Division, 77, 90, 111
14th Panzer Division, 229, 231, 233, 235
14th Rifle Corps, 95
15th (Sivash) Rifle Division, 177, 179
40th Rifle Corps, 261
41st Rifle Corps, 262
42nd Rifle Division, 12
43rd Army, 10–11, 80, 86, 152, 228, 259
44th Guards Rifle Division, 129, 179
45th Infantry Division, 71, 89, 104–05, 111, 117–23, 125–6, 133–4, 136, 138, 242, 258
45th Rifle Corps, 37
47th Army, 57, 81, 164–6, 168, 175–6, 186, 213, 220–2, 237
48th Army, 57, 84, 152, 186
49th Army, 151, 237, 262
50th Army, 81, 151, 254
51st Army, 152–3, 229, 231, 235
52nd Security Division (German), 90
53rd Infantry Division, 99
53rd Rifle Corps, 118, 180
57th Infantry Division, 89, 99, 101, 111, 128, 148–9, 242, 258
413th Rifle Division, 137
417th Rifle Division, 236

279

548th *Volksgrenadier* Division, 234
549th *Volksgrenadier* Division, 234
551st *Volksgrenadier* Division, 234
Feldherrnhalle Panzergrenadier Division, 90, 149, 242, 253, 257
Felke, H., 140
Felzmann, M., 186
Fifteenth Army, 68–9
Fifth Air Fleet, 239
Finland, 17, 34, 74, 79, 160, 201
Finnish War, 192–3, 246
First Air Fleet, 77, 239, 247, 252
First Army (German), 66
First Army (Polish), 82–3, 206–07, 213, 220, 222, 243
First Baltic Front, 10, 30, 63–4, 73, 79–80, 83–6, 95–6, 147, 152–3, 158, 161, 203–04, 227–30, 236, 243, 259, 261–2
First Belorussian Front, 8, 38, 54, 55, 57, 60, 72–3, 79, 81–5, 88, 97, 104, 110–11, 114, 118, 120, 123, 146, 152–3, 156, 158, 161, 163–4, 174–5, 190, 204, 207–09, 218, 220–1, 224–6, 237, 247, 259, 262
First Panzer Army, 50, 55
First Parachute Army, 64
First Ukrainian Front, 15, 29, 38, 39, 54–5, 62, 72, 86, 155–6, 163, 186, 204, 207, 225
Fogel', Ya.Ya., 262
Foreign Armies East, 53, 69, 76, 114, 208, 223
Fourteenth Army, 66
Fourth Air Fleet, 239
Fourth Army, 13, 50, 69, 70, 73, 78, 86–9, 93, 95–7, 99, 110–15, 120–1, 126, 140, 143–4, 146–7, 151, 153, 157, 161, 163, 171, 208, 213, 215, 225, 241, 244
Fourth Panzer Army, 86, 115
Fourth Ukrainian Front, 15, 62, 91
France, 50–2, 66–8, 78–9, 191, 205, 225, 238
Franek, F. von, 214, 218, 258–9
'Free Germany' National Committee, 112, 140
  see also National Committee for a Free Germany
Fricke, G., 132
Frieser, K.H., 51, 72–3, 75, 89–90, 104, 145, 147, 156, 158–9, 163, 208, 213–14, 215, 222, 225
Friesner, J., 161
Fritsch, W., 70
Fw 190 (fighter bomber), 89

GDR (East Germany), 254, 258
  see also East Germany
GDR People's Police, 257
Galicia, 244
Gamann, A., 122, 133, 137, 255
Gartsev, I.A., 180–1
Gaudecher, G. von, 177
Gehlen, R., 53–4, 70, 76, 208, 223
General Lee (tank), 12
General Staff (French Army), 197
General Staff (German Army), 116, 158, 161
General Staff (Red Army), 2, 13, 23, 26, 28–35, 38, 53–4, 81, 83, 93, 155, 197, 207, 223
German National Democratic Party, 257
Germany, 17, 41, 50–3, 66, 69, 74, 109, 116, 127, 161, 176, 192, 205–06, 238
Gestapo, 182
Gihr, G., 101–02, 138, 256
Gille, H., 170, 172, 174, 178, 182, 187
Gluzdovskii, V.A., 40
Golikov, F.I., 61, 62
Gollwitzer, F., 94–5, 255
Gomel', 76, 258
Gorbatov, A.V., 259
Gordov, V.N., 2, 4, 23, 26, 34–9
Gorodok, 30, 86
Great Patriotic War, vi, 63
'Grif', Operation, 228
Grille (self-propelled gun), 127, 139–40
Grodno, 109, 117, 152–3, 161, 175, 258
Grossdeutschland Panzergrenadier Division, 50, 90, 160, 175, 228, 231, 233, 235, 239
Gryzlov, A.A. 83, 93
Guderian, H., 68, 161, 227–8Gulf of Riga, 227, 233
Gumbinnen, 203
Gusev, N.I., 164

He 111 (bomber), 89
Hahne, H., 253
Hamann, Gen., 116
Harpe, J., 115
Harteneck, G., 156, 163, 171–2
Hausser, P., 145, 197
Heinrici, G., 50, 65
Hermann Göring Parachute-Panzer Division, 175, 213–20, 222
Heusinger, A., 72, 73, 160, 161
Hewel, W., 52
Heyne, H.W., 255

INDEX

High Command Reserve (Soviet), 98, 248
Hilfswilligen (*Hiwis*), 116, 124, 127, 186, 211, 212
Himmler, H., 253
Hitler, A., 41, 49, 51, 52–4, 67–70, 73–4, 76, 78, 80, 87, 90, 93–7, 107, 113–16, 141, 145, 158–61, 175, 182, 187, 192, 195, 205–06, 230, 237–9, 254
Hitter, A., 255
Hoffmeister, E. 99, 102, 116–18, 121, 124, 133–4, 136–8, 256
Home Army (Polish), 82, 206–07, 213, 220, 226
 see also Polish Underground Army
Hornisse (self-propelled gun), 88
Hummel (self-propelled gun), 127, 135, 140
Hungary, 212, 228

Il-2 (assault aircraft), 39, 247, 251
Il-4 (assault aircraft), 247
IS-2 (tank), 107, 168, 209, 215–16, 218, 221–2, 228,
 see also Iosif Stalin (tank)
IS-122 (tank destroyer), 113
Iasi-Kishinev Operation, vi, 213, 226, 244, 246
Ikonnikov, I.A., 37
Il'nitskii, Ya.T., 20, 22–3, 25–6, 30–2
Insterburg, 203
Iosif Stalin (tank), 98, 232
 see also IS–2
Italy, 17, 51, 66–8, 79, 175, 213–4

Jagdpanzer IV, 140, 168, 176–7, 214–16, 218, 222
Jelgava, 228, 235–6
Jodl, A., 49, 78–80
Jordan, H., 66, 103, 107, 114, 127
Ju 87 (dive bomber), 89
Ju 88 (bomber), 89
Juttner, Col, 106, 124, 132, 135–6

KV (tank), 12, 13, 98, 100, 224, 229
KV-122 (tank), 169
Kaganovich, L.M., 202
Kalinin Front, 1, 64
Kalisz, 204
Kalmykov, A.S., 181
Kamenets-Litovskii, 170–3, 182
Kamera, I.P., 23, 25–6, 34, 38–9
Kaminskii, B., 253–4

Karelia, 74
Karelian Isthmus, 74, 252
Katukov, M.Ye., 160
'Katyusha', 185
Kaunas (Kovno), 73, 96, 152–3, 161, 203, 208, 230
Keitel, W., 237
Kempf, Operational Group, 41
Kessel, M. von, 93, 106, 120, 122, 127–8, 130–3, 137–40, 142–3, 248
Kesselring, A., 68
Khalkhiin-Gol River, 61–2, 246
Khar'kov, 41
 Battle of, 64
Khazanov, D.B., 249, 251–2
Kholm, 64
Khrulyov, A.V., 34
Kiev, 64
Kiev Military District, 257
King Tiger (tank), 109
Klammt, G., 258
Kleist, E. von, 67
Kleffel, P., 234
Kluge, G. von, 67, 206, 238
Klyaro, I.V., 261
Knobelsdorf, O. von, 229, 234
Kobrin, 54, 156
Konev, I.S., 29
Königsberg, 69, 73, 154, 234
Korsun-Shevchenkovskii Operation, 55
Kotinskii, A.Yu., 44
Kovel', vi, 51–4, 69–70, 72, 76, 78–9, 86, 93, 153, 158, 163–4, 166–7, 169, 174, 176, 190, 194, 208–09, 224–5
Krasnov, I.G., 261
Krebs, H., 72, 163, 170, 237–8
Kriegsmarine, 68
Krylov, N.I., 111
Kryuchyonkin, V.D. 11
Kryukov, V.V., 156
Kuban' River, 48
Kurdyumov, V.N., 192, 193
Kurochkin, P.A., 82
Kurowski, E. von, 258
Kursk, Battle of, 55, 63–4, 225
Kuzbass, 200
Kuznetsov, F.F., 1, 2, 26, 32, 81

Lake Balaton, 146
Latvia, vi, 78, 153–4, 227, 253, 259
Lazarenko, I.S., 262

Leibstandarte, 196
  see also 1st SS Panzer Division
Lemm, H.G., 139, 143
Leningrad, 50, 64, 210, 243
Leningrad Military District, 192
Lepel', 20, 83, 86, 108, 115, 147
Lida, 79, 110, 152
Liepaja, 228
Lindemann, G., 72–3, 77, 161
Litvinov, M., 201
Lithuania, vi, 78, 147, 150–1, 153–4, 230, 253, 262
Lodz, 190, 204
Lomza, 203
London, 226
Long-Range Aviation, 175, 246
Lublin, 69–70, 72–3, 156, 170, 175, 186, 207–10, 225–6
Lublin-Brest Operation, 210
Luchesa River, 27
Luchs (light reconnaissance tank), 176
Luftwaffe, 8, 49, 53, 68, 77, 89, 137, 169, 205–06, 213, 215, 230, 238, 246–8, 251–2
Luninets, 54, 87, 152
Lutzow, K.J. von, 106, 116, 120, 121, 256
L'vov, 53, 54, 69, 71, 79, 225
L'vov-Sandomierz Operation, 74

MGB (Ministry of State Security), 38
MVD (Ministry of Internal Affairs), 254, 256, 258
MZA (small anti-aircraft artillery), 108
Magnuszew, 213, 220, 222, 237
Makarov, M.G., 122, 135
Malenkov, G.M., 1, 2, 13, 17–20, 22, 28, 34–5, 38, 57, 61, 63, 81
Manstein, E. von, 67, 225
Manteuffel, H., 233
Marder II (tank destroyer), 127, 130, 176
Marder III (tank destroyer), 127, 214, 218, 222
Marienburg, 203
Mariompol, 152
Martinek, R., 253
Martsinkevich, V.N., 262
Maultier (half-track truck), 140
Mecklenburg, 66
Mekhlis, L.Z., 2, 24–5, 33–4, 38
Memel (Klaipeda), 203, 228
Michaelis, H., 254
Mikoyan, A.I., 34, 202

Ministry of Foreign Affairs (Germany), 52
Minsk, vi, 19–20, 39, 48, 54, 70–1, 73, 75–7, 79, 83–6, 89, 94, 99, 107–15, 125, 132, 134, 139, 142, 144–8, 150–3, 167, 194, 196, 224, 254, 256, 258
Minsk-Mazowiecki, 215–16, 218–19, 221
Minsk Operation, 110
Mitava, 235
Mlawa (Melau), 127, 203
Model, W., 67, 72–3, 78–9, 93, 111, 114–15, 137, 142, 157–61, 163, 171–2, 175, 208–09, 213–14, 220, 223, 230
Modlin, 213, 215
Mogilev, vi, 20, 50, 65, 73, 80, 83–5, 94, 96–7, 101–02, 104–05, 126–7, 139, 143, 147, 194–5, 254, 256–7
Molodechno, 77, 83, 87, 109–10, 112–13, 115, 144–6, 148, 150, 152, 157
Moldavia, 228
Molotov, V.M., 202
Moscow, 54, 62, 70, 99, 107–08, 153, 198, 201, 210, 225, 241, 254–8
  Battle of, 55, 65–6
Moscow Military District, 91, 256
Muhlenkamp, J., 167, 168–9, 171–2
Muller, V., 111–12, 130, 142, 148, 257–8
Muller-Bulow, K., 256
Munich, 66
Mussolini, B., 68

NKVD (People's Commissariat of Internal Affairs), 63, 158, 196, 257
NSDAP (National Socialist German Worker's Party), 193
IX Air Corps, 238
IX Army Corps, 89, 95
9th Guards Rifle Corps, 81, 186
9th Luftwaffe Field Division, 242–3
9th Panzer Division, 52, 240
9th SS Division (*Hohenstaufen*), 194, 238, 239
9th Tank Corps, 104, 123, 129–32, 135, 259
19th Panzer Division, 187, 214, 217, 220, 222
19th Rifle Corps, 81
19th Tank Corps, 228, 229
91st Rifle Corps, 81, 223
95th Infantry Division, 89, 111, 242, 254
96th Infantry Division, 31
96th Rifle Division, 117, 119–20
96th Rifle Corps, 81
Nagyatad, J.S., von, 256

INDEX

Narew River, 110, 176, 203, 204, 206, 213, 215, 237
Narva, 227
Narva River, 50
Nashorn (self-propelled gun), 96, 165
National Air Defence Forces, 93
National Committee for a Free Germany, 254, 255–8
  see also 'Free Germany' National Committee
Neman River, 142–3, 150, 152, 153, 161, 249
Netherlands, 64, 238
Neumann, P., 191–7
Nevel', 80
Niepold, G., 71, 116, 141, 142–3, 235
Nikolaev, 152, 153
Ninth Army, 66, 70, 71, 73, 76, 88–9, 93, 96, 99, 101, 103–04, 107, 111, 114–16, 119–21, 125, 127–8, 130, 132–7, 139–41, 143, 153, 156, 161, 186–7, 195, 208, 213, 215, 222, 225, 241, 256
Normandy, vi, 51–3, 66–9, 72, 74, 79, 90, 154, 190, 194, 206, 208, 238–40, 246, 262
North Africa, 67–8
Norway, 17, 54
Novogrudok, 152
Novyi Bykhov, 83
Nowy Dwor, 155

OKH (*Oberkommando des Heeres*), 70, 73–6, 90, 94, 151, 234, 239
OKW (*Oberkommando der Wehrmacht*), 49–51, 69, 74–6, 241–2
100th Rifle Corps, 95
102nd Infantry Division, 89, 173
102nd Rifle Division, 120
104th Infantry Division, 31
105th Rifle Corps, 177, 183
108th Guards Rifle Division, 100, 125
110th Infantry Division, 89, 99, 242, 258
110th Rifle Division, 211
114th Rifle Corps, 81
120th Guards Rifle Division, 126, 262
121st Rifle Corps, 81
125th Rifle Corps, 81, 218
129th Infantry Division, 71, 89, 163, 176
129th Rifle Division, 134
132nd Rifle Division, 57
134th Infantry Division, 71, 89, 99–102, 105, 111, 118, 122–3, 125–6, 131, 133, 243, 253

139th Rifle Division, 254
144th Rifle Division, 19
153rd Rifle Division, 12
157th Rifle Division, 12
158th Rifle Division, 19
160th Rifle Division, 59
164th Rifle Division, 12, 19, 255
170th Infantry Division, 145
173rd Infantry Division, 216
173rd Rifle Division, 35, 245
174th Rifle Division, 20, 245
179th Infantry Division, 31
184th Rifle Division, 19
192nd Rifle Division, 20, 245
194th Rifle Division, 26
196th Infantry Division, 242
197th Infantry Division, 89, 242, 253
Ochsner, W.F., 258
Oder River, vi, 74, 150, 153, 160, 238
Odessa, 78–9
Okulicki, L., 226
Oliwa (Kiwerski, J.W.), 82
Orel, 255
Orsha, 1, 3, 11, 13, 15, 17–18, 27, 33, 35, 39–40, 77–8, 80, 83, 85, 87, 96–8, 107–09, 150
  Operation, 14–16, 18
Osipovichi, 84, 99, 116, 126, 135–6, 138, 152–3
Oslikovskii, N.S., 96, 110, 143–4, 146, 160
Ostroleka, 203
'Overlord', Operation, vi, vii, 53, 206, 262

Panther (tank), 109, 116, 143–6, 160, 165, 168, 172, 176–7, 182, 184–5, 214–16, 222, 239
Panyvezys, 152
Panzer II (tank), 116
Panzer III (tank), 116, 127, 141
Panzer III (flamethrower tank), 127
Panzer IV (tank), 109, 116, 124, 127, 129–30, 138–41, 143, 146–7, 167, 172, 176–7, 182, 184, 214, 216, 218, 222, 228, 239
Panzer 38(t) (tank), 127
Panzerfaust (anti-tank weapon), 121, 124, 165
Panzerjäger (tank destroyer), 176–7
Panzer Group West, 68
Parichi, 99, 119, 131
Paris, 198, 200
Peschel, R., 253

283

OPERATION BAGRATION: AN INCOMPLETE TRUTH

Pfeiffer, G., 253
Pflugbeil, K., 77
Phillip, E., 100, 105, 253
Pilsudski, J., 209
Pinaev, V., 164, 169
Pinsk, 87, 152, 161
Pistorius, R., 253
Plan 'Blue', 225
Plato, A.D. von, 144–6
Pliev, I.A., 104, 142, 172, 174, 183
Ploesti, 50, 252
Pokrovskii, A.P., 1, 11, 22, 25, 29–32, 34, 38
Poland, vi, 50, 52–3, 127, 154, 211, 227, 243–4, 253, 255
Poles'ye, 166
 see also Pripyat' Marshes
Polish Committee of National Liberation, 206–07, 226
Polish Underground Army, 219
 see also Home Army
Politburo, 199
Polotsk, 78, 83, 86–7, 95, 96, 115, 146
Poplavskii, S.G., 37
Praga, 204, 208, 213, 215, 217, 219, 222, 237, 248
Prague, 62
 Operation, 38
Preussisch-Eylau, 203
Prinz Eugen, 233, 234
Pripyat' Marshes, 54, 69
 see also *Poles'ye*
Prokhorovka, 145
Proskurov-Chernovtsy Operation, 55
Pulawy, 175, 208–09, 262
Pultusk, 204, 237

RKKA Naval Administration, 201
RONA (Russian National Liberation Army), 201, 253
Radzievskii, A.I., 208–09
Radzymin, 186–9, 213, 215, 220
Ragulya, I.L., 262
Raseiniai, 65, 203, 227–8
Rastenburg, 205
Raus, E., 230, 234–5
Rava-Russkaya, 79
Red Army, vi, 8–9, 17, 24, 41, 45–6, 50–6, 60, 62–3, 65, 74–6, 78–9, 82, 89, 94, 104, 117–18, 147, 150, 156, 158, 162, 174, 177, 185, 196, 206, 208–10, 212, 222, 224–6, 235, 244–6, 262

Red Army Air Force, 248
 see also Soviet Air Force
Red Army Personnel Administration, 61
Red Banner Baltic Fleet, 201, 202
Reich Air Fleet, 238, 239
Reich Labour Service, 88
Reinhardt, G.H., 65, 80, 94–5, 160–1, 230
Rhine River, 67, 169
Riga, 78, 95, 111, 141, 161, 177, 203, 227, 234, 236
Riga Operation, 237
Rodin, A.G., 24, 33
Rogachev, 54–5, 84, 96, 104–06, 126, 131
Rogachev-Zhlobin operation, 55
Rokossovskii, K.K., 54–5, 63–4, 71, 82, 104, 121, 156, 164, 175, 178–80, 208, 213, 215
Romanenko, P.L., 180
Romania, vi, 50, 52–3, 69, 79, 206, 212, 226–8, 236, 252
Rome, 213
Rommel, E., 67
Rossosh', 64
Rostov-on-Don, 64, 66, 145
Rotmistrov, P.A., 11, 70, 78, 96, 107–10, 113, 145, 160, 207, 227
Rudkin, F.N., 155, 164, 168
Ruhr, 50, 206
Rundstedt, G. von, 66–8
Rzhev, 66, 225

SMERSH, 13, 29, 30, 34, 35
Sd.Kfz.7 (armoured personnel carrier), 124, 135
Sd.Kfz.10/4 (armoured personnel carrier), 133
Sd.Kfz.222 (transport), 176
Sd.Kfz.232 (armoured car), 176
Sd.Kfz.250 (armoured personnel carrier), 176
Sd.Kfz.251 (armoured personnel carrier), 176
SU-57 (self-propelled gun), 107–08, 113, 209, 215–16, 218, 222, 229
SU-76 (self-propelled gun), 100, 107–08, 113, 123, 129–30, 133, 136, 165, 169, 184, 209–10, 215–16, 218, 221–2, 229
SU-85 (self-propelled gun), 107–08, 113, 123, 129, 131, 133, 209–10, 215–16, 218, 221–2, 229
SU-122 (self-propelled gun), 129, 229
SU-152 (self-propelled gun), 100, 107–08, 113
SU-M-10 (tank), 113
II SS Panzer Corps, 52, 72, 238–9
II Army Corps, 257
VI Army Corps, 66, 89, 95, 99, 253

INDEX

2nd Cavalry Corps, 81
2nd Guards Cavalry Corps, 175–6, 213, 221, 227
2nd Guards Army, 55, 152–3, 229, 261–2
2nd Guards (Tatsinskaya) Tank Corps, 3, 27, 96, 98, 113, 143–4, 151
2nd Rifle Corps, 38
2nd Tank Army, 156, 175, 187, 209–10, 212– 218, 220–3, 226, 237, 248, 258
6th Air Army, 81, 247
6th Cavalry Division (Mongolian), 61–2
6th Guards Army, 10, 11, 38, 76, 80, 84, 86, 95, 152, 229, 262
6th Guards Corps, 227
6th Infantry Division, 71, 89, 104, 111, 118, 122–3, 133, 136, 138, 242, 255
6th Luftwaffe Field Division, 89, 242, 253
6th Panzer Division, 50, 90, 97, 160, 162
6th Tank Army, 226
7th Guards Cavalry Corps, 81, 156, 209
7th Infantry Division, 66, 89, 172, 173
7th Panzer Division, 67, 175, 228–9
16th Air Army, 107, 121, 247, 252
16th Army, 64, 247
16th Guards Rifle Division, 98
16th Panzer Division, 166
16th SS Division (*Reichsfuhrer SS*), 194
16th Tank Corps, 212–15, 217–19, 237, 258
17th Rifle Division, 117
60th Sevsk Rifle Division, 60
61st Army, 81, 152, 156, 186
61st Rifle Corps, 81, 223, 262
62nd Rifle Corps, 262
62nd Rifle Division, 12, 245
65th Army, 84, 118, 122, 152, 173–4, 177, 181–4, 186, 262
65th Rifle Corps, 33
69th Army, 57, 81, 175, 223, 262
69th Rifle Corps, 257
69th (Sevsk) Rifle Division, 128, 177–9
71st Guards Rifle Division, 262
73rd Infantry Division, 213, 217
73rd Rifle Division, 59
70th Army, 57, 81, 156, 175
70th Rifle Corps, 37, 81
73rd Infantry Division, 208, 214–16, 220, 258
75th Guards Rifle Division, 131, 184
77th Rifle Corps, 81
78th Assault Division (German), 77, 89, 96, 98, 111, 148–9, 242, 256

707th Infantry/Security Division, 71, 89, 99–103, 111, 122, 127, 133, 243, 256
Salmuth, Hans von, 68, 69
San River, 73–4
Sandomierz, 53, 225
Sarny, 81
Saucken, D. von, 111, 143, 216, 228, 235
Scheller, W., 253
Schmalz, W., 215
Schulenburg, F.W. von der, 238
Schunemann, O., 252
Schurmann, P., 89, 98, 149–51
Schweppenburg, L.G. von, 68
Second Army (German), 66, 69–70, 86, 88–90, 107, 125–6, 140, 156, 158, 161, 163, 166, 170–1, 173–5, 182–3, 186–7, 208, 213, 215, 225, 241, 254
Second Army (Polish), 226
Second Baltic Front, 38, 84, 86, 95, 153, 204, 227, 229
Second Belorussian Front, 38, 55, 64, 79, 81–5, 96, 110–11, 114, 151–3, 155–6, 158, 161, 175, 203–04, 207, 225, 237, 254, 262
Second Panzer Group, 68
Second Ukrainian Front, 29, 55, 81–3, 146, 213, 226–7
Second World War, 197, 201–02
Serock, 204, 213, 215, 237
Seventeenth Army, 69
Seventh Army, 68
Shaposhnikov, B.M., 225
Shara River, 152
Shcherbakov, A.S., 2, 81
Sherman (tank), 107–09, 113, 172, 188–9, 209, 210, 215–18, 221–2, 229, 232
Shimonaev, A.I., 2, 29, 81
Shtemenko, S.M., 2, 81, 93
Siauliai, 73, 152, 227, 229, 233, 236
Siedlce, 170, 175–6, 187, 204, 208, 213, 215
Siegfried Line, 153, 206
Silesia, 205
Simonov, K.M., 11, 77, 159 Sivakov, I.P., 262
Sixteenth Army, 64, 233
Sixth Air Fleet, 89, 230, 239, 248, 252
Sixth Panzer Army, SS, 146
Slonim, 54, 110, 152
Sluch' River, 75
Slutsk, 84, 99, 112, 115
Smirnov, Ye.I., 245–6, 249
Smolensk, 13, 19, 65, 70, 76
  Battle of, 55

OPERATION BAGRATION: AN INCOMPLETE TRUTH

Sokolovskii, V.D., 1–2, 13, 17–18, 23–6, 28–30, 32–4, 38, 40
Sosnkowski, K., 82
South-western Direction, 64
South-western Front, 64
Soviet Air Force, 247–8, 252
  see also Red Army Air Force
Spain, 46
Spas-Demensk, 31
Stalin, I.V., 1–2, 34, 37–8, 53–4, 61, 63, 73, 81–4, 93, 95–6, 145, 153–4, 164, 192–3, 197, 201–02, 208–09, 219–20, 223–7, 252
Stalingrad, vi, 1, 52, 161, 243
  Battle of, 55
  Counteroffensive, 55, 225
Staraya Russa, 64
State Defence Committee (GKO), 38, 81
Stavka (of the Supreme High Command, VGK), 1, 8, 13–14, 23–5, 27, 31–2, 34, 37–40, 53–4, 64, 80–3, 91, 110, 114, 145, 147, 151, 153, 155–6, 158, 164, 169, 203–04, 206–07, 213, 225–7, 237, 247
Steinkeller, F.C. von, 257
Storch (aircraft), 171
Stug III (assault gun), 88, 126, 165, 222, 240
Stug IV (assault gun), 167–8, 240
StuH (howitzer), 240
Svencionys, 152
Svisloch', 83, 85, 102, 123, 135–7, 139, 141, 152–3
Svisloch' River, 110, 123, 136–8, 140–1, 256
Sweden, 201

T-34 (tank), 12–13, 100, 107–08, 113, 117, 123–4, 128–30, 132–4, 138–9, 165, 169, 184–5, 188–9, 209, 213, 215–18, 222, 228–9
T-34 (flamethrower tank), 100
T-60 (tank), 12
T-70 (tank), 12
X Air Corps, 238
XII Army Corps, 65, 89, 96, 111, 148–9
XX Army Corps, 89, 140, 156
XXIII Army Corps, 89–90, 172–4, 182–3
XXIV Army Corps, 68
XXVII Army Corps, 66, 89, 96, 98–9, 148, 257
XXX Army Corps, 69
XXXV Army Corps, 89, 99, 102, 106–07, 116, 120, 126–7, 256
XXXIX Panzer Corps, 89, 96, 97, 216, 228, 233, 235, 253

3rd Air Army, 10, 247, 251–2
3rd Army, 55, 118, 153, 203, 237, 259, 262
3rd Guards Army, 38
3rd Guards Assault Air Division (Soviet), 81
3rd Guards Cavalry Corps, 110–11, 143, 146, 151–2, 155
3rd Guards Mechanized Corps, 110–11, 113, 143–4, 146, 151, 153, 227, 229–30, 248
3rd Guards Tank Corps, 107, 108–09, 186, 228
3rd Tank Corps, 209, 212–21, 237
3rd Panzer Division, 68,
3rd SS Panzer Division (*Totenkopf*), 186, 217
  see also *Totenkopf* SS Panzer Division
10th Army, 81
10th SS Panzer Division, 238–9
12th Infantry Division, 89, 111, 139, 254
12th Mechanized Corps, 65
12th Panzer Division, 72–3, 97, 111, 115–17, 125–6, 137–43, 157, 175, 227–8, 233, 235
12th Reserve Division (Hungarian), 89–90
12th Rifle Division, 56
13th Guards Rifle Corps, 261–2
20th Artillery Division, 98
20th Panzer Division, 66, 71–2, 73, 88, 90, 93, 97, 101, 103–07, 111, 114, 116, 120–3, 126–35, 138–43, 159, 225, 231
21st Guards Rifle Division, 95
21st Army, 12
22nd Army, 227
22nd Guards Rifle Corps, 10, 228
23rd Guards Rifle Corps, 96, 262
24th Infantry Division, 96
24th Panzer Division, 50
25th Panzergrenadier Division, 88, 89, 96, 98, 148, 150, 242
25th Rifle Corps, 81
26th Infantry Division, 66, 169
28th Army, 64, 84, 122, 152, 186
28th Jäger Division, 143
28th Rifle Division, 95
29th SS RONA Division, 157, 253
29th Tank Corps, 107, 109, 144, 228
30th Army, 57
30th Infantry Division, 65
31st Army, 23, 26, 28, 32, 39–40, 85, 99, 144, 151, 244, 245
31st Infantry Division, 89, 148, 242, 258
33rd Army, 2–4, 11–12, 19–20, 23–4, 26–7, 33, 35–8, 151, 153, 208, 228
35th Infantry Division, 71, 89, 111, 118, 127–8, 174

INDEX

35th Rifle Corps, 259
36th Infantry Division, 71, 89, 104–06, 111, 117, 119–20, 123, 128, 131–2, 134–6, 138, 140, 242, 255
37th Rifle Division, 177, 179–80
38th Guards Rifle Division, 58
38th Rifle Corps, 81
39th Army, 33, 80, 85, 147, 155, 203, 228, 255
200th Rifle Division, 95, 261
201st Security Division, 89
203rd Security Division, 89
206th Infantry Division, 89, 94, 242, 255
211th Assault Air Division, 249–50
211th Infantry Division, 89
212th Infantry Division, 228
215th Rifle Division, 19
218th Rifle Division, 60
220nd Rifle Division, 244
221st Infantry Division, 90, 145
222nd Rifle Division, 19, 245
236th Infantry Division, 31
239th Infantry Division, 31
239th Rifle Division, 95
242nd Night Bomber Division, 81
246th Infantry Division, 89, 242, 256
247th Rifle Division, 20
250th Rifle Division, 100
251st Rifle Division, 20
252nd Infantry Division, 89, 95, 228, 253
256th Infantry Division, 89, 108, 242, 254
259th Fighter Division, 249, 250–1
260th Infantry Division, 89, 111, 148, 243, 258
267th Infantry Division, 89, 148–9, 242, 253
269th Rifle Division, 125
277th Rifle Division, 37
283rd Infantry Division, 111
286th Security Division, 89, 108, 111, 243
290th Infantry Division, 96
290th Rifle Division, 12
292nd Infantry Division, 89, 183, 185
296th Infantry Division, 71, 89, 111, 122, 126, 133, 243
299th Infantry Division, 89, 108, 111, 242
307th Rifle Division, 59
311th Rifle Division, 95
314th Night Bomber Division, 249–51
323rd Rifle Division, 100–01, 259, 261
331st Rifle Division, 20, 245
332nd Assault Air Division, 249–50
332nd Rifle Division, 259
334th Bomber Division, 249–50, 252
335th Assault Air Division, 249–50
336th Fighter Division, 81
337th Infantry Division, 12, 89, 111, 242
342nd Infantry Division, 166–7, 169
343rd Rifle Division, 262
346th Rifle Division, 234, 236
348th Rifle Division, 261
352nd Rifle Division, 32, 245
354th Rifle Division, 178
356th Rifle Division, 122, 134–5, 179
357th Rifle Division, 228
367th Infantry Division, 125
369th Rifle Division, 262
378th Rifle Division, 95
383rd Infantry Division, 71, 89, 102, 104, 105–07, 111, 116, 118–19, 122–3, 131, 133, 136, 138, 242
385th Rifle Division, 257
390th Field Training Division, 88, 90
391st Security Division, 90
Tauroggen, 229
Ternopol', 63, 79, 94
Third Air Fleet, 238–9
Third Baltic Front, 38, 86, 95, 227
Third Belorussian Front, 11, 39–40, 63, 73, 79–81, 83–4, 85–6, 97, 110–11, 114, 145, 147, 151–3, 155, 158, 161, 203–04, 207, 225, 230, 236–7, 244, 247
Third Panzer Army, 65, 70, 73, 76, 78, 80, 88–9, 94–6, 111, 114–15, 140, 143, 146, 157, 160–1, 208, 225, 230, 234–6, 241
Third Ukrainian Front, 83, 213, 226–7
Tiger (tank), 77, 88, 108–10, 113, 143, 145–7, 176–7, 222, 228, 239
Tile, A., 233
Timoshenko, S.K., 192–3
Tippelskirch, K. von, 50, 65, 66, 86, 96–7, 107, 111–13, 115, 147, 159, 206
Todt Organization, 192
Tomzov, A., 164, 169
Totenkopf SS Panzer Division, 50, 90, 170, 175–6, 187–9, 220, 222, 239
 see also 3rd SS Panzer Division
Transylvania, 228
Traut, Hans von, 96, 98, 149, 256–7
Tresckow, H. von, 156, 163, 170, 182, 253–4
Trowitz, A., 258
Tsaikov, K.A., 262
Tukhachevskii, M.N., 209

287

OPERATION BAGRATION: AN INCOMPLETE TRUTH

Tukums, 207, 227, 229, 233–6
Twenty-Fifth Army, 64
Tyrol Army, 66

US Army Air Force, 53
USSR, 72, 147, 154, 201–02, 235, 256–8
Ukraine, 18, 78
Union of German Officers, 257
Unrhein, M., 233
'Uranus', Operation, 1

V-1, 233
V-2, 233
Valentine (tank), 107–09, 113, 222, 229
Vasilevskii, A.M., 8, 54–5, 64, 93, 153–4, 204, 225, 227, 236
Vatutin, N.F., 55, 62
Vedeneev, N.D., 212
Velikaya River, 50
Velikie Luki, 65
Vienna, 192, 198, 259
Vileika, 83, 102
Vilnius (Vilna), 110, 145–6, 150, 152, 154, 160–1, 207, 220, 226
Vistula River, 69, 74, 79, 91, 153, 175, 196, 204, 206–09, 213, 215, 222–4, 237, 247
Vistula-Oder Operation, vi
Vitebsk, vi, 1, 3, 17–18, 27, 32–3, 35, 65, 69–70, 73, 75–6, 78, 80, 83, 85–6, 94–5, 114, 164, 253, 255
  Operation, 13–14, 16, 18, 64
Vladimir-Volynskii, 54
Vlasov, A.A., 201, 253
Volckers, P.G., 257
Volkovysk, 125, 139, 140, 153, 262
Vol'skii, V.T., 207
Vormann, N. von, 107, 141
Voronezh Front, 225
Voronezh-Kastornoe Operation, 63
Voronov, N.N., 25, 26, 34
Vyaz'ma, 225

Warsaw, 53, 69–70, 72–3, 140, 153–4, 160, 175, 177, 182, 186, 188, 206, 208–09, 213–17, 219, 222–3, 225–6, 237, 253, 258
Warsaw Uprising, 218–19, 223, 226, 253
Wehrmacht, 49–51, 89–90, 147, 153, 157, 160, 162, 169, 175, 196, 208, 225, 233, 235–6, 241, 243, 246–7, 254–8, 262
Weidling, H., 128
Weiss, W., 66, 163, 170–1, 173
Wespe (self-propelled gun), 116, 127, 140
Westphalia, 169
Western Bug River, 54, 73–4, 142, 152, 168, 173, 175, 177, 179–81, 183–6, 190, 213, 215
Western Dvina River, 73–4, 78–9, 83, 86, 96, 161
Western Front, 1–3, 6, 11, 13–15, 17–25, 27, 29–34, 36, 38, 40, 55, 64, 81
Westphal, S., 237
Wiking SS Panzer Division, 51, 90, 167–8, 170–2, 174, 175, 177, 181–4, 186–94, 196–7, 201, 213–14, 220, 222, 239, 244
  see also 5th SS Panzer Division
Willys (jeep), 180
Wroblewski, R., 12, 117, 121, 127
Wustenhagen, A., 254

Yakimovich, A.I., 262
Yegoshin, T.F., 259
Yenshin, M.A., 59
Yeremenko, A.I., 55, 95

Zakharov, G.F., 55, 64, 111, 151
Zeitzler, K., 76, 94, 161
Zhitomir, 81
Zhizdra, 31
Zhlobin, 54, 104–05, 120
Zholudev, V.G., 259–61
Zhukov, G.K., 8, 29, 39, 54–5, 61–4, 71, 77–8, 84, 93, 110, 154, 159, 180, 202, 204, 210
Zutavern, K.L., 254